RUSSIAN RESEARCH CENTER STUDIES 56

THE FAMILY IN SOVIET RUSSIA

THE FAMILY IN
SOVIET RUSSIA

BY H. KENT GEIGER

HARVARD UNIVERSITY PRESS

CAMBRIDGE · MASSACHUSETTS

1968

The Russian Research Center of Harvard University is supported by a
grant from the Ford Foundation. The Center carries out interdisciplinary
study of Russian institutions and behavior and related subjects.

This volume was prepared in part under a grant from the Carnegie Corporation
of New York. That Corporation is not, however, the author, owner,
publisher or proprietor of this publication and is not to be understood
as approving by virtue of its grant any of the statements made or views
expressed therein.

To my father and mother,
Homer and Flora Geiger

FOREWORD BY ALEX INKELES

THE FOUNDING FATHERS of sociology in Europe saw the family as one of the central elements of society, both reflecting its setting and in turn influencing the functioning of the larger system of which it was a part. They viewed the family as an institution, and studied its interaction with other institutions — political, economic, religious, cultural. In America, however, sociologists were more interested in the inner life of the family. They saw it less as an institution and more as a pattern of interpersonal relations. Their curiosity was roused to understand why young people choose one rather than another in courtship and how they adjust to each other in marriage. The study of the family became much more psychological. The completeness of the shift in attention was reflected in the title of a book called *The Family: From Institution to Companionship* (New York: American Book Co., 1945), written by one of America's leading sociologists, Ernest W. Burgess, and his disciple Harvey J. Locke.

This tendency in American sociology is not difficult to explain. In American social structure the individual nuclear family predominated. We had no tradition emphasizing the large, extended family, and little experience with powerful aristocratic dynasties capable of dominating the political and cultural scene. Hence it seemed less compelling to study the interrelation of the family and the society. Our cultural tradition emphasized the individual's right to privacy and sharply limited the rights of society to interfere in the sphere of family life. And our values of individualism and the pursuit of happiness legitimated a conception of family life as mainly a means for pursuing individual happiness rather than for fulfilling society's purpose.

Like every scientific perspective the individual-centered study of the family has its virtues. It heightens our awareness of aspects of stability and instability in family life that are overlooked by the institution-centered approach. But like every scientific perspective it also has its marked limitations. These become painfully evident when we turn to study the family in societies other than the United States and Western Europe. No account of the family in the Soviet Union can even remotely do justice to the facts unless it is systematically oriented to examine the impact on the family of events in the larger society. In the Soviet case the critical features of the family's social setting were the profound and rapid pace of social change that the Soviet Union experienced after 1917 and the ideological imperative that shaped official policy toward the family. These two forces, themselves complex and changing, provide the central focus for Dr. Geiger's study of the Soviet family. Through a detailed analysis of Soviet sources he traces for us the dramatic unfolding of the history of an idea — that of "the withering away" of the family — and of attempts to embody it in government policy. The inadequacy of the marxian conception of the family; the resistance of individuals and families to government policies, and their abuse and personal exploitation by still others; the consequences of these policies for society; the awkward efforts to adjust policy to social reality and the demands of the times; the final abandonment of radicalism for a conservative, even bourgeois, family policy; the later return to a modified liberalism, are all traced for us in detail by Professor Geiger. In his review of marxian theory and Soviet policy on the family, he brings to light the exalted and the mean, the imaginative and the stupid, the boldness and the timidity, the dogmatic rigidity and pragmatic flexibility manifested at different times by different leaders, and he does so with a dispassionate objectivity and thoroughness which will surely make this the definitive account of Soviet family policy for many years to come.

Yet Dr. Geiger's work has implications that go far beyond the Soviet scene. His analysis contributes to restore the study of the family as a central element in the analysis of the institutional framework of all large-scale societies. It will take its place alongside such standard works as Conrad Arensberg and Solon T. Kimball's *Family and Community in Ireland* and Marion Levy's *Family Revolution in Modern China* as one of the basic books for the study of the family in modern society. It is on the basis of such work that we may hope to build that truly comparative study of society which Comte, Spencer, and Durkheim all set as the main task of sociology, and which William Goode has recently attempted in *World Revolution and Family Patterns* (New York: Free Press, 1963).

Professor Geiger gives ample attention to communist ideology, government policy, and institutional response, yet does not neglect the meaning of these processes for the individual family member. There is no necessary conflict between a strictly sociological account of family affairs and one that is sensitive to socio-psychological issues. Indeed, we may argue that knowledge of the institutional setting of the family is the best guide to the critical personal problems that face the individual family member. Dr. Geiger uses this approach to great advantage in his analysis of the adjustment problems of the millions of women left without any hope of marriage by the large number of deaths of men in the course of revolution and war; in his examination of the efforts of husbands and fathers to maintain their authority over wives and daughters now able to earn their own living; and his exploration of the conflict of the generations, one oriented to tradition and often resisting Soviet influence and even authority, the other eager to follow the model of "the new Soviet man." These accounts are richly illustrated with quotations by participants in Soviet family life which Dr. Geiger has drawn from a surprisingly wide variety of studies dealing with the intimate details of daily life in Soviet families. Thus he gives us not only an account of policy on the macroscopic level, but also enables us to see the effects of that policy as it impinges on the individual and his intimates in the microcosm of the family.

Of course, no one who takes up this book will willingly put it down until he gets an answer to the overarching questions: Has the Soviet experiment with the family worked? Has Soviet society succeeded in transforming human relations in the family by its prior transformation of the social relations of production through socialism? Professor Geiger addresses himself to these questions in his concluding chapter. Not a few will be unwilling to accept his conclusion, but they will not find him lacking in frankness or forthrightness in stating it.

Cambridge, Massachusetts
September 1967

AUTHOR'S PREFACE

THERE IS ROOM for argument on how important the family is in modern life, but few today feel that the family is slated for disappearance. Yet Karl Marx and Friedrich Engels did entertain this view, and many of their Soviet followers were convinced that the family was a dying institution. To respond to this unusual situation my account begins with the marxist theory of the family and the story of how the Soviet communists confronted both it and the existing family of the society they took over.

The perspective is changed in Parts III–V. We move from the summit of ideological concern and national policy down to the grass-roots level of daily life. Some readers may wish to skip quickly over Parts I–II to assume this perspective. Since there has been little done on the family by Soviet sociologists and since daily life has in any case been one of the least known aspects of this generally secretive, closed society, a detailed discussion of my sources appears in the Introduction.

The families discussed are almost all from the Slavic majority of the population, Great Russians, Ukrainians, and Belorussians. The family systems of each of the national and ethnic minorities has its origin in a distinct sociocultural starting point, but the patterns of change point to the emergence of a common "modern" family system. In most respects the direction of change and the accompanying problems are similar to those experienced by the Slavic peasantry. For this reason, as well as to avoid the tedium of encyclopedic compass, I have omitted any separate treatment of ethnic or national differences in Soviet family life.

I have also elected to forego in this book systematic cross-national comparisons of Soviet family patterns with those found in the American family, the Israeli kibbutz family, and so forth. This does not mean that such systematic comparison is not feasible or that it is counter to my taste. Good comparative analysis must await, be based upon, and follow after less ambitious studies such as this one.

I am very much obliged to the institutions and individuals who have aided me in the preparation of this book. The Russian Research Center of Harvard University supported me as a graduate student and later as research fellow and provided materials, stimulation, and encouragement, in addition to financial assistance, for many years. Tufts University, the

Center for Slavic and East European Studies of the University of California at Berkeley, and the Russian Area Studies Program of the University of Wisconsin have also provided free time and other assistance indispensable to completing the study.

Among individuals I am most indebted to Dr. Malte Bischoff for his consent to allow me full use of his excellent doctoral dissertation, to Professor Alex Inkeles for encouragement, incisive criticism, and the writing of a foreword, and to my wife, Mildred, for typing and editing assistance.

For careful reading and detailed critical comments I am grateful to Professors Robert V. Daniels, Robert A. Feldmesser, Ira L. Reiss, Ezra F. Vogel, and the late Meyer F. Nimkoff. This final version has profited greatly from their comments.

For general impressions or for criticisms of particular portions of the manuscript I am grateful to Professors Alfred C. Clarke, Peter H. Juviler, Alfred G. Meyer, Barrington Moore, Jr., Talcott Parsons, Alice S. Rossi, and Gordon F. Streib

H.K.G.

Madison, Wisconsin
September 1967

CONTENTS

TABLES

THE FAMILY IN SOVIET RUSSIA

ABBREVIATIONS IN THE TEXT

A   Life-history interviews, Harvard Project on the Soviet Social System.

B   Family-life interviews and questionnaires, Harvard Project on the Soviet Social System.

Bi   Malte Bischoff, "Die Struktur and die Wandlung der sowjetischen Familie (um 1950): die Familie in der sowjetischen Gesellschaft."

Ka   E. O. Kabo, *Ocherki rabochego byta.*

Ku   P. I. Kushner (ed.), *Selo Viriatino v proshlom i nastoiashchem.*

Nov   Joseph Novak, *The Future Is Ours, Comrade: Conversations with the Russians.*

Ro   Alice S. Rossi, "Generational Differences in the Soviet Union."

Tr   Leon Trotsky, *Voprosy byta.*

INTRODUCTION | SOURCES AND METHOD

To MY KNOWLEDGE there is not yet in existence a complete statement and adequate analysis of the views of Marx and Engels on the family. Perhaps the two chapters presented in Part I will help to fill the gap. For this section on "The Marxist Theory of the Family" I have relied almost entirely on the original writing of Marx and Engels. For Part II, dealing with one aspect of the response of the Soviet rulers to Marx and to the responsibility of running a very unmarxist society, I have relied upon the words of the regime's spokesmen, from the highest level — Lenin and such colleagues as Alexandra Kollontai, Anatole Lunacharski, S. N. Smidovich, and Emelian Iaroslavski — to the lowest level — officials of the party and government, professors of historical materialism, journalist-polemicists, and people whose letters to *Pravda, Izvestiia,* and other newspapers have been published. I have also used English-language materials such as the journalistic accounts by Ella Winter, Jessica Smith, and Susan M. Kingsbury and Mildred Fairchild; the excellent writing on Soviet legal history by Harold J. Berman, Vladimir Gsovski, and John N. Hazard; and various other published and unpublished writing by Western authors.

For the sociology of the family, Parts III–V, I have used four main sources of information. First, the materials collected and analyzed by me and other members of the Harvard Project on the Soviet Social System. This project was sponsored by the Russian Research Center of Harvard University and was designed to secure as thorough a canvas as possible of the experiences, opinions, values, and backgrounds of the large but rapidly dispersing body of former Soviet citizens living in the Federal Republic of Germany in the postwar years. A complete description, detailed report of findings, and a discussion of problems connected with sampling, data collection, analysis, and control of bias may be found in Alex Inkeles and Raymond A. Bauer, *The Soviet Citizen.* See especially Part One, "Objectives and Methods," pp. 3–64.

Several different subprojects, with corresponding subsamples of the nonreturner population, were contained within the larger Harvard Project. The two that have been most useful in the preparation of this book were the extended life-history interviews, 329 in number and designated in the text with the letter "A," and the 123 interview and questionnaire investigations dealing specifically with family life, which were my own responsibility. Fifteen of this latter group were interviews conducted by me with, in three cases, Russian-speaking assistants; the rest were lengthy paper-and-pencil questionnaires filled out by the respondents, and then extended or supplemented, when appropriate, by further interviewing by me. All material cited from this group is identified in the text with the letter "B."

The information described above was gathered in 1950 and 1951 and subjected to analysis in the following years. In addition to my own materials, reports, and published articles, and the life-history interviews mentioned above, I have made use of some of the psychological interview protocols and several unpublished memoranda. I am especially indebted for ideas and occasional interview excerpts (identified by "Ro" in the text) to the excellent monograph by Alice S. Rossi, "Generational Differences in the Soviet Union," submitted as a project report in 1954 and later as a doctoral dissertation to the Department of Sociology, Columbia University.

A second body of data has furnished a remarkably lively collection of first-hand impressions of Soviet family life gained by people playing the role of naïve participant observers. After World War II, a large number of Germans who had become Soviet prisoners of war were not permitted to return home. They stayed on in the USSR, most often in camps, but frequently enough in villages or cities, where they were put to work in the Soviet economy and lived in close contact with the Soviet population. Many of them were able to live in Soviet families or to observe them closely.

Their return home to the Federal Republic of Germany reached a crescendo several months after the death of Stalin. Between September 1953 and August 1954 some 10,000 former members of the German armed forces were permitted to repatriate. For the next two years the knowledge of Soviet family life accumulated by a selected portion of them was systematically explored by a German sociologist, Dr. Malte Bischoff. His findings were presented in a doctoral thesis, "Die Struktur und die Wandlung der sowjetischen Familie (um 1950): die Familie in der sowjetischen Gesellschaft" (Structure and change in the Soviet family around 1950: the family in Soviet society), submitted to the Faculty of Economic and Social Sciences of the University of Hamburg in 1956.

Bischoff's information comes from a total of 104 different observers, selected from an original sample of 1,500, largely on the basis of their familiarity with Soviet family life. The observers wrote lengthy monographs on the lives of 219 different Soviet families. These monographs were then supplemented by interviews conducted by Bischoff with the same respondents, and by a series of additional memoranda containing their general observations about family and social life in the USSR. Excerpts from these case history materials are identified in the text with the letters "Bi" and page numbers referring to Bischoff's dissertation. As is the case with the Harvard Project respondents, when the age of a respondent is mentioned it refers to his age as of 1950, which was also the median year of observation of the Bischoff sample of Soviet families.

The third group of materials on which Parts III–V of this book are based consists of Soviet publications. They are of two types. The first consists of philosophical and journalistic writing by Soviet newspaper workers, jurists, party and Komsomol officials, representatives of government agencies responsible for public affairs touching on family life, and ordinary citizens telling of their experience and opinions. These accounts are in the main anecdotal and didactic, but they do often have the merit of furnishing local color and drama and they occasionally furnish clues to important patterns.

The second type of Soviet publication is more properly scientific. At its best the reporting and analysis is on a par with that of modern social science in the Western world. Three such works that have been helpful are Leon Trotsky, *Voprosy byta* (Questions of daily life), a strikingly frank and detailed report based on the observations of middle-level party workers called to a conference in Moscow in 1923; E. O. Kabo, *Ocherki rabochego byta* (Sketches of the daily life of workers), a study of the budgets and home life of Moscow working-class families in the middle of the New Economic Policy period conducted by a team of anthropologists and statistical workers; and the more recent *Selo Viriatino v proshlom i nastoiashchem* (The village Viriatino in past and present), edited by P. I. Kushner, a high quality ethnographic account of a kolkhoz village, Viriatino, Sosnovski district, Tambov region, about halfway between Moscow and Stalingrad (now Volgograd). Excerpts from these three books are referred to in the text by the first two letters of the name of author or editor, "Tr," "Ka," and "Ku," and page number. References to the Trotsky book are to the Russian edition.

During the final revision of the manuscript a Soviet textbook of reasonable quality became available, *Brak i semia v SSSR* (Marriage and family in the USSR), written by A. G. Kharchev, the leading specialist on this topic in the Soviet Union. His book was useful mainly for its reporting of a number of recent studies, some conducted in the Leningrad area by the author himself.

In addition to these major works, I have been helped by other scientific or near-scientific publications, such as the occasional articles on family life in such journals as *Semia i Shkola* (Family and school) and *Sovetskaia Etnografiia* (Soviet ethnography).

Finally, I have used the writings of my predecessors and colleagues in the field of Soviet studies. Special mention should be made of the book by Joseph Novak, *The Future Is Ours, Comrade,* a sprightly reporting of everyday life and opinion in recent Soviet times by a former national of an eastern European country. Excerpts are identified in the text by the letters "Nov."

Such a heterogeneous and unorthodox body of sources requires some analysis. The Soviet nonreturners are, of course, largely political refugees, many of whom were badly treated in the USSR. However else they may differ from the Soviet population itself, they are certainly more anti-Soviet. Does the presence of such feelings rule out the possibility of their giving an objective account of family life? I think not, because, among other reasons, in many instances it is not clear what kind of pattern of behavior or belief would be considered hostile to the regime. Did, for instance, the actions of the Soviet regime weaken the family or strengthen it? The Project respondents themselves do not agree upon the correct answer, and sometimes the most virulently anti-communist will point out that the inner solidarity of the Soviet family is the measure of its opposition to the regime. Indeed, an obstacle more handicapping to my efforts to employ refugee respondents was the inability of many people, most often those from working-class and peasant backgrounds, to describe, analyze, and compare their experience and family lives. For instance, a peasant who became an unskilled worker was asked to tell how the relationship between his wife and himself differed from that between his father and his mother. His answer: "Father had his wife and I had mine" (292 B 4).

I now feel particular appreciation for the fact that the Harvard Project materials concern the family life of people who were later to become political refugees. For one thing, I have renewed my confidence in what I have learned from them by virtue of the remarkable extent to which the conclusions of the Bischoff study and much of the Soviet material agree with those of my own initial study of refugees. At the same time I have become more fully aware of the opportunity my data have offered to explore precisely that part of family life about which we know least, and about which political refugees are most qualified to give information — namely, what happens to the family under a revolutionary and oppressive political dictatorship.

Two considerations on the use of refugee testimony are worth noting. In the first place, a good proportion of the Harvard Project respondents were by no means particularly disaffected or otherwise unusual while living in the USSR. A minority but still a considerable proportion would have shared the sentiments of a young woman who would have preferred not to be a refugee: "I would never have come to Germany by myself. I was sent here as an *Ostarbeiter*. Had I been able to, I would have remained in the Soviet Union, had not the Germans sent me out. I never really had anything against the regime, although I didn't like certain parts about it, but I never had anything against it" (631 A).

In the second place, by far the greater part of my account is concerned not with the question of generalizing numbers or proportions directly from sample to population, that is from the Harvard Project directly back to the Soviet population. Rather it has been my main interest to investigate intrasample subgroup differences, or, more generally, social patterns. In the present case, 90 per cent of the discussion in Chapters 5 through 11 concerns qualitative patterns and themes and differences among families on various social class levels. In most cases such patterns and themes as have been discovered can be presumed to characterize the Soviet population, as well as my samples, with much more certainty than can quantitative estimates. For instance, I would not seek to estimate the exact proportion of religious believers in families on different social class levels on the basis of my sample data. But I do not hesitate to argue that the information gained from the Harvard Project samples is good enough to establish (1) the (very probable) existence in the USSR of social class differences in religious attitudes and (2) the (very probable) inverse relationship in the USSR between social class level and the tendency for strong religious commitment to be characteristic of family life.

Bischoff's sample of families observed by German prisoners of war, when combined with the materials of the Harvard Project, as far as I am aware exhausts the total resources of systematic non-Soviet investigations of family life in the USSR. Compared with the "B" sample of the Harvard Project materials (the subsample of 123 interviews and questionnaires devoted entirely to family life) the Bischoff sample has three advantages. First, it does not consist of political refugees, but of ordinary Soviet citizens living in ordinary families, many of which are still going concerns in the contemporary USSR. Correspondingly one has the distinct impression that politics, political discussions, and political differences play a less important role. Their family lives seem more apolitical, also more disorganized, than those of the Harvard Project group. A second advantage is the fact that outside observers rather than the family members themselves are doing the reporting, and hence some of the less normative and less conscious sides to family life can be touched upon. Not only deviant behavior but many of the sensitive areas of husband-wife relations are reported more adequately by the outside observers than they could have been by the participants themselves.

A third advantage of the Bischoff sample has to do with time and social class perspective. His sample consists entirely of postwar families; mine were families whose experiences in the USSR were mostly prewar. And his sample has a greater variety of marginal and lower-class families than I was able to get together. Both the temporal and special social perspectives have been invaluable.

Soviet, Russian-language sources, as I have noted, fall into two groups, the less scientific and those that are reasonably objective. In reading Soviet publications and trying to evaluate the information contained in them, several things must be borne in mind. Allegiance to the doctrines of Marx, Engels, and Lenin has precluded certain kinds of hypotheses and investigation. It is a safe bet that no sane Soviet citizen will propose publicly or attempt to test the hypothesis that there is an association between the private ownership of productive property and the solidary quality of the relationship of spouses. This question has already been decided on grounds other than social scientific and is not open to investigation. Similarly, it has been a rule since the Revolution to investigate and report on only those issues that promise some political advantage.

No clearer evidence of the politically imposed bias in virtually all Soviet materials can be found than the working of the "imperative-indicative," in which statements are made in the form of assertions which are in function hortatory and in fact frequently false. Although things have improved since the death of Stalin, even the best work being done in the USSR is not free of such bias. One begins to wonder when the announced purpose of a series of ethnographic research projects is "to investigate the decisive transformation of the kolkhoz village." Even the best social scientific publication yet to appear, the 1958 book edited by Kushner on the village Viriatino, is bound by the compulsion to find examples of progress, improvement, and reform in the village and to evaluate negatively such "survivals from the past" as keeping the farm animals in the kitchen in the winter time and all family members eating from the same wooden bowl at mealtime. Sometimes, one suspects, the ethnographers are victimized by falsifications in the past which have by now become historical truth. Thus, it seems most unlikely from what we know of the peasant attitude toward religion that, as claimed in the book by Kushner: "In 1933 the huge majority of the population of Viriatino came out in favor of closing the church in the village" (p. 230).

We can expect the quality of Soviet social science to get better and better, but the insecurity bred by Stalinism cannot be undone in a short time. Nor can the Soviet regime be expected quickly to forswear its aversion to such survivals as religious faith, patriarchal relations in marriage, and so on. For the present, then, and for some time in the future, there is doubt that the Soviet people, even if approached by objective researchers, will give frank answers to questions about their beliefs and behavior in these areas. As long as the conduct of private life is by official definition a matter of public concern in the USSR, the Soviet citizen who divulges information unfavorable to himself remains politically vulnerable.

How, then, does one use materials about Soviet family life that are of Soviet origin? In general, with great caution, and in contrast to the interpretive emphasis used with materials from refugees, by accepting more quickly published material that is unwelcome to the regime, and by treating with skepticism events and facts that favor its policies and goals.

I have as a rule tried to confine my reliance on the fourth group of materials, various English-language sources, published and unpublished, to factual matters. Knowing the shaky basis for many of the broad generalizations made about Soviet social life, I have by and large ignored them, even if they agree with those generalizations that I myself have concluded are valid.

I have been to the USSR twice, for several weeks in 1956 and again in 1958. I do not count it a strong asset to have been able to travel in the USSR, for Soviet families often are as closed as is their society. My opportunities to observe Soviet family life directly were limited in the main to the public side — parents walking in the park with children, a couple eating in a restaurant, vacationers traveling on the train, and so forth — but this limitation did not preclude entering into frequent and occasionally revealing conversations about family life. These observations and conversations in the USSR undoubtedly enriched and sharpened my ability to work with the more systematically gathered materials upon which this book is based. And, of course, there is nothing in the pages to follow that my own experience while in the USSR would lead me to question.

I

THE MARXIST THEORY
OF THE FAMILY

In some ways what men believe to be true is more important than the truth. The statements of Karl Marx and Friedrich Engels about the family, though they were often false or misleading, have had great influence on the way the Soviet rulers have dealt with the Soviet family and have also influenced, we may be sure, the Soviet man in the street.

Since the time when the notions of the founders of marxism were elevated to social dogma, their scientific validity, or lack of it, has ceased to be of primary importance. I shall therefore often be more interested in exploring the relation of an idea to other ideas, especially to the underlying structure and spirit of Marx's and Engels' thought, than to the real world it purports to represent.

The positions, inconsistencies, and errors of marxism have all been significant because they constitute a large portion of the prologue to the present Soviet attitude toward the family.

ONE | THE FAMILY FROM THE
ARMCHAIR OF MARX AND ENGELS

WHEN MARX AND ENGELS wrote about the family from time to time over a forty-year period, they described the family as they saw it about them under capitalism, discussed the family in the past, and were interested in the family's future. The main point about the family which drew their interest was the relation of husband and wife and the way it is affected by property relations and other aspects of economic life in the larger society. The most complete discussion of the marxist theory of the family was published by Engels in 1884, after Marx's death, in the book *The Origin of the Family, Private Property and the State, in the Light of the Researches of Lewis H. Morgan.*[1]

Although Engels was the author of this work, he noted in the preface to the first edition that Marx himself had hoped to undertake the task and had made extensive extracts which he, Engels, had reproduced "as far as possible." Actually, many of the ideas in *The Origin* can be found in the first joint work of the two writers, *The German Ideology,* not published during their lifetimes. Quite clearly, then, this, like most other products of their collaboration, was in the main a joint work of the two founders of marxism and points to an impressive unity and continuity over four decades in the basic outlines of their thought.[2] Knowledge of this collaboration makes the involved exposition easier to follow. There were apparently some differences between the two men about the family, but since we are unaware of precisely what they were,[3] for the purposes of this book their ideas will be assumed to be both in agreement with one another and of mutual origin.

The Marxist Approach to the Family

One of the conclusions to which Marx and Engels were led, with the support of Morgan's researches, was that the family assumed many different forms as it evolved through history and thus constitutes a "series in historic development," as Marx wrote in *Capital.*[4] They also felt that these different forms were in rough correspondence with the principal stages of social development postulated in their vision of human history.

The final typology, developed largely by Morgan and endorsed by Engels (presumably also by Marx), included four major forms of relations between the sexes.

The first form was a stage of unrestricted sexual freedom or complete promiscuity. In the beginnings of human history, in fact, as man became human in the transition from the animal, there was no family or marriage whatsoever.[5] The second form was group marriage, which developed very early and had several subtypes. The main characteristic of group marriage as a whole was the absence of the incest taboo, and the earliest subtype in Engels' system, based on his understanding of the moiety system of the Australian aborigines, was essentially "mass marriage" whereby "not the individuals, but the entire groups are married, moiety with moiety" (p. 38). Since there were in existence only two moieties, the range of sexual choice was indeed a wide one. The next subtype was the "consanguine family," with mating taboo between the generations but in which "brothers and sisters, male and female cousins of the first, second, and more remote degrees, are all brothers and sisters of one another, and *precisely for that reason* they are all husbands and wives of one another" (p. 32, Engels' italics). The third and highest subtype was the "punaluan family," whose essential feature was "mutually common possession of husbands and wives" by a number of the same sex, same generation, consanguineal relatives on one side, but in which the incest taboo, already effective between generations, was now extended to brother and sister and to opposite-sex cousins (p. 34 et passim).[6] It is interesting to note that the social mechanism proposed by Morgan, and endorsed by Engels, which was to explain the gradual extension of the incest taboo and thus the gradual evolution of the relation between the sexes, was simply the principle of natural selection: "the tribes among whom inbreeding was restricted . . . were bound to develop more quickly and more fully" (p. 34).

The third major form of relationship between man and woman was the monogamous family, corresponding to civilization, the era of history in which Marx and Engels were most interested; this form will be discussed at length. Finally, the whole spirit of Marx's and Engels' thinking provides a fourth major type, which I shall call simply "the pattern of the future," under communism. Hence, there are four main stages in the "historical series": sexual promiscuity, group marriage, monogamy, and the pattern of the future.

The variable element in these forms does not correspond very closely with that of the main typology of evolutionary social orders developed by Marx and Engels and expressed in terms of the division of labor and property forms: primitive communism, slavery, feudalism, capitalism, and socialism.[7] In fact, the correspondence of family form with the major historical epochs of Morgan is also forced: to the period of savagery corresponds group marriage, to barbarism the "pairing family," and to civilization monogamy (pp. 47, 66). In the pairing family, neither fish nor fowl, one man lives with one woman but polygamy and "occasional infidelity" remain his right, though not hers. Furthermore, the marriage tie can be easily dissolved by either partner (p. 41).

Engels notes that the pairing family had already been appearing in group marriage or even earlier, and also that it is a "form of monogamy" (pp. 40, 25). Consequently, it is best considered a transitional form between group marriage and monogamy. Moreover, since the principle of natural selection had taken full responsibility for the earlier development of the family, as the really central principle of the tide of history began to take over the pairing family also represented the transitional form between primitive communism and slavery. With the rise of private productive property, the temporary alliances of the pairing family were no longer adequate. When property existed and had to be transmitted, heirs were needed. Hence still another transitional form appeared, this time a clear subtype of the monogamous family, the patriarchal family. It is the first family form to be found in written history (pp. 50–53).[8]

The concept of a transitional family form will be encountered once more in the proletarian family. First, however, the reader should understand that the rather tortured system of types to which Engels (and Marx) subscribed has, it is agreed at present, little validity as a chronological series. It is perhaps most useful simply to note the main theme and key principle of the relations between the sexes before the advent of private property. The theme is the progressive narrowing of the "circle of people comprised within the common bond of marriage, which was originally very wide, until at last it includes only the single pair, the dominant form of marriage today" (p. 276). The key interpretive principle is natural selection. There is also a trace of another mechanism, a product of the rationalistic spirit of the times — the surrender of the "woman's" right to complete chastity before marriage and of monogamous intercourse in marriage for the observance of monogamy (partial at least) on the part of the man (pp. 10, 46–47).

The family owes its origin, it would seem, to the operation of these two principles. In the beginning there was only promiscuity and then came group marriage (pp. 15, 30). Later the pairing family, combining characteristics of both group marriage and monogamy, appeared before the rise of history's main determining principle, private property.[9]

Although the monogamous family, the only one found in civilization, represents a higher stage of historical development than the earlier forms, Engels (and apparently Marx as well) was quite fascinated by the sexual lot of primitive man. Group marriage, for instance, he said, "seen at close hand, does not look quite so terrible as the philistines, whose minds cannot get beyond brothels, imagine it to be" (p. 39). "The Australian aborigine," Engels continued, "wandering hundreds of miles from his home among people whose language he does not understand, nevertheless often finds in every camp and every tribe women who give themselves to him without resistance and without resentment" (p. 58).

With civilization, however, "monogamous marriage comes on the scene as the subjugation of the one sex by the other." In fact, while "a great historical step forward," it, "together with slavery and private wealth . . . opens the period that has lasted until today in which every step forward is also relatively a step backward, in which prosperity and development for some is won through the misery and frustration of others" (p. 58).

As the social role of the man in using tools and transforming things into property for other than immediate consumption assumes the center of the stage, it leads to the form of monogamy known to the present. But a difficulty is presented by the fact that Engels sometimes uses the concept monogamous family to refer variously to the pairing family (in a matrilileal gens [clan] in which women are dominant), to the patriarchal family, to the family of the bourgeois, to the proletarian family, and even to the family of the future, while elsewhere he uses it to refer quite exclusively to the bourgeois family under capitalism. I shall avoid this difficulty by concentrating on family types in relation to the structure of property relations.

Clearly, Marx and Engels felt that property played the central role in civilized society, and it was indeed the civilized historical present in which they were most interested. But the image of the future, as they saw it, also constitutes part of the marxist heritage with which the Soviet regime had to deal. Hence, I shall examine at length their concepts of the bourgeois family under capitalism, the proletarian family under capitalism, and the family in the society of the future, when private property ownership would be abolished. The details of each of these types reveal important aspects of marxist thought, as does the role played by the family in Marx's and Engels' social theory, historical materialism.

Marx and Engels eagerly seized upon the ideas of Morgan, ideas which later research has shown to be inaccurate or, at best, unprovable hypotheses, because he, in the name of respected scholarship, supported some of their ideas which were most bitterly contested by their contemporaries: the central role of the forms of economic development and private property in causing social change, the notion that society develops or evolves in a relatively orderly fashion through a series of stages, and a concept of which more will be said later, the "survival." Marx and Engels were particularly happy to analyze the family because it was such a small, manageably observable unit — "a society in microcosm." If it could be proved that the various family forms constituted a historical series, the point would lend not inconsiderable support to their contention that society, too, had had and would take different forms in past and future. Hence the founders of marxism were most receptive to the ideas of a man who, in the modern verdict, is adjudged as no more than another nineteenth-century evolutionist now thoroughly discredited on empirical grounds.[10]

The Bourgeois Family Corrupted

Marx and Engels spoke of the family life of the bourgeoisie in terms of greed, oppression, exploitation, boredom, adultery, and prostitution. The bourgeois family was quite corrupt, but, and this was for them a main point, it pretended to be something quite different. In fact, "boredom and money are the binding factor, . . . but to this . . . dirty existence corresponds the sacred conception of it in official phraseology and in general hypocrisy." Again and again they stress that the bourgeois family is in a state of de facto dissolution (Auflösung). The "inner bond" of the family ties of "obedience, piety, marital troth" were all gone. Nothing was left but "property relations" and their consequences.[11]

Thoughts of property and money, the spirit of exchange, dominated the ties of the bourgeois with his wife and with his child. Future husbands haggled with future fathers-in-law over the size of the dowry, while fathers and sons sparred greedily over the question of inheritance. Under these conditions there could be no true love between husband and wife, a fact institutionalized, claimed Marx and Engels, in the "marriage of convenience." Hence, marriage among the bourgeoisie amounted to forced cohabitation, or, as a favorite phrase had it, *de facto* prostitution, in which the woman "only differs from the ordinary courtesan in that she does not let out her body on piece-work as a wage worker, but sells it once and for all into slavery" (p. 63).

In addition to exploitation of the helpless wife — both of her labor in "open or concealed domestic slavery" as "head servant" in the household, and of her body as producer of an heir or simply as an object of loveless lust — there were broader developments. The first, about which Engels seemed rather ambivalent, was adultery. The second, about which he had nothing good to say, was prostitution. Both were said to be part and parcel of bourgeois family life, an assertion that is apparently to be understood in quite a literal sense. Of course, Marx and Engels conducted no field studies on these matters, but Engels confidently describes the supplanting of feudalism by the bourgeois social order in France: "The 'right of the first night' passed from the feudal lords to the bourgeois manufacturers. Prostitution assumed proportions hitherto unknown. Marriage itself remained, as before, the legally recognized form, the official cloak of prostitution, and was besides supplemented by widespread adultery." [12]

Another concept derived from this situation is the notion of "an exclusive attitude" toward other families.[13] Though a minor theme in the thought of Marx and Engels, it is found repeatedly at both beginning and end of their careers and serves to introduce an idea which came to be more central in the early years of Soviet history — the family as a divisive force in the larger society.

Within the family, as Engels' memorable aphorism put it, the husband is the bourgeois and the wife is the proletarian. And it was not only property ownership which brought inequality of power. In the bourgeois family the husband earns the living and supports the family, a situation which, said Engels, "in itself gives him a position of supremacy" (pp. 65–66). From this twofold advantage of the bourgeois husband, Marx and Engels deduced, came the "domestic slavery" of the wife and all the other sad consequences it entails. The fact that there are some differences between the various types of bourgeois families, that sometimes the German philistine's wife revolts and "wears her husband's trousers," that the French husband often "wears horns," and so on, are all minor eddies in the pool of bourgeois pestilence (pp. 60, 63).

Nevertheless, the concept of the family was indispensable to the bourgeois in order to preserve control over his property. For this reason the greedy, lusty bourgeois fiercely defended the idea of the family as embodied in law and religion. Nothing was the equal, avowed Marx and Engels, of the hypocrisy of bourgeois morality.

The Proletarian Family

The marxist image of the proletarian family is ambiguous. Perhaps it is akin to a more general ambivalence in marxist thought toward wealth, power, and other things of this world. While there was no question about the depravity of the bourgeois in his relation to wife and children, or about the reason for it, the social relations of the proletarians were free of the corrupting influence of private property. The proletarian was, for instance, more generous than the bourgeois; although he was poor, beggars turned to him, wrote Engels, rather than to the stingy bourgeois.[14] On the other hand, the proletarian family was poverty-stricken. Since the worker was at best an exploited wage earner and at worst a member of the "reserve army of unemployed," his family lacked not only property but income. Food, clothing, and decent shelter were short. The emergence of capital accumulation, monetary exchange, commercial competition, and the concentration of property ownership had left him helpless and exposed. His lot was one of starving, stealing, and suicide, and in his family life were drunkenness, brutality, and sexual irregularity. In fact, his family was "torn asunder by modern industry" to the point where there occurred a "perpetual succession of family troubles, domestic quarrels, most demoralizing for parents and children alike." Engels repeatedly used such phrases as "the ruin of all domestic relations" or asserted that "no family life was possible." He did not blame the workers for this, though; since they were denied all other privilege by the system which gripped them, no one could blame them for turning to those pleasures which were left, drink and sexual indulgence. "The workingmen, in order to get something from life, concentrate their whole energy upon these two enjoyments, carry them to excess, surrender to them in the most unbridled manner." [15]

The breakup, factual dissolution, or practical absence (all terms used synonymously by Engels) of proletarian family life was owing in the first instance to economic need, but also to one of its immediate consequences — the employment of women and children in industry. Under the conditions of capitalism painted by Marx and Engels, the liberating influence of social production was only a portent. At the moment proletarian women and children were exploited mercilessly, with long hours, low wages, and unbelievable working conditions. Thus, said Engels, the employment of women breaks up the family. As the mother grows away from the children, they are neglected and grow up as savages, and are then, of course, unprepared to form and maintain decent families when they become adults. So the cycle repeats.[16]

From this central thesis, Marx and Engels deduced several subsidiary patterns. The proletarian tends to marry early as a means of self-protection, for then, in true Darwinian fashion, he can procreate many children and put them to work in the sweatshops and the mines. The fact that "the absolute size of the families stands in inverse proportion to the height of wages . . . calls to mind the boundless reproduction of animals individually weak and constantly hunted down," wrote Marx.[17]

Moreover, complained Engels somewhat incongruously, the employment of the wife is likely to "turn the family upside down." A situation is created in which the husband cannot find work, but his wife can because she will work for less. Thus he sits at home while she becomes the breadwinner. Engels then treats the reader to the "outrageous episode" of poor Jack who must sit at home and mend his wife's stocking with the bodkin while she is off at work.[18]

But, in positive terms, the absence in the proletarian family of the original source of all the trouble, private property, can have only a salutary effect, in view of the havoc it creates among the bourgeois family. In deference to the logic of their analysis of the bourgeois family, Marx and Engels also conclude that among the proletarians the family is "based on real relations" (reale Verhältnisse). In the beginning of their collaboration real relations seem to mean several more or less vaguely stated natural or environmental conditions — not only property but social, ecological, and physiological factors. A typical excerpt refers to the "real body of the family" and includes relationships given by "the presence of children, the construction of the contemporary city, formation of capital." [19] In Engels' later writing, however, real relations increasingly mean personal preference and mutual love, or as Engels liked to call it, true or mutual "sex love."

Engels also asserted that marital equality existed in the proletarian family. This situation results from the absence of property and also from the fact that the wife is frequently employed, two conditions which give her the power to dissolve the marriage if she wishes and also bring her the position and respect associated with a productive economic role. Among the proletarians, who regard the norms of religion and laws as no more than embodiments of bourgeois interest, "if two people cannot get on with one another, they prefer to separate." Obviously there is also no reason for adultery, prostitution, or religion, and they "play an almost vanishing part" (p. 64).[20]

The positive side of the proletarian family thus contains true love, marital equality, willingness and freedom to divorce on appropriate occasion, and disregard of the traditional morality as merely an expression of class interests. In all of these, as well as in the determining conditions, freedom from property ownership and the employment of the wife, the proletarian family approaches Marx's and Engels' image of family life under communism.

Under capitalism there are important differences, to be sure. When Engels says that the family is still an "economic unit of society," he refers to the continuing fetter imposed upon the wife by the tasks of housekeeping and the care of children. These place her in a position in which "if she carries out her duties in the private service of her family, she remains excluded from public production and unable to earn; and if she wants to take part in public production and earn independently, she cannot carry out her family duties" (p. 65).

In spite of this seemingly crippling defect, in his last major work Engels paints a positive picture of the proletarian family. Freely contracted marriage and true love are the rule. Perhaps there is, concedes Engels, "something of the brutality toward women that has spread since the introduction of monogamy" (p. 64), but he apparently now thinks of it as a pure survival, with no source in the conditions of proletarian life.

In general, Engels' thoughts on the proletarian family constitute a clear example of the conflict between analytical principles that work in opposite directions. On the one hand, there is the corrosive effect of exploitation and poverty: "The great overturn of society through competition, which dissolved the relationship of the bourgeois among themselves and to the proletarians into relationships of money, changed the various 'sacred things' listed above into items of commerce, and destroyed for the proletarians everything natural and traditional, for example, family and political relationships together with their entire ideological superstructure." [21] Turning the coin over, the absence of private property makes social equality and love possible: "Sex-love in the relationship with a woman becomes, and can only become, the real rule among the oppressed classes, which means today among the proletariat" (p. 63).

In his first work, *The Condition of the Working Classes in England in 1844,* Engels emphasized the first principle and neglected the second. In his last work, he emphasized only the liberating absence of private property among the proletarians. There is scarcely a reference to the dire effects of poverty in the entire book. Because of his tendency to impute concreteness to an analytical notion, Engels' propositions have outstripped him, a flaw that frequently appears in the writing of Engels and Marx. In this case, the interpretive principles clash in the direction of influence they are supposed to exert to such a degree that one of them tends to push the other completely out of the picture.[22]

The Pattern of the Future: Equality, Freedom, and Love

Under communism life would be better. Classes would disappear, the state would be unnecessary and would wither away, and the antagonisms between town and country and between physical and mental work would end. There would be no such deadening division of labor with its strict and narrow work specialization as existed under capitalism, and there would be no religion, because the social contradictions from which it had risen would have disappeared. Marx and Engels were quite explicit about what would happen to the family under such conditions. A good part of it would disappear, consigned like the state to "the museum of antiquities." Propertyholding, work, consumption, and the rearing and education of children would be surrendered to society. All these activities, according to the founders of marxism, in one way or another breed inequality within the family and hence oppression, marital or parental.

Curiously, other than to note that all children would be reared on a communal basis,[23] Marx and Engels had little to say about the future relationships of parents and children. Apparently they would not continue to live together, because society was to rear and educate. Whether they would see each other and, if so, how frequently are questions left unanswered. It is only asserted that the communal rearing of children would bring "real freedom" among all members of the family.[24] The union of man and woman clearly would continue to be a close one, however. The promise discernible in the proletarian family would then be unmistakably fulfilled, and its two defects, poverty and maintenance of a private household, would have ended. Women would have been drawn into the liberating sphere of "social production" and freed from the domestic slavery of the individual family household. As a first approximation, then, it seems that under communism the family would disappear, but marriage would remain.

Rather than marriage, perhaps the word love should be used — love purified and exalted, free from all economic considerations which "exert such a powerful influence on the choice of a marriage partner. For then there is no other motive left except mutual inclination" (p. 72). But would inclination not lead to the "free love" or "sexual communism" that horrified the nineteenth century. Engels replied to this criticism early in his career, in 1847, by answering the question: What will be the influence of communist society on the family?

It will transform the relations between the sexes into a purely private matter which concerns only the persons involved and into which society has no occasion to intervene. It can do this since it does away with private property and educates children on a communal basis, and in this way removes the two bases of traditional marriage, the dependence, rooted in private property, of woman on the man and of the children on the parents. And here is the answer to the outcry of the highly moral philistines against the "community of women." Community of women is a condition which belongs entirely to bourgeois society and which today finds its complete expression in prostitution. But prostitution is based on private property and falls with it. Thus communist society, instead of introducing community of women, in fact abolishes it.[25]

In other words, it will be nobody's business but the man and woman concerned; and, since things can hardly get worse, they have to get better.

Later a more substantial clue was given. Relations between the sexes would revolve around the nature and significance of love, about which

Engels had very definite ideas. He considered it "by its nature exclusive." Hence, a marriage based on it would be an "individual marriage" (p. 72). But he did not see such a bond as indissoluble: marriage would continue only so long as love continued, and "the intense emotion of individual sex-love varies very much in duration from one individual to another, especially among men" (p. 73). Obviously, then, and Engels makes this explicit, if love comes to an end or is supplanted by a "new passionate love," separation will benefit all concerned. Divorce will not be needed, however, only separation. As a matter of course, under such conditions both adultery and prostitution will also disappear, for they will simply be unnecessary. Complete sex equality, complete freedom of choice, perfect love — such was the promise of communism.

Further than this — the emergence of those features of family life which were emphatically absent in the bourgeois monogamous family — Engels did not go, but he reiterated his stand of the early years with these words: "But what will there be new? This will be answered when a new generation has grown up . . . When these people are in the world, they will . . . make their own practice and their corresponding public opinion about the practice of each individual and that will be the end of it" (p. 73).

Moreover, in the family of the future, after the abolition of private property ownership and the assumption of social responsibility for children, there would be no anxiety about the material consequences of unwanted pregnancy. Similarly, illegitimacy would carry no stigma, for society would care for legitimate and illegitimate alike. And, of course, there would be no anxiety about inheriting and bequeathing wealth.

The thoughtful reader will perceive some difficulties in these formulations. Parenthood, for instance, is given short shrift. The question of mutuality in love, a very troublesome matter, and the related fact that in Engels' own words men are "by nature" more polygamous than women are not adequately settled (pp. 10, 46–47, 73).[26] Neither is the question of whether there will be individual dwellings for men and women.[27]

But the founders of marxism had written in *The Communist Manifesto* that "the theory of the Communist may be summed up in the single sentence: Abolition of private property." [28] And now, it seems, they were seeking to be consistent in drawing out the implications of this commitment. Hence the concepts of the family and marriage were greatly overshadowed by the concern with liberation of the individual from all external constraint. The family of the future was essentially a naturalistic unit rather than a social institution, for social relationships were regarded as little more than the extension of the individual's potentialities for equality, freedom, and love.

TWO | HISTORICAL MATERIALISM AND THE FAMLY

THE FAILURE OF Marx and Engels to clarify the exact relation of the family to historical materialism left the main axiom of historical materialism unbowed but led to weakness and ambiguity in the marxist theory of the family. As a result, the gates were open wide for a rich tide of supplementary theories as well as legislative experimentation in the post-revolutionary USSR.

On the Withering Problem

Historical materialism clearly extends priority, if not exclusive reign,[1] to the influence of economic factors. In the causation of social change, the "mode of production" is seen as the prime mover. In marxian terminology, the conditions constituting this force have come to be designated as the "base" (*Unterbau*) and the phenomena of change which are dependent upon it as the "superstructure" (*Überbau*).

Although this conceptual scheme dramatizes effectively the determinist facet of Marx's and Engels' theories, it is unfortunate and misleading and does not reflect the best thinking of the two originators of marxism. Not only does it suggest an overly rigid notion of the direction in which causal influence is exerted from base to superstructure but it also leads to an unproductive dualism in ordering social forces. That is, it suggests only two conceptual dimensions: the economic (sometimes, more broadly, materialistic) base and all those other phenomena dependent on it, the superstructure. Actually, Marx and Engels most frequently thought in terms of a three-dimensional scheme made up of cultural forms or patterns of social institutions, the proper realm for "survivals"; social relations as they "really exist" (for example, in the proletarian family under bourgeois capitalism); and economic or materialistic conditions.[2] Unfortunately, because of the base-superstructure scheme, apparently taken from the building trade, and because of the presence of careless or elliptical statements in which Marx and Engels seem to be working with a dualistic scheme, in marxist theory only the first and third elements can be identified with certainty as superstructure and base. The middle element, social relations, responds to changes in the third and also can be seen as itself causing changes in the first. Hence, it can be located according to desire either in base or in superstructure.

Marx and Engels made use of Morgan's term "survival" to refer generally to components of an outmoded superstructure. The state, law, religion, morality in general were all part of that superstructure, and, consequently, since superstructural elements were presumed to be the result of contradictions at a lower level, they would all disappear under communism. The fate Marx and Engels assigned to the family was not unrelated to their general discussion of life under communism. Their interpreters have frequently contended that they felt the family was also part of the superstructure, and hence that it took a form which was essentially a function of the state of economic forces at a given moment in history. As such, the family not only was a totally dependent institution, and therefore unimportant, but would ultimately disappear completely.

This conclusion is supported on at least four grounds. First, Marx and Engels do occasionally speak quite plainly of abolishing the family, as in the following: "That the abolition of [the] individual [household] economy is inseparable from the abolition of the family is self-evident" (*Ideology*, p. 18).[3] Another is found in the *Communist Manifesto*: "Abolition of the family! Even the most radical flareup at this infamous proposal of the Communists. On what foundation is the present family, the bourgeois family, based? On capital, on private gain. In its completely developed form, this family exists only among the bourgeoisie, but this shape of things finds its complement in the practical absence of the family among the proletarians, and in public prostitution. The bourgeois family will vanish as a matter of course when its complement vanishes, and both will vanish with the vanishing of capital" (*The Communist Manifesto*, p. 77).

Secondly, Marx and Engels suggest an analogy between social classes and state on one side and spouses and family on the other. The state, clearly a superstructural element that was developed by the bourgeoisie to protect its property interests inevitably falls with the fall of classes (*Origin*, p. 158). The family would suffer the same fate, for its function apparently was analogous to that of the state. It was an institution to protect the husband's interest in exploiting the wife. He was the bourgeois and his wife the proletarian.

Thirdly, at both the beginning and the end of their writing careers Marx and Engels made statements that seem to treat the family as a survival from an earlier era. The cultural ideal (or social institution) of the family no longer corresponded with the underlying reality they saw. Thus, Marx wrote that under capitalism the exercise of parental control over children became anachronistic, indeed evil. "The capitalist mode of production, through the dissolution of the economic basis for parental authority, made its exercise degenerate into a mischievous misuse of power" (*Capital,* I, 535). And Engels felt the accepted relationship between man and wife was no longer possible in a case where the wife took outside employment. In fact, their relationship was turned "upside down"; the reason — "simply because the division of labor outside the family had changed" (*Origin,* p. 147). Such instances could easily be multiplied, for time and again the founders of marxism seemed to forget the complexity of the conditions and forces determining a given concrete phenomenon and to attribute the properties of necessity and sufficiency to a single factor.

Finally, the student of marxism knows that the pattern of the future is not without its precedent in the past. The merging of future and past is especially prominent in *The Origin.* Ostensibly on the basis of Morgan's research into the North American Iroquois and other preliterate societies, Marx and Engels concluded that primitive man was in a happier condition than his civilized cousin. They wrote of the Iroquois:

And a wonderful order [*Verfassung*] it is, this gentile order, in all its childlike simplicity! No soldiers, no gendarmes or police, no nobles, kings, regents, prefects, or judges, no prisons, no lawsuits — and everything takes its orderly course. All quarrels and disputes are settled by the whole of the community affected, by the gens or the tribe, or by the gentes among themselves . . . . Although there were many more matters to be settled in common than today — the household is maintained by a number of families in common, and is communistic, the land belongs to the tribe, only the small gardens are allotted provisionally to the households — yet there is no need for even a trace of our complicated administrative apparatus with all its ramifications . . . There cannot be any poor or needy — the communal household and the gens know their responsibilities towards the old, the sick, and those disabled in war. All are equal and free — the woman included . . . And what men and women such a society breeds is proved by the admiration inspired in all white people who have come into contact with unspoiled Indians, by the personal dignity, uprightness, strength of character, and courage of these barbarians. [*Origin,* pp. 86–87.]

Against the "simple moral greatness" of the old "gentile" society Marx and Engels juxtaposed the corrupt civilization they saw around them, with its "base greed, brutal appetites, sordid avarice, selfish robbery of the common wealth" (*Origin,* p. 88). The cause, of course, was the development of private property and classes, as Marx and Engels had long since concluded. Morgan's research was doubly attractive to them because it detected a pattern of life in the past which corresponded in many respects with the hopes nourished by Marx and Engels for the future and hence united a happier future with a happier past in a comforting similarity. This point is explicitly stated on the last page of *The Origin,* where Engels cites with approval Morgan's judgment of the coming "next higher plane of society," and even underlines the book's concluding words: "It will be a revival in a higher form, of the liberty, equality and fraternity of the ancient gentes" (p. 163).

The unification of the two utopias — past and future — is not without significance to our interest. For, "under the gentile order, the family was never an organizational unit [*Organisationseinheit*], and could not be so, for man and wife necessarily belonged to two different gentes" (*Origins,* pp. 90–91). This statement anticipates the ultimate prediction of Marx and Engels. It almost but not quite explicitly indicates that there will be no family under communism. Again, Engels resorts approvingly to ideas of Morgan:

> When the fact is accepted that the family has passed through four successive forms, and is now in a fifth, the question arises whether this form can be permanent in the future. The only answer that can be given is that it must advance as society advances, and change as society changes, even as it has done in the past. It is the creature of the social system, and will reflect its culture. As the monogamian family has improved greatly since the commencement of civilization, and very sensibly in modern times, it is at least supposable that it is capable of still further improvement until the equality of the sexes is attained. Should the monogamian family in the distant future fail to answer the requirements of society . . . it is impossible to predict the nature of its successor. [*Origin,* p. 74.]

This passage very strongly implies that the monogamous family will indeed fail to answer society's requirements in the future.

All of the above lends support to the view that Marx and Engels felt that the family would wither away. However, passages can also be found which suggest that they thought of and used the term family in two distinct senses: (1) to refer to the social relations clustering around the facts of sex and age differences, sexual attraction, sexual intercourse, and reproduction; and (2) as a strictly cultural or institutional entity, a survival of the past in relation to the conditions appearing on the scene with modern bourgeois capitalism. Examples of the second usage have already been given, and the following is an example of the first, more general, connotation: "Modern industry, by assigning as it does an important part in the process of production, outside the domestic sphere, to women, to young persons, and to children of both sexes, creates a new economic foundation for a *higher form of the family* and of the relations between the sexes" (*Capital,* I, 536; my italics).

This semantic problem caused difficulties similar to those brought on by the dualism suggested in the concepts of base and superstructure. The family would indeed wither away if the term meant the cultural form of the detested "monogamous family of civilization," but it would not wither, at least not entirely, if the term referred to the observable clustering of certain kinds of behavior and social relations around sex, age, and reproduction.[4] In addition to the semantic confusion, there were other complexities.

Underlying Thought-Models: An Emerging Multi-Factor Theory

Marx's and Engels' major concept was the central place of economic factors in social change. But the world of facts is stubbornly complex, and the marxist treatment of the family has been particularly shaky because of certain facts relating to biological ties and to sexual reproduction which seem to be materialistic but yet are not economic. This clash of social theory, with its inherent press toward completeness and closure, and the world of observable facts resulted in two fissures, possibly a third, in the structure of economic determinism, both of which are of the greatest interest for students of marxism and students of social theory in general. Two of these "underlying thought models" are presented in some detail in this section, and a third is briefly alluded to. Neither of the first two was ever made very explicit in the writing of Marx and Engels, thus have led to considerable confusion and uncertainty among marxists about the role of the family in historical materialism. The third analogy is almost entirely latent.

As noted previously, the tendency in Marx's and Engels' writings on the family is to treat the family principally as a function of economic developments. Throughout Engels' major work on the subject there are references to the determining effect of property relations, the division of labor, the employment of women, and, as an extension of the latter, a kind of "reflection" theory of the family. For example, Engels argued that as wealth increases, the man overthrows the traditional order of inheritance — reckoned in the female line, according to him,[5] a fact which "was the *world historical defeat of the female sex*" (*Origin,* p. 50; Engels' italics). Two different but closely related economic factors are held directly to influence the positions of husband and wife: an increase in wealth, with subsequent change in the inheritance role, and the wage-earning work role of the husband. In both cases an advantageous economic position is seen as inevitably leading to unbalanced personal power which in turn leads to oppression and inequality. This mode of analysis is certainly consistent with the main thesis of Marx and Engels' thought.

At first sight, then, it does not seem inconsistent to find such depictions of the family as the following, in which Engels is speaking of the monogamous family: "It is the cellular form of civilized society, in which the nature of the oppositions and contradictions fully active in that society can be already studied" (*Origin,* p. 58). Such descriptions can easily and conveniently be interpreted simply as elements in a reflection theory of the family, for they are explained entirely by the portrayal of the economic circumstances reigning in society as a whole.

But this leads us to our first underlying analytical model. Early in their career the two collaborators spoke of the "latent slavery in the family" (*Ideology,* p. 21), and in *Capital* Marx wrote about a division of labor in the family which "spontaneously developed" and which depends upon or is caused by "differences of age and sex" (pp. 90, 386). Surely these must be reckoned as references to a noneconomic factor, unless Marx and Engels are simply being elliptical, which seems unlikely. To call "differences of age and sex" aspects of property relations, or of economic forces of any kind, would be stretching the meaning of this latter concept to the breaking point. More likely, Engels and Marx saw age and sex differences *in themselves,* that is, as facts of nature, as a source of inequality (ultimately of power) and oppression. From this point of view, then, insofar as Marx conceived them to be capable of variation, as is implied by the use of the term slavery (which obviously could not be eternal), family relationships can be seen as a superstructure over a biological base.[6]

A further analogy, also focusing on a biological fact, is found in the earliest exposition of historical materialism made by the two writers (*Ideology,* pp. 16–27). There they assert that three basic premises[7] support their analysis: (1) the production of material things to enable man to live; (2) the infinity of human needs — as soon as one is satisfied, new needs appear; and (3) reproduction.[8] They then continue their exposition to develop the idea that to each mode of production or industrial stage — see premise (1) — there corresponds a "mode of cooperation" or "social stage." This mode of cooperation (*Weise des Zusammenwirkens*)[9] is, they say, itself a force of production (*Produktivkraft*) and thus becomes also a condition (fact, moment, premise), the fourth, of the historical process.[10]

These ideas were considerably refined in later writings. The important fact in the present context is what appears to be the assignment by Marx and Engels of an independent and fundamental role to the process of reproduction, premise (3). There is little doubt that this is what they meant. They wrote: "The production of life, both of one's own in labor *and of fresh life in procreation,* now appears as a double relationship: on the one hand as a natural, on the other hand as a social relationship" (*Ideology,* p. 18; my italics). If *The German Ideology* were the only place in which such an idea was presented, one would be inclined to assume that they later thought better of it. But the notion recurs in similarly explicit form in the last major work of the founders of marxism, *The Origin of the Family,* and again in a letter of September 21, 1890, from Engels to Bloch. In *The Origin* Engels referred to the earlier book and repeated with approval the following: "The first division of labor is that between man and woman for the propagation of children" (p. 58). Engels did not propose to abolish this division of labor, though he may have wished to, but he did consider reproduction to be of such importance to historical materialism that it receives explicitly equal weight with production. In the preface to the first edition of *The Origin of the Family,* he wrote:

According to the materialistic conception, the determining factor in history is, in the final instance, the production and reproduction of the immediate essentials of life. This, again, is of a twofold character. On the one side, the production of the means of existence, of articles of food and clothing, dwellings, and of the tools necessary for that production; on the other side, the production of human beings themselves, the propagation of the species. The social organization under which the people of a particular historical epoch and a particular country live is determined by both kinds of production; by the stage of development of labor on the one hand and of the family on the other. The lower the development of labor and the more limited the amount of its products, and consequently, the more limited also the wealth of the society, the more the social order is found to be dominated by kinship groups. However, within this structure of society based on kinship groups the productivity of labor increasingly develops, and with it private property and exchange, differences of wealth, the possibility of utilizing the labor power of others, and hence the basis of class antagonisms: new social elements, which in the course of generations strive to adapt the old social order to the new conditions, until at last their incompatibility brings about a complete upheaval. In the collision of the newly-developed social classes, the old society founded on kinship groups is broken up; in its place appears a new society, with its control centered in the state, the subordinate units of which are no longer kinship associations, but local associations; a society in which the system of the family is completely dominated by the system of property, and in which there now freely develop those class antagonisms and class struggles that have hitherto formed the content of all *written* history. [Pp. 5–6; Engels' italics.]

Apparently Marx and Engels were inclined somehow to look upon reproduction as part of the base. It seems quite clear that they were on the verge of an analogy between the mode of production and the mode of reproduction, to which would correspond, respectively, two separate and parallel sets of modes of cooperation or social stages.

The social stages which correspond to the different stages of development of the mode of production were of course the stages in the historical development of society: primitive communism, slavery, feudalism, and so forth. The social stages which presumably would correspond to "variations" in the mode of reproduction were the different forms of social relationship, group marriage, monogamous family, and so on, which Marx and Engels saw as clustering around sex and reproduction, a line of thought much encouraged by Morgan.

The analogy is obviously faulty, since the process of reproduction is hardly a variable in the same sense as the process of production. Moreover, Marx and Engels never developed it in any explicit and systematic way, and to their followers it has proved to be either embarrassing or mystifying. Heinrich Cunow, for example, found it "almost incomprehensible how Engels could have made such a mistake," and soberly asserted that the "production of men" had always been accomplished "in the same way and with the same means." [11] His colleague, Karl

Kautsky, noted that the phrasing in *The Origin* corresponded almost word for word with that in *The German Ideology* and found it "very remarkable" that nothing more was said about it in the intervening years.[12] Even Lenin, in reply to criticism by the sociologically inclined N. K. Mikhailovsky about this phrase of Engels' was not able to give an effective defense or explanation.[13] Nor have efforts by Soviet theorists been very successful. For some time it was simply dismissed as a mistake or an inaccuracy on the part of Engels, while more recently the view has been taken that Engels' reference in *The Origin* to the determining importance of reproduction was meant to refer to the earliest period of human history, when "people were still more like beasts than people" and the means of production had little influence on their relations.[14]

In fact, however, a careful reading of the quotation above makes such an interpretation dubious. The forthright manner of its presentation and the persistence of the idea over forty years of more or less continuous thinking and polemical activity by the two founders of marxism strongly suggests that the family was not seen by them as of the same ilk as the state, religion, and so forth — that is, as an element of the superstructure dependent entirely on contradictions arising out of material circumstances — and that they felt the family, insofar as it was a part of the superstructure, was "originally tied" with a base other than an economic one.

It is not impossible to conclude from this review that Marx and Engels were for their time unusually acute sociological analysts and were close on the track of the essentials of modern sociological theory. In these scattered comments they seem to be moving in the direction of a multifactor theory of the determination of concrete social structure. Thus their thoughts about the family tended to lead them in a direction opposite to that in which they wanted to move, which was toward economic determinism, a single-factor theory. But Marx and Engels were moralists and political activists as much as they were social theorists, and these interests had their influence on the theories they developed. Admittedly, even the most indignant of men are unlikely to become very exercised over the injustice arising from the division of labor in reproduction.

According to still a third pattern, implicit in the writings of Marx and

Engels, the family can be analyzed in terms of an analogy with the main axiom of historical materialism. This belief extends the parallel between the mode and relations of production (in the economic realm) to the mode and relations of reproduction. In both cases important needs are involved, certain objects can satisfy those needs, and rights are at stake. To the need for food, clothing, and shelter correspond the sexual need of the individual and the (derived) need of society for new members. To the means and instruments of production correspond the sexual characteristics and organs of men and women. And to the economic commodity and to property rights correspond both sexual satisfaction and sexual rights and the fruit of intercourse — a new life — and parental rights.

Carrying the analogy further, the element corresponding to socialization of the means of production is clearly the socialization of the bodies of men and women and of their children or, if one prefers, the abolition of private sexual and parental rights. And, of course, to the economic greed and exploitative nature of the bourgeois correspond the sexual jealousy and sense of parental ownership which are part and parcel of the institution of the monogamous family.

Marx and Engels were clearly willing to consider a certain abolition of parental rights, since under communism the rearing of children would be the responsibility and right of society as a whole; but the abolition of sexual rights (which they tended to see as simply the right of the husband to his wife's body) was another matter. As a problem in their scheme, it was solved by means of an image of what would happen once women were freed from their economic and legal inferiority. Marx and Engels apparently felt that once women had obtained a position of equality with men, there would be no need for any kind of rights, for natural man and natural woman would engage in sexual relations strictly according to mutual inclination. This naturalistic humanism protected them against the charge of proposing a onesided socialization of women. They did not, however, envisage the possibility that in the future society women themselves might wish, in numbers large or small, to treat their own bodies as public property, in which case the criteria of both naturalism and mutuality would be satisfied. Their presumption that sexual love is individual is one of the unscientific elements present in their ideas.

Personal Values at Work

This is not the place to enter into a thorough discussion of the role played in marxism by the values of Marx and Engels, but so many of them do touch on the marxist image of the family that it is essential to spend a few pages on them. Many, as we shall see, were carried over, sometimes with added vigor, to the post-revolutionary Soviet scene.

In the first place, Marx and Engels were iconoclasts. This general attitude did at times enable them to undertake analysis of topics and problems which to their contemporaries were still sacred and not proper subjects of discussion. They were, for instance, interested in the problem of incest and both were sufficiently emancipated to be able to think and write reasonably, if not always correctly, about it. The main conclusion to which they came, as we have seen, was that in the more primitive era of man's history incest was common and that it was the extension of the incest taboo to a wider and wider circle of relatives which accounted in the first place for the emergence of the family as an institution of civilization. But their critical attitude occasionally became radical to a fault. Marx and Engels simply did not like the family, a fact we shall discuss in more detail later. For instance, in defending his conclusions about the existence of a "primitive social stage of sexual promiscuity," Engels severely debunked the main family institution of the present, monogamous marriage. Such a typical passage as "And if strict monogamy is the height of all virtue, then the palm must go to the tapeworm which has a complete set of male and female sexual organs in each of its 50–200 proglottides, or sections, and spends its whole life copulating in all its sections with itself" (*Origin*, p. 28) definitely steps over the boundaries of ethical neutrality, the position of the social scientist, into the realm of social criticism.

In addition to their iconoclasm, Marx and Engels shared an attitude which might be called promethean humanistic ethical universalism. Their deep indignation about unjust conditions and institutions was coupled with a magnificently hopeful attitude toward man's ability to overcome them. Nothing so aroused them as exploitation of any kind, sexual as well as economic. The well-known feudal *jus primae noctis,* for instance, repeatedly drew Engels' ire. Again, differences in sex and age which led to differences in rights and power within the family were dubbed "latent slavery"; indeed, being born into a particular family or a particular class is characterized as a "fetter" and an "accident" (*Ideology*, pp. 70–71). In their opposition to such fetters and accidents, the two founders of marxism might be said to be against not only tradition but the tyranny of nature itself.

This very eagerness to gain absolute equality of rights, an end to all exploitation, led Marx and Engels to one of their most central and pervasive errors: the consistent presumption that in human relations inequality of power leads always to abuse of power. This revealed their Darwinian heritage but also anchored a major weak point in their system. The concept clearly is closely related to their ethical position, manifested repeatedly in their writings in diatribes against wealth, against power, against all privilege, traditional or natural, and explains why property relations are so central to their theory. Since property is easily detachable from the individual, it was obviously the key starting place for the redemption of man. The view that property should be detached is quite clearly their central value judgment. Only "primitive, natural communal property" met with their favor (*Origin*, p. 57). In their analysis of the family this value element is quite manifest not only in respect to property but also in respect to other natural inequalities that are central to the family, those of age and those of sex. Marx and Engels quite consistently defended the weak against the strong: children were defended from exploitation at the hands of parents, and woman was even more fiercely defended against the same fate at the hands of man. Perhaps this is one source of their enthusiasm for Charles Fourier's idea that the emancipation of women was the best general index of the moral progress of civilization: "The development of a given historical epoch is best of all defined by the relation between the progress of woman and freedom, since in the relations between woman and man, the weak and the strong, is most clearly expressed the victory of human nature over bestiality. The degree of feminine emancipation is a natural measure of the general emancipation." [15]

There are, of course, other broad guidelines in the ethics of Marx and Engels, more minor or more diffuse. Many seem to parallel central conceptions of Western monotheism,[16] but to pursue them in detail would take us too far afield.

One value area that must be taken up is the attitude of the founders of marxism to the question of sexuality and love. Marx had little to say on this matter, and perhaps on this point there was considerable difference between him and Engels. If personal experience is relevant, Marx led an ordinary, if troubled, family life, whereas Engels formalized in marriage only the relationship to his second consort, and did that in the last moments of her life in 1878.[17]

Throughout *The Origin* it is obvious that sex and love are strangers in the city of marxism. Other than in the more or less implicit analogical models discussed above, they are irrelevant to the central concerns of historical materialism. In fact, they are awkward and embarrassed strangers. Sex, especially its "highest form," individual sexual love (p. 62), is highly idealized. Not only is the supposedly unrestrained and "generous" sexual life of savages favored, as contrasted with the hypocritical restrictions of civilized society, but, and quite consistently, even adultery is granted considerable praise (pp. 68 ff.). In the ancient world, as in the Middle Ages, it was only in the free choice of adulterous unions that true love was found; and among the married in the time of capitalism, wrote Engels, it was an irony of history that while the rising bourgeoisie proclaimed the love marriage as a human right, it was only the oppressed class, the proletariat, that was able to enjoy it (p. 72). But, to be more specific, Engels defined sexual love as follows: "Our sexual love differs essentially from the simple sexual desire, the Eros of the Ancients. In the first place, it assumes that the person loved returns the love; to this extent the woman is on an equal footing with the man whereas in the Eros of antiquity she was often not even asked. Secondly, our sexual love has a degree of intensity and duration which makes both lovers feel that non-possession and separation are a great, if not the greatest, calamity; to possess one another, they risk high stakes, even life itself" (p. 68).

The Emergence of the Category Love

When so many pages of fervent admiration for sexual love find their way into a work which purports to be dealing with human life and history as it actually is, one may suspect the writer's interest in a value that is above and beyond the reality of life itself. Possibly the placing of sexual love on a pedestal, even more than other features of marxism, represents a disguised plea for what Marx and Engels saw as natural man. Or perhaps it, along with Engels' rather compulsive insistence on absolute equality between the sexes, is simply a reaction formation against a deep-lying hostility and lack of trust toward women, especially bourgeois women — women of his own social class. And his declarations in favor of love may be so vigorous partly because he felt himself that his view was suspect. Certainly his position brought him face to face with several difficult problems which he could escape only with the most tortured explanations and devices.

While such interpretations are not unreasonable, the introduction and use of love in the unfolding of historical materialism suggests still an additional view. In *The Origin* Engels speaks of love as a historical emergent: "Here a new element comes into play, an element which, at the time when monogamy was developing, existed at most in germ: individual sex love. Before the Middle Ages we cannot speak of individual sex love" (p. 68).

But surely ancient man and woman cannot have been so unfortunate. Individual sex love actually plays a different role, more purely syntactical, in the historical materialism of Marx and Engels: it is designed or, better, concocted to set the limits between socialized and personal property and between public and private life. In fact, love seems the savior of monogamy. In speaking of the future society, Engels asserts that "prostitution disappears; monogamy, instead of collapsing, at last becomes a reality also for men" (p. 67).[18] Further: "Can prostitution disappear without dragging monogamy with it into the abyss?" The answer is yes, and the reason is the "new element . . . individual sex-love" (p. 68).

Marx and Engels were distracted from their main goal, perhaps even embarrassed, by the common tendency of the time to impute to them, and with some reason, an espousal of sexual communism. Of their genuine and imagined opposition to the various established institutions of society, none aroused more moral indignation than the idea of communal sexual property. As we have seen, the idea of the socialization of the means of production could easily be extended to include *sexual* property (reproductive property!) as well.

All in all, then, one can safely guess that individual sex love was in part a makeshift device used by Engels to save the semblance of the family as an expression of individual freedom in the imagined society of the future and to draw the line, however dimly and unconsciously, between public and private rights. Man's right to love was at least partly recognized, and the whole question anticipated a central dilemma of divided loyalty in the Soviet era.

Marx and Engels as Sociologists

The ambitious scope of marxism is one of its most distinctive features. Marx and Engels were preachers and prophets as well as social analysts, and it is now clear that one of their greatest errors was ultimately one of prophecy. The revolution did not in fact first occur in the most wealthy and developed countries, under conditions of ripened capitalism, and the development of marxism in poor, backward Russia necessarily strained their ideas.

Nevertheless, much respectable social theory can be found in Marx's and Engels' writing. In fact, their richness of insight and fertility of imagination, along with plenty of the artist's ambiguousness, makes reading them a continual source of intellectual novelty. Some of their best, and most general, theorizing concerned the family, and, in addition to the thoughts already discussed, several other aspects of their work will complete the picture and also suggest why their ideas have been sometimes welcome, sometimes not, in the USSR.

First, the concept of "survival" (German *Überbleibsel,* Russian *perezhitok*) is as prominent today as ever in the Soviet lexicon. As popularly used in the late nineteenth century by such evolutionary anthropologists as Morgan and Edward B. Tylor, the term referred to a social custom or pattern which ostensibly served no useful purpose but continued nonetheless to exist. It was analogous to the "sport" of biological theory and hence was of interest in the first place simply as an item of curiosity, but in Morgan's thought it was also methodologically central: the detection of survivals in the present seemed a foolproof means of studying the past. Modern theorists believe that a true non-material cultural trait which serves no live purpose is quite rare, if it exists at all, and the concept of the survival therefore plays little role in modern ethnological or sociological theory.[19] Perhaps it should do so, but the main problem in its use is that no adequately precise criteria have been devised to bring assurance that a particular pattern does not have some as yet undiscovered and unsuspected latent function. A pattern that does have such a function is, of course, not a survival. And the modern Western social scientist, more modest and cautious than his father and grandfather, is likely to suspend judgment for lack of evidence.

But the "survival" of the nineteenth-century evolutionary anthropology fitted neatly into the panorama of Marx and Engels. It was exactly the sort of concept they had in mind when speaking of the "political or religious nonsense" which only cluttered up man's chances to understand the "materialistic connection of men with one another" (*Ideology,* pp. 18–19). Insofar as the survival and historical materialism made a happy union, the concept did epitomize an important, and valid, proposition of Marx and Engels: that cultural forms change more slowly than the economic and other conditions of man's life.

Marx and Engels also developed important theories about the source of survivals in social contradictions and about their conservative function, to the extent that they had one, as a means of social control. Thus, "the rights of the children had to be proclaimed, because their parents were exploiting them" (*Capital,* I, 535); and of the bourgeois family in general, wrote Marx: "Its befouled existence is set off by the sacredness of the idea of the family in official parlance and in everyday hypocritical locutions." [20] Engels provided a not entirely dissimilar analysis of the incest taboo; since it arose out of the "contradiction" between the sexual attraction of relatives and the (supposedly) deleterious effect of inbreeding, it served as a restraining institution in its province in the same manner that the state functioned in its sphere.

Marx and (particularly) Engels also anticipated modern multifactor sociology in their usage of explanatory mechanisms. As soon as a theorist undertakes to develop a theory of history, he must be prepared to offer interpretations of concrete events, and, in the case of evolutionary theory, of transitions from one stage to another. In detailing the stages through which the family had passed, and the reasons for the passages, Marx and Engels came closer than anywhere else in their work to breaking completely away from their tendency toward monistic economic determinism. More than once Engels had to take recourse to such social mechanisms as natural selection (to explain why the punaluan family replaced the consanguine and why the pairing family replaced the punaluan family), or adaptation (to explain population growth, changes in social organization, and so forth), or even a bargaining process whereby women exchanged their social supremacy in the communistic household for the "right of chastity, of temporary or permanent marriage with one man only" (*Origin,* p. 46).

Actually, Marx's and Engels' theorizing about the history of the family has had little influence upon the thinking of most marxists. Clearly, in their thinking the family was not very important; other institutions, other forces, other problems held the center of attention. Second, their writing about the family was not focused; it was often ambiguous and contradictory. Third, some of their thoughts about it do not correspond with economic determinism.[21] Since the latter was for many the most appealing aspect of marxism as a social theory, the path of least resistance was simply to forget about those parts of their writing on the family which came closest to multifactor theorizing. Thus, the well-known marxist theoretician of the German Social Democratic party, Heinrich Cunow, asserts that in ranging "the production of men" alongside "the production of the means of life" Engels "breaks completely away from the unified nature of the materialist view of history." [22] For him, as well as for his even more eminent colleague, Kautsky, this idea of Engels (and Marx) was simply a mistake. On the other hand, Kautsky's analysis of the family in one respect is a significant improvement on Marx's and Engels' and does approach a multifactor theory; for him sexual life was a relatively constant factor in history, one which is "independent of the latitude of productive forces." [23]

Marx and Engels hated private property; it was corruptive and had to be done away with. To the extent that they wished to emphasize this, both writers were logically forced into the position of opposing the family mainly because it was a basic propertyholding institution. In Soviet times the family came to be seen more and more in terms of the diversion of loyalty, as the carrier of an antagonism between the individual and revolutionary society. Though this was a relatively minor theme in Marx and Engels,[24] it was to become a major one in the post-revolutionary Soviet Union.

THE SOVIET REGIME

CONFRONTS THE FAMILY

The play written by Marx and Engels was first presented in Russia in the years following the October Revolution. But the theater, unfortunately, was not well suited to the aim of the playwrights, and some of the essential props were missing. Nevertheless, it was decided to go ahead with the production. After some time it became apparent that revision was needed, but the authors had such close friends in high places that the needs of the audience and the caustic comments of critics were little heeded.

THREE | PROBLEMS OF THE TRANSITION PERIOD

MARX AND ENGELS believed in a direct transition from "ripe" capitalism to communism and gave little reason to anticipate a revolution in Russia. Among the Bolshevik leaders the most fertile minds undoubtedly understood that many of the ideas of the founders of marxism were not always relevant to the particular problems of what came to be known as the "transition period," [1] but literal allegiance to those ideas was so strong that the struggle between the marxian ideological heritage and the necessity of attending to immediate requirements eventually constituted a prominent theme of early Soviet social history. In addition to the interplay between emerging social problems of the day and principles generally shared among the communists, one finds a noticeable difference within the party itself. On questions of family and sex life, as in other areas, there developed a left wing and a right wing.[2] The former was more radical, more literal in interpreting marxist ideas, and more anxious to rush them into practice. The right wing, more conservative and more practical in modifying inherited ideas in the interest of effectively solving current difficulties, also tended to be rather more interested in solving, or ignoring, such questions on the grounds of personal tastes, which in the marxist lexicon referred broadly to all aspects of life not dealt with in the concepts of historical materialism.

It took considerable time for this division of opinion to become apparent, however, because neither Lenin nor the party as a whole took much interest in it. More important concerns filled the minds of the Bolshevik leaders.[3] There was a great deal of sympathy for Engels' clear distinction between the realm of public life and the realm of private life, and it was not immediately apparent that the marxist theory of the family would lead to difficulties.

In the first decade or so after the Revolution it was rather generally though vaguely agreed that the family was not worth much as an institution and would eventually disappear. Such thinking and writing as was done on the subject seemed to be motivated by two main considerations: the first to appear was simply the desire to explain, clarify, support, and elaborate the ideas of Marx and Engels, while the second, which developed later, was to try somehow to come to terms more directly with the problems of disorganization of family and sexual life that were developing but were hard to analyze in terms of the marxist theory of the family. Concurrently, of course, decisions had to be made and workable policies formulated, and often the practical right hand did not seem to be letting the ideological left hand know what it was doing.

In Pursuit of the Marxist Theory of the Family

Perhaps the most lively question posed by the writing of Marx and Engels, and the one receiving the most ambiguous response, was on the future of the family: Would the family, like the state, religion, and other institutions, wither away with the attainment of the classless society? More specifically, three questions, or at least three elements of the issue, seemed to be at stake here: Would the family disappear at some future, unspecified, time? If so, what implication did this have for the young socialist society; that is, would the disappearance or withering begin immediately? And again, if so, should the party and its followers take an active role in bringing about such a process? Among the positions taken on the far left was that of the leader of Bolshevik feminism Alexandra M. Kollontai, who tended to answer all three with a vigorous yes. On the far right were those who, like the German Social Democrat, Karl Kautsky, argued that the family would not disappear, now or in the communist future, and that in any case little could or should be done by the communists themselves, for such action would be "unmarxist." For example: "The communists see the only lever to a real transformation of human relations in a change of the productive base, the economic foundation of social life, over which the various ideological forms constitute multiform superstructures in which are clothed human consciousness, morals and customs." [4]

Somewhere between these two extremes, but closer to Kollontai, the views of the majority can probably be found. In the years between 1917 and 1934 most party members apparently subscribed to the following formulations, written by an influential member of the Leningrad party organization:

Bourgeois ideologists think that the family is an eternal, not a transitory organization, that sexual relations are at the basis of the family, that these sexual relations will exist as long as the two sexes, and since man and woman will both live under socialism just as under capitalism, that therefore the existence of the family is inevitable. That is completely incorrect. Sexual relations, of course, have existed, exist, and will exist. However, this is in no way connected with the indispensability of the existence of the family. The best historians of culture definitely have established that in primitive times the family did not exist . . . Similar to the way in which, together with the disappearance of classes, together with the annihilation of class contradictions, the state will disappear, similarly to that, together with the strengthening of the socialist economy, together with the growth of socialist relationships, together with the overcoming of earlier pre-socialist forms, the family will also die out. The family is already setting out on the road to a merging with Socialist Society, to a dissolution into it. [But] an openly negative attitude toward the family under present conditions does not have sufficient grounding, because pre-socialist relationships still exist, the state is still weak, the new social forms [public dining rooms, state rearing of children, and so forth] are as yet little developed, and until then the family cannot be abolished completely. However, the coordination of this family with the general organization of Soviet life is the task of every communist, of every Komsomolite [member of Communist Youth League]. One must not shut oneself off in the family, but rather, grow out of the family shell into the new Socialist Society. The contemporary Soviet family is the springboard from which we must leap into the future. Always seeking to carry the entire family over into the public organizations, always a more decisive overcoming of the elements of bourgeois family living — that is the difficult, but important task which stands before us.[5]

To summarize, the family will eventually die out, is in fact starting to do so now, but nonetheless will be needed for the duration of the transition period, and the party and its followers should take an active role in helping things along, mainly by setting a good example.

Preconditions for the new social ordering of the relations between the sexes were required. The most crucial was the entrance of woman into social production, which would give her economic independence and hence social equality. Her work in social production would then have to be balanced by society's assumption of the responsibilities of childrearing, supplying and preparing food, washing clothing, and so on. All such patterns — the entry of women into the labor market, the socialization of household chores, the assumption of public responsibility for childrearing — were originally subsidiary links in the causal chain leading to the end of the family, and to equality and freedom for the individual, but in early Soviet writing they tended to assume the status of end-goals in themselves, and to be justified in their own terms.

Lenin himself elaborated slightly the position of Marx and Engels on social equality for women. He was as strongly opposed as they, perhaps even more so, to the individual household with its "stinking kitchen," and, like them, asserted that only socialism and an end to small households could "save woman from housewifery." [6] Also, like Fourier, Marx, and Engels, Lenin saw in the liberation of women, the weaker sex, a symbol of a more general liberation, though he placed more stress on the psychological factor of participation in social production as a source of personality development, which would then serve generally to put women on a more equal footing with men. Conversely, Lenin seemed more irritated with the specific nature of the housewife's tasks than Marx and Engels had been when they had confined themselves more to the general factors of property relations in the family and the wife's entry into social production. Lenin wrote: "Women grow worn out in the petty, monstrous household work, their strength and time dissipated and wasted, their minds growing narrow and stale, their hearts beating slowly, their will weakened." [7] In this, he continued, it is not only the woman who suffers: "The home life of a woman is a daily sacrifice to a thousand unimportant trivialities. The old master right of the man still lives in secret. His slave takes her revenge, also secretly. The backwardness of women, their lack of understanding for the revolutionary ideals of the man, decrease his joy and determination in fighting. They are like little worms which, unseen, slowly but surely rot and corrode." [8] These subtleties constituted a relatively small shift of explanatory emphasis. For the rest, Lenin agreed that the development of public restaurants, crèches, and similar facilities was crucial, and that the abolition of the small household economy was, in the words of one of his colleagues, E. A. Preobrazhenski, "theoretically indisputable for every Communist."

Further arguments in support of the socialization of household chores were that the maintenance of an individual household was uneconomical and perpetuated the small, isolated, shut-off family unit, a source of hostility toward the new socialist way of life. During the 1920's, considerable effort was expended in the calculation of how many hours of labor were required to run an individual household, and a comprehensive survey of the life of Moscow workers conducted in

1923–1925 reported that some twelve working hours per day were needed, on the average, to carry on individual family life.[9] At one time it was estimated that in Russia 36,000,000 work hours were spent every day only on the preparation of food in individual households, whereas centralized production would have required only 6,000,000 work hours.[10] Later, in the middle of the First Five Year Plan, the complaint was made that 30,000,000 individuals were giving their full time to unproductive household work.[11]

As a corollary to such information, the liberation of women in itself was seen as a condition for economic development. Thereby the family became by implication a direct obstacle to the "development of the base." [12] Trotsky went even further, reversing the usual order of precedence in the marxist theory of the relation between family and economic life: "Until there is equality in the family, there will be none in social production." [13]

The rearing of children by society was hailed by all not only because it saved time and released the mother for outside work, but because it could be more scientific, more rational, more organized than rearing within the individual family. Some carried the argument even further and contended that in a society organized around a collective work system it was more appropriate to accustom a child from the earliest years to life in the collective rather than to train him in the individualistic small family. Kollontai's early formulation is characteristic: "The contemporary family, as a specific social collective, has no productive functions and to leave all care for posterity in this private collective cannot be justified by any positive considerations . . . Logically speaking, it would seem that care for the new generation should lie with that economic unit, with that social collective, that needs it for its further existence." [14]

To many observers the most striking feature of early Bolshevik family theory concerned the future of parent-child relations. Marx, Engels, and even Lenin had left the field open for the most radical pretensions of the leftists. Perhaps it is significant that neither Engels nor Lenin ever became a father. In any event, the writing of Marx and Engels clearly disregarded the positive contribution to society of motherhood and fatherhood. As a result, A. V. Lunacharski, Commissar of Education, could write in the early 1930's: "Our problem now is to do away with the household and to free women from the care of children. It would be idiotic to separate children from their parents by force. But when, in our communal houses, we have well-organized quarters for children, connected by a heated gallery with the adults' quarters, to suit the requirements of the climate, there is no doubt the parents will, of their own free will, send their children to these quarters, where they will be supervised by trained pedagogical and medical personnel. There is no doubt that the terms 'my parents,' 'our children,' will gradually fall out of usage, being replaced by such conceptions as 'old people,' 'adults,' 'children,' and 'infants.' " [15] Kollontai, prominent opponent of motherhood, saw it as an unjust burden and, in her zest for feminine emancipation, seemed to want to see women and men placed in identical social roles.

At times the radical image of the future took on very concrete form. In a series of publications of the late 1920's L. M. Sabsovich urged an immediate and complete change in all phases of everyday life — a radical cultural revolution. He advocated complete separation of children from parents from the earliest years and said that those who argued for recognition of such concepts as the natural biological tie between parents and children, were "soaked in petit bourgeois and 'intelligentsia-like' prejudices." [16] He held that social and economic factors accounted entirely for the feeling of exclusive love toward one's own children: in the future society there would be only love for children in general. Moreover, he pointed out that since the child was the property of the state, not the individual family, the state therefore had the right to compel parents to surrender their children to special "children's towns" to be built "at a distance from the family." [17] This was but one element in a broader scheme devised by Sabsovich for the construction of a new type of "socialist city" (the contemporary form of city was a "capitalist invention") in which not only work but all aspects of leisure and consumption activities were to be organized on a collectivist basis. The family dwelling would be completely eliminated, to be replaced by individual rooms for individual persons (though married persons could have adjoining rooms). Sabsovich urged that such reorganization of life into a "truly socialist" form start immediately: "Down with so-called 'transitional forms'!" The workers should not be furnished with gas, electricity, and other conveniences, but instead provided with a thorough socialist reconstruction within the next five to eight years.[18]

We may doubt that such views were widely shared. One opponent of Sabsovich referred to "various strange ideas about home life under socialism," such as, "all individual home life (not only family life) will disappear under socialism," and, "the whole life of a person, physical and mental, can be lived within the collective." [19] Nadezhda Krupskaia, Lenin's widow, noted that children belonged neither to parents nor to the state, but to themselves. Furthermore, the state was due to wither away, and "the parental sense will not be suppressed, but will flow in another channel; it will afford much more joy to children and to parents." Hence, parents would be justified, she wrote, in refusing to turn their children over to children's towns in the manner proposed by Sabsovich.[20]

All in all, on the level of ideology the first decade or so of post-revolutionary thought brought a rich and often quite interesting tide of theories about the family. With no official party line on the subject, the writings of Marx and Engels were ambiguous enough to elicit a variety of theories, and the emerging problems seemed to justify the number of them evoked.

Property and Inheritance

Some marxist ideas about the family found concrete embodiment in the realm of legal actions. Since marxist thought insisted so vigorously on the corruptive influence of private wealth, it was only natural that its presumed power should be curtailed. On April 27, 1918, it was decreed: "Testate and intestate succession are abolished. Property of an owner (movable as well as immovable) becomes after his death the domain of the Russian Socialist Federated Soviet Republic." [21] Other legal measures were taken to forestall immediately the detested "marriage of calculation." The 1918 family code proclaimed that "marriage does not establish community of property" and that "agreements by husband or wife intended to restrict the property rights of either party are invalid, and not binding." [22]

Nevertheless, the retreat from the abolition of inheritance began immediately, even in the very decree in which it was abolished. Though succession was repealed in principle, immediate relatives who had been living with the deceased were permitted to inherit if the value of the estate did not exceed 10,000 rubles, close relatives who were incapable of working were to receive an amount necessary for support, and so on. This situation was an early example of one which was to become prototypical: the Bolsheviks were simply not in a position to carry out their declared aims. In 1919 the Commissariat of Justice decreed that the 10,000-ruble limit did not apply to peasants' farmsteads, in 1922 the Civil Code explicitly permitted inheritance up to 10,000 rubles to specified persons, and in 1926 the upper limit was abolished entirely. However, hostility to the principle of inherited property continued and was expressed by a strongly progressive inheritance tax until 1943, when the tax itself was abolished. All that remained after that was a fee, progressive but never higher than 10 per cent.[23]

The abolition of the concept of community property of husband and wife was also a source of trouble to the Soviet leaders. Motivated largely by the desire to abolish marriage for money, the decree seemed a logical corollary to the marxist devaluation of household labor. All agreed in principle that women must be drawn out of the home and into social production, but the difficulty was that many married women could not, or would not, be so drawn out. There were large families to care for, there were not enough crèches and kindergartens, and there was unemployment during most of the years of the New Economic Policy from 1921 to 1928. But in those families where the wife did not work, such goods and money as were acquired after marriage could be interpreted as the legal property of the husband. In case of divorce, a phenomenon of increasing frequency in those days, the purpose of the law — to protect both spouses, but especially the woman, from exploitation — could boomerang to the disadvantage of the housewife. Thus, practice showed that laws of good intention could lead to bad results. So, in 1926 the principle that property acquired after marriage is community property of the spouses was restored to the code of laws on marriage and family.

One of the main functions of private wealth in most societies, whether accumulated or inherited, is to provide for times of sickness, old age, or other need for self or relatives, and the 1918 code recognized that legal responsibility for maintenance of children, the aged, and the invalid would have to continue for a time. In the 1918 decree on inheritance, for example, certain relatives (if propertyless and disabled) were authorized to receive, from an estate exceeding 10,000 rubles in value, a sum necessary for self-support. This exception was justified by a condition — "until a decree for universal social insurance is issued." [24] Although the idea of societal support for the individual was central to marxist socialism, it is an index of developing problems that in the 1926 code the individual's legal responsibility for support of needy relatives, instead of being narrowed, was widened to include brother, sister, grandparents, and grandchildren.[25] Presumably "marriages of calculation" continued with much the same frequency as before, though as time went on the determining factor came to be more a matter of selecting a husband who was a "big specialist" rather than wealthy.[26] The continuing importance of money in family life was also shown by the large number of lawsuits about problems of alimony.[27]

Parents: A Hotbed of Traditionalism

Though the theme is barely present in Marx and Engels, largely because of the limited importance of the transition period in their thinking, it was not long before their Soviet followers decided that the family was definitely not on the side of the Revolution. Kollontai put it very well: "The family deprives the worker of revolutionary consciousness." [28] She, like many of her colleagues, fulminated against the "small, isolated, closed-in family" and awaited the time when first loyalty would be to society, while family, love, all of personal life would come second.

Such theorists saw not only that in the family the spirit of acquisition and the sense of private property were born and nourished, but also that the family was intimately connected with religion. Life's most significant personal events — birth, marriage, and death — were after all those of family life, and somehow even the most convinced Communists found it hard to see the revolutionary "Dead March" supplant a Christian burial. Among the rank and file clearly there was nothing to take the place of the church, as the party members complained among themselves, and so the struggle against religion often was carried over into antagonism toward its everyday social context — the family.

One can gain an understanding of the spirit of the time by looking more closely at the strand of bolshevik social thought which might be called "totalism." The search for a total, though as yet voluntary, monopoly of the individual's personal loyalty is an early harbinger of the political totalitarianism that came later. The rationalistic Bolsheviks simply had no use for the "anarcho-individualistic disorganization" of the family, which demanded loyalty and time that they felt to be due the Revolution and the Cause. In fact, one influential party leader, A. A. Solts, even pointed to a contradiction between sexual needs, a "very individual matter," and the building of a collective society.[29]

The intractability and hostility of the family were demonstrated when it became apparent that it was not only the peasant and worker masses who stubbornly clung to their traditions. Trouble developed in the party itself. The old-fashioned family explained why workers did not join the party in the first place, and family pressure as well as church weddings caused misunderstandings among party members and exclusions from the membership ranks.[30] There was some discussion in the early years about what to do with Communists who took wives from an "alien class." In those years revolutionary political activity, especially at the lower levels, was a masculine one to which wives often responded with lack of enthusiasm. In 1923, one author argued, probably with considerable truth, that since only 10 per cent of the party members were women, the bulk of party wives must be politically unresponsive and "philistine." [31]

This situation led to an interesting conflict between the marxist principle of sex equality in the family and the Communist's obligation to impose his communist ideas. The outcome of this dilemma suggests the relative importance of the two norms: "We have the right to demand and we must demand from party members that the spiritual supremacy in the family belong to them — communists." [32]

In still another way, not at all foreseen by Marx and Engels, the family presented problems. It is the family, and the older generation, complained a writer in 1927, through which "the filth of the old world is passed to the youth." [33] Here, then, were a myriad of relatively inviolable self-oriented groups with an acquisitive attitude toward property, too often professing belief in religion, showing sexual self-indulgence, and even harboring open hostility to the new order. Truly the family seemed to be the enemy of everything the Revolution represented. It is little wonder that the bulk of bolshevik theorizing placed the family in the same boat with prostitution; in the future, both would disappear. The concept of the family as "the most conservative stronghold of the old regime" [34] therefore reinforced the more doctrinaire thought inherited from Engels, that the monogamous family was not worth much even in itself because of its internal structure.

To a considerable extent, perhaps, the family was also a favorite scapegoat. Many party leaders were surprised and chagrined to find that the workers, to say nothing of the peasants, were often neither enthusiastic about the Revolution nor much interested in the new way of life.

The family was most likely slated for extinction anyway, and its deep conservatism could account for the fact that bolshevism was not accepted more quickly. Thus, attacks on the family helped assuage the conscience of the more democratic and utopian-minded in the party.

The "family" is of course a rather abstract notion, but the individual persons who make it up could be held more immediately accountable. The targets of the most direct and concrete hostility were parents. They were seen as conservative or even reactionary toward the new way of life: mothers were religious and fathers were drunken or obsessed with private property. Since classical marxism, as we know, had nothing positive to say about the parent-child relationship under any circumstances, its relative silence about the tender love of mother and child, the closeness of father and son, and the like could be called upon for support. Actually, Marx and Engels tended to depict the parent-child relationship under capitalism in only one way: as tainted with exploitation. Perhaps they found it even more hopeless than the relationship between husband and wife, for if the latter tie was to be redeemed and purified in the future society, the same could not be said of the former because the state would rear the children.

Then, too, there was a certain inviting feasibility about destroying the family by attacking the parents. If parents could somehow be bypassed, the children could be used for the purposes of the regime. They were accessible to influence in the schools, their unformed minds were still suggestible, and they represented the future, for which hopes were high. As early as the Second Komsomol Congress in 1919, Komsomolites were being urged to split young people away from their parents, to induce, as one phrasing put it, "a psychological stratification in the rural family, drawing rural youth over to the side of the toilers' government." A resolution of the Congress urged Komsomol members to give special help to young Cossacks "who are rising up against their fathers." [35]

In the mid-twenties, an active party publicist, A. B. Zalkind, urged in books and pamphlets that children should respect their fathers only if their ideas were correct; neither respect nor obedience was due a reactionary father. Children who had parents with lagging revolutionary consciences were asked to criticize and reform their mothers and fathers. Parents, in turn, were to adopt a new and comradely attitude toward their children.[36] To give teeth to the new image of parent-child relations, speakers and writers announced that the use of physical punishment by parents was forbidden.[37] Indeed, a 1927 publication of the Commissariat of Justice described Soviet law as, among other things, "a new law which categorically denies the authority of the parental relationship." [38]

At the Seventh Congress of the Komsomol in 1926 Krupskaia urged upon the delegates the importance of the Young Pioneer organizations in the task of rearing the new generation. "The Pioneer detachment," she asserted, "must be, for the Pioneer, something like what the family used to be." Six years later, at the Ninth Congress in 1931, one delegate asserted that the Soviet regime had done away with the "fetish of the family, the subordination to the parents," and that children were now concluding "social contracts" with their parents. Contrasting the interests of the regime with those of the individual family, she continued, "We have taught children to proceed from higher interests — from the interests of the proletarian class." A resolution of the Congress spoke of the "extension of our influence in the family through the children themselves." Along with parents, schoolteachers were demoted. In 1931 a prominent party leader urged that leadership in the schools be exercised predominantly by the organized children.[39]

During these years some children actually brought their parents into court. The most dramatic episode, which colored the tone of the entire era, was the case of Pavlik Morozov, who when he took the side of the regime in the war being conducted with the peasantry denounced his own father and was subsequently killed for that act. He became an official martyr, and *The Great Soviet Encyclopedia* tells the story this way:

Morozov, Pavlik (Pavel Trofimovich, 1918–1932) — A courageous pioneer who, after selflessly struggling against the kulaks [rich peasants] of his community during the period of collectivization, was savagely killed by a kulak gang. The pioneers were carrying on an active struggle against the kulaks. M. exposed his own father, who had been at that time (1930), chairman of the village Soviet, but had fallen under the influence of kulak relatives. After telling his representative of the district committee of the party about how his father was secretly selling false documents to exiled kulaks, M. then testified in court in his father's case, and labelled him a traitor. The kulaks decided to settle matters with M. He was killed, together with his younger brother, on September 3, 1932, in a forest, by kulak bandits. The name of Morozov was given to the kolkhoz which was organized in Gerasimovka after his death, and also many other kolkhozes, pioneer palaces, and libraries." [40]

A more vigorous symbolization of the discrediting of the older generation, the rising power of youth, and the regime's willingness to trample family loyalty underfoot could hardly be devised.

These policies were not without their effect. As the power and the responsibility of the parent were gradually being relaxed, the rearing of children was becoming, it seemed, more and more a function of the larger society. But the new soicety was not equipped to deal with such a heavy duty. Ideological pretensions had again outrun institutional capacities, and to the extent that parental authority declined, Soviet children were more and more on their own, for the authority of youth organizations and "society as a whole" was largely chimerical.

Social Equality for Women

The equalitarian reformist zeal of the early years must not be underestimated. After all, the traditional form of the parent-child tie was considered unsatisfactory by the bolsheviks not only because parents were apt to be conservative or reactionary toward the new regime, but also because it epitomized the old moral system — based on blood ties and sympathy for relatives. Hence, just as in capitalist society, this tie bred further inequality by virtue of the differential capacities of parents to give their children education and a suitable general upbringing. But the epicenter of communist equalitarian aspirations was in the relation between the sexes. After the abolition of private property ownership, the assumption of family functions by the state, and the engagement of all women in social production, a situation was to arise in which "marriage will no longer have the appearance of a family as its obligatory consequence." The author of this phrase went so far as to allege that the separation of the kitchen from marriage is "a more significant historical event than the separation of church from state." [41] In fact, as we have seen, there was not a little sentiment in favor of residential separation of husband from wife. As one radical young woman wrote in an "open letter," "It is precisely a separate life [of husband and wife] which creates full 'equality of rights' for both parties, guarantees spiritual growth, liberates the woman." [42]

Many were in disagreement with this, but all were willing to vote for the desirability of economic independence for women. In countless pamphlets, posters, and speeches Russian women were urged to enter the factory and office. Since this goal could obviously be achieved only gradually, it soon became clear that an additional measure was needed: motherhood deserved special economic support. As Kollontai, the most enthusiastic proponent of independence for women, had written even before the Revolution, only with "all around security of motherhood" could marriage be cleansed of that "bourgeois scum," that calculated self-interest which had nothing in common with love. A later writer, with a fine flair for phrasing, carried on the Kollontai tradition by referring to the need of a "social correction factor for the biological inequality of the sexes." [43]

In addition to its programs, proclamations, and exhortations, the new regime did actually take some important legal measures. It repudiated the conservative, patriarchal Church, decreeing that henceforth only civil marriages were to be legal. It granted substantial freedom of marriage and divorce to all except near relatives. Mutual consent was the main requirement for marriage, and for divorce the desire of either of the spouses was deemed sufficient cause. The new freedoms were taken with sufficient seriousness by enough people so that in a few years the divorce rate began to rise, and the complaint could be made that the courts were "buried under alimony cases." [44] Actually, even the party itself played a role in the trend, since from time to time members were encouraged to look closely after the political education of their wives and to divorce those who were hopeless laggards.[45]

In addition, full equality of legal and political rights was accorded to women in the marriage relationship. Alongside those securing freedom of choice in marriage and divorce, several provisions attracted considerable attention at the time because of their symbolic importance, especially those providing that the wife "need not follow the husband" in case of change of residence and concerning the surname to be taken by the woman after marriage. The former is best interpreted as an expression of resentment against an explicit provision of Tsarist law which did require the wife to follow the husband if he should for any reason change his residence; it was easy for communist thinkers to see this as intentional and unjust interference with the right of the wife to pursue an occupational career independently, and hence as constituting the real underpinning of inequality. The article on surnames gave three possible choices: husband's, wife's, or joint surnames. For some reason, in the first code of laws on marriage and family, permission was not given to allow each party to retain his or her premarital name. This lack aroused some criticism at the time and was suitably amended in 1926.

Once women had also been accorded full rights to vote, to participate in public associations and activities, and, of course, to enter into occupational life, or social production, on a basis of full equality with men, the problem was then seen as one of persuading women to seize their new opportunities. A special section of the party, the Women's Section (*Zhenotdel*), occupied itself mainly with the task of drawing women into broader public activities. However, no special rights were accorded at this time to women for those "biological infirmities," pregnancy and childbirth.

In addition to such positive measures as these, the fight was carried on against "survivals of the old regime." The chief targets relevant to sex equality were the Church, the Islamic tradition with institutions perpetuating the inferior status of women such as the bride price, and those basic attitudes of the population, especially among the peasantry, which were so strongly linked to the old patriarchal mores. The prevailing communist attitude toward sexual jealousy was particularly revealing. It was seen as an extension of the private property spirit: "Nowadays it is one of the worst crimes to kill a woman for jealousy, because we are trying to free our women, not regard them as the property of man any more. If a man kills his wife or lover out of jealousy, he is given the maximum penalty — ten years — and in Central Asia he is shot." [46]

But good marxists regarded such details as minor, for their central verbal commitment was to the development of facilities which would accord *de facto* release from kitchen and children. Virtually every public utterance on family and women from the time of the Revolution forward was to be permeated with this thought. Unfortunately, with the exception of the period known as War Communism, when ration cards were issued on the basis of employment, the drift of women into social production was very slow. It was no secret that for many there were no opportunities. During the New Economic Policy (NEP) period, and in glaring contradiction with the goal and intention of the party, unemployment was widespread, and those women who could find work often faced the unsolved question of providing for children and maintaining the household.

In spite of repeated assertions of the intention to establish communal kitchens, dining halls, laundries, and a network of children's homes and crèches, it was hard to accomplish much. The extensive communal institutions of War Communism could not be continued for financial reasons,[47] and owners and managers of private enterprise during the NEP period were reluctant to invest in such uneconomic ventures as crèches and public restaurants. In the press, side by side with the stated intention of doing better, there were constant complaints about the insignificant extent of communal feeding. For example, the party's leading publicist on such affairs, Emelian M. Iaroslavski, counted "public dinners" served on November 1, 1925: 20,000 in Moscow, 50,000 in Leningrad, and 67,000 in the provinces, a total of 137,000. At the same time he noted that only three out of 100 children were coming to the crèches. All the rest were being reared entirely by individual families.[48] With the end of the NEP period further efforts were made in the direction of socializing the family's functions, but as resources and personnel were committed to the "harder" part of the Five Year Plan, the claim of establishing crèches and public dining rooms began to sound more and more hollow.

This problem concerned quality as well as quantity. In the early communal facilities the food was bad and poorly served, often in crude, unpleasant surroundings. The children's crèches were dirty and understaffed and, as one writer put it, "the public laundries tear and steal more than they wash." [49] Reactions were understandably negative, and the tendency of some of the party theorists to identify the institutions of War Communism as a first step toward the achievement of the idealized classless society could hardly have been more ill conceived. All in all, it was a poor beginning, and the population was skeptical about such communal activities for years afterward.[50]

Apparently there was little improvement in later years. Various expert estimates and surveys established in the early 1930's that few in the population were interested in communal housing, and that Russian women did not care about communal dining halls and were avoiding the crèches, while the "better-placed workers" who ate in the public dining halls were glad to return to their family dining tables as soon as rationing was abolished (in 1935).[51]

Within the family nobody could be certain whether women were becoming more nearly equal, but many opinions were expressed. Some pointed to greater sex equality in everyday life as an accomplished achievement of the Revolution. More writers stressed the slowness of change in everyday living and complained about the continued presence of prostitution, "calculation in marriage," and the fact that "men remain superior and continue to exploit the women." [52] An especially bitter pill was the discovery of a new social type, the party member who was reactionary in domestic life. One woman wrote to the newspaper about her husband, an important activist, who had forbidden her to work or engage in political activity: "And in those very meetings which he forbids me to attend because he is afraid I will become a real person — what he needs is a cook and mistress wife — in those very meetings where I have to slip in secretly, he makes thunderous speeches about the role of women in the revolution, calls women to a more active role." [53]

A widely recommended proposal for correction of the "temporary" inability of the state to take over the family's functions was that men share women's household work. In 1920 Lenin, in commiseration with the much pitied housewife of marxist theory, had complained to Zetkin: "So few men — even among the proletariat — realize how much effort and trouble they could save women, even quite do away with, if they were to lend a hand in 'woman's work.' But no, that is contrary to the 'right and dignity of a man.'" A few years later E. O. Preobrazhenski, noting that there was as yet no socialist childrearing available, called for an "elementary equality" between man and woman in discharging this responsibility, asserting that in no case should the burden lie fully upon the woman. In later years others carried on the theme: Lunacharski wrote that he would shake the hand of a comrade — an "honest Leninist" — who would rock the baby's cradle so his wife could go out to a meeting or to study. And Krupskaia, lamenting in 1928 that the rationalization of daily life was still not complete, urged that all members of the family share the housework. She was glad to report that: "The new is already starting to break into the pattern of daily life; even now one sees a grown worker take a child out for a walk, a husband help a wife at home." One suspects, however, that the Soviet husbandly masses were as a rule little inclined to take over duties that in other bolshevik speeches were described as trivial and properly social rather than familial functions. Possibly the problem is best epitomized by the experience with the new freedom about surnames. As of 1928 ninetenths of the women marrying were still taking the name of the husband, and cases in which the man would take the wife's name could "be counted absent." [54]

Probably closer to reality was the view held by some that the first decade or two of Soviet history saw a worsening rather than an improvement in the status of Soviet women. The great mass of women, illiterate and submissive, were little interested in their new freedoms and equality. Legal rights were often completely unappreciated. Peasant women, for example, rarely sought alimony in the event of divorce. In urban families the right to work, if it existed in the form of a concrete opportunity, was more often seen as a financial necessity than as a new freedom.

Without replacing childrearing, food purchase and preparation, and the like by the family, the Revolution simply brought an additional burden to women. They remained tied to the family and home and often, in addition, had to work in a factory or office. Studies made in these years showed that women were on a day-to-day basis generally busier than men. Since they could spend less time in public or political work, study, and even sleep, they were less able to develop themselves and become the equals of their husbands.[55] Trotsky wrote in 1937: "One of the very dramatic chapters of the great book of the Soviets, will be the tale of the disintegration and breaking up of these Soviet families where the husband as a party member, trade unionist, military commander or administrator, grew and developed and acquired new tastes in life, and the wife, crushed by the family, remained on the old level. The road of the two generations of the Soviet bureaucracy is sown thick with the tragedies of wives rejected and left behind." [56]

All in all, it was the men who profited most surely and immediately by the new freedoms intended to bring equality to women. The women who remained tied to the family often seemed more liable to exploitation after the Revolution than they were before. Perhaps the most spectacular, if relatively rare, variety of male who exploited the situation was the crafty peasant who married a peasant girl in the spring to get himself an extra harvest hand and divorced her in the fall to save the expense of feeding her over the winter.[57] Much more common was sexual exploitation.

The Sex Problem

Though they originated in the most admirable of motives and were based on years of socialist thinking about the proper pathways to individual freedom and social equality between the sexes, the regime's doctrinal position and policies with regard to the family caused a sex problem. The devaluation of family life and the introduction of such policies as easy divorce, free abortions, and *de facto* marriage (in the 1926 code), had their repercussions. Of course, responsibility for the social patterns of the 1920's and early 1930's cannot be placed entirely at the door of the bolsheviks: war, civil strife, poverty, and the general atmosphere of revolutionary social reconstruction also contributed, perhaps crucially, to the disorganization. Nevertheless, the party must bear considerable responsibility, for the sexual problem is very closely connected with an important marxist principle — that promise of complete freedom in private life which plays such a prominent role in Engels' writings.

Correspondingly, the predominant view in the early years was that family life was not a public function and that sex life was "outside the area of regulation of the Communist Party." [58] Indeed, the strength of feeling can be gauged by a statement made in 1923 by Lunacharski, Commissar of Education, to the effect that the state regulation of a person's life was one of the "dangers threatening communism." Furthermore, "the morality of communist society will be found in the fact that there will be no precepts; it will be the morality of the absolutely free individual." If there will be freedom in personal life, then, said Lunacharski, there will be a great variety in the relationships found, and so much the better. Paraphrasing Engels, Lunacharski foresaw not only the absence of the government regulation of private life, but "no pressure of public opinion is permissible either; there must be no 'comme il faut'!" Moreover, "all of this or most of this applies also to our own time; in relation to so-called sex life there can be only one precept: it is necessary to defend the weak in that unique type of struggle which boils in the soil of love." But even this is not moral regulation, he argued, but a juridical matter. For the rest, said Lunacharski, "all the freedom possible." [59]

To most party members these statements seemed good marxist doctrine. In spite of growing opposition to the idea, a scholarly monograph published as late as 1929 could cite both Marx and Engels as authorities for the strict separation of private and public life.[60] It therefore also seemed appropriate to hold that sex life was an individual matter, entirely outside the party's purview. Sofiia N. Smidovich, an influential feminist and party member, wrote on the subject: "We are inclined to excuse a lot, to close our eyes about a lot, when the matter concerns so-called personal life. 'You can't do anything about a given act from the point of view of communist ethics,' we often say. 'Where is it written that a communist can have only one wife, and not several?' . . . And not a little more is heard and said in such cases. We are apprehensive lest we fall into dogmatism, carry on like the priests, and so on." [61]

It was not long, however, before some among the party leaders came to the conclusion that "freedom in private life" was easily interpreted by the masses as an invitation to sexual misbehavior. Arguments were soon put forth in favor of "interference in private life": "It is not hard to see which is socially more expedient — to treat 'personal life' as an inseparable part of some whole, defining a person in all his manifestations, or to close our eyes on 'personal life,' supposing that one or another Morgunov, Romanov [noted sexual exploiters of the times], and others can't be avoided." [62] The cases used as a basis to urge interference in private life all center on young women who are exploited by men. Interestingly, what was at stake here was essentially the "mutuality problem" so glaringly overlooked by Engels in his formulation of sex love. These young women continued to love their masculine partners after the latter had grown tired of them, thus making themselves liable to exploitation.

By 1927 even Lunacharski, who in 1923 had justified sex freedom in the name of natural man ("The slogan, Back to nature! Back to the animal! is quite appropriate."), was in a much more sober mood: "That which until the present has been called private life cannot slip away from us, because it is precisely here that the final goal of the Revolution is to be found." [63]

The best-known defender of sexual freedom, Alexandra Kollontai, differed from her fellow communists in her willingness to follow to their logical ends the implications of current thinking about such matters and thus to arrive at conclusions which seemed incorrect, but could not be refuted within the limits of marxist theory. First of all a feminist, she devoted considerable effort to writing about the equality of men and women and in proposing ways to achieve it.[64] Throughout her polemical and fictional writings, polygamous sex interests are defended as a right of women as well as men. She became best known, however, as a champion of love as a feeling, to be distinguished from the sex act. Writing in 1923, she drew this picture of the proper communist approach to the question: "The morality of the working class, insofar as it has already crystallized . . . consciously discards the external form in which the love relation of the sexes is cast. For the class problems of the working class it is completely a matter of indifference whether love takes the form of a prolonged and formalized union or is expressed in the manner of a transient tie." This clear denial of the validity of institutional forms was carried out in the name of "full, many-sided love" or, to dramatize the concept, the "winged Eros." Kollontai's basic idea was clearly that love is to reign supreme, and sex is to be its servant. Sex without love is taboo: "The ideology of the working class does not place any formal limits upon love. But on the other hand the ideology of the toiling class already thoughtfully takes a stand on the content of love, toward the shades of feelings and experiences which tie the two sexes. And in this sense the ideology of the working class will persecute the 'wingless Eros' (vice, one-sided satisfaction of the flesh with the aid of prostitution, transformation of the 'sex act' into a self-oriented goal from the pool of 'easy pleasures') much more strictly and mercilessly than bourgeois morality did. 'The wingless Eros' contradicts the interests of the working class." [65]

Along with feminism and the enshrinement of love, another major strand in Kollontai's thought was the notion that love was eventually to change its form, was to be generalized to the collective:

In the achieved communist society, love, "the winged Eros," will appear in a different, transformed, and completely unrecognizable form. By that time the "sympathetic bonds" between all members of the new society will have grown and strengthened, the "love potential" will have been raised, and solidarity-love will have become the same kind of moving force as competition and self-love are in the bourgeois order . . . the stronger the new humanity is linked together by the firm ties of solidarity, the higher will be its spiritual-mental ties in all regions of life, creativity, and the smaller the place which will remain for love in the contemporary sense of the word. Contemporary love always sins in that, absorbing the thoughts and feelings of "the two loving hearts" it at the same time isolates, separates off the loving pair from the collective. Such a separation of "the loving pair," the moral isolation from the collective, in which the interests, tasks, aspirations of all members are interwoven in a thick network, will become not only superfluous, but psychologically unrealizable. In this new world the recognized, normal and desirable form of relations of the sexes will probably rest upon a healthy, free, natural (without perversions and excesses) attraction of the sexes, on a "transformed Eros." [66]

It is not hard to imagine the effect that this sort of argument had on meetings of factory workers, peasants, and young Komsomol groups. More widely shared was the much simpler notion that the old sex morality was part of the corrupt bourgeois superstructure. In the words of Preobrazhenski: "How about the so-called spontaneous amoralism, quite widespread among a part of our proletarian youth? If one looks upon it as a negation in practice of bourgeois and petit bourgeois morality and practice, and a dispersing of the 'non-class' fog over class norms, then this 'amoralism' is, in essence, marxist, the historical-materialist relation to the morality of other classes." [67] In any case, the permissive aura of these theories presaged the trouble ahead.

Regarding sexual life itself, in 1920 an article published in a nationally distributed party journal asserted that "an unimaginable bacchanalia is going on," and that "the best people are interpreting free love as free debauchery." [68] The actual extent to which sexual promiscuity seized the country is not known, but there was no shortage of persons ready to point to various bits and shreds of evidence and to draw the conclusion that disorder prevailed. Smidovich reported a conversation with a Komsomol member who asserted that he found it unnecessary to visit prostitutes: "I don't have to, because I can have any Komsomol girls I know whenever I want them." Another defender of feminine virtue reported the existence of a "League of Free Love" in the Ukraine. Demyan Bedny, poet of the Revolution, wrote a satire, "Seriously . . . and Not for Long or The Soviet Wedding," and "Young Correspondent" Koltso wrote to a newspaper about how "sleeping" had become a profession and that one Ivanchuk had a record of 80.[69]

In any event, there was wide agreement that an extraordinary amount of pre- and extra-marital sexual activity was taking place. At the Fourteenth Party Congress, N. I. Bukharin felt called upon to denounce what he referred to as "decadent and hooligan groups with names such as 'down with innocence' and 'down with shame.' " That such sentiments were prominent among communist youth themselves is also suggested by the title of a popular Komsomol song of the times, "Away, Away, with the Monks." [70]

On the other hand, if those who believed in sexual freedom represented a left wing, there was also a right-wing deviation. Among this group one could find ascetics, "people taking it as a duty to deny themselves the satisfaction of their sexual needs." [71] Though the fight for communism twenty-four hours a day could lead to a radical separation of sex from love, for which there was no time left, and thus to a matter-of-fact-promiscuity, it might also lead, quite logically, to a complete denial of sexuality as well as other forms of self-expression, such as drinking, dancing, games, recreation in general. The latter tendency produced an interesting social type who was "dreadfully serious; he does everything according to the program. He even sleeps according to the program [and] in him everything cheerful, alive, hides itself underground; he and the Komsomol, too, . . . have begun to freeze over." One writer characterized this as a professional disease of the Komsomol activists, who consequently became "onesided in their outlook on life." [72] Again, this trend was reflected in organizational rules. One young woman, in organizing a party cell, decided, along with several comrades, that the Program of the Communist Party prescribed an "ascetic mode of life." Several years later it was reported that a newly organized youth commune had prohibited its members the right to a sexual life.[73]

Finally, still another unacceptable variant of the conduct of sex life was the return to bourgeois marriage. Weak-willed "philistines" retired to the narrow family circle and gradually left their circle of comrades.

When, soon after the Revolution, some of the party leaders began to feel troubled about the situation, they had only minimal factual information. Lunacharski pointed out in the mid-1920's that he could rely only on indirectly derived impresisons received from individual observations, events reported by others, and "reflections of life in literature." [74] Thus even the question of who exactly was being promiscuous was not clearly settled. It was taken for granted, naturally, that it was primarily the young people, but writers differed about whether worker youths were more unrestrained than peasant youths, Komsomol members more promiscuous than nonmembers, and so on.[75]

University students tended to be in the ideological vanguard, and more independent of the control of traditional communities. They were also scrutinized more frequently because of their accessibility, and surveys showed that not only behavior but opinions and theories about sex were showing a luxuriant proliferation among them.[76] Such theories and opinions have considerable interest as examples of the popular culture of the day. They were primarily justifications for sexual freedom, ranging from the most transparent and unadorned to the most sophisticated and disguised of rationalizations. The simplest, most traditional, and probably most widespread had little to do with marxism or the Revolution; it was simply the view that sexual abstinence was injurious to the health: "This is for some reason considered an indispensable truth . . . (I will not try to judge how we in the North have developed these African passions.) . . . Somebody heard it somewhere, where he doesn't know!" The likelihood is, it would seem, that concern for health is also a rationalization — working in the service of a still deeper-lying factor, the sex identity of the Russian male. As the same writer tells it, in another place: "Often a raw youth, to show he isn't 'some kind of girl' drinks up for bravery in the company of those who are like him, then goes to visit the prostitutes and starts the shameful page of his life." [77]

Most of the theories about sexual freedom sprang up in connection with marxist thought and with the Revolution; and a good proportion of them share the axiom that communism and greater sexual freedom went hand in hand. Thus at Saratov in 1918, the "right of private ownership of women" was abolished by decree, and in a remote part of one of the Ukrainian provinces the "League of Free Love" was said to have "hid itself under what were supposed to be 'principled motives of the Communist Program,' requiring complete freedom, and in the first place, 'sexual freedom.' " [78] Eight more or less distinct varieties of this popular subject of everyday folklore may be identified.

1. *A gift of the Revolution.* The view that sexual freedom was simply a pleasure to be enjoyed to the full, as a gift of the Revolution, was found among at least some of the simple peasantry. It is revealed, for example, in a *chastushka* (popular verse) of the time: "Now there are new rights and you don't have to get married. Just stand at a table in the committee room and sign up." And some of the university students believed that "a correct communist life . . . will be to live with one woman, and at the same time both she and I ought to feel free in relation to each other." [79]

2. *The glass-of-water theory.* A slightly more sophisticated and much better known outlook had a respectable position among many nineteenth-century socialists and was outlined most succinctly by Bebel. Sexuality was elevated in a relative sense. That is, it was separated off from love and accorded independent legitimacy. Love in turn tended to be denied completely or to be regarded as a "physiological phenomenon of nature," as a Komsomol organization's circular put it.[80] At the same time, however, this theory also devalued sexuality as a simple and inconsequential action akin to drinking a glass of water.

This view was connected with a certain tendency to link material property and sexual property; that is, sharing the wealth tended to include, by generalization, the latter kind of property as well as material property. Apparently the notion was widespread. Lunacharski spoke of the "extraordinarily broad currency of the glass-of-water theory," and a 1927 poll of students in ten institutions of higher learning at Odessa revealed that in answer to the question, "Does love exist?" only 60.9 per cent of the women and 51.8 per cent of the men answered yes. Moreover, opposition to the theory often seemed suspiciously conservative and could easily be associated with bourgeois morality, and philistinism (*meshchanstvo*).[81]

3. *Elemental nature.* Closely related to the glass-of-water theory was the more defensive stress on sex as one of the aspects of daily life that cannot be changed or controlled. As described by Smidovich, "It is put in me by nature. I have to satisfy my instincts." This approach is, of course, perfectly legitimate for any careful reader of Marx and Engels, who exalted natural man, as did at least some of their authoritative followers.[82]

4. *A symbol of opposition to the old order.* Among the more politically conscious members of the population there was a strong tendency in the first two decades of Soviet history to equate sexual restraint with the bourgeois and aristocratic classes, along with polite manners, personal cleanliness, and fineness of language, to say nothing of neckties, jewelry, and elegant clothing. Sexual promiscuity, then, took on a certain aura of patriotism, so to speak, as a revolt against the moral vestiges of the old way of life, as a "revolutionary protest against the former philistine morality." [83]

A variant of this theme concerned the patronage of prostitution. For the Komsomol member, visits to prostitutes were in violation of marxist dogma. In consequence, sexual freedom with his feminine comrades assumed a virtue of its own.[84]

5. *The heroic soldier of the Revolution pose.* A more pragmatic basis for justifying sexual freedom was linked with the crusading ideal of serving the cause of the Revolution and communism: "We have no time to settle down with a family; we are too busy . . . Fatigue, the over-straining of forces suffered during the time of the Revolution, has made us prematurely old. The usual confines of age and all kinds of norms are not suitable for us." A variant stressed the maintenance of ideological purity: "How can I enter a permanent union with a girl when she might turn out to be a philistine after a time?" [85]

6. *Poverty justifies promiscuity.* The study of Odessa students revealed that 19 per cent of those analyzed (some 2,328 respondents out of 3,500 given questionnaires) did not have a private bed to themselves,

and that 52 per cent of the men and 45.5 per cent of the women asserted that they did not get enough to eat. Hence, if it was true that sexual promiscuity was most pronounced among university students, they could explain their devotion to sexual freedom as a purely practical response to poverty and the inability to establish a family, and as "ideologically" quite justified. Some of them were likely to quote Marx: "It is not the consciousness of people that defines their existence, but the contrary, their existence defines the forms of their consciousness." [86]

7. *Free love as part of the new way of life.* In the marxist lexicon "free love" is an ambiguous notion. In the writing of Marx and Engels it is best interpreted as referring to the separation of love from economic concerns — in which case a more adequate expression would be "freed love." But it can also literally mean, as it has to many interpreters, that the old ethical norms do not apply to the relations between the sexes and that love follows nothing more than mutual inclination. The latter view, which can also be justified by reference to the marxist classics, particularly to *The Origin* of Engels, was of course very popular among those who were interested in justifying sexual freedom. Their thinking was picturesquely paraphrased by Lunacharski in 1927:

Husband, wife, children — husband and wife who bear and rear children, this is a bourgeois business. A communist who respects himself, a soviet person, a leading member of the intelligentsia, a genuine proletarian ought to be on his guard against such a bourgeois business. "Socialism," say such 'marxists,' "brings with it new forms of relationship between man and woman — namely free love. A man and a woman come together, live together while they like each other — and after they no longer like each other — they part. They are together for a relatively short period, not setting up a permanent household. Both the man and woman are free in this relationship. This is the transition to that broad public society [*obshchestvennost*] which will replace the small philistine nook, that little philistine apartment, that domestic hearth, yes that stagnant family unit which separates itself off from society! "A genuine communist, a soviet person," they say, "must avoid a pairing marriage and seek to satisfy his needs by *changez vos dames,* as they said in the old cadrille, with a definite changing, a freedom of the mutual relations of the husbands, the wives, fathers, children, so that you can't tell who is related to whom and how closely. That is social construction.[87]

Such views, reflecting a liberal but on the whole not inaccurate interpretation of a tendency in Engels' thought, were supported by arguments that sometimes took a direction that calls to mind the implicit invitations to analogy of marxist theory. A recent Soviet discussion recalls how "back in those days" partisans of the "free love" theory argued that if private ownership of the means of production corresponded with monogamy (understood as private ownership of women), public ownership of the means of production should correspond with free love, that is, public ownership of women.[88]

8. Sex and love as base and superstructure. The more inventive minds among the youth, attracted simultaneously to the marxist way of thinking and to the appeals of the flesh, soon began to propose a sophisticatedly "marxist" formulation of the whole problem. Rather than being parallel to the drinking of a glass of water, and hence without further significant consequence, the sexual attraction of two humans was said to constitute the "base" of love. And since sexual love between man and woman enjoyed a high moral position in the thought of Marx and Engels, the marxist could easily conclude that the determining, and therefore truly important, aspect of the matter was sex. A student observes: "The basis of love is the sexual attraction of two individuals for one another. If some 'misunderstanding' enters into the sexual relationship, then the whole poetic superstructure falls to pieces." Of course, the ultimate result in terms of personal behavior was not dissimilar to that of those who preferred their sex without any poetry. An even more liberal adaptation to the spirit of marxism was found in the theory that "eroticism defines consciousness," one of several "alien theories" about sex referred to by Iaroslavski.[89]

It is clear that the effort to define the nature and origin of love brought, as it still does, much interesting discussion but no very solid conclusions. The older generation tended to see it as more closely related to reproduction and childrearing, while the younger theorists were likely to connect it more closely with sexuality as a materialistic and hence proper pleasure of the individual.[90] In any event, the most consistent marxists were sure that sex was not a base for the family, for any reader of Engels' last book could see that in primitive times the family did not exist (and, consequently, perhaps would not in the communist future.[91]

The justification of sexual freedom in the name of marxism aroused considerable indignation among some of the party leaders. They suspected the obvious existential basis of such theorizing.[92] Lunacharski paraphrased the young man wooing the reluctant virgin as follows:

" 'Well,' she says, 'what if I do, and you leave me, and I get a baby. What do I do then?' He answers, '. . . what philistine thoughts! What philistine prudence! How deeply you are mired in bourgeois prejudices! One can't consider you a comrade.' " Lunacharski continues, "the frightened girl thinks she is acting like a marxist, like a leninist, if she denies no one." [93]

Most of the population, one suspects, and a good proportion of the inner circle of the older comrades themselves urged the youth to abstinence or at least to moderation in sex behavior. But it is most revealing that no good marxist theoretical arguments immediately at hand could provide a reasoned and principled underpinning to the case for self-discipline in sex, especially in a land where the old social order had been overturned and where the canons of Marx and Engels were supposed to guide the way to communism.

It was increasingly clear that sex had become a complex social problem. There were not only the continued presence of prostitution and the usual transgressions and indiscretions of youth, but also a good number of mature adults, including many party members, who were "enjoying the new freedom." Stories circulated about sexual exploits of herculean proportions, about men with twenty wives, each with a baby.[94] This problem was of the sort most painful to serious marxists, for it involved exploitation of the weak by the strong. In fact, the parallel between the individual freedom and sexual exploitation of the female of these times and the individual freedom and economic exploitation of the proletarian worker described in classical marxism is quite striking. Both freedoms were purely formal.

As early as 1923 the essential facts of the case were recognized in this frank analysis:

The new quality of all social relations, the new style of life, already created under capitalism and not at all by us long ago made the new forms of marriage indispensable. They are characterized by our freedom, by the absence of any restraint whether that be juridical restraint or the power of economic relations. In principle we separated marriage from economics; in principle we destroyed the "family hearth," in which was centered the power of economics, which independently of juridical norms, transformed marriage into an externally forced union and sentenced woman to a many-sided slavery. We destroyed the hypocrisy of the family hearth. We said that marriage ought to be a union of love, and not a juridically or economically required union. We said that marital ties must not be converted into marital "bonds," that is, into marital chains which connect the husband with the wife like one chain gang member to another. But we carried out the resolution on marriage in such a manner that only the man benefited from it, and the woman was left in a tragic position . . . the woman remains tied with chains to the destroyed family hearth, to the ruins of the family hearth. The man, happily whistling, can leave it, abandoning the women and children.[95]

If women were forced to conceive and then were abandoned by husbands who wanted to live according to the new way of life, opinion studies showed quite clearly that the two sexes actually held different views about sex and love. It was mainly the men who wanted sexual variety, or at least sexual gratification, whereas the women tended much more to be interested in love. Thus the double standard continued to prevail, and writers began to stress the fact that "the girl is the person who suffers." [96]

There were two main views on the role of the new regime in these unfortunate developments. One group held that the law itself was at fault: it did not accord sufficient protection to the woman. The other side put responsibility not upon the law, which was plainly well intentioned, but upon people's abuses of the law. The anticipated assumption by the state of responsibility for childrearing, they believed, would clear up the problem.[97]

Finally, while only a minority of the population indulged in the new sex freedom, they were sufficiently numerous to be troublesome and many were in social positions of high visibility. The attitude of the majority of the population varied from one individual to another and from social group to social group, of course, but it seems fair to say that the main response was widespread moral indignation. Freedom of divorce and abortion, for instance, seemed to many an open invitation to sex debauchery. Attitudes about sex and family attitudes were very deeply rooted, and the "good intentions" of the party leaders were rarely recognized. In fact, quite the contrary was true. The average citizen was apt to see the communist and his way of life not as a model of virtue and principle, but as purely and simply licentious. As a sociologist reported in a book published in 1929, "A reaction has been observed in our country against such . . . sexual anarchism, at times reaching as far as the resurrection of the fine morality of the priests." [98]

The Plight of the Children

As I have already shown, among the Soviet communists it was a foregone conclusion that parenthood was a declining occupation that was to be replaced by social rearing. Upbringing of children by the state would not only free the women for work but also provide a more effective means for rearing better citizens. The "program maximum" of the early years was expressed by Z. I. Lilina, wife of G. E. Zinoviev, in 1918, in words which were to become famous: "We must rescue these children from the nefarious influence of family life. In other words we must nationalize them. They will be taught the ABC's of communism and later become true communists. Our task now is to oblige the mother to give her children to us — to the Soviet State." [99] That this was not idle talk was proved by an immediate legal measure, the prohibition of adoption by childless couples in article 183 of the original family code of 1918. The Bolsheviks did not wish to support the creation of new families and thus reinforce the parental role.

The assumption that state rearing of children would be widely established was not actually borne out by subsequent events. Instead, during the turmoil and chaos of the Civil War the young society's resources proved inadequate. The need for state institutions was in fact growing because of the tide of children rendered homeless by the death, destruction, and mobility of the times, but there were too few children's homes, crèches, and kindergartens, and in those few that were set up conditions were very bad. Lack of space soon led to restrictive admission policies. Crèches and kindergartens became in effect emergency care institutions, into which only "complete orphans" or the children of the poorest workers were taken.[100]

Apparently facilities were so poor and personnel in such short supply that it proved impossible to stop the alarmingly high death rate of babies entrusted to the care of the state. In the city of Moscow, as early as 1924, babies were being farmed out to private families by arrangement with the Moscow Soviet, although party representatives showed little enthusiasm for the idea. But the head of the Department of Motherhood and Infancy of the Commissariat of Health stated that health was more important even than the "principles of social training." She explained that collective education could be only partial because funds were lacking, because methods had not been worked out to organize it, and because the population was not ready for it.[101] In *Izvestiia* of January 2, 1926, it was announced that "many homeless children" were being "settled" amongst the peasantry.

The realities of the early years after the Revolution forced a quick retreat from principles. Poverty forced the organizations responsible for children to settle them in private families, and adoption was again legalized in the 1926 family code.

But such actions did not strike at the roots of the evil. They could not, of course, prevent the extended period of revolution and civil war that produced so many orphans, but even after those social convulsions had ended, they could do nothing to restrict the number of orphans already present.

Another problem, which seemed potentially more permanent but was basically more susceptible to ameliorative action, was abortion. The figures for Moscow, Leningrad, and other large cities were pronounced "massive" and "horrifying" by some of the more respected older party members. Smidovich wrote that she had seen young women who had undergone four or five abortions within a year.[102] While abortion was of course regrettable, it was also "understandable" to the same writers who were dedicated to social equality between the sexes. Vinogradskaia wrote in *Pravda,* July 26, 1923, quite reasonably, that women turned to abortion so they could stay at work and "keep up with their husbands." Existing conditions made motherhood a handicap, and many Soviet wives in those days, as today, were forced to choose between motherhood and social equality.

A corollary of the rise in the abortion rate was the fall in the urban birth rate. As early as 1926 Lunacharski expressed anxiety that this would be a decisive factor in reducing the enthusiasm of those who still favored the abolition of the family forthwith. He argued that it was only thanks to the peasantry, not yet touched in such degree by "pseudo-revolutionary ideas" so as to reflect them in their family life, that the birth rate had not suffered even more.[103]

A problem with long-run implications was abandonment. A "constant chain of wanderers" through the undermanned and numerically scanty state institutions created a feeling of helplessness among the personnel assigned to deal with them.[104] Although no tallies of the number of homeless children are reliable, estimates for the year 1922 ranged as high as 9,000,000, and the number was obviously great enough to cause serious concern.[105] Not only did the homeless children present a pitiful spectacle, become diseased, and die, but they gradually became a public menace, roaming the streets in gangs and committing every crime and violent act. Among the peasantry in the countryside, where there were practically no government institutions or other responsible agencies, abandonment often took place in the forest and was in fact infanticide. It was nevertheless a lesser evil in the eyes of the village peasants, who were intolerant of illegitimacy.[106]

Dislocation and poverty were major factors here, but there were clear indications that the problem of abandoned children might become permanent. A writer presented this vignette of the situation: "As has been rightfully indicated already in the press, there exists among our youth a licentious, an irresponsible, attitude to woman and the consequences of marriage. He marries several times and produces babies, but who is going to rear them and what will happen to them — about that who cares, for we are 'growing into the future,' for 'we are communists, and in communist society there is no family.' This is an abscess, bourgeois depravity of its own kind turned upside down." [107] Of course, nonsupport was illegal, but only in a formal way, not as a part of the ethos supported by the party at the time. "Support" was legally defined for divorced persons as a proportion, depending on the number of children, of the wage earner's income, and even this responsibility was often disregarded. Solts wrote in 1926, "Right now there are among us many party members who refuse to support their children." [108] Easy divorce, a matter of firm principle, was beginning to show its seamy side.

In about 1925 a Communist's wife wrote a dramatic letter to the newspaper concerning her husband's behavior. He had another woman, had already left his family several times, and now wanted to go for good. But, wrote his wife, his sick son worshipped him and needed a father. She continued: "If the matter concerned me alone, I would have left long ago. But there is a sick child involved. I have really worn myself out. But you can't allow the child to see that his father is carrying on with another woman right in front of his eyes. The child loves his mother and his father, too. Tell me, in what way are children guilty in all these dramas? If there were social rearing, then it would be another matter. But there is not enough room for even the full orphans . . . Later on things will be fine. But now, in the transition period — what can one do?" [109]

What seemed to many the best way out of the impasse, contraception, was not suitable for a number of reasons. The methods and devices available were often ineffective; the people, especially the peasantry, 80 per cent of the population, were not used to them; and, as a matter of principle again, it did not seem right to manufacture and distribute birth control devices and information. For one thing the birth control practiced by the bourgeois pair in capitalist society had been scornfully derided by Lenin as defeatism. For another, government sponsorship of contraception would have struck the population as still another effort to introduce sexual libertinism. To the party leadership, things seemed bad enough already on the home-life front. As a result little was done to produce or publicize contraceptives.[110]

All in all, individual sex love was proving an inadequate support for a lasting tie between husband and wife, to say nothing of that between father and children. And it was becoming increasingly evident that fathers, about which Marx and Engels had little good to say, were very important. The social problems of the early years were a fitting prelude to the new family policy of the 1930's and thereafter, in which the major legitimate function of the family became that of rearing the children.

FOUR | NEW THOUGHTS AND POLICIES: REVISING THE MARXIST THEORY OF THE FAMILY

BY THE MIDDLE of the 1920's public as well as private expressions of concern about the social problems connected with family life were becoming more frequent. In discussions held at the highest levels of the party and government, divorce and abortion figures were cited and references were made to such further problems as the link between the growing number of orphans and the "current sex ethic," which was believed to be associated with the "disintegration of the family." [1] In 1926 a publication based on letters written to *Pravda* by women readers about their personal problems was aptly titled "Painful Questions," for that phrase expressed both its content and the author's conclusion: "The human documents presented below produce a painful impression. There is an aura of inconsolability about them. They invariably end in urgent questions to which it is not easy to give a simple and satisfactory answer." [2] At about the same time, such Bolshevik leaders as Iaroslavski and Lunacharski began to assert that there was great interest in and desire for new advice about moral problems, especially sexual ones, among the youth: "Each of us has been repeatedly approached by students, by Komsomolites, with an invitation to give a report on the subject of 'the sexual question,' 'sexual relationships,' 'marriage and the family,' 'the problem of sex,' etc." [3] Among some of the people, it was argued, there was a growing dissatisfaction not only with the current arrangements of marriage and family life, but also with the formulations of Marx, Engels, and their more orthodox Soviet followers. A recurrent complaint was that the communists gave no answers to the concrete questions asked of them. One of Trotsky's respondents, for instance, told of a lecturer on the subject "Marriage and the Family" who began by announcing, to the general chagrin of his audience, that he would talk about nothing but Engels' *Origin of the Family*. Another reported that the workers "think that we [communists] are deliberately silent on the question, and we really are." [4] Several years later the problem was still pressing. "Current problems need current answers," argued the young, "and we have had enough of the prescriptions of the future." A sharply worded example appeared in an "Open Letter to Comrade Smidovich": "When the new base is laid, then relations of the sexes will be wonderful. That's true. But what do you say we should do while waiting for the 'new base'? . . . let us not argue about principles; here we are in agreement with everything. Let us speak instead about the earthly utilization of heavenly principles." [5]

Such reactions marked the beginning of the end of the first phase of the regime's policy toward the family. By and large it was, for almost the entire first decade, an era of individual freedom, and the party's policy remained one of hands-off. During the first five years, there simply was no explicit and concrete line about the conduct of daily life, for relatively little attention was paid to it. As Trotsky wrote in 1923, the fact was that "the party did not and could not accord specific attention to questions of the everyday life of the working masses. We have never thrashed out these questions concretely as, at different times, we have thrashed out the questions of wages, fines, the length of the working day, police prosecution, the form of the state, the ownership of land, and so on. We have as yet done nothing of the kind in regard to the family nor in general the personal, private life of the worker." [6] As a result, it must have seemed to many that since the communists had no answers, such questions were being solved quite simply by the youth themselves.[7]

Theoreticians in Debate

As the party became aware of the growing dissatisfaction, it came to see that the first step toward a more active party role in everyday life was recognition of the existence of social problems; the second was explanations of what had happened that would put the growing difficulties into some kind of marxist perspective. The writings of Marx and Engels were unfortunately of little help, but Soviet theorists nevertheless made occasional efforts to show that Marx and Engels had not really meant to say that the "family in general" would disappear but only the "bourgeois family," or that they had opposed "sexual communism," which some writers sought to equate with what was now called "disorderly sexual relations." [8]

In 1927 a work that purported to be a thorough coverage of the views of Marx and Engels on the sexual question was published by D. B.

Riazanov, Director of the Marx-Engels Institute, whose ideas had also been presented earlier in the course of the prolonged discussions carried on in 1925 and 1926 about the new code of law on the family and marriage. Riazanov's central argument was that Marx, in his early writings, opposed sexual promiscuity. He asserted that in a manuscript unpublished until 1927 Marx referred to: "the sanctification of sexual intercourse by its exclusiveness, the linking of intercourse with legal norms, the moral beauty transforming the demand of nature into a force of spiritual unity, the spiritual essence of marriage." However convincing this statement was at face value, Riazanov had to admit lamely that it was written by Marx in his presocialist days when "Marx was not a communist and undoubtedly not a marxist." Riazanov attempted nevertheless to surmount such a substantial obstacle by pointing to later work in which Marx attacked "vulgar communism": "Finally, this government [vulgar communism] seeking to contrast general private property with private property, is expressed in a completely bestial form when it contrasts marriage (which is, of course, a recognized form of exclusive private property) and the communal ownership of women; when, as a consequence, the woman becomes for it social and under-valued property." There is nothing in common, continued Riazanov, between satisfaction of a need such as for food with a need for sexual intercourse. Satisfaction of the latter involved another human being directly, and "man is the highest being for man." Marx saw, he said, that "human feelings become more and more humanized and include spiritual and practical feelings (will, love, etc.) which arise thanks only to the being of their object-humanized nature." Riazanov also pointed out that some forty years later Engels came to the same conclusions: that individual sex love was an emergent in the process of historical development, that it was "by its nature exclusive," and that it was an indication of "the greatest moral progress." [9]

Though Riazanov made about as much effective use as anyone could of materials left by Marx and Engels, he himself seemed to realize that his position was weak, for as often happens in the absence of a really convincing argument his ideas were buttressed by name-calling and an appeal to the living authority of Lenin and Kautsky. He stated that "Lenin shared fully his exposition" of their views and cited Kautsky to the effect that "economic development will make the carrying on of the individual household more and more unnecessary, will more and more undermine the economic basis of the family. Does this mean that the family itself will disappear? No. There is already a new, higher basis for it — individuality . . . Together with individualism, a type of individual sex love will grow which will find satisfaction only in a union and mutual life with one definite individual of the opposite sex." [10]

None of this seemed very relevant by the mid-twenties, however, for the feeling was developing that some problems were urgently in need of solution and that life itself, coupled in the view of some with "the best from the inherited past," would have to show the way.[11] This attitude opened the door, if not to "anti-marxist" ideas, at least to approaches that were outside the scope of Marx's and Engels' theory of the family.

In dealing with contemporary social problems, some of the older party leaders tended to ascribe the sex problem, which was at the head of the list, to the natural impulsivity and impatience of youth. Iaroslavski wrote: "No matter how much many Komsomolites want to quickly transform all of life into communist harmony (and such moods — give us the commune immediately, give us a communist way of life immediately — are found among our youth), we must not forget that the social system in which we are living is a transition one." In the same sentence, however, Iaroslavski put his finger on the most significant factor: not only were young people naturally impatient, but the transition period in Soviet Russia was assuming certain properties not foreseen in classical marxist writings. "The transition period in our economy and in all of our construction has thrown a significant part of our youth off the rails. They have been torn away from the customary conditions of existence, but have not yet become strong in the new ways." [12]

Any good marxist could see that economic backwardness and poverty were the roots of such difficulties. "We need socialist accumulation," wrote Trotsky. "Only under this condition will we be able to liberate the family from all the functions and cares which now oppress and destroy it." [13] A solution to the sex problem, wrote Iaroslavski, is linked with a "new type of family" and an improvement in the position of women, but, he continues, "here we must say quite plainly that without a radical reconstruction of our entire economy, we cannot solve this question properly." [14]

As it also became evident that the transition period would last for some time, the issue was seen to be not merely economic. Family life and sexual attitudes change very slowly, and if some of the youth were too far ahead of the times, most of the rest of the population seemed too far behind. As one writer put it, "superstructures (and of course

daily life is a superstructure) are very sluggish, tightly organized."
Preobrazhenski even argued that older people, even party members,
were not able to change, that they were "too spoiled by capitalism"
to be able to live under communism.[15]

Such sober reassessments pointed up the fact that communism was
still distant, but the ideal image of a communist society continued to
induce many to overlook the limited possibilities of the present. Critical
voices were ranged against these attitudes however. Already in 1923 one
writer analyzed the sex problem in this way: "Our youth are struggling
with the contradictions between our principles and our institutions. They
are crippling them. We must act!" And, in 1926 Solts complained that
many proposals made at the discussion of the draft law on marriage
and the family were "based on idealistic principles, that is, upon conditions which are conceivable only in a communistic society: people are
free, the sex union is free, we do not interfere. But we are marxists.
We know that without taking account of the material base nothing can
come of it." [16]

Once this point had been understood, it was not difficult to conclude
also that the monogamous family was still needed. Lunacharski, thinking
better of some of his earlier thoughts, went through a revealing meta-
morphosis. In 1927 he wrote that yes, there will be a great amount of
individual freedom later, but "not now!" He continued: "People can
come together, and then part. This depends upon circumstance and
upon temperament. One person finds another who will be a friend for
his entire life, but the next does not; one person has one kind of temperament, a kind of personality such that he gets an especially great joy
out of the serious building-up in life of a deep and specially chosen union
with another individual, but the next prefers a flashing, fleeting transition from one to the next. Both the first and the second are possible
in socialist society, but in our society of the transition period? No. In
our society the only proper form of family is the prolonged pairing
family." [17]

To Lunacharski, a man of principle, the concessions to the realities
of the transition period were obviously unpleasant. The right to divorce,
for instance, was very important to him: "We consider that both man
and woman ought to be free in their fate." But, he continued, it ought
to be a rare occurrence, "perhaps once in a lifetime, perhaps twice, if
you are really so unhappy." He who made a mockery of the freedom
to divorce was to be shamed by public opinion as a person who is a

"daily life counterrevolutionary." The question of abortions was approached in the same manner: the watchword for many people in arranging their sex life should be restraint, but "we are not hypocrites, and sometimes abortions are necessary." [18]

Other writers, such as Smidovich and Iaroslavski, argued that not only would the family continue to be important for some time, with new and stronger bonds being created between man and woman, but that the promised freedoms were too costly for the proletariat. "Individual sex love," it appeared, was foundering in the mire of sex debauchery, and the latter term (*raspushchennost*) was becoming more and more popular. As Smidovich said, "The transition period is a period in which the proletarian state, socialist elements, and public society, will become manifest, and not laxity and all sorts of 'freedoms,' the cost of which the proletariat well knows." [19]

The idea of natural man was becoming less popular, and already by the mid-twenties some well-known party members wanted, as apparently Lenin had, to see less freedom and a little more responsibility. For a considerable period, until Stalin ended intellectual controversy in Russia, the rightists attacked the leftists for "refusing to modify their principles," for their "spontaneous surrender to nature," and for "waiting for manna from heaven." The following is a sample of statements reflecting the latter flaw: "The new man will come by himself, will come about on the basis of the new socialist system. Without a new economy you can't build a new man in any case. What is there, then, to get excited about? The time will come and all the filth, all the force of habit will disappear by itself." [20]

The rightists, in turn, were accused by the leftists of wanting to give up the gains of the Revolution, of bourgeois philistinism and the like. N. V. Krylenko's statements rebutting opposition to the legal recognition of *de facto* marriage, a topical question in the year 1926, provide a good example: "We hear arguments from the lips of our opponents, and accusations about us that we want to 'destroy marriage,' 'destroy the family,' 'legalize polygamy.' How these arguments smell! And won't the more acute readers catch in them the smell of other arguments, which once were spread against us from the core of the most reactionary strata? Isn't it desirable by custom to add to these accusations for company also the accusations that we want to 'destroy religion' or 'destroy the state'?" [21]

The antagonists on either side found it difficult to sustain a high level of debate, and the discussion frequently declined to the level of simple name-calling. A vicious attack against Kollontai's theories about the winged and wingless Eros by a member of the editorial board of the journal in which her article was published took her to task for an un-marxist preoccupation with love. It labeled her an idealist, a petty bourgeois feminist, and a "socialist intelligentsia philistine," in addition to the less serious charges of being a sloppy thinker and an irresponsible writer: "How is it possible, considering oneself a marxist and a revolutionary, to talk so much about the Eros of love and sexual morality . . . The problem of love does not have in our life one tenth of the significance that Comrade Kollontai wants to give it in her articles, vainly wasting here her pathos and enthusiasm. It is really shooting at sparrows with a cannon." [22]

A later apology in the pages of the same journal sought to soften the condemnation of Kollontai herself, but it confirmed the theoretical differences: "Differing from Comrade Kollontai in the solution of questions of morality, sex, and daily life posed by the Soviet scene, the editorial board considers it indispensable to emphasize that Comrade Kollontai remains a distinguished fighting comrade." [23]

Even Riazanov, the party's expert on marxism, buttressed his scholarly position by calling his radical opponents lowbrows, "on as low a cultural level as the passionate-sweet baboons from the nobility or the bourgeoisie, or those mobile types from the working class whom the workers neatly call 'factory bulls.' " [24] Preobrazhenski summed up the whole first phase of argumentation in a much quoted passage:

Concretely, is it possible to pose an answer from a point of view of proletarian interests to the question, what forms of relationship of the sexes will be most compatible, if not with the present social relations and social interests, then with the relationship of socialist society: monogamy, transitory ties, or the so-called disorderly sexual intercourse? Until the present the defenders of one or the other point of view in this question have been more likely to base all manner of arguments upon their personal tastes and habits in this area, rather than to give a correct sociological and class-based answer. He who liked more the somewhat philistine personal family life of Marx, and he who, by inclination, preferred monogamy attempted to dogmatize the norm of the monogamous form of marriage, selecting medical and social arguments. Those who incline to the opposite attempt to hand out "temporary marriages" and "sexual communism" as the natural form of marriage in the future society and moreover sometimes the carrying into practice of this type of relations between the sexes is proudly viewed as a "protest in fact" against the bourgeois family morality of the present. In fact such a posing of the question shows that people are recommending their own personal tastes to communist society and representing objective need in terms of their own personal sympathies.[25]

Such, it seemed likely, would often become the lot of disputation when marxism could not point the way to the proper conduct of life in the transition period.[26]

Preobrazhenski was quite correct. Personal tastes, along with deeper lying impulses, did seem important factors in calling forth opinions. Even Lenin took a strong stand against the glass-of-water theory, though he also asserted that it was "repulsive to poke around in sexual matters." He vitiated the effect of his conservative views even more by contending that questions of sex and marriage were simply not very important at the time (1920) and admitting that he had been "accused by many people of philistinism in this matter although that is repulsive to me." [27] Presumably, among his accusers were some whose opinion was important; Iaroslavski noted in 1926 that in the views he expressed on this subject at the Third Congress of the Komsomol in 1920, Lenin "somewhat differed from other communists." [28]

The arguments eventually centered around two major substantive emphases. The leftists in the party tended toward the humanistic side of marxism, and the leninists sought to elevate the success of the Revolution, the class struggle, and the building of communism into the supreme value of the time and to deduce maxims of personal conduct from that value. Among the defenders of the first emphasis was Lunacharski, who had early argued that the only normative restriction on complete freedom in sex life should be the precept that "it is necessary to defend the weak [the child and the woman] in that unique type of struggle . . . in the soil of love." [29]

Within the wing of social theorists who gave precedence in their hierarchy of values to the Revolution, to the party, to the cause, several subthemes were emphasized. One of the earliest stressed eugenics and was proposed by Preobrazhenski, ordinarily ranked as a leftist, but in this respect occupant of a transitional position between left and right. In his book, *Morality and Class Norms* (1923), he argued that once sex life is separated from the family "it becomes a social question first and foremost only from the point of view of the physical health of the race." From this argument he drew the conclusion that the norms of sex conduct ought to be left to medical science. He insisted, however, that in principle society had the right to regulate sexual life in the interests of improving the race through artificial sexual selection. But this eugenicist approach had no practical consequences, for the shortage of facilities and medical personnel made it impossible even to take the simple step of requiring a medical test for marriage.[30]

Other arguments in favor of interference on behalf of society were more down-to-earth, stressing restraint in sex, as in the use of tobacco and alcohol, as a factor in the conservation of health. Further, excessive sexual activity took time and strength which then were not available for work and for the party. From this argument it was only a short step to the most coherent post-marxist theory developed in the realm of sex life.

The Theory of Revolutionary Sublimation

Lenin was the prime mover in the view that the Revolution demanded more discipline and less freedom. It was understandable, if regrettable, Lenin wrote, that sexual relations were problematic: "The desire and urge to enjoyment easily attain unbridled force at a time when powerful empires are tottering, old forms of rule breaking down, when the whole social world is beginning to disappear." But, he continued, the Revolution "cannot tolerate orgiastic conditions . . . no weakening, no waste, no destruction of forces. Self-control, self-discipline, is not slavery, not even in love." Lenin also argued that sexual promiscuity was not simply a "personal and private affair," but a social matter because "a new life arises. It is that which gives it its social interest, which gives rise to a duty toward the community." This hardly profound but fundamental reminder was to become the cornerstone of the new family policy. Finally, as mentioned above, Lenin did not hesitate to express his own personal tastes. He disposed of the glass-of-water theory by pointing out that the normal man prefers not to drink out of the gutter, nor out of a glass "with a rim greasy from many lips." [31]

Though Lenin set the tone for the most forceful principled argument against sexual freedom, it remained for Aaron B. Zalkind, a Sverdlovsk professor, to translate it into more explicit and concrete terms. In a series of articles and books published between 1923 and 1930 Zalkind presented a reasoned case for conservatism in sex.

He claimed that his argument had three most immediate goals: the welfare of posterity, the proper distribution of "class energy," and orderly mutual relations within the (proletarian) class.[32] The theoretical novelty of his proposals centered in the notion of energy. Defending the view that both sexual activity and social activity drew from the same pool of energy, he argued that where socially constructive activity was not possible, energy tended to flow into sexual interests and activities. Hence all of bourgeois society was suffused with sex, for in the exploitative capitalist system, the rich develop great sensitivity to sexual affairs and spend a great part of their time and energy on sex. The poor follow suit, for they are unable to spend excess energy constructively, and the results are the sexual poisoning of the human organism, the "sexual inflation" characteristic of capitalism, and the symptoms of excessive sexuality among children: onanism, extreme curiosity about sex, and early amorousness. To the "opium of religion" corresponded the "dope of sex." [33]

On the other hand, continued Zalkind, under the dictatorship of the proletariat excessive preoccupation with sexual matters could not be tolerated, for it was "robbing the Revolution." It was necessary that sexual interests give way to a return of social interests, that that which had been stolen from the working class be given back to it. In fact, argued Zalkind, in a manner reminiscent of Kollontai, one must draw closer to the social collective than to the love partner. Indeed, in designating sex activity as energy stolen from the working class and the Revolution, Zalkind went further than Kollontai, who had argued that people were not yet able to center all their love interests on the social collective, and that therefore individual sex love, purified of any economic aspect — her winged Eros — was for the time quite permissible. Zalkind, less generously, contended that it was necessary to take back from sex all it had stolen from human creativity, and to give it its rightful due, which was a "serious affair," but ranking far from first place.[34]

Zalkind asserted that his theory of revolutionary sublimation, in which he made selective use of the ideas of Freud,[35] was a logical result of the basic principles or criteria of proletarian morality: collectivism, organization, dialectical materialism, and activism. In the service of these basic principles — and their operational equivalent, "revolutionary expediency" — sexuality had to take second place. Most important, sex was not a private affair; the proletarian class had the right to interfere with the sex life of its members. In fact, Zalkind informed his readers that "every joy must have a productive purpose," and "a genuine citizen of the proletarian revolution should not have unnecessary sexual feelings." [36]

Zalkind did not leave things at this abstract level. He presented a list of twelve "norms of sexual behavior" that included such standards as sexual life should not start early, continence should be observed before marriage, and the sex act should not be repeated frequently. These norms were claimed to be deductions from the more general principles of collectivism, organization, and the like, and from the principle of "revolutionary expediency." Zalkind also looked ahead and argued that sex life in the future communist society would have many of the same characteristics as the life he recommended to his contemporaries. Sexual relations would be richer, more tender, more modest, more organized, and would involve less frequent repetition of the sex act and less variety of partner.[37]

In his enthusiasm for applying the principle of revolutionary expediency, Zalkind arrived at a position about the feeling of jealousy that did not displease the radical leftists. With his concluding recommendation, "Struggle against the feeling of jealousy," there was general agreement, but Zalkind's rationale was less acceptable. Instead of opposing sexual jealousy as a form of the property motive or the spirit of bourgeois possessiveness, or as a transgression against the right of the individual to his own freedom, which were the orthodox views, he placed the class struggle first. "If my partner leaves me for a person more valuable to the class struggle, my protest is anti-class, shameful." [38] This view was apparently too extreme, and he was taken to task for it. Bukharin, for example, mocked this particular idea as "scum from the cauldron of philistinism." [39] In general, however, Zalkind's revolutionary norms of sex conduct received widespread attention in the twenties as a serious effort to come to terms theoretically with a situation that was becoming more and more disturbing to the party leadership.

Zalkind did not argue his case purely from abstract principles; he strengthened it by pointing to the problems connected with undesired pregnancies and births. Moreover, his appeal to another aspect of revolutionary expediency, authority ("Lenin and others among the best party members are with me" [40]), was doubtless correct. The theory of revolutionary sublimation presented two features attractive to the Soviet leaders, several of whom went on record in favor of it. Iaroslavski, for example, wrote in 1926: "The youth are not attracted to the laws of nature, to the fact that these elements of inner sexual secretion, generally speaking, signify the same things as the elements of our nervous energy. And since the line of satisfaction of sexual needs at times seems both the most pleasant and the easiest, for it is the line of least resistance, this energy — extraordinarily precious nervous energy — is spent precisely on sexual life and not for the intellectual work of the brain, for current business, for the huge struggle awaiting the young generation which will, in the opinion of all of us, build communism; for this they have few powers left." [41]

The revolutionary sublimation theory seemed to offer a solution not presented in established marxism, one which struck at the root of some of the most pressing social problems of the day. Thus, it seemed an important starting point in the struggle to work out some kind of ethical system for the everyday life of the transition period, to which Marx and Engels had devoted little attention.

In his writing Zalkind did not refer to the marxist classics, and with good reason, for he proposed the overthrow of two of Engels' most important principles. Engels had written of the moral superiority of individual sex love; it would "engender a feeling stronger than for life itself." Equally central was the principle of no interference in private life. All in all, Zalkind's approach represented an application of the bolshevik tendency to reverse the traditional marxist view of the role of base and superstructure: "The proletariat, attempting now to build a social economy in organized fashion, cannot fail to interfere also in a different social disorder, because a badly adjusted superstructure (even the sexual part of the same daily life superstructure) often can be reflected in a crudely negative fashion on the healthy development of the base itself (that is, the economy)." [42]

Zalkind's theory was also an elaboration on the clearly emerging Machiavellian ethic of Lenin. In Lenin's own words: "We say that our morality is wholly subordinated to the interests of the class struggle of the proletariat. We deduce our morality from the facts and needs of the class struggle of the proletariat." [43] To go from the "facts and needs of the class struggle" to the concrete rules of proper conduct in private life seemed for some time an unbridgeable gap, but Zalkind's concept of a limited pool of energy, which could be drained in the service of social or personal goals, provided the crucial link.

It remained only to add the positive side to the act of sexual sublimation. As a proper channel for the expression of the excess of youthful energy, the party leadership recommended sports, exercise, the cultivation of intellectual and cultural interests, and, of course, participation in organized political life. Apparently the theory of sexual sublimation also fitted in well with the inclination of some in the party, including Stalin, to undertake a task of such proportions that the ascetic heroism of the Revolution, its sense of sacrifice and self-denial, would be again repeated. From this point of view, the Five Year Plan era was a massive project in sublimation, for after an inverse relationship had been postulated between progress and sexuality, between heroic struggle and unhealthy preoccupation with the realm of private pleasure,[44] the sex problem could fade into the background — in a word, take care of itself. And, quite consistently, during the entire five years of the First Five Year Plan virtually no attention was paid by Stalin's regime to it or to other problems linked with family life. By 1934, however, new developments suggested that the theory of revolutionary sublimation had not been enough to turn the course of events in the desired direction.

The New Family Policy

In family policy there were some minor retreats from principle during the very first years of the regime's life, such as the exception made of estates worth 10,000 rubles and less in the law prohibiting inheritance and the repeal in 1926 of the prohibition against adoption. It was also generally recognized that some in the party and many in the population never approved of the radical marxist ideas about family life. Finally, a slow but unmistakable shift can be discerned in the tenor of most of the published materials during the second half of the 1920's. Nevertheless, during the first half of the 1930's policy continued as before, until the great turning point came, between 1934 and 1936, when official propaganda directed its attention to the family with vehemence. The press filled with editorial and didactic material, posters appeared, party members were told to set a good example, and laws were passed that explicitly represented a new policy. On the theoretical plane the tolerant and future-oriented nature of the earlier writing now gave way to a more exhortatory and moralistic tone, which represented for the first time a very definite and unified line. The accumulation of fifteen years of experience had led to a decision at the highest level.

At this time a new figure, Anton S. Makarenko, with the obvious blessings of Stalin, rose to national prominence. School teacher, camp director, writer, and educational philosopher, he spent the years from 1920 to 1935 working with the abandoned, neglected, homeless waifs (*bezprizorniki*). This task was not easy, for many of his charges had become thoroughly criminal and depraved. But he was remarkably successful in helping them organize their thoughts and behavior, raise their hopes and self-respect, become economically productive and independent, and often return to society as useful citizens. The story of his experiences was told with considerable literary skill in two books, *Pedagogicheskaia Poema* (*An Epic of Education* or, as most commonly translated, *The Road to Life*) and *Flagi na Bashniakh* (*Flags on the Battlements* or *Learning to Live*), first published in 1933–1935 and 1939, respectively.

As director of camps for homeless children, first under the auspices of the Kherson Regional Department of Education, Ukrainian Soviet Socialist Republic, and later (1927–1935) under those of the Soviet secret political police, Makarenko instituted a demanding and strict — even martial — camp regimen. The young people, he found, usually responded with relief and pleasure to the end of their previous self-destructive anarchism and to incorporation into highly organized, militaristic yet self-governing groups or collectives, which performed under his own close supervision and active participation. Makarenko's faith in his method, his unusual patience and skill, and his considerable warmth and charismatic leadership eventuated in Soviet society's most genuine, even dramatic, example of the creative power of the organized collective. His pragmatically oriented conquest, at least in principle, of one of the new society's greatest social problems together with his unconcealed contempt for the "progressive," "child-centered," and experimental pedagogical theories of the 1920's and early 1930's, and for the olympian "bureaucrats" who sought to give life to such "abstract ideas and principles" [45] brought him into continuing conflict with educational officials. By 1935, however, experimentalists had been repudiated, the new party line supported discipline and traditional pedagogy, and fame with honor came to Makarenko. Since his death in 1939 his influence has continued to grow to the point where, like Marx, Engels, and Lenin, an institute has been established to carry out research on him and his work.

Makarenko also became the most authoritative writer on the family to emerge in the Soviet period. *A Book for Parents,* written in 1937 and published in 1940, presents in the form of short stories and instructive episodes with commentary the thesis that "in moulding their children, modern Soviet parents mould the future history of our country and, consequently, the history of the world as well." [46]

The main themes have a familiar ring. The family is, or should be, a collective in which the parents, with loving but strict authority, prepare their children for life in Soviet society. Among the principles Makarenko recommended were consistency, unanimity of parental requirements, orderliness, and great respect for the children coupled with high expectations placed before them. By learning to accept and carry through ever more difficult tasks willingly, the children would learn discipline, and by coming to accept the values imposed upon them by their parents, delegates of the larger society, they would become properly dutiful. The content of duty was made up of official Soviet values: heroic work effort, faith in the party and its ideas, and, of course, collectivism.

The parents' responsible leadership was all-important; they had to unswervingly and devotedly set themselves before their children as examples by, for instance, firmly pursuing worthy goals. Makarenko recommended large families because the true collective spirit could not develop with only one child in the family. In general, Makarenko's ideal Soviet family was close to a mirror image of the total society, thus "every attempt it [the family] makes to build up its own experience independently of the moral demands of society is bound to result in disproportion, discordant as an alarm-bell." [47]

The eager acceptance of Makarenko's ideas is symptomatic of both the type of social problem and the characteristic solution of the Stalin era. Discipline, duty, and subordination of the individual to group values as defined by unquestionable authority was exactly to the taste of Stalin, who was, moreover, quite ready to look upon his peoples as delinquents and moral defectives. But as a man of his era, Makarenko merits appraisal in his own right. In some ways he was a paradox: a man who was intensely involved, protective, and warmly human with his *bezprizorniki,* who at the same time took as ideal types the officers of the dreaded and detested secret police; a strict disciplinarian in his camps who was nevertheless in constant feud over his authoritarian methods with his superiors in the educational field and in the higher administrative echelon; a Soviet writer on the family whose books carry hardly a reference to the views of Marx, Engels, or Lenin; and a man of creative literary capacity who was remarkably anti-intellectual, in this respect much like his spiritual father, Maxim Gorky.[48]

In the present context, however, Makarenko's ideas about the family are most interesting. Focusing on the difficult task of combating individualism in order to produce citizens who would find no contradiction between their needs and society's, he supported and rationalized the authority of Soviet parents at a time when it had become increasingly clear that some kind of authority was badly needed. Nevertheless, one cannot escape the suspicion that he continued to feel distrustful toward the family and probably would have preferred to find some other solution to the organization of life in his ideal Soviet society. His field experience with delinquent and homeless children could well have suggested that a social collective other than the family could adequately perform the function that the family in the hard times after the Revolution had failed to perform.

Probably as a matter of practical politics, Makarenko saw that no matter what future policy would bring, the family was going to have to rear a lot of children in the years ahead. His work also made him very conscious of the defects and failures of Soviet parents. In this sense, then, the man who showed how effective the nonfamilial social group can be in forming and changing the human personality had no alternative other than to recommend the family for the job.

As other Soviet writers began to refer to the family as a basic cell, the foundation of Soviet society, or, following Makarenko, a small collective, it was urged upon the populace that strengthening of the family had become one of the basic rules of communist morals. The urge to domesticity, previously regarded as something of a social crime, as petty bourgeois philistinism, was now praised. Soviet wives and mothers could hear and read that achieving a "comfortable home life" was a legitimate and even praiseworthy goal. By the late 1940's points of view were published that even more directly contradicted Marx, Engels, and Lenin. For instance, household work, described by Lenin as petty, drudging, and monotonous, was now redefined as "socially useful labor." The activities of father and mother in the role of parents, instead of being dominated by the "exploitative attitude," "ignorance," and "individualism" of the traditional marxist view, now became socially important — and hence matters of patriotism. For the children, love for parents became an ethical absolute; in contrast to the earlier conditional love urged upon them, Soviet boys and girls now were told to love and respect their parents, even those who were old-fashioned and did not like the Komsomol. To fortify the newly recognized importance of parenthood and set the tone for his subjects, Stalin's propagandists began to laud the sober and stable family lives of such great examples as Marx, Lenin, Liebknecht, and Chernyshevski.[49] Stalin himself engaged in a most unbolshevik act in 1934 when, to the accompaniment of full publicity, he visited his old mother in the Caucasus; previously the Soviet press had published virtually nothing about his personal life.

On the legal side, parents were accorded specific new liabilities. In the spring of 1934 a decree was passed denouncing hooliganism and urging parents and teachers to supervise their children more rigorously. Parents became liable under criminal law for the delinquent acts of their children and also were made subject, by legislative enactment, to considerable social pressure for lack of adequate supervision of their children. The militia were empowered to fine neglectful parents up to two hundred rubles without court action, parents were to be financially responsible for their children's misdemeanors, parental neglect cases were to be reported to the place of parent's occupation, and a procedure was set up to transfer children into children's homes if parental supervision could or would not be exerted.[50] The pressure on the children themselves was also increased. Minors from the age of twelve were to be held accountable for criminal acts such as larceny, violence causing bodily injury, and murder, and from the age of fourteen, jointly liable with their parents for civil damages.

The new responsibility of parenthood was even reflected in a reduction in scheduled operation of crèches for preschool children, which were opened each day only for the period that covered the mother's work shift and the time she required to deliver and call for her children.[51] The change in attitude could also be traced in fictional literature, for unsuitable ideas expressed in earlier editions of novels were changed or left out in editions published after the new family policy. For example, in Bruski, volume IV, by F. I. Panferov, the original sentence, "I know the party is not concerned with family matters," disappeared in later editions, along with similar passages.[52]

The rehabilitation of parenthood went hand in hand with a new propriety in marriage and sexual life. While previously the terms marriage and man and wife had been indiscriminately used to apply to the most casual and temporary alliance,[53] the Soviet propaganda machine now began to distinguish between sexual frivolity and marriage, the latter being "in principle a lifelong union with children." Instead of seeking to separate marriage from the family, which had been the tendency earlier, the joys of motherhood and fatherhood now were closely tied to marriage.

Again, the new policy was reflected in both legal measures and less explicit changes. One of the main problems in the domestic law of the first fifteen years concerned the recognition of a state of marriage in the event of litigation about the disposal of property, alimony suits, and so on. The 1926 code, passed after considerable discussion, gave legal status to *de facto* or common law marriage, and was widely considered for this reason to be a more radical code than the first one promulgated by the new Soviet government in 1918. From the mid-thirties, however, the balance of relative significance attached to *de facto* and to registered marriage began to shift back, and finally in 1944 only the latter was recognized as legally binding. The seriousness with which Stalin wanted his people to regard permanent, registered marriage was manifested in the unmarxist sanction imposed by the law upon a child born outside such a union: he was to be without the right to claim the name or estate of his (biological) father and thus could easily be identified as illegitimate. In combination with the natural tendencies of men and women, and the abolition of legal abortion, the 1944 law thus introduced the likelihood that many Soviet citizens would in the future occupy this unfortunate status and help reinstitute a concept — illegitimacy — which Soviet and other marxists previously had considered a bourgeois prejudice.

Efforts were also made to stress the positive side. The locale of marriage registration, the *ZAGS* or civil registry office, was to be brightened up, and local officials were urged to see that the registration procedure took on some of the solemnity of the marriage ceremony. Local industries were authorized to manufacture wedding rings, and presumably the venereal disease posters occasionally to be found in ZAGS offices were also removed.[54]

The new sacredness of marriage had several corollaries. It implied a fresh attitude toward sexual expression, one opposed to the original attitude, which had been very rationalistic. Since, for example, medical science could not prove that incest was physiologically harmful, the criminal code had said nothing about it. Similarly, homosexuality had not been illegal for the first seventeen years of Soviet rule. According to the prevalent official attitude adultery was entirely a private matter, and hence hardly cause for concern. Even bigamy was punishable only in the Moslem areas of Central Asia where the bolsheviks wanted to stamp out polygamy as a "survival of the past." [55]

Actually, earlier Soviet justice had not been entirely unresponsive to sexual deviance. Defined in a very special way, it was closely associated with the concept of exploitation. The conditions under which rape could occur, for example, stressed the regime's desire to give legal support to sex equality. A husband could (and still can) be prosecuted for the rape of his wife, and in the days of easy marriage, a man who entered into that state solely to gain sexual access, and with intent to divorce subsequently, could also be prosecuted for rape. Similarly, article 154 of the criminal code provided for the conviction of an employer who forced a female employee into sexual relations.[56]

But, after marriage had been made newly important, the regime took a much more stern position toward sexual deviance, especially that which could destroy a marital union. Homosexuality was made a criminal offense in 1934, and an energetic nationwide campaign against sexual promiscuity, quick and easy marriage, bigamy, adultery, and the exploitative approach toward women was carried on during most of 1935 and 1936. On August 11, 1935, *Pravda* printed a story about a drunkard with three wives and another about a woman who quarreled with her new husband on the way from the *ZAGS*, and returned there, within an hour of the marriage, to divorce him. Bigamists, exploiters, deserting husbands and fathers, and the more innocent but still wayward young persons too easily mistaking infatuation for love were all busily exposed. One can imagine the rueful feelings of Iaroslavski, that veteran counsellor who only a few years earlier had pointed out that it was unbolshevik to be forever "looking under the bedsheets." [57] Many, we may be sure, inside the party and out, still held to the view that sex activity was part of private life and no concern of the party's.

If "so-called free love and loose sexual life are altogether bourgeois and have nothing in common either with socialist principles and ethics or with the rules of behavior of a Soviet citizen," and if "marriage is the most serious affair in life," as *Pravda* commented in 1936,[58] then it seemed logical to introduce a new conception of love. The priority given by Engels to individual sex love had already been devalued by some writers even before the new family policy. One line of thought sought to play down the natural, presumably sexual, basis of love as described by Engels, and to substitute common work, participation in building communism, and shared cultural interests as a basis for marital love.[59] A variant of this trend was simply to reduce or even deny the importance of love as an experience and as a unifying bond. During the First Five Year Plan the almost complete lack of attention given to the family in the official mass media was paralleled by the expression in the literature of the time of such sentiments as "It's work that matters, not wives," and by such period types as Uvadiev, a party secretary in Leonid Leonov's novel, *Sot* (1930), who banished smoking, drinking, and tenderness from his life, looking upon love as "merely a fuel to treble his strength on the next day's path." [60] Even later, when love had again become more legitimate, it still occupied a low rank on the scale of officially recommended priorities. It was not as important as, say, labor and struggle.

More significant was the effort to introduce a distinction, completely overlooked by Engels, between love and infatuation. Operationally, it was a simple distinction to make: love was a lasting tie, and infatuation was not.[61] Mutual sexual attraction, so central in Engels' scheme of things, was thus newly labeled, and natural man's freedom was defeated by the rule of discipline and responsibility.

For the first two decades after the Revolution the regime used only advice and persuasion, but by 1935 Stalin was ready to resort to more concrete inducements. For men and women who insisted upon "mistaking infatuation for love," penalties were assigned. The laws of 1935–36 provided relatively mild sanctions, fees of 50, 150, and 300 rubles for first, second, and subsequent divorces, and, probably more important, required entry of the fact of divorce in the personal documents of those involved. Though considerable success in lowering the divorce rate was claimed immediately,[62] even heavier sanctions were introduced in 1944. A judicial process of divorce was instituted, and the fees for divorce raised to at least 500 rubles and at most 2,000 rubles. In the judicial process the lower court was required to make every effort to effect a reconciliation; if this proved impossible, the case was to be carried to a higher court, which was the one that could actually grant the divorce. Consequently, the Soviet citizen who wished to divorce was faced with substantial ideological, financial, and judicial obstacles. Freedom of divorce, to many communists one of the most prized achievements of the Revolution, had become for the majority of the Soviet population little more than a formal right without content.[63]

Another achievement of the Revolution, equally dear to feminists and to large sections of the poorly housed urban population in the USSR, was the right of women to legal and free abortion. The 1920 enabling decree referred to the "gradual disappearance of this evil" and pointed to "moral survivals of the past" and "difficult economic conditions" as the main reasons why women still felt compelled to resort to abortion. By 1936 the "survivals" and "difficult conditions" had hardly been wiped out, and it was also clear that the Soviet State was not preparing seriously to take responsibility for childrearing upon its own shoulders. Nevertheless, after a nationwide discussion in which many expressed opposition, abortions were made illegal in that year.

All in all, this move seemed a crushing blow to the idea of sex equality, and also to one of the few areas of personal freedom remaining to Soviet citizens. To be sure, provisions were added to grant material aid allowances to mothers of large families and provide more maternity services, and the people were promised that within eighteen months the number of nursery beds for children would double and the number of permanent kindergartens increase threefold. The exposed position of the Soviet mother was further recognized by raising to two years' imprisonment the penalty for divorced fathers' refusal to pay alimony in judgments awarded for the maintenance of their children.[64] In 1944 the responsibility of unmarried fathers was curtailed, but at the same time assistance to mothers was made more generous, and also extended to unmarried mothers.

To sum up, all these measures make it clear that responsibility, reproduction, and childrearing were in favor and that stable marriages, large families, and self-discipline were now more important to the regime than individual freedom, sex equality, and ideological consistency.

Equally as fascinating as the story of how Stalin's regime decisively changed its position on the family is the question of why it did so. A great deal has been written on the subject, and many writers have concluded that the Soviet experience proves that the family cannot be dispensed with. This conclusion is certainly too strong, but it is difficult to establish a definitive interpretation. Perhaps all the evidence on why the new position was adopted will never come to light, for it may be that Stalin simply made a personal decision which he never bothered to explain to his colleagues or to justify in any other form.[65] Interpretations of the new family policy offered by both Soviet and Western analysts are often overly monistic, assigning exclusive weight to only one condition or reasonable cause. It is more likely that the switch in policy was overdetermined, and that at least five sets of conditions were at work: (1) the specific and concrete social problems of the kind described in the preceding chapters, which called for attention to the family's function of social control; (2) the concessionary mood of Stalin's regime, anxious to gain a measure of popular unity and loyalty among the people, who were by and large in favor of the new, more conservative family policy; (3) a new international situation with a reassessing of the Soviet Union's immediate future on the world political scene and the link between family life and birth rate; (4) the general shift in Soviet policy toward discipline and control over individual freedom, which may simply have swept the family, as it did other institutions of social control and indoctrination, back into a more legitimate status; and (5) a significant and explicit reorientation in Soviet marxism, stressing the active role of the superstructure in inducing social change.[66]

Several of the social problems faced by the Soviet regime can quite easily be linked with the family. One of the earliest to appear was the gross lack of consistency between the proposals of ideology and the requirements of real life. Since the latter also tended, incidentally, to be more immediately reflected in the norms of the Soviet legal order than in the ideological sphere, these two features of the Soviet system were sometimes out of phase both with one another and with the requirements of successful social organization. For example, though ideological opposition to adoption and to inheritance was quite pronounced, legal support for both concepts was found to be necessary at an early time. Similarly, although the ideological commitment to sex equality was strong, responsibility for care and support of children continued to rest primarily upon the mother both in the normal pattern of everyday family life and in the allocation by court order of the custody of the children of divorced parents. Hence, a certain disharmony or lack of congruence between ideology on the one side and both life and law on the other became a more and more troubling social problem.

Soviet law confronted a series of difficulties as it tried to enforce those ideologically determined principles that did appear within reach. The close interconnection between the various facets of human affairs is well illustrated by the vexed relationships in family life between two goals of early family policy: individual liberty, such as freedom of divorce, and sex equality. Full freedom of divorce, in the absence of social rearing of children, inevitably led to the unfair burdening of the divorced mother, and a considerable portion of the discussion about family life in the USSR has regularly been concerned with technical problems of making certain fine points of ideological principle legally workable even while jeopardizing the attainment of others. Thus legal problems were part of the background of the new family policy, and the advent of the latter afforded the regime a noticeable increment in immediate, if not long-run, administrative convenience. This became most apparent in 1944 when all legal trace of the *de facto* marriage concept ended with the declaration that only registration could make it legal.

Obviously, human suffering itself, the sexual exploitation of women, abuse of the freedom of divorce, and similar matters were part of the explanation. Once again, however, since women had been exploited in this fashion for almost two decades, the relative importance of this factor was clearly low. The questions of homeless children and juvenile delinquency were more important, for both could be laid at the door of irresponsible parents. Studies conducted by Soviet specialists in Leningrad and Moscow strongly suggested that spending leisure in an unorganized way outside the family was characteristic of juvenile delinquents. The leading Soviet expert on family law, Sverdlov, also attributed the rise of the new family policy partly to the problem of juvenile delinquency.[67]

In an even broader sense, the welfare of the children was at stake. As increasing numbers of fathers were absent and mothers employed, upbringing became problematic, and Soviet writing became quite explicit about the task of the family: "The main importance of the family comes from its work of preparing the new generation for communism." In an official apologia published in 1936 it was argued that the idea of state rearing of children, now identified as "Kollontai's theory," was harmful because it "unwittingly" vindicated parents who did not wish to trouble about their children.[68]

The word "unwittingly" also seems to be a key to the change in policy. The Soviet man in the street undoubtedly was hard pressed to distinguish between what was appropriate in the "socialism" of today and what in the "communism" of the future. In time the confusion was cleared up by a more emphatic distinction between the two eras: the term communism was applied only to the future society, for earlier the people apparently believed, as one writer put it as early as 1926, that " 'the new way of life' is distinguished from 'the old' in the fact that there should be no family at all, neither new nor old." [69] This belief was characterized simply as "wrong thinking," and the new family policy sought to avoid it by specifying what was permitted and what was not in a completely unambiguous fashion. And more sophisticated rascals would now be prevented from the "attempt to hide their acts of exploitation behind an empty 'leftist phrase.' " [70]

The list of social problems could be extended,[71] but the second major circumstance in the great policy change must be considered at this point. Although the extent and fervor of the people's opposition to the radical policies of the early years cannot be definitely established, it seems quite likely that most of the peasantry felt little attracted to free divorce, legal abortion, and other practices. Such kinds of freedom — perhaps individual freedom in general — had little to recommend themselves in their social and cultural context. Among Russian peasants the word for freedom, *svoboda,* sometimes seems to call up an image akin to anarchy, as shown by the reply of a peasant refugee to a question about the proper way of requiring discipline from a child: "Children must obey their parents, but in a free state like the USSR this is impossible" (100 B 6). Sexual freedom was a much more serious matter in the peasant villages than in the cities, for behavior of all kinds was more visible to all and the consequences of sexual intercourse much harder to avoid or hide.

Evidence from refugees suggests the general unpopularity of the central plank of the original bolshevik program for the family, free divorce. Three out of four among those questioned recorded their approval of the legislation which made the procurement of divorce considerably more difficult. Reactions to some of the more detailed provisions of the law are significant. While it is not possible to vouch for the representativeness of these views, they suggest prewar attitudes. As to the substantial expense involved: "(It costs a lot of money to get a divorce.) That is good. There will be less prostitution" (296 B 20). As to the long and difficult court process: "People just say, 'Right now we are not getting along, so let's get a divorce.' It brings depravity to the people. It should go to the court, to make a person think. If not, he just pays a couple of rubles and gets a divorce. That is not good" (279 B 41). To be sure, proof that most features of the new family policy met with approval, even if it could be found, would not indicate that such a fact had been taken into account by Stalin.

Still, and in spite of Stalin's notorious lack of esteem for public opinion, in times of war or other crisis concession to popular demands is a legitimate bolshevik tactic, and it is probable that in the year 1944 the regime was fully prepared to make any concessions necessary to help unify the population and end the war quickly. Indeed, the tendency to make such tactical concessions appeared as early as 1934 when, in connection with the trend toward the united front policy, symbols of popular appeal — for example, such words as "motherland" and "patriot" — were rehabilitated after many years of official proscription.[72]

A third set of conditions responsible for the new family policy appeared with the new situation in international politics, especially the rise of Hitler's national socialism, which posed a military threat to the USSR. Hitlerism seems largely responsible for the prohibition of abortion. One of the reasons for repealing the right to legal abortion given at that time, concern for the health of mothers, obviously camouflaged the desire for a rise in the birth rate. "We have need of people," observed a leading Soviet official.[73] The regime's leaders had long professed to be aware that prohibition of the manufacture and consumption of alcoholic beverages had proved ineffective in the United States. There was every reason to believe that the prohibition of abortion in Russia would produce similarly undesirable reactions, but the policy was nevertheless put through. This fact suggests how anxious Stalin must have been to arrest the sharp decline of the Soviet birth rate. More people meant more soldiers and more workers, and it seemed that the USSR would be needing both.

An even broader frame of reference has sometimes been called up to explain the new policy. In this view, after the Five Year Plans and the frenzied drive for collectivization had exhausted and even seriously disorganized the Soviet people, the rapidity and scope of the effort demanded and the social changes induced had brought with them the reactions often found in times of stress — extreme mobility, waves of crime, and other types of disorderly personal behavior — to the point where the stability of the Soviet social order itself was endangered. This situation required the imposition of a thoroughgoing new social discipline, and the family can be seen to be only one of several instruments of social control and social coardination that Stalin's regime put to work in the mid-thirties in the interest of personal discipline and social stability. The other main agencies for controlling and disciplining children, school and youth organizations, were also reconstituted, though in a more traditional fashion, with greater stress on regimen and discipline. Similar trends occurred in law, in the armed forces, and in industry, for it was necessary to regroup and reorder the chaos in human relations which the frantic pace and desperate struggles of the preceding years had brought about. This was a time for the stabilization of social relations.

Before turning to the ways in which the new policy was framed in the ideology, I should mention one interpretation which has enjoyed some popularity though I myself do not find it compelling. The proponents of this view assert that the family policy of the first fifteen to twenty years was designed largely to divert the control and influence of hostile parents away from youth and that, in the course of time, as political opposition to the regime diminished, the attitude of parents became sufficiently positive so that the regime was, with equal wisdom, able to support the family. In brief, this theory argues that official policy toward the family corresponded to the regime's evaluation of the political attitudes of Soviet parents and its opinion of the ways in which the family rears its children: if parents are seen as against communism, the regime tries to weaken the family; if the parents are in favor of the regime, it tries to strengthen the family.

The most glaring shortcoming of this interpretation is that it disregards the fact that the time of the inception of the new family policy corresponds quite closely with the likely point of maximum political disaffection among the population. Forced collectivization had just been completed, the living standard in the cities had dropped to a point much below that of 1928,[74] and the purges and terror were about to reach a high peak. At such a time Stalin could hardly expect that Soviet parents were making special efforts to rear loyal young communists.

The final consideration at issue in an analysis of the new policy on the family poses the issue somewhat differently. It is curious that although published accounts of the change have made every effort to explain why it occurred, none as yet has considered why it took almost two decades for the regime to decide that the family was of sufficient importance to deserve explicit support. Marxism and its hold over the regime provide an explanation. Three features of marxist thought are involved: a value premise, a proposition relating two parts of social structure at a concrete level, and the marxist view of how social change occurs — all of which served for many years to obstruct direct participation by the party in the guidance of family behavior.

The value premise, which goes back to Engels, is the insistence on a separation between public and private life, the latter being the realm of individual freedom. In spite of the theory of revolutionary sublimation and sporadic assertions by various influential party leaders to the effect that there must be "in principle" no such separation, a strong undercurrent of opinion supported it (and still continues to do so). That noninterference in private life, which has usually meant quite specifically family life, is preferred by the Soviet population at large goes without saying. It has also been common in the thinking within the party,[75] which is understandable both because party leaders have always maintained a remarkably rigid wall between these two sides of their lives and because no firm line on such things was taken until 1935. When the policy did change, with official dogma supporting the monogamous husband, the responsible father, and the joyous mother, who set aside leisure time to spend with the family, and so on, it was possible for an official apologist to claim that the leftist theories of the early years had gone uncriticized. Though this is not strictly accurate, after Stalin's accession to power, we must remember, "criticism" had taken on a new meaning; it was now equivalent to condemnation.

Equally influential was the proposition that sex equality could be gained only through the abolition of the women's responsibilities for childrearing and housekeeping. The regime's commitment to sex equality was very strong, and to support the family by praising these two activities was to fly in the face of elementary marxism.

Finally, the fact that the marxist theory of social change clearly assigns the more active role to the economic base had made it very difficult for marxists to forsake the idea that morality is no more than epiphenomenal. The dilemma this heritage has visited upon the bolsheviks is revealed clearly in an excerpt from a book edited by Iaroslavski in 1924: "The fundamental question which occupied us earlier, before the October Revolution, was the question of whether communist morality can be worked out in the absence of a communist system, since morality, just as all other ideological norms, is only a superstructure over one or another foundation of the economic setup of the region." [76] When morality was regarded as "only a superstructure," it made little sense to try to set up a moral code for family behavior until a communist base could be brought to life. Thus, insofar as such behavior was not determined by economic factors, it was the realm of private life, and could properly be relegated to the category of "matters of no concern to the party."

By the mid-thirties it had become quite clear that the economic base for a radical withering of family life was not forthcoming. At that point a new ethos was pressed into service, and aspects of Lenin's thought were made definitively explicit under Stalin. Most significantly, the superstructure, now a "socialist" one, was assigned an active role in fomenting social change. Indeed, just as in Soviet economic life, classical marxism was stood on its head, and the Soviet state under Stalin proclaimed the still continuing campaign to bring the Soviet social order into conformity with its own ideological (that is, "superstructural") conceptions. The official view of the role of the family in this quest is revealed in the following authoritative formulation, published in 1936: "The increased attention which is lately being paid in the U.S.S.R. to the struggle against all sorts of traditions of exploitation in family life is to be explained, not by any strengthening of these traditions, but by the fact that they are now in striking opposition to the whole socialist system of our state in which socialism has become the social form of existence of the multitudes." [77]

There were other varieties of apologia. Among the writings of those who sought to justify the new family policy in ideological terms, the most dignified tone is found in the works of Krupskaia, Lenin's widow, who confined herself to the unrationalized essence of the new line: "It is possible to solve this question [the proper conduct of family life] only on the basis of communist morality." [78] She also referred to the "great expense" to the Soviet State that was involved in the new decree on the support of motherhood.

No authoritative writers attempted to find justification for the new family policy in Marx, Engels, or Lenin, and the efforts that were made by little-known persons seem quite clumsy, internally contradictory, and embarrassed.[79] Evading theoretical argumentation of any sophistication, they relied on indoctrination, and especially upon that peculiar Soviet form that has been aptly termed the "imperative-indicative." Clearly, the truth was too awkward to be faced, and had to be covered up.[80]

The imperative-indicative, which has suffused almost all Soviet writing on the family since the 1930's, is actually a form of socialist realism — that is, a form of mass persuasion. As such it both hides the truth and formulates a course of action: "In socialist society . . . conditions are created which allow woman to combine harmoniously an active participation in productive and social life with the performance of her family function, her duties as a mother"; "Our youth in the choice of a life-friend — wife or husband — know only one motive, one impulse: love. The bourgeois marriage of pecuniary convenience does not exist for our growing generation"; "Motherhood has become a joy, . . . our women and children are the happiest in the whole world"; and "In socialist society personal interests and the interests of the family are harmoniously united with the interests of all of society." [81]

One searches in vain for honest and clear analysis in this literature. It sometimes seems that falsehood and obscurantism know no limits. For example, works published in the late 1930's claimed that "the founders of marxism established that socialism brings with it a strong and healthy family," [82] that "when Engels said that under communism the 'relations of the sexes will become a private affair which will concern only the interested persons, and into which society cannot interfere,' he had in mind not the independence of personal family interests from social interests, but only the independence of woman, her right to free choice of husband without constraint, her right to free divorce, the absence of a slave-like dependency of the wife on the husband and the children on the parents." Moreover, the latter writer continued, "Marx declared forthrightly that the proletariat will interfere in the personal relations of the sexes, in the mutual relations of man and woman to the extent that they break the rules of communist communal life." [83]

Use of scapegoats also became common: "The enemies of the people, the vile fascist hirelings — Trotsky, Bukharin, Krylenko and their followers — covered the family in the USSR with filth, spreading the counter-revolutionary 'theory' of the dying out of the family, of disorderly sexual cohabitation in the USSR, in order to discredit the Soviet land." [84]

Along with such examples of intellectual prostitution, a tone of moral disapproval and the threat of greater severity of sanctions for the "moral survivals of the past" developed as the logical consequence of a stronger role for the superstructure in bringing about change. Survivals now were divested of any legitimate ontological status in the official ideology and consequently became simply examples of personal failure among the Soviet people. The list of taboos was widely advertised, and the Soviet citizen was left in no doubt about what was expected of him. Among the most prominent survivals connected with Soviet family life were sexual dissoluteness, hasty marriage, frequent divorce, wife-beating, the woman's giving up work and study after marriage, adultery, failure to give economic support to aged parents, and "looking upon a wife as a possession." These shaded over easily into other areas of behavior linked with family life, such as religious belief and practice, desire for personal wealth, and the consumption of alcohol, and included the most trivial as well as the most serious of derelictions. The concept of survival gradually became simply a label, a device for calling attention to what the party and government considered undesirable. Nonetheless, until recently the description of such survivals and the vignettes of model behavior have been almost the only published material on family life since the 1920's bearing any relation to reality.

In two respects, however, the Soviet conception and use of survivals requires further comment. First of all, survivals tend for several reasons to be masculine vices: (1) men in general engage in more visible and disruptive forms of deviant behavior than do women; (2) husbands are most often held responsible for the extent to which social equality between spouses — the marxist keystone to a proper marriage — has in fact not been realized; and (3) Stalinist oppression seems to have damaged the male personality more than that of the female (in ways discussed more specifically in Chapter 9).

Survivals also pose for the regime the interesting dilemma of accounting for their continued existence many years after the achievement of socialism. For almost two decades the main explanations have been that the "remnants of the former exploiting classes of Tsarist Russia linger on," that "consciousness lags behind economic development," and that the survivals are nourished from without by the "capitalist encirclement." [85] In the Soviet frame of reference these all seem temporary causes, for the conditions described are expected to terminate. In fact, the main function of the notion of survivals is to shift the responsibility for discrepancies between the ideal and the real from the state of the Soviet economy to the shoulders of individual Soviet citizens. The notion is apt to be a permanent fixture, for it provides the regime with a freedom of maneuver not permitted by the classical marxist formulation, but, as time goes on, survivals will very probably become more and more identical with the patterns of social deviance in any modern society. Their official status in the formal ideology will continue to perform a valuable function, serving as justification for the Soviet regime's persistent interfering in all sides of individual life — for, in a word, its totalitarianism. To give one recent example, it has become quite usual to blame Soviet juvenile crimes upon the irresponsibility and mistakes of the delinquent's parents, and the conclusion which emerges might be expected: "In connection with this, the interference of public organizations into family upbringing must be considered an appropriate and beneficial phenomenon." [86]

Post-Stalin Problems and Trends

The new family policy began in the mid-thirties and was brought to full scope in the legislation of 1944. In the decade following there were no significant changes, but since the death of Stalin some momentous new developments have occurred. Illegal abortion was the first portion of the new policy to fall. In 1954 the Presidium of the Supreme Soviet annulled criminal responsibility of women for obtaining an abortion, and in 1955 rescinded the rest of the law originally passed in 1936. Three factors were given in explanation: (1) the broadening of measures to encourage motherhood and protect infants along with continuing growth in the social consciousness and cultural level of women; (2) a desire to afford women a chance to decide for themselves about motherhood; and (3) a desire to avoid the injuries being sustained by women in illegal operations performed outside hospitals.[87] The first reason is mainly window-dressing, since much the same claims were given as the pretext for making abortions illegal in 1936. The second seems somewhat gratuitous in view of the evidence that many women were already making their own decisions outside the law, as suggested by what one observer characterized as "the real reason" [88] — namely, the third — which appeared to be tacit recognition that legal prohibition of abortion could neither eradicate the practice nor raise the birth rate. A further, though unstated, factor was probably the wish of the government leaders to end profiteering by unscrupulous abortionists, both with and without medical training. The combination of great demand for illegal abortion and the great risks attendant upon it often led to very inflated prices. As one might gather from the lack of public discussion or official commentary accompanying the new decree, "it is as if the regime, with a shrug of the shoulders, chose what seemed to be the lesser of two evils in a highly complicated human situation." [89]

A second development, of the greatest consequence for family policy as well as for all of Soviet society, was the denigration of Stalin and the cult of personality, which led the way to sharp social commentary and criticism of a kind that had not been possible since the 1920's. Newspaper reporters, belle-lettrists, and writers of letters-to-the-editor were able to deal much more honestly with a wide range of social problems, including those touching on family life. For instance, the post-Stalin decade witnessed a host of films, plays, novels, and short stories dealing quite exclusively with the complexities of private life — with love, personal and family happiness, marital conflicts, and a much broader range of mixed and antisocial emotions. The writings of Antonov, Panova, Kazakov, Nagibin, and Voronin, for instance, evoke an image of human nature and social relations much more complex — often irrational and tragic — and quite in contrast with the enthusiastic, virtuous, and psychologically uninteresting "positive heroes" of the previous quarter-century.[90]

Even the law itself, promulgated in the name of people, party, and the sacred cause of communism, lost its untouchable quality. A 1960 newspaper discussion of the 1944 law on the family referred to it as "obsolete" and as containing "decayed norms." [91] Indeed, one of the most popular topics concerning family and married life in the daily press in the 1954 to 1963 decade was the lack of correspondence between the 1944 law and the code of morality and actual life of the Soviet people. The main target of criticism was the heavy administrative and financial barrier to divorce, which forced a great part of the population into evasions of the law and de facto marriages.[92]

Some of the writing shows a remarkable degree of indignation and concern over social justice — remarkable, that is, within the framework of the usual practices of the Soviet press. Especially attacked has been one of the main instrumentalities of the new family policy, that which made the woman entirely responsible for the support and rearing of children born out of legal wedlock. "A bitter feeling arises when one realizes that certain provisions of the law of July 8, 1944 . . . aid in the revival of the shameful view that women are the guilty parties in the 'fall from grace' of man. They aid in spreading narrow views that indiscriminately brand any woman who has dared to have a child 'without a husband.' " [93] Such indignation is considerably justified, for the 1944 law did indeed clearly imply that women were to be held primarily responsible for the population's sexual and reproductive behavior, and that the possible injustice to men that might arise out of wrongful imputation of paternity was of greater evil than the combined weight of failure of mothers to receive support for children and the application of the label "unmarried mother" to a good part of the population.[94]

An equivalent measure of antagonism has been directed against the stigmatization by the 1944 law of millions of Soviet children as illegitimate. The children of mothers who were literally without husbands as well as those who had husbands but had to live with them in *de facto* or unregistered marriage were identified in their personal documents with a dash in the place of the father's name. Moreover, they had neither the right nor the opportunity to take their father's names. The man on the street, it seems, considered both categories as illegitimate, and school children were to be heard addressing certain of their peers as, "Hey you, fatherless." [95]

I have been unable to locate more than one or two published defenders of this provision. One writer argued in 1960 that "what changes should be made in the law code is not a pressing question to the millions . . . [who] . . . do not feel the weight and severity of the law because they do not violate it" and, furthermore, that those who do are "uninhibited, slovenly, sensual," the true fault lying in "egotism" and "immorality." The overwhelming majority, however, have clearly been in agreement in condemning the legal buttressing of illegitimacy as an "astonishingly unjust" article of legislation, "in contradiction to the very spirit of Soviet society." [96]

Finally, ardent adherents of social logic discovered a corollary set of most distressing anomalies. From time to time the Soviet organized public found it necessary to heap scorn on unmarried fathers who had, by refusing to marry, incurred no legal responsibility whatsoever. This practice, it appeared, was giving a " 'legal' right to sexual promiscuity for some and the responsibility for it to others," and the 1944 law prolonged the helpless and exposed position of the Soviet mother which had been one of the most unsavory consequences of the earlier, easy-divorce policy. There was also the tragicomic spectacle of the mass adoption by men of their own children, who were otherwise "illegitimate," born to them by their own "wives," whom they could not marry because of inability to get divorces from their previous (legal) wives. Finally, who could fail to be rendered uneasy, if also impressed, by the juristic sleight-of-hand shown by some judges in their attempts to circumvent the law of 1944 in such cases, in order "to find any basis at all — however shaky or naïve — for arriving at a just decision." [97]

All in all, the time was indeed ripe when, "in response to many letters of inquiry," a new law on marriage and the family, several years in preparation by a representative subcommittee of the Supreme Soviet, was revealed in February 1964 and went into effect on December 10, 1965.[98] It was admitted that the existing (1944) legislation contained "certain flaws." Readers who were not already well familiarized with them could discover what they were by studying the changes. In the future birth certificates issued for children born out of wedlock would no longer show a line drawn through the place for the father's name; paternity outside marriage would be made subject to voluntary admission and, "in certain cases," to the determination of the court; obligatory public announcements in the newspapers of the filing of a divorce action would be ended;[99] and divorce cases would be heard and decided only in the people's courts.

The changes clearly represent a compromise position; the post-revolutionary pendulum has come to a vertical rest. There is apparently to be no complete "return to the principles of Lenin," that is, absolute free divorce as some have urged, but the most pressing sources of injustice and trouble appear to be at an end.

A third development of the post-Stalin years may prove in the long run to be the most significant of all: the growing fund of accurate information about family life, and the rise of new methods and personnel to gather more such information in the future. To be sure, most published information is still markedly selective in its choice of problems and often biased in the use of facts and arguments. At this time no scientific investigations are being made of the effect on family life of the cult of personality, for instance, nor are there any serious efforts to describe and compare Soviet family life in terms of social class differences. And the rhetoric of the imperative-indicative too often continues to mislead the naïve and vex the instructed. Western readers, and presumably Soviet as well, often find it difficult to disentangle what is from what ought to be, and the post-Stalin regime seems unlikely to revoke publicly the peculiarly marxist view of truth. The West, of course, has learned to attach a special label to the phenomena likely to develop out of the "unity of theory and practice": the principle of the "self-fulfilling prophecy." Thus, the commonly found assertion that "the marriage of calculation has become a most rare phenomenon, and peace and love in the family the customary occurrence," is no more than a canon of marxism; unproven or untrue;[100] but a didactically useful, or functional, item serving to decrease the number of such marriages, and to embarrass those who are still calculating. Needless to say, this view of the relation between action, belief, and published material constitutes a most formidable barrier to the spirit and method of dispassionate sociological inquiry. The social fact as we know it and the cultural revolution as the Soviet rulers wish it do not harmonize well.

Nonetheless, in many respects the secrecy and dogmatism of the past have given way to such a degree that one may forecast a genuine qualitative change in the self-originated knowledge about the family in Soviet society. I shall cite three specific trends. First, national statistics of interest to marriage and family life are now being published. Though these are not always released in the most clear or usable form, it is of some interest to learn that about half of the Soviet families with children have only one child, that the USSR had a crude marriage rate of 12.1 per thousand in 1960, and that the average Soviet family size in 1959 was 3.7 persons.[101] Secondly, the daily press has become a much more frank, interesting, and reliable source of sociologically relevant information. For example, in 1956 reporter Kiselev divulged that while investigating the problem of divorce he had uncovered evidence of a large number of "*de facto* divorces" which never appeared in any statistical tabulations, and, moreover, that he had talked with "dozens" of persons, not one of whom had approved of the current divorce situation.[102]

For another example, in a 1960 article on "Unusual Children," reporter Kotovshchikova divulged facts of explosive potential for Soviet family policy. A Soviet sociologist finds they "have the significance of the most convincing sociological experiment." [103] The reporter starts her story with a description of a rosy-cheeked, attractive little girl of five who, though quite normal in appearance, did not talk at all. She then reveals that the girl had been reared in the state institutions for children, in an infants' home, and, later, in a children's home. Furthermore, continues Kotovshchikova, the graduates of a certain Leningrad children's home were doing poorly in school; their first-grade teacher told the director, "It's very hard to work with your children. They don't understand the simplest things!" The author refrains carefully from overgeneralizing or overstating her case, but the message is indeed clear: some factor in the institutional homes for infants and young children resulted in retardation of development. Regarding speech retardation, for instance, "in the infants' homes there are extremely few conversations with grown-ups, and for the most part they do not have an individual make-up, but a group one (in which the attention of the listener is always more spread out than in individual interaction)." [104]

A third source for the rapid increase in Soviet sociological knowledge about the family in recent years has been a higher rate of research and publication in the established discipline of ethnography.[105] Furthermore, concrete or research sociology has been established as a respectable endeavor, complete with institutes of research. Though attention is largely focused on the sociology of work, some research is being conducted on family life.

The results of sociological research on family life can be communicated only if the basic axioms of historical materialism are bypassed. This is justified in two different ways. First, there is a tendency to refer to certain phenomena and events as natural categories, that is, as independent of the main concerns of marxist analysis. In sociological discussions of the family there are references to the "natural-instinctual basis" of parental, filial, and sexual love, and the assertion that "a peculiarity of marital-family relations is the fact that they have an immutable natural foundation in the form of the differences of the sexes." [106]

A second device is found in the extension of the conceptual linkage tracing the types of influences between the base and the superstructure. "The dependency of marital and family relations upon the base does not signify in all cases a direct and immediate connection between them. The forms of marriage and the family are *directly* determined by the nature of the moral relations in the society and the legal norms, but morality and law, in their turn, depend upon the entire political and cultural life of the society." Such an argument indicates that among the factors appropriately considered to influence family life, in addition to the economic base, are moral and legal norms and "the entire political and cultural life of the society" or, more specifically, economic relations inside the individual family itself, public opinion, religion or atheism, the position of the woman in society, and the ideas, principles, standards, sentiments, emotions, experiences, wills of the individuals concerned. Finally, to encompass every possibility, "class, national, moral, esthetic and legal relations can also in one way or another make themselves felt in the life of a family." In addition to such structural categories, certain idiosyncratic factors, which no account of the vicissitudes of the Soviet family could afford to omit, now also exert legitimate influence: "In particular periods of history a great influence upon marriage and the family has been exerted by such factors as the disproportion between the male and the female population, wars and the moral upheavals connected with them." [107]

A general conclusion to this newly enriched view of the sources of family life may be found in one important assertion: "This complexity of the mutual links of marital-family relations with social life has as its consequence the relative independence of the development of marriage and the family in respect to changes in the economic base of society." [108] With the "marxist theory of the family" pigeonholed, the assertion of a vital determining link between property ownership and other parts of the base on the one hand and the nature of the family on the other has become a ritual postulate, relegated to propaganda service. Henceforth it will be possible to extend significantly the variety of topics amenable to research without prejudicing the still living dogma of the superiority of socialism and socialist institutions over capitalism. As of 1964, however, when comparing the Soviet family with that of America, the leading Soviet writer, Kharchev, still felt compelled to find evidence that the Soviet family is in various ways "superior";[109] unbiased international comparisons are not yet close at hand in the USSR.

A further development, also connected with the demise of stalinism, focuses on life in the future in lively and speculative discussions that are evocative of the intellectual atmosphere of the 1920's. Just as forty years ago, differing positions are taken by the radical visionaries and the more prosaic defenders of common sense and tradition, and two central problems are at issue. Regarding the first, the matter of childrearing, an eminent spokesman for the radical position, Academician S. G. Strumilin, states the case as follows:

The advantages of public childrearing are so great and so obvious that every public expense, on any scale, for *all* the country's children is justifiable . . . The collective of children, especially if they are guided without pressure by the experienced hand of a pedagogue, can contribute much more of the best social habits to the rearing of a child than the most kindly and loving mothers . . . In according the public forms of childrearing unconditional preference over all others, it is our job in the very near future to extend these forms at such speed that after 15 or 20 years they will be available from the cradle to the high school graduation certificate — for the entire population of the country. Every Soviet citizen, upon emerging from a hospital as a baby, will go to a crèche, from there to a nursery school maintained day and night or to a children's home. From there he will go to a boarding school, from which he will depart with a ticket into independent life — to go into production or for further study at his chosen speciality. Naturally, children's institutions ought to be organized in every residence building under the same roof with the adults but in separate premises with special service personnel and with the full cost of maintenance born by the state as in the boarding schools.[110]

Strumilin's proposals, orthodox dogma not too long ago, have evoked a storm of controversy and a discussion likely to continue for some time. At the present moment three main issues seem to be at stake.

The first centers on the extent and mode of participation. Are "all" the country's children to participate? Will "every Soviet citizen . . . go to a crèche, from there to a nursery school maintained day and night"? In short, will attendance be compulsory? The strong sentiment on the part of many parents against full-time rearing by the state is based on the suspicion that absence does not usually make the heart grow fonder. A worker says, "We have a great need for boarding nurseries, but the fact that my son is becoming alienated from me is so painful that I can't even talk about it. I call him 'Sasha, my son.' But he just runs away. No! I have to spend at least an hour or two each day with my son. Otherwise it's impossible, otherwise I can't stand it." [111] Actually, such fears ought to have been laid at rest by the fact that the issue was settled, as much as the current explicit party line can settle a controversial matter, by the 1961 party Program. The Program promises maintenance of children free of charge at children's establishments "for every family" at an early date, but only "if they so desire" or "if parents wish." [112] One can safely predict that if this position is maintained, and if excessive pressure behind the scenes is not applied, even in the distant future a large number of parents will eschew boarding schools and similar institutions and prefer to keep their children with them at home, especially when they are young.

The second issue concerns the uncertain effect upon young children of institutional rearing. In contrast to the implication given by Strumilin that public rearing provides "great" and "obvious" advantages, some evidence and some weighty opinion to the contrary have now appeared. An authoritative example of current doubts is given by the Director of the Laboratory of Higher Nervous Activity in the Child, Pavlov Institute of Physiology, USSR Academy of Sciences: "The question of the rearing of children in infants' homes and crèches has tremendous significance to the state. It is a matter of the formation of a generation which is full-valued in the neuro-psychological sense. By the way, it has been shown by numerous observations that the retardation of the development of children in infants' homes and partly in crèches (especially in the 24-hour-a-day groups) is compensated for in later years with difficulty and incompletely." [113] The USSR's leading family sociologist, A. G. Kharchev, also ranges himself against Strumilin in judging indispensable the role of the family in childrearing: "Because of its deeply specific quality and the uniqueness of the influence of the family on the child, it is an indispensable factor in normal childrearing. Children reared without its participation are much more subject to the danger of one-sided or retarded development than those who are members of family collectives." [114]

A third issue stems from a contradiction between two aspects of Soviet ideological speculation. The 1961 party Program promised an ever greater reduction of working hours — a six-hour, six day or a seven-hour, five-day week in the 1960's and still shorter in the decade of the 1970's.[115] Moreover, it predicted a rise in the level and convenience of living such that off-work time will become more genuinely free. But it has become increasingly apparent that both parents and children find being with each other a matter of joy rather than a burden.[116] Why, then, ask some Soviet people, should plans be made to divest them of the chance to spend their free time in the way many of them most prefer? We might aphorize their feelings toward the ideal of a further spread in public upbringing as, "No, that would be moving in the wrong direction!"

To sum things up, the outlook at the moment for a continuing increase in total, full-time childrearing by the state is dimmer than at any time since the Revolution. Both it and the communal organization of family life, the "abolition of the individual family household," seem on their way to permanent repose. The most authoritative recent reassurance at hand is the declaration by Khrushchev in 1961, in his report on the new party Program: "People who say that the significance of the family drops during the transition to communism, and that it disappears with time, are absolutely wrong. In fact, the family will grow stronger under communism. Completely disencumbered of family considerations, family relations will become pure and lasting."

The new Soviet sociology has not ventured into the complexities of systematically probing public opinion on this subject, but some indication of the people's state of mind was given by a recent report of audience reaction to the melodrama, *Story of a Salvaged Love,* which was performed at the Pushkin Theatre in 1964. When a "modern" student, in love with her handsome professor, suggested the idea that "in a hundred years husbands and wives will be friends, not parents, and society will bring up their children" the line, according to one observer, received the biggest laugh of the evening.[117]

Another major problem, still unsolved, is presented by the idea that under communism both individual freedom and sex love are supposed to reach full flower: how is the latter — which, as Engels pointed out, gives rise to inclinations "variable in intensity and duration" — to be reconciled with the continued existence of the family? One answer stresses a growing "moral factor," expressed as strengthened feelings of mutual love, loyalty, and friendship to one's spouse and loyalty to an established family even in the face of a new love. Communism is to lead to the greatest increase of the role of this moral factor in family life, as in all other affairs. Thus, during an epoch of freedom in marital-family relations there will also be present the most complete, developed, and stable monogamy.[118] The patent contradiction is transcended by the transformation and perfection of man, by "a new man who among other things will harmoniously combine spiritual wealth, moral purity and a perfect physique." [119] Under communism marital conflicts and divorce based on the termination of the feeling of love (*issiakaniia liubvi*) will therefore become "incomparably more rare than at present, because among the factors exercising influence over marital-family relations there will no longer be vulgarity, nor meanness, nor frivolity." [120]

The opposing viewpoint is closer to that of the marxists of days past. The spokesman for this side, Academician Strumilin, venerable dean of Soviet economists as well as social philosopher, refers to a future in which a "new, strong and worthy love" between a man and a woman other than his wife and the mother of his children will not have to end tragically. He continues: "All such grave conflicts and collisions between an active individual love and duty to society, or between love for a woman and concern for the fate of one's innocent children are quite comprehensible under contemporary conditions and cannot be disregarded. Still and all, this is not the norm, but rather deviations from it. Under the conditions of communism means will be found to reconcile the interests of family and society." [121] To some, at least, love in the communist future is still bright with the promise of naturalistic freedom, just as it was to Engels and Alexandra Kollontai. And, it seems, in the USSR there are still "not a few people" who think that with the development of Soviet society the family will gradually die out, along with the state, law, and other social phenomena inherited from class society.[122]

ADJUSTING TO THE
OUTER WORLD

At this point the focus on the Soviet leaders' thoughts, problems, and policies can be dismissed, and crucial events and trends of the Soviet scene viewed from inside the family. From this perspective, I shall discuss the ways in which collectivization, the great purge, and the other massive economic and social changes of the past forty-five years have influenced the fate of individual Soviet families, the manner in which the family has been organized to fit into the class system, and the problems it has encountered.

My attention will be fixed at a point midway between large-scale societal developments and trends, on the one hand, and the vicissitudes of the individual Soviet citizen on the other, and I hope to convey a clear notion of the typical experiences and the general flavor of Soviet family life. I shall then be prepared to move to a more detailed inspection of married life and parent-child relations.

FIVE | WHAT THE REVOLUTION BROUGHT TO THE FAMILY

THE OCTOBER REVOLUTION set in motion what has been called "the greatest social experiment in history." The entire world has been deeply interested in the succession of highly dramatic events in the USSR, but the Soviet people were the actual actors and directors of the play, the guinea pigs of the experiment. For some years stunned disbelief, caution, and eager hopes were mingled, but later, as time passed, the Revolution, the Communist Party, marxism, and the Soviet leaders become deeply loved by some and bitterly hated by many more.

Even now, when both the initial attitudes and the subsequent sharpness of feelings have worn off, questions of interpretation and evaluation remain — questions such as whether the Revolution was "inevitable," whether Lenin and his followers have brought more good or more evil to the world, whether communism represents the nascent future or an anomalous throwback. These questions are still momentously controversial in most parts of the world, including the Soviet Union itself.

Evidence of the complexity of the problem is provided by the very frequency and vigor of calls for Soviet patriotism, dedication to the cause of communism, renewed faith in the ideas of Marx and Lenin, and continued forcible repudiation of doubt by the leaders. One is most impressed by the still controversial nature of the Soviet regime and its works at those times when the genuine political views of ordinary Soviet citizens become known.

Against this important background feature, the Soviet family can best be introduced in the context of the two sides of the main controversy on the national scene — in terms first of the injury and then of the good brought to the people by the regime. Both injuries and benefits have been mediated to and through the family, and many of the most memorable events and policies of the years since 1917 have their poignant reflections in the experiences shared by the members of Soviet families in their efforts to adjust to change.

A discussion later in this chapter will center on the situation of that unique minority of the Soviet system, the politically underprivileged.

Their forced assimilation through a "prototype experience" will be viewed as a model telling in bold relief much about what it has meant to live in a society in a time of revolutionary change. Finally, an analysis of a preliminary confrontation between Soviet society and the Soviet family will reveal the extent to which they have been in sharp competition for the loyalty of the individual, to whom the question has appeared as: Where is home?

A Multiplication of Catastrophes

There is a homicidal cast to Soviet history. Estimates of the number of untimely deaths are staggering — nine million in the First World War, twenty million in the Second, with additional millions who perished in the Civil War and from famine, epidemics, forced deportation of kulaks, and the persecutions of Stalin's Terror and labor camps. According to one Western scholar, Soviet population losses, if birth deficits suffered during the World Wars are included, come to approximately 100,000,000 in some forty years.[1]

Although all have suffered, most of the victims have been men. The 1959 census shows twenty million more women than men in the Soviet Union and in the age group thirty-two and older almost twice as many women as men. This fact alone demands that two easy stereotypes about the USSR be called into serious question. It is sometimes said that the Soviet Union is a land of youth, but in reality it is more a land of women. The second stereotype, inherited from what now seems, inside the USSR, a distant past, sees the Soviet Union as a land of free love, though in reality it is much more a land of broken families.

These two realities indicate the significant fact that a very great proportion of Soviet families are headed by women. In the village of Viriatino, subjected to intensive study in 1953, a breakdown of the distribution of the 456 families showed that women made up 44.5 per cent of the total number of heads of households, and that the modal type (67 families) was a two-person family headed by a woman.[2]

Life itself is of course the most precious possession, but other things are also dear, and catastrophe has visited Soviet families in several guises. The October Revolution itself turned the old social order upside down, and the various other revolutions, both episodic and continuing, have suppressed and actively persecuted entire groupings because of their undesired positions in the social structure. As a sample, one respondent explained that his father, a civil engineer, was arrested "only because he belonged to the bourgeoisie." "He was given the verdict — exile for 5 years to any of the smaller cities of Russia. They called this punishment 'minus 5,' which meant that he could not live in any of the five largest cities of the Soviet Union. Before his release he asked the judge why he was being punished, and the answer came: 'Listen, citizen. You are a man of the past, and we don't need people of your kind around. Be glad that the Soviet Government is merciful' " (1578 A 7). A detailed accounting of all groups and categories involved would detract from the main theme of this discussion. It is more important to understand the consequences inside the family of the precipitate declines in status that have been so frequent. Two further examples of the categories of families involved include suggestions of what it has meant to the family to be of the "former people" or "alien elements," as they were called.

My father was refused a passport because he was a kulak. He was required to leave the village and go to some other place in the Kharkov Region 50 kilometers away. He just had to leave; they did not tell him where he was to go. So he left. But he was still persecuted, to the point where he could not talk to his family. He went to live with some comrades who were in the same position as he was. He left us without even telling us where he was going. [314 A 32]

My father was the son of a very plain and ordinary priest. This certainly did not help him. He was referred to as a "son of a priest," and the fact that his father had been of very humble peasant stock did not help him at all. We were disfranchised. We were thrown out of our house and told to go wherever we wanted. We lived in a house that was fit for chickens. We could not do anything. We had no prospect of decent work. [1109 A 6]

Even when members of such men's families remained alive, they suffered separation, dispossession, and loss of such civil rights as were accorded to the population.

Particularly revealing is the case of the kulaks, who were the main victims of Stalin's most unpopular reform, the collectivization of agriculture. As has so often been the case, Soviet social reconstruction was paid for in the coin of individual suffering and broken families. In the official language the "liquidation of the kulaks as a class" paved the way for "building socialism in one country," but in the language of the people the Soviet power took their possessions, caused famine, and scattered them and their families to the four winds.

For these peasants family life often simply ceased to exist. Husbands and wives, parents and children were separated from each other as well as from their land. Unable to enter a kolkhoz or to farm other land, and with no occupational skills but those of the farmer, those kulak men who remained alive and free often drifted to newly active construction sites, where they worked at unskilled labor and lived in barracks. Their wives, considered by the regime to be more backward than hostile, sometimes went to the cities to work as servants or at other unskilled jobs and occasionally journeyed to live with relatives. Kulak children were often adopted, taken in by more fortunate relatives or neighbors, or added to the population of homeless children.

The fate of the priesthood has been similarly hard. Heavy taxes, public ridicule, quasi-legal persecution for conspiracy against the state, denial of alternative opportunities for work and for the education of their children, and sometimes physical destruction were the lot of the Russian priest until the Second World War.

These kulaks and clergy have been especially prominent among the groups persecuted, I suspect, because of their social visibility and also their relative inability or unwillingness to adapt to the new Soviet order. The story about the priest continues: "Throughout the entire . . . Soviet Revolution and the Soviet regime he continued his religious work. The peasants loved him . . . At one time, while we were living in that village on the Dniester, someone offered to get my father across the river. My father refused to flee. He said he would stay to face his fate as God had willed it" (1109 A 8).

As important as these typical catastrophes — the physical destruction or separation of the family members and the radical decline in status with loss of material possessions, civil rights, and opportunities — has been a profound sense of insecurity and, at times, even dread. This pattern, perhaps the most distinctive of all Soviet experiences in daily life, developed early, in the form of efforts to settle accounts with the ruling classes of Tsarist times, became more striking in the drive against the kulaks, and gradually rose to the frenzied destruction and horror associated with the peak of the great purge of 1936 and 1937, the *Ezhovshchina*. By then the term "enemy of the people" was being applied to long lists of loyal party members condemned out of hand by the all-powerful Stalin. The circle of families affected was constantly widened, but for many it was only the culmination of a trend that had begun earlier with the Revolution and the Civil War, events that left the Bolsheviks, party of the minority, in command of a people toward most of whom they felt little sympathy. Since that time Stalinist terror has relented, and has even been "explained" as the time of the cult of personality, but its traces are still to be found, and the reality of fear remains a crucial factor in many Soviet homes.

For many in the population the Soviet period ushered in a sense of protracted conflict with the political rulers — a peculiar type of civil war between the regime and the people. The sides were, of course, quite unequal, but the powers of passive resistance and spiritual independence are great, and it is stilll true today that many Soviet citizens look upon their government and leaders with aversion and think in terms of "we" (the people) and "they" (our oppressors in the Kremlin). Largely responsible was Stalin's terrorism and the climate of fear it caused. A fifty-six-year-old nurse tells: "We all trembled because there was no way of getting out of it. Even a communist himself can be caught. To avoid trouble is an exception" (490 A 21).

Though much of the activity was hidden from the eyes of the outside world, there were some very public signs. For instance, in June and July of 1934 legal measures were introduced which, in effect, converted the Soviet citizen's close relatives into hostages. The laws established criminal liability for members of the family of a "traitor to the home-land" or a deserter from the armed forces. Sentences were meted out even if the treason or defection was not known to those who lived with the traitor or were dependent of him. As law this policy remained on the books for some time after the death of Stalin, apparently until the appearance of new criminal codes in 1958, though Soviet jurists criticized it before then and in 1957 a Western legal scholar was assured by the Deputy Procurator General of the USSR that it was "no longer applied." [3]

Again and again measures that the Soviet rulers regarded as progressive steps toward a better society were experienced by the people as intense cultural deprivation. The two most prominent examples are the reorganization of peasant life on the collective and state farms and the officially sanctioned opposition to the church and religious institutions, both of which were extremely unpopular with the great majority of the population. The response to agricultural collectivization is indicated in the following account by a party member who was also a peasant in

1930: "When we were told of collectivization . . . I liked the idea. So did a few others in the village, men like me. The rest of the village was dead set against it . . . Well, we got going . . . I called a village meeting and I told the people that they had to join the kolkhoz, that these were Moscow's orders, and if they didn't they would be exiled and their property taken away from them. They all signed . . . and felt as though they were being sent to jail." [4] Since that time the Soviet peasants have continued to chafe under the collective farm system, resenting those who forced it upon them, and extreme poverty and economic insecurity have added greatly to the burdens of institutional deprivation. To many, life on the kolkhoz has seemed like forced labor mainly because of its social organization: "Before the Revolution he [respondent's father] was master on his fields. He worked when he wished to. No overseer stood behind his back and pushed him to work like a donkey. Under the Soviet regime we became slaves" (1664 A 24).

Turning to the other main form of institutional-cultural oppression, the Soviet regime has always been unfriendly to religion as faith and ideology, and to the church as an organization. Though formally church and state are separate, and freedom of religious worship is supposedly guaranteed, in fact churches have been destroyed or withdrawn from use, and continuous streams of antireligious propaganda have been emitted by Soviet agencies and institutions. Every Soviet schoolboy learns that religion is the opium of the people, unscientific and reactionary, and party and Komsomol members are expelled for entertaining religious superstitions or prejudices.

Thus the formal right of religious worship has been made a mockery through action behind the scenes, purportedly at the behest of the toiling masses but in reality through decision by the party at the highest level. A notion of the extent to which the people were deprived of religious facilities in the prewar years can be gained from scattered facts and figures on the number of churches destroyed, withdrawn from use, or not replaced. In 1936, for example, *Izvestiia* reported that some of the fastest growing of the new cities, including Magnitogorsk, Karaganda, and Stalinsk, had no churches at all. Of all the many forces brought to bear in the effort to wipe out religion this elimination of places of worship has clearly been the most destructive. A young worker from a peasant background reports the story in barest outline: "From 1933 to 1942 I never went to church. There was none in the city in which I lived" (117 A 27). In Moscow in the year 1942 there were an estimated seventeen churches remaining in use by parishioners, in comparison with a total of at least six hundred before the Revolution.[5] During the postwar era, in connection with the new favor which the church gained, many damaged churches have been rebuilt or repaired, and new ones constructed. As of the late 1950's it was reported that there were 20,000 to 25,000 churches functioning, about half the number at hand in 1917.[6]

In addition, the party has periodically undertaken campaigns to discredit and obstruct what it contemptuously refers to as the practice of cults, and for a young person, in particular, to be identified as a believer involves a serious stigma in Soviet public life. Similarly, even though the clergy were given legal status equivalent to that of other citizens in the 1936 Constitution, a move said to have been sponsored by Stalin himself, even heavier repressive pressure was simultaneously imposed against individual members of the clergy. The considerable shortage of priests is a problem that continues today.

Eastern Orthodoxy is a faith with little explicit theology, ritual-centered to an exceptional degree. With no church in which to worship and with no priest to administer, for many Soviet people there just has been "no religion." The relevance in the political thoughts of a good many of the Soviet people is suggested by the words of a young man describing the view of his mother: "She thought that the communists were anti-Christ and atheists. She believed that men could not live without God and that people who were against God were against her" (110 A 108).

To sum up, Soviet history has brought many traumatic and deprivational experiences into the lives of the people, and a good share of these have been shared as family tragedies and misfortunes. The men — husbands and fathers in families — have been killed, separated, and greatly handicapped by denial of status and opportunity. The women — wives and mothers — have been hard pressed to carry on. Stories of a destroyed family like the following are often heard. The narrator's father was a peasant separated from his family and could neither rejoin nor help support those he left behind. As a result: "My mother had to work very hard; she was employed in excavation for building foundations. For this work she received one half liter of soup — not soup, really, but water — and 200 grams of bread each day. She did not get any money at all. This was not enough to maintain me and my brother, so we had to go to a children's home. All the children there either had no parents — many of their parents had died in the famine — or they were children like myself, whose parents could not feed them or who did not know where their parents were" (314 A 32).

In those families where all were able to survive and remain together, the outer society seemed threatening and improvident. In some periods and for some families arrest by the political police represented the ultimate misfortune. It was hard to anticipate calmly the possibility of arrest. Nevertheless, some provided in advance a dramatic symbol of the people's mood — the packed suitcase, ready to take along if the secret police knocked at the door — and some others thought of the economic security of those who would be left behind. One bookkeeper, relatively affluent, reported that he kept "only small sums" of money in the savings bank in order not to attract attention, but that "we had larger sums at our disposal just in case of trouble — so in case I should be arrested my daughter would have some support. Money was kept at home . . . I was always expecting an arrest and I wanted my daughter to keep the money by her, in case of emergency" (8 B 4).

Aside from such practical measures, some reactions were purely individual, like those of a forty-five-year-old mining foreman from a city in White Russia who was described as "very anxious," in constant fear that his former life as a kulak would be uncovered. His mind was chiefly on food, and all his thoughts were directed toward assuring the nourishment of his family. He spoke mostly about eating, for "eating his fill" was for him the most important consideration (Bi, 219, 306). Probably the search for gratification from the most accessible sources of human pleasure has been a major response to the hard lot of Soviet daily life. Eating, drinking, and sexual activity have doubtless attained greater general esteem, along with a sense of gratitude for the mere chance to live in a complete family.

Finally, insecurity in the presence of a threatening political environment frequently draws people together, and the evidence suggests that the catastrophic experiences of Soviet life have often had the effect of strengthening the sense of comfort and unity that family members have found in each other. It may even be true that while the suffering imposed by Soviet history has destroyed many specific families, it has also strengthened the family in general. For the family seems to profit from the adversity of the individual, especially when the source of injury is clearly located "on the outside," and the political leadership can be blamed. Thus, the best data available when subjected to statistical analysis suggest that political deprivation of the family (defined operationally as the execution, disappearance, or prolonged imprisonment or exile of one or more family members other than the respondent) increases solidarity among those who remain in the family. On the other hand, deprivation of a purely economic nature seems to have the opposite effect, as if there were a tendency for family members to blame each other.[7] Concretely, of course, the sources of the two forms of deprivation tend to merge, and both have often been laid at the door of the Soviet regime, leading to a district differentiation in the minds of many of the people between the harsh, threatening outer society and the haven of home: "At home we felt secure and safe. At home we wept, we smiled, we criticized or cursed those who made us poor and hungry" (1664 A 24).

Benefits of the Revolution

Foremost in the long list of benefits of the October Revolution put forth by the party and government are major institutional innovations. Most important are economic measures, such as abolition of the private ownership of productive property, national economic planning, and an end to wage slavery, economic crises, unemployment, and the exploitation of man by man. New institutions have also appeared in the countryside, where agricultural work was organized into large-scale collective and state farms, eminently praiseworthy in official view because they facilitated the introduction of heavy machinery, scientific method, and coordination of crop assortment and growth on a mass scale. Collateral activities — scientific research and development, training of professional manpower, and even cultural affairs — are directed by plan to the maximum extent feasible. The market as a distributive mechanism is derided and its function restricted as far as possible.

It is claimed that these structural changes have made it possible to organize Soviet society more rationally, that they afford Soviet man a heretofore unavailable opportunity to bring the basic forces influencing his life into conscious control and will ultimately provide him with material abundance, social security, cultural and leisure opportunities — in fact, the chance for all-around self-development of his personality.[8] As the political orators like to say, summing things up with a flourish, the October Revolution and the victory of socialism in the USSR have ushered in a new era in the history of mankind.

These changes and associated claims are of the greatest importance in that they constitute a kind of institutional return to the people, payment extended, in exchange for the sacrifices exacted by the Revolution, and it would be a grave error to dismiss lightly the fact that they have been and are highly valued by many Soviet citizens. Even in the face of dire stalinist oppression the achievements of the Revolution have found their adherents. In the words of a young refugee who found Soviet life hard but nevertheless had in the main a "positive attitude towards the regime": "I thought that all the difficulties were connected with the sacrifices which were necessary for the building of socialism and that after a socialist society was constructed, life would be better" (110 A 107). Moreover, these achievements were not only experienced as promises for the future. The young man continues: "I also felt that there was much that was positive. Even in the present life" (110 A 107).

Analyzing the statements of refugees and current members of Soviet society, there seem to be three general classes of benefits that must be taken into account: in general terms, sympathetic identification with communism, status advances, and increments of social justice and security made generally available to the population at large. The first, alluded to above, involves a sense of largesse derived from identification with the accomplishments of the regime. One recent case can be seen as a kind of rehabilitation of pride, corresponding with the end of the cult of the individual. A man, forty-five years old, a "minor clerk in an unimportant job" in Moscow, married, father of three children, "just a plain man, neither a saint nor a scoundrel" according to his brother, "decided to join the party after the Twentieth Congress. He told me then that though he wasn't one of those who had destroyed socialism, he would be glad to try and repair it, working together with other people like himself" (Nov 135).*

Behind such sentiments lie three considerations. Along with a general approval of the desirability of socialism comes the very considerable success of the regime in meeting both the tasks it has imposed upon itself, as in its economic growth, and the challenges visited upon it from without, as in the war with the Axis; to these correspond the readiness to identify with the system and to share the glory of prodigious achievement. The third consideration is a composite of the two preceding,

* From *The Future Is Ours, Comrade,* by Joseph Novak. Copyright © 1960 by Doubleday & Company, Inc. Reprinted by permission of the publisher.

involving the future prospects of the Soviet system and producing a sense of inevitable triumph, in which the party, the government, the people, and their system are "in step with history." This general feeling of confidence and security has been termed by one observer "optimism about progress" — "a trust in the overall development of society, a conception of unceasing, further economic expansion, a sense of power, and national pride." [9]

The sense of certainty and inevitability, seemingly so foreign to the Western world today, is most striking. The author of a recent account asserts that all his informants from the Soviet working class considered the present system not only stable but final, the most common argument being this one: "The USSR came into being as the result of the operation of historical law, therefore nothing can overthrow it. Marx, Lenin and Stalin predicted a long time in advance what would happen, and this always did happen" (Nov 86–87).

The second class of benefit, status advances, is more concrete. The overthrow of the upper classes, the scattering of the kulaks, and similar practices, while probably never equally balanced, found at least some compensation on the scales of justice in terms of advantages gained by other groups. This was, after all, a revolution in the name of the oppressed masses and seemed to many of them to be just that. In its earliest years Soviet history brought status gratuities to the urban proletarians and to the poor peasantry. Because of their spotless class backgrounds, they benefited from a general opening of doors previously closed to them. In the words of a twenty-six-year-old chauffeur from a peasant background: "Among my relatives . . . there were not any kulaks. My father had fourteen brothers. All were alive . . . Under the tsar they lived very badly. When the Soviet power came, most of them joined the party, more than half . . . They lived in the city as workers under the Soviet power. Because the Soviet power gives life only to those who talk well, who propagandize, and who lived badly under the tsar" (138 A 21).

A political career beckoned to those with clean background, and for many brought rapid mobility and psychic satisfaction. A thirty-three-year-old army officer of proletarian background tells of his own life: "Once I had been in the Komsomol, it was the natural thing to move ahead into the party. Besides that, entrance into the party was considered a great honor. The government was showing you its trust and that it considered you to be a man capable of bearing responsibilities and of being an example to other people" (110 A 108). Here gratuitous status advance begins to merge with advance through achievement. The latter form has come increasingly to predominate as the Revolution has aged and Soviet society stabilized.

Even today, however, the shortest route to social and economic advance is probably the political, and in a totalitarian system orthodox political attitudes continue to play a major role. In words calling to mind the power of positive thinking, a Soviet citizen explains that "Here, a man can reach the highest positions in society if he is always positive. And he can easily be positive by active work in social and political organizations" (Nov 88). At the same time, economic growth and an expanding labor market played a strong supporting role in the rise of the status level of the Soviet masses, but further attention will be given to this in the next chapter; here I shall focus mainly upon the politically significant side of status advance.

As a result of the Revolution, the status of ethnic minorities advanced in relation to the Slavic majority, and women were declared equally eligible to participate fully in the life of the new society and to receive a greater share of its rewards. A young woman tells of her desire to exercise her new prerogative to study for an occupational career: "You see, in the Soviet Union that is the way they brought us up. At meetings and at lectures they constantly told us that women must be fully equal with men, that women can be flyers and naval engineers and anything that men can be" (85 A 15).

The third category of benefit is perhaps the most important, for it corresponds rather closely with desires held by peoples everywhere. Into this category fall institutional forms according social justice, well-being, and security to the people — all that is signified by the term welfare state. Clear examples are the generous provision to the people of medical services, the growth of the Soviet educational system, and the development of new facilities and opportunities for pregnant women, the aged, young children, and other categories of the population needing special support. Such benefits must be further analyzed according to both the extent to which they satisfy universal human aspirations and the extent to which they are perceived as accomplishing this task in a fashion morally superior to that of the Tsarist past or the capitalist outside world.

The valuation of distributive justice seems quite prominent in the informal culture. Indeed, an early and continuing source of support for the Revolution has been found in the degree to which privilege, opportunity, material wealth — all the things to which the general label "benefit" has been attached — have been distributed impartially, irrespective of ascribed social characteristics. Immediately after the Revolution this source of gratification was perhaps at its strongest. In the words of a woman who compares the old times with the new, in the simplest possible terms: "In the old times a peasant could not get a higher education. Now he could and he could also do some better work. People were very happy to see that the old families now had to go to work just as they did" (85 A 14).

It is quite likely that most Soviet citizens still think of their country as the world's leader in defending the poor and oppressed, and as the place where ethical universalism finds its highest expression and staunchest defense. Such thoughts reflect propaganda as well as reality, for the Soviet leaders lose no opportunity to publicize the equal status of Soviet women, the privileges of Soviet children, the absence of racial discrimination and animosity, and the brotherly solidarity of all Soviet citizens. Indeed, the last party Program claims that equal distribution of the total social product increases in and by itself the resulting total utility. In the future, "Soviet people will be more prosperous than people in the developed capitalist countries even if average incomes will be equal, because in the Soviet Union the national income is distributed fairly in the interest of all the members of society." [10] Probably this unproven claim is accepted on faith by the great majority of the population.

The dispensation of benefits has affected the Soviet family primarily by accelerating the process of adaptation inside the family to the changing circumstances of the outer society. Such a link applies, of course, most strongly in the case of those families whose members profited most and who expressed in their own lives the acceptance of the Revolution. Both the connection between societal changes and family change and the role of status advance as the activating mechanism are expressed in the words of a young man: "My father, of course, was very much in favor of my joining the party. He felt we were living like the new family of a new society" (110 A 108).

Adapting to Soviet Reality

The foregoing may serve to suggest two prominent goals of the Soviet family: to avoid catastrophe, or to survive or diminish it if it could not be avoided, and to profit, so far as possible, by the more attractive features of the new society. Both adaptations have been strongly and explicitly held and in combination have fed back into the larger society behavior that adds up to a profound change in the nature of that social system.

The point is well-illustrated in terms of ideological orientations. Virtually all sources agree that the past forty years have seen a decline in religious faith in Russia. No statistics on the distribution of religious believers have been made public since 1937, but at that time Iaroslavski, head of the League of Militant Atheists, estimated that about two-thirds of the urban adult population over sixteen called themselves atheists, and that in the countryside from one-half to two-thirds were believers.[11] A recent estimate by a prominent Western observer has it that at least half of the Soviet population has broken with religion, and the best study of the question with refugee opinion data revealed a striking generational trend toward the weakening of religious faith.[12]

A trend of opposite direction has been observed in respect to the Revolution and the Soviet regime, but acceptance of the Soviet system, while generally upward, has had sharp declines. It has probably taken the form of a W-shaped curve, with the high points in the 1920's, during World War II, and at the present moment. The feet of the W are mired in the forced collectivization, purges, and forced labor camps of the 1930's and in the postwar years, when stalinist policy tightened things up again after the wartime relaxation.

These, of course, are very broad trends and, while important, they obscure almost as much as they reveal about Soviet family life. The avoidance of catastrophe and the acceptance of the various benefits offered have not been equally possible for all. If members of some families felt they were marching in step with the times, others felt like the auto mechanic whose father had been a kulak — "We were different from others because we lived in eternal fear because we were considered to be of an alien class" (92 B 2) — or like the Jewish couple of more recent times who were sensitive to an increase in Soviet antisemitism. They, reports the observer, "were very close to each other, in part because of the feeling they shared of constant threat from society" (Bi 171).

The social and cultural milieu itself has played a significant role in determining variations in change inside the family. In the villages, for instance, the old faith is still alive. In Viriatino in the mid-1950's, almost every peasant hut had its icon, and the words of a peasant woman, "I don't want people to come into our home and find no icon" (Ku 230), suggest that its display was socially mandatory. In the cities icons can also be found, but the atmosphere is much less receptive. A young worker reports quite differently: "My mother was a very devout woman, but religion was forbidden in the Soviet Union. My mother kept an icon in one corner. There were many intelligentsia living around us and of all of our neighbors, none of them had any icons, and they laughed at us for having one . . . I do not have any religious feelings. I saw how the neighbors were laughing at us" (452 A 25).

Contrasting cultural predispositions and social milieus add to the differentiating force of the direct actions of the regime itself. The result is a rich proliferation of spiritually distinctive families. One person says, "My family was very religious . . . My father went out of his way to be religious" (127 A 22), while another explains that in his family "the question of religion, as of something archaic, did not come up" (604 B 9), and in still another the parents are vigorous "practicing atheists." The same can be said for political attitudes and other indicators of the family's cultural atmosphere.

Alongside the trend of change itself, then, must be ranged an extended array of different types and patterns in family life, many of which suggest change in process or show signs of the strain associated with rapid change. The diversity exists in several forms. First there are many families with abnormal membership composition. Occasionally, the Soviet family approaches a caricature, as in those rare cases when the children are quickly after birth turned over with no regret to the state, or when there is a remarkable amount of make-do involved. A Ukrainian, reared as a peasant, tells how his wife, father, and two youngest children died in a famine, leaving him with an eleven-year-old daughter. He was an unskilled laborer, and took his daughter to live with him in a barracks filled with men of similar occupation: "Well, I just asked the manager of the barracks to give me a bed in the corner, so she slept in the upper bunk and I slept down. I hung up a sheet between the corner and the rest of the barracks . . . A daughter with no mother. What should I do with her? . . . They proposed sending her to a children's home. But it was terrible there. There was no order . . . so a comrade said to me, 'It is better if your daughter stays with you. We will help a little bit and it will be better than sending her away.' . . . (Was it bad for the child to be with a lot of men?) Yes. Very. They swear a lot, like workers will. But there was no other way out.

I was absolutely unable to get a family home" (279 B 10–14). Secondly, since religion does not disappear all at once, but in a lingering and dissociated way, there are a great number of families in which religious orientations, images, and practice occur in various muted and distorted forms. Thus, Soviet religion today often seems quite restricted, episodic, and makeshift. Although refugees often reported religious faith among the members of their families, accompanying qualifications nullified the effect of their statements. A young coal miner says of his mother, a collective farmer: "My mother believed in God and she never said anything against Him, but she had not completely surrendered to the priests" (456 A 22). A restricted quality is also suggested by the extent to which the higher status groups fail to allow their religious orientations to exert influence on other aspects of their lives. In white-collar and intelligentsia families, for instance, attitudes toward religion seem to bear little relation to "attitude expressed inside the family toward the Soviet regime," whereas in worker and peasant families, where religious faith is generally stronger, the association between a positive attitude toward religion and disapproval of the Soviet regime is quite pronounced.[13] The acme of such "religion-in-transition" is reached in the cases of party members who secretly baptize their babies at night,[14] or in the peasant families where the portrait of Lenin and the holy icon stare at each other from opposite corners of the room. A peasant woman explains: "Lenin is for this life; the saints are for the other. Lenin gave bread to the people, but only God can give peace." [15]

The significance of religion is always greatest at the time of the major events of family life. Although there is no church in the village of Viriatino, virtually all infants are baptized and the dead given Christian burial. Indeed, the investigators concluded that one of the main reasons religion continues in the village is the service it renders to these "great moments" of family life. They were especially impressed with the "extraordinary vitality" of rites connected with death.[16]

On the other hand, the Soviet ethnographers were intensely interested in ritual behavior the meaning of which none of the peasant villagers could explain, behavior that seemed to have little religious significance, patterns that were followed "just by habit." A typical example, in the words of a villager: "We consider faith outmoded. But we observe the [religious] holidays with food and rest from work" (Ku 231). The makeshift quality of Soviet religious practice is seen most clearly in the patterns resulting from the shortage of facilities for worship and ceremony. A bookkeeper, of peasant origin but urban residence, tells of a substitution: "I was compelled to have my children baptized by a Lutheran priest even though I myself am Orthodox. This was more convenient since there wasn't any Orthodox priest around" (499 B 8).

Similar admixtures can be found in political sentiments: both belief and doubt, partial and episodic enthusiasms, formal patriotism with substance, and loyalty in the midst of anti-Soviet anecdotes — in short, all the muted tones, combinations, and contradictory elements found in religion. Analogous to the icon of the religious family are the political portrait, the statuette of Lenin, or the writings of Marx in the pro-Soviet family. And corresponding to the view that religion is archaic, with the occasional Sunday afternoon visit to the museum of science and atheism, is the phenomenon of political alienation, and the anti-Soviet anecdote, that peculiarly effective device by which the people hold at a distance the absolute demands of totalitarian rule. Political opinions are a more private concern of the family than are religious beliefs. They ordinarily are kept from neighbors, for they expose to danger, and even within the circle of close relatives political attitudes are not to be taken lightly. A young woman whose father was a Kiev physician and whose uncle was an army officer and a staunch partisan of the regime observed: "We could never tell an anti-Soviet anecdote in his presence. Not that he would report on you, but simply that he would tell you you were not politically conscious enough" (431 A 21).

Close examination reveals occasional scraps of evidence to suggest that political faith may be suffering some of the same transmutations that can be observed in Soviet religious life. For example, one man attempts to explain why, like so many of his fellow Soviet citizens, he has faith in Soviet justice even though he is also very conscious of its defects: "A man is only a man. He must have faith in the justice of the authority under which he belongs. If we doubt this, what is left? How will we live without this faith? Do you really believe that faith in injustice helps you in life better than faith in justice, even if you don't think everything is right and proper?" (Nov 137)

These various combinations and contrasts permeate the family, and indeed all of Soviet life, for they reflect a poorly integrated social system. Outer social and cultural developments have been so rapid and often so coercive in their effect that the different parts of less complex units and structures have changed at markedly differing rates. This is true not only of the family, but also of informal groups and cliques and of the individual personality.

One need not search far to find dissonant elements in the psyche of Soviet man. The individual's reaction to the Soviet scene frequently has been political disaffection, certainly a normal response to much of what has occurred but one which has also been a liability, which has brought various subsequent mechanisms of coping and defense into play. One example can be seen in the life of a thirty-seven-year-old widow who was living with two children and her mother and working as a construction engineer. This attractive, energetic woman, a party member, had "critical feelings": "Since she was conscious of her critical feelings, she lived in constant fear of the MVD and forced herself to exhibit the utmost reserve in her dealings with all persons . . . This fear also led her to assume a certain mask; she was a party member, zealous and emphatically interested . . . She was also a very hard worker in her job, [but] . . . She felt insecure in the city, and also in her party position" (Bi 191–2).

Similar signs of rapid, stressful change in the larger society can be seen in informal social groups, the clique of friends and circle of acquaintances. One of the most alarming aspects of social life under Stalin was the extent to which people could not trust each other, together with the general feeling that such relations, which are particularly appreciated in the traditional culture, had been spoiled. Of course, the fact that different persons held varying political viewpoints accounts for some aspects of the problem, but more important was the degree to which Stalin's police were "secret." Too frequently the *seksot,* the "secret worker" or informer, was used as a means of political control, and the threat of betrayal for a chance remark supported the view that friendship was somewhat dangerous. The feeling that one had to be very careful about new acquaintances also led to a Soviet brand of "gallows humor": A man telephoned the local secret police representative. "My wife and I want to give a party tomorrow night and thought we should notify you in case you want to send someone out." The official asked, "How many will be there?" The man answered, "Fifteen." The official replied, "Don't worry. In any group that large there's bound to be someone working for us." [17]

The nature of informal organizations in Soviet social life reveals much about what has happened in the country's history. One refugee respondent perhaps summed it up more accurately than he realized when he compared two different types of social stratification. Things really were not too different after the Revolution, he felt, for "In Tsarist times there were the rich and the poor; under the Soviet power there were the party members and the non-party members."

Social stratification in the USSR has always had a strong economic basis, but it is also important to remember the extent to which it has a political foundation and to realize that political stratification is a keen reflection of rapid societal change, expressing the diversity of fortunes associated with it. In the Soviet political class system there have always been two extremes. At the top the most highly placed party families form a social stratum whose subculture is reinforced by social distance from the rest of the people. A Soviet common man, a fifty-year-old Ukrainian supply worker, sees the life of party members and their families this way: "They got full legal and actual rights to rule the country. As a mode of life they have to keep apart from the rest in order not to compromise the party. They must be loyal instruments of the party policy. They have to live in a circle of their own. They form a caste behind a little iron curtain" (74 A 32).

At the other extreme is the milieu of the déclassés, the dispossessed, and the alienated. Between the two, the political middle class is comprised of the masses who are ambivalent, apathetic, perhaps too tired, too fearful, or too busy to think. A working-class woman tells of her attitude toward the Soviet system: "I gave no special thought to such questions in the USSR and did not concern myself with it. I only knew that it was necessary and that I had to work" (100 B 8, 9).

Political beliefs also function as a poignant indicator of changing times inside the family. Typically, for example, children are less religious and more admiring of the Soviet regime than their parents, and men more than their wives. The following description, offered by the young army officer quoted earlier, was probably quite characteristic inside many Soviet families for some time after the Revolution: "[My father] brought me up in the Soviet spirit, teaching me that the Soviet Union had opened the road to opportunity for the Russian worker and peasant . . . My mother on the other side was a religious woman, and so was always against the regime" (110 A 102).

In brief, a look inside the family reveals the same marks of rapid change that can also be found in other parts of Soviet society and in the Soviet personality structure. There are indications that accepting the new and forsaking the old has not been easy: the changes in religious orientation, political attitude, and so on which have taken place have produced a surprising proliferation of contrasting types and poorly integrated structures. Such developments have tended to destroy guidelines for the individual's conduct of life, and Soviet informal social life sometimes can be not too inaccurately characterized by the phrasing of a former participant — "a consciously created chaos." The challenging fact is that underneath the totalitarian façade of order and control lies a quite different world.

Becoming Legitimate: A Prototype Experience

In the study of great social upheavals exact statistics establishing precisely how many persons or families are directly involved are not always relevant. For example, in America during the Great Depression most men were able to keep their jobs, and most families were not struck directly by unemployment, but the fear of losing one's job and the sense of insecurity it brought were nevertheless quite common and had definite effects on society. In the Soviet Union an analogous experience occurred, by coincidence, mainly in the same decades as the economic trauma on the other side of the globe. Like the loss of employment in America, the first stage in this Soviet experience was also involuntary, deprivational to the individual, and seriously crippling to the family. Moreover, while it was "lived through" by a minority (though a substantial one), just as in the American depression there was a great deal of vicarious participation. To some degree the entire Soviet population has felt its influence as a personal one; the forces at work have so arranged themselves that they symbolize one major kind of relationship between Soviet family and Soviet regime.

The experience, which is shared by the family as a whole, has two parts. The first is loss of political status, becoming an alien element, a political suspect, or at worst an enemy of the people. The second part involves the recovery of status legitimacy through methods by which Soviet families have become reabsorbed into the main body of Soviet society.

The families corresponding in the political class structure to the poor and hungry at the bottom of the Soviet economic hierarchy were at first the clergy, landowners, merchants, military officers, and, to a lesser extent, professionals, intellectuals, and civil servants — in fact, all well-off persons in Tsarist Russia. In later years the kulaks and, in practice, anyone once arrested were added to the number of such "people of the past." In 1935 family background in itself was officially declared insufficient cause for persecution, and at the Tenth Congress of the Komsomol the First Secretary, A. K. Kosarev, reported that the ranks of that organization were to be enlarged; even the offspring of the "alien classes" were now to be accepted, for Stalin had proclaimed that "the son is not responsible for the father." [18] But the arrests continued and even increased in the years immediately following. Then in the postwar era a new crop of aliens appeared, those who had willingly or under force collaborated with the Germans by becoming war prisoners, working in the German economy, or simply failing to flee to the East or join the Soviet partisans. After the deterioration of relations with the West and with the founding of the new state of Israel, still another category was added, the Soviet Jews.

Loss of the status of good citizen is hard to bear in terms of an individual's own welfare, but it has also ordinarily stigmatized his entire family. Many of the same problems have had to be faced by such families: fear of persecution, the unpleasant social aspects of pariah status, and a dim future for adults and children alike.

The most immediate result was frequently economic. A worker in a medical dispensary reports: "After my father's arrest my mother was forced to start working to support the family . . . [and] we led a miserable life until we finished our studies and began working. We were hungry and cold" (426 B 2). Economic deprivation is a consequence of second-class status, but even as the members of certain families are denied by society, they also deny themselves. This denial takes two forms: a lack of extra effort and initiative in study and work because of anticipated rejection and, secondly, inability to engage in what might be termed legitimate illegal activities. The Soviet people tend to look with some tolerance upon petty speculation, pilfering of government property, black marketing, and the like — matters that are illegal in the regime's view but that, as side activities, have been extremely common in the USSR. Such behavior is indeed criminal, however, and second-class families are ordinarily too fearful to try to supplement family income in this way. Thus their living standard is lowered all the more by their sharper sense of political insecurity.[19]

Often the future chances of the children seemed fatally injured. A young man tells how his father got along all right in the USSR until the early years of World War II, when he was arrested. The arrest meant more than the loss of a father, for the sense of spoiled identity comes through strongly: "I started to understand differently from before. I understood that all the doors from now on would be closed to me. Whether I wanted to study more or get a job after the study. As a son of a repressed person I could not move anywhere. Gradually there began to develop a hatred against all this. I don't know how it came about. Equally gradually and there was not any more such a desire to study or to acquire anything. I studied but everything was indifferent to me" (125 A 44).

Such circumstances provided a great incentive somehow to become legitimate; second-class citizenship appeared as a double and triple handicap. The Soviet regime early provided its own preferred channel to full-valued status — the formal renunciation — and for some time after the Revolution many seemingly chose to divest themselves of the stigma in that way. Perhaps the most typical form in the early years involved a split between parents and children. The facts, and a likely explanation, are furnished by a refugee respondent: "The children, wanting to go ahead in life, often renounce their parents. In 1928, 1929 and 1930 and even later one could find a notice in a newspaper as follows: 'I, Nicholas Ivanov, renounce my father, an ex-priest, because for many years he deceived many people in telling them that God exists, and that is the reason I am severing all my relations with him'" (1035 A 37).

As time went on, and the struggle between Stalin's regime and the people increased in intensity, political arrests became more frequent, and more and more families lost their men, leaving the prime responsibility for renunciation with the wife. In refugee case histories the welfare of their children was always in the forefront of the parents' thoughts, and sometimes renunciation — the formal severance of the marital tie — seemed almost routine. In the words of an architect's daughter: "After my father's arrest, my mother was given the opportunity of renouncing my father, which she did, because she had to support me. She took her maiden name again" (1451 A 5).

Public appearances are deceptive, however, as is so often the case in the USSR. The apparent willingness of Soviet citizens to sacrifice loved ones for personal advantage, which awakened so much moral revulsion on the part of outsiders, often proves on closer inspection to have been no more than sham public ritual, entirely or in good part devoid of such meaning to the actual participants. The case of a fifty-year-old doctor, arrested in 1938 and subsequently released, is similarly instructive: "My son had to renounce, as did my wife, and when I came back my son simply said that I was arrested by mistake and now I was back at work again. My wife renounced me at a public meeting and said that she was separated from me . . . before I left I told my wife to renounce me as she was an artist and director of a museum and I knew that unless she renounced me she would lose her post and how would my son continue to live?" (40 A 15) In a different variation, an NKVD worker tells how he prepared for his arrest even before it occurred by persuading his wife to enter into a "prophylactic divorce": "In 1941 my father's brother escaped from his exile and came to me. By my order he was given a passport. This was discovered and I was dismissed from work. Seeing before us an inevitable destruction and jail, so as not to tie my wife by marriage we took a divorce and she went back to her parents. I proved the necessity of divorce to my wife and she agreed with me, since there was no hope of return for me" (147 B 5).

The path thus provided by the Soviet regime for those who wished to cleanse themselves of their family associations and turn with purified background toward the future clearly reflected the low esteem in which the rulers held the family during those years. The citizen obviously found it distasteful to be forced to repudiate those nearest and dearest to him. The resulting conflict of loyalties in most cases could end only in conversion of public renunciation into an empty form, with inner feelings continuing as before. "Our fathers were arrested as enemies of the people. We became fearful of mentioning their names; they forced us to renounce them, but we continued to love them." [20]

Another way to become legitimate in the USSR follows an underground pattern, with only the principals being aware of the transition in status. The individual could simulate a reliable past, often taking on a new identity complete with name. A twenty-eight-year-old woman remarks that it was quite possible to conceal an unfavorable class background: "After my father was dekulakized and my mother took me to Odessa she lived under her maiden name and nothing in our records ever indicated that we were of kulak origin" (449 A 9).

The problem of records and personal documents was surmounted by counterfeiting expertise. It is in harmony with the political nature of Soviet society and the kind of illegal entrepreneurship to which it gives rise that such talent should be turned to the production of fake internal passports, birth certificates, and other documents rather than to bogus money as in the United States. A worker tells a brief history of his life: "When my father was arrested, I left [home], without getting any documents. Later on I got false documents which I bought for ten rubles, and since 1930 I lived under an assumed name" (325 A 37).

The unsettling events and administrative disorder of the times contributed a great deal to the opportunity for such activity. An army officer of "alien" background reports: "I am from Moscow, but I indicated in all official papers that I was from Kiev. My brother said he was from Warsaw. Now when they inquired in Kiev, they could not find anything. During the Civil War all archives in Kiev were destroyed. This trick is used very frequently in the Soviet Union" (136 A 5). It is important that adults have a proper pretext for changing their social and political identity, and the most useful occasion has been a change of job involving a move of substantial distance. Thus, in the USSR economic opportunity has often meant a chance to combine a new job with a clean political slate.

There were other occasions appropriate to Soviet "political passing." For example, a distinctive marriage of convenience could from time to time be observed. A young refugee respondent compares the background of her father, from the peasantry, with that of her mother, from an "old, well-known pre-revolutionary family," and draws this conclusion: "My mother came from an old royal family. It is my belief that she married my father chiefly to hide her own social origin" (85 A 13).

Changing identity is easier in the younger years, and the primary benefits of legitimate status, new opportunities for education and careers, accrued mainly to the young people. Consequently, most examples of the change were doubtless found among the youth. A man whose father was a kulak, recounting the unpleasant circumstances of his early school years, states that even a move to the city with his mother in 1932 did not help but that another move and other steps did: "To end this situation my mother sent me to my aunt, who had no son, and I took my aunt's name . . . I got a birth certificate very simply by going to see a doctor in the town and saying that my birth certificate had been lost, and he made me out a perfectly legal, regular statement . . . This made me a real proletarian and from that time I had no difficulties about my past within the Soviet Union" (143 A 23). To summarize, three simultaneous steps had to be taken: a change of residence, as an individual or a family group; a change of public identity, involving an alteration of name, place of birth, and such; and falsified documents to prove new identity.

"Passing" is a form of social assimilation. In the USSR, as in any other place, life has constrained the individual to act in a fashion conforming with his interests as he sees them shaped by external circumstances, and, as we have briefly seen, this process affects Soviet family life in several ways. Above all, however, "passing" is an individual experience, and while the black mark can be hidden from the eyes of others, sometimes even from the eyes of intimates, it cannot be hidden from oneself. The Soviet version of the marginal man — one whose place in society is legitimate, whose family life is perhaps satisfactory, but who himself is the victim of an unassailable malaise — is typically political. A secret police colonel's testimony completes the prototype experience. In the years before World War II, his life pleased him in all but one respect: "I had a good perspective, because I had a good record, but there was one matter which worried me all my life. In the Soviet Union much attention is paid to the social origin and to the social position of a man. My social position was all right. I occupied a good post and I had been a volunteer in the Red Army, but my social origin was not so good. I had come from a privileged class and I lived in a constant fear. I thought all the time: 'Suppose it will be discovered suddenly. Then all I have desired, all I have built for myself and for my family, my life, my career will suddenly collapse' " (136 A 10).

Where Is Home?

The Revolution was carried through by a political party acting in the name of a class for the ultimate benefit of individuals taken collectively — the toiling masses. Established institutions were smashed or bypassed and only at a later time allowed partial rehabilitation. As we have shown in earlier pages, the guiding spirit of marxism scorns established institutions and cultural values, admires the rational, conscious individual, and looks to the eventual emergence of men living together in freedom and equality. The original marxist paradise was essentially a paradise of individuals, with social institutions inherently suspect. A later emphasis brought the needs of the Revolution itself more to the front, and loyalty to it and to the various entities purporting to embody it — society, party, Soviet State — became crucial. Efforts were begun to draw the individual from his former institutional contexts — church, community, family — and into the party, the work-collective, and the largest and best collective — the new Soviet socialist society.

Both established families as concrete social units and the man-in-the-street's image of the family suffered from this change. Some individuals began to feel either guilty or defensive about what Soviet writers derided as a "cozy little bourgeois nest" or the "isolated family hearth." Others took pride in their separateness and resented the interference of the regime in private affairs. Even today the "happy Soviet family" has a hollow and sloganistic ring: the regime is still not quite willing to admit the family to full status and prefers to deal directly with the individual whenever possible.

As individuals many have experienced in Soviet life a sharp competition between the regime and the family for loyalty and time. Different men and women have decided the problem in different ways, but the whole question has continued as a controlling influence in Soviet daily life, and, however decided, the Soviet citizen has always had a jealous society waiting outside the door.

Rather than forming a unitary pattern, responses have been varied, but in all cases the attitude of the man has been the initial determining factor. To start with the response that came first chronologically and was basically reactive, expressing aversion for the Revolution and regime, the "alienated family" can be seen to have several characteristics. A blemish of some kind in the man's sociopolitical status confers second-class citizenship on the whole family, and both he and his family show antipathy or lack of interest in politics and current affairs; thus a doctor's wife reports: "Our family lived its own life. Communist politics, questions of education, did not interest us" (86 B 2). In such families work and career ambitions also amounted to little; in the words of a coal miner, age forty-five and of kulak origin: "Ours was a Soviet family that lived and worried about one's daily needs. Not everyone could have aims or work on a career, especially if one was of an origin that we were" (329 B 2). Not only politics and work, but social relations in general are limited; a collective farmer says, "My family avoided knowing many people . . . We always tried to keep aloof, and yet to help others" (285 B 2). Some denied any friendship ties whatsoever, like a woman bookkeeper, married in 1924, who states: "I preferred not to acquire any friendships and to live within the closed circle of our family" (13 B 5). Such "former people," to apply the term often used to describe them, live mainly with and for each other according to the ways they knew in the past. They are usually aloof and sometimes exhibit a sense of superiority. A woman gynecologist in whose family several members suffered repression says: "We lived very harmoniously, in a close union. We were also a very religious family. We never lost our God nor our conscience" (306 A 38). The main goal shared by the family and each individual is security. Disenchantment with the greater society breeds a feeling of no future, a strong desire to lead what is known in the USSR as the quiet life, and a number of strong beliefs, partly true, partly stereotype, which support a life of alienated seclusion. Their fellow citizens, Soviet institutions, and the whole system strike them as ruthless, immoral, and generally distasteful.

Secondly there is the "inner émigré" family whose members enter into the larger society only partially. Those who seek to emigrate in spirit are not ordinarily proletarians by background or current status. Many of the intelligentsia, old and new, who are not full converts to communism live in families that are linked thus to society. The key feature is well described by the wife of a university professor: "He always worked. Always . . . His work filled out his life . . . Work gave him a chance to escape the reality of Soviet life. We called it the inner emigration. We emigrated from our surrounding life into our work. If you work very well as a specialist you can live and escape from the Soviet power . . . [and] the purpose is to get away from the party" (139 B 6–7). These men and women escape both political and, one suspects, familial involvement. Their main goal and satisfaction in life is occupational achievement. They are very busy at their jobs, which allays the tendency of the local communist representatives to complain that such people are inactive politically. For "émigrés" themselves such a self-image is a convenient one, for it enables them to satisfy fundamental needs of both self and family while holding society at bay.

It should be made clear at this point that both the foregoing modes of family response to the Soviet order occurred only within a minority of the people. The majority carried on their lives after the Revolution just as before, with minimum consciousness of pressure from the larger society. Neither alienated nor involved beyond a minimum level, they have remained indifferent to the dilemma of family versus society. Such men lack sensitivity to the political side of the Soviet system and have no feeling of being saved by, or escaping into, work. They live in peace with a middle or low-level job, and keep reasonably busy in the routines of daily family living. Typical is the behavior and outlook of a forty-two-year-old Stalingrad painter: "He was not a bit interested in politics, yet the children were members of the young Pioneers. He read no newspaper and took no part at all in political functions. But in all this he had not a bit of a bad conscience and felt completely free, since he did his work well, and concerned himself otherwise only with his family" (Bi 179). Their families have legitimate status but are apathetic in politics, accept work as part of life but get no special meaning or pleasure from it, and lead uneventful social lives. Like citizens of other countries, the men like sports, hunting and fishing, television, and the like; for the rest, they seek any way to break the monotony, sometimes even as passive spectators to political affairs. They are apt to be very family-centered, and to look upon society, the party, the state, and similar institutions as distant entities from which one gets what one can. The father lives mostly for the present but may be future-oriented in thinking about his children. Family life is ordinarily traditionalistic, and the question of how to distribute spare time, energy, and loyalty between family and society does not even come into his mind as a problem.

The final type of response is also that of a minority — but the only one in which the conflict between family and society is solved by favoring the latter, as the Soviet leaders would have it solved. In such families the man is highly dedicated to his public, usually political, role. His background is ordinarily spotless and his current status elite or near elite; he plays an active role in work or politics or both. Demands on his time, abilities, and loyalty are intense. As a secret police official put it: "I worked almost all 24 hours. I never had any rest. . . . I had to work as much as my superior ordered me to" (147 B 2, 3). The extreme involvement of such men in the outer society determines most other aspects of their lives. Their informal social life is highly restricted and quite instrumentalized, and there is likely to be no free time. For instance, a chemist and his wife were party members but "lived for their profession and their work. Everything else was subordinated to it." The observer continues: "They had few outside interests, for work constantly came first. And because they had set a deadline for their research, they worked until they were practically no longer able to because of fatigue. The only balancing features were chess and a small garden. Even when they had guests, which happened rarely, they were always professional colleagues, with whom then only technical conversations were held. Both were party members and participated regularly, but completely passively, in political functions" (Bi 177).

A similar emphasis can be seen when the family is that of a full-time party official. One active and very devoted party worker's attitudes suggest his almost total immersion: "Free time meant little to the husband . . . He used his free time almost exclusively for honorary public activities. Social visiting, even within the family, was restricted almost entirely to party friends . . . The husband saw cultural needs as a part of political interests; he subordinated them to the latter" (Bi 212).

Such families often show an unusual degree of adaptation, with personal family, and societal goals all apparently coinciding. The party, the factory, and the kolkhoz, rather than the family, serve as home. For the man described above, the party serves as a kind of family. As he liked to put it, the party had raised him, educated him, and made him an official. Even his personal identity is closely bound up in the party: though others considered him Jewish, he "did not consider himself a Jew, or a Russian, but a Bolshevik" (Bi 212). If the occupational commitment is extreme, sometimes political activity is not essential, though of course a proper political attitude is always present and strongly affects the self-image. In one particular case, a hard-working, successful factory director was not a party member but nonetheless looked upon himself as "a non-party fighter for the great cause" (Bi 177). Sometimes, of course, there is evidence of some compulsiveness, as in the behavior of an MVD captain stationed in Moscow who "had few opinions of his own, but was rather an absolute 'party man.' He seemed . . . more eager than industrious, more busy than genuinely active . . . [and] worked from early until late, very often also at night" (Bi 311). Another trait that is quite important in its implication for family life is asceticism. A young man tells of his father, one of the "twenty-five thousanders" recruited in 1929–1930 from the urban proletariat in order to help in the collectivization process. Some 70 per cent were party members. "Father never drank and almost never smoked. He did everything and gave everything to the party" (417 A 23).

Moreover, conscious effort is expended in living, in family and marital life, so as to avoid shutting off the family from society. There are many ways to do this, even behind the doors of the home and in the most personal affairs of the family members. Political literature and symbols are displayed, children are named after revolutionary heroes or slogans, "revolutionary rites" (Komsomol weddings, factory committee christenings, and the like) are substituted for religious ceremonies, and so on. In this respect, too, the dedicated person and his family differ greatly from the mass of the population. In Viriatino, for example, the Soviet ethnographic team found that there were only three non-Christian funerals in the 1952–1956 period. They were those of the teacher, the chairman of the village soviet, and a man who lived in the city but returned to his village for burial. Both the latter two were party members.[21]

The final characteristic, hinted at earlier, requires some extended comment, for it reveals the basic point of strain in the dedicated family. The man is confronted most forcefully by the dilemma of family versus society, and it is he who must, so to speak, make the basic choice. Bischoff's data show that the idea of the primacy of society over family was approved more, but also rejected more, by the men than by the women in the families observed. Women were more indifferent to the idea, probably because most of them had decided early in life that the aims and responsibilities of family life came first. Only if the husband makes his choice in favor of society and is impressed into service, does the wife confront a stressful situation, for she and the family are likely to be neglected.

Such a source of neglect has become somewhat legendary in Soviet popular culture. In spite of all efforts by party and government to bring about sex equality, Soviet husbands and wives are frequently placed in situations that act upon their personalities in such contrasting ways that their paths become ever more separate. A worker who joined the party, became "interested," "developed," and was torn away from his wife, also a worker but one who did not join the party, had the difficulty explained as follows: "Both of the workers . . . had emerged out of countryside poverty. Both had had difficult childhoods and uncultured ways of life, but whereas the army and public service had drawn the husband out from that way of life and he had begun to make much progress, his wife remained, during the most difficult years, a semi-qualified, illiterate worker with three children on her hands and had to carry on a constant struggle for existence. She never took any part in public work" (Ka 49).

From this situation have come two important Soviet social types. The first is suggested by the example above, the backward wife, who cannot keep up with her husband intellectually and politically. Though in less sharp form, this problem has been common not only in the most dedicated families but at all levels, for Soviet women, having had to continue as mothers and housewives, have rarely been able to take full advantage of their formal equality with men in economic and political life.[22]

Complementing this first type is the husband of the backward wife, whose intense societal involvement has given rise to the proposition that "A party husband is a poor husband." For example, when a government official, active on an All-Union committee, married late, his prospective wife's parents had some doubts about him: "My wife's parents looked at me without too much pleasure, thinking that as a responsible official I would be too sovietized and a bad husband" (131 B 7–8). The inadequate-husband theme is also found in the widely accepted idea that members of the party marry only late in life; earlier they have time for sexual ties and perhaps love, but not for family life.

Poor husbands and backward wives, priests and victims of the Revolution apparently were troublesome and numerous enough to help provoke the "new family policy" of the mid-thirties. Though the new party line and legislation kept many estranged spouses from divorcing, it did not solve the basic problem. The wives of busy, politically co-opted husbands were thenceforth more likely to remain married to them but still had to devise means for adjusting their own lives.

Two extreme forms of adjustment can be found. A wife might also devote her life to work and politics, arranging to deal with home and family as best she can. Sometimes this is successful, but often the appearance and atmosphere of family life are depleted, as in the case of a woman, forty, married to a political police officer, also forty. Both worked and both were party members, but "she had little interest in their home. In spite of her frequently expressed demand for cleanliness in her work (which her work, furthermore, reflected), the dwelling was very disorderly and poorly cared for" (Bi 184–185).

The second extreme places emphasis on the other horn of the wife's dilemma. She becomes as wifely and motherly as possible, relinquishing any substantial direct involvement in the outer society, leaves such activities to her husband, makes the best of her traditional sex role, busies herself with the household and with keeping up appearances and spirits, and does not hold an outside job. This reaction is found in the wife of a prominent Moscow factory director. He is forty-one, she thirty-two, and though they have no children she is neither employed nor politically active. The main interest she expressed was in her luxurious five-room apartment near the Kremlin and in maintaining her own personal elegance. Her concern with the world outside the USSR is seen in her questioning of the observer: "How would a factory director's wife live in Europe?" (Bi 175)

The wives of successful men in an open-class society are under some considerable temptation to exhibit the measure of their husband's achievements in their own style of life. Though consumption is not supposed to be conspicuous in the USSR, it is nonetheless visible from time to time. Even in the countryside — in the village of Viriatino, for example — the ethnographic team complains of a muted but still communicable form of it: "In some materially secure families, including those of certain activists, women avoid working on the kolkhoz and do not reach the established minimum number of workdays, something which has a negative effect on work discipline" (Ku 249).

For an intelligent, able-bodied woman not to work in the USSR is somewhat illegitimate in the official view, and status display is downright bourgeois. Yet the wife in a dedicated family does make a valuable contribution. She is complementary to her hard-driving husband in the sense that much of her energy has to be used to support the internal emotional life of the family, to which her husband is able to contribute so little. It should also be noted that it would often be difficult for her to hold a position at a level commensurate with that of her husband, but awkward to work at a lower level.

Inside the Kremlin, without doubt, a wife's nonemployment may have become in itself a symbol of high social status. In the official language, this is a "survival," but, we would add, one which is deeply implicated in family life and, like many other survivals of Soviet daily life, likely to continue for some time. The family in which the man chooses most strongly the direction of society rather than family often contains a woman who does the opposite. Very probably this is one reason why so little is known about the wives of prominent Soviet men, and also serves as one source for some high-level favoring of the idea of a continuing strict separation between public and private life.

The common element in the multiformity of patterns traced in preceding pages reduces to a family confronting simultaneously the threat or reality of disaster and the promise of better, adjusting to these by accepting new values but paying the price in terms of a certain loss of integrity and functional capacity. Serving as it does as a battleground between older traditions and ties and the newer demands of the outer society, the Soviet family calls to mind the trials and triumphs of the immigrant family of an earlier era in America. Departed from the old, not fully accepted by (nor accepting of) the new, straining to balance the contradictory requirements of adjustment to the large society outside with ministration to the established patterns and needs inside, such a family combines cautious hope for the future with heavy scars from the past.

SIX | HARDSHIP AND OPPORTUNITY:
THE FAMILY IN THE CLASS SYSTEM

IN 1928 THE SOVIET living standard was not radically out of line with that of countries in comparable stages of development. The bulk of the peasants conducted their lives and work in traditional patterns, as yet undisturbed by the forced collectivization and resettlement soon to come. It could not be said that the urban population was prosperous, yet contrasted with the situation in countries like Austria, Czechoslovakia, Italy, France, and Germany, they were fairly well off. For example, the purchasing power of hourly wages in terms of food shows that only the latter two countries were better off than the USSR (Table 1).

TABLE 1. Purchasing power of hourly wages in terms of food, USSR and eight other countries.

(USSR = 100)

Country	1928	1936–1938	1951–1952
USSR	100	100	100
Austria	90	158	167
Czechoslovakia	94	142	—
Denmark	216	304	344
France	112	283	200
Germany	142	213	233
Great Britain	200	192	361
Italy	86–98	108	144
United States	370	417	556

Source: Chapman, p. 176, adapted from Solomon Schwarz, *Labor in the Soviet Union* (New York, 1951), pp. 131–132, 175–178, 234–238.

In October 1928 the First Five Year Plan for industrial development was launched, the party under Stalin decided to collectivize agriculture, the Soviet people had to start tightening their belts, and from that time the Soviet living standard fell. Real wages of nonagricultural wage earners and salaried employees dropped by from 22 to 43 per cent between 1928 and 1940, and — largely as a result of World War II —

were approximately 50 per cent of the 1928 level in the year 1948. They did not begin to approach the 1928 level until around 1952.[1]

In the countryside the living standard was lower than in the cities from the beginning. One estimate puts the real per capita income of urban households at approximately 1.7 times that of rural households in 1928.[2] After the collectivization of agriculture things became worse; the peasants' real income per capita probably declined by more than 20 per cent[3] between 1928 and 1937, though this figure masks the catastrophic decline in the early years of the 1930 decade. In those years hunger and even famine came to Russia just as in the old days. Even in the better years the peasants had to struggle for their lives at minimum levels of subsistence.

Generally there can be no doubt that clothing, shelter, services, transport, food itself have been scarce and poor — that life has been hard. Though usually hidden by misleading propaganda, an occasional Soviet statistic is revealing. When at the Twentieth Congress of the party in 1956 the decision was made to increase the production of consumer goods over the level of 1940, the magnitude of increase aimed at — three and one-half times — suggests how things must have been in that year. Moreover, it is important that during much of Soviet history the situation was growing worse instead of improving. Even though the improvement of the past decade has been substantial, for most of the Soviet people it has been a rather new experience, and it is too early to go very far in assessing its effects on family life. The predominant over-all fact in Soviet history, and the predominant orienting point in Soviet family life, has been the pinch of a low living standard. This is an important fact, but only as a starting point for further analysis.

The second fact to be considered deals with the reflection in ideology of the first. When real wages began to decline in the late 1920's the Soviet regime quickly ceased publication of detailed statistics on retail prices, the cost of living, and real wages. At the same time, statements were released designed to convey to the population and the world an impression of a continuous and rapid rise in living standards. Thus when during the First Five Year Plan there was in fact a precipitous decline both in rural and in urban areas, a rapid increase in material welfare was claimed. Similarly, during the Second Five Year Plan it was claimed that workers' real wages doubled, and in the postwar years comparably impressive but inaccurate statements are at hand, such as a sixfold rise in real income from 1913 to 1953.[4]

Thus, at a time when the average standard of living in the USSR was declining in both an absolute and a relative sense (that is, in respect to those other countries with which it preferred to compare itself; see Table 1), great effort was being exerted to persuade the population that the opposite was the case.

A third factor in the unfolding story is social differentiation. In spite of average poverty, Soviet society is highly stratified into distinct and recognizable social classes. For the first fifteen years of the Soviet era bolshevik hostility to the old upper classes, antagonism to any kind of privilege, and the desire to see "every cook rule the state," as Lenin had written, combined in favor of the worker and the poor peasant. In those days a humble background was an advantage, and there was considerable sentiment inside the party in favor of social leveling. In 1931, however, Stalin put an end to any desires or hope for the prompt realization of an equalitarian society by labeling wage equalization "leftist," "bourgeois," "equality mongering." Promotions, graduated wages, and other material benefits were needed, he argued, to reward the individual worker according to his qualifications and to promote the learning of scientific and industrial techniques.

By the middle of the First Five Year Plan the idea of substantial differences in living standards was being vigorously encouraged. Wages and other perquisites were henceforth to be distributed according to the worth of work done. A system of modern social classes emerged that took ever more firm shape during the 1930's and became, as it is today, one of the most important determining influences in the life of the Soviet person. Soviet differentials in earnings have been roughly similar to those found in capitalist countries, though of course the gross inequalities of wealth often found in capitalist society were ended along with the abolition of private ownership of the means of production.[5]

There are, then, three starting points for analysis: a notable, indeed often increasing, *de facto* scarcity of the necessities of life; a myth, ardently fostered by the rulers, of increasing prosperity; and a pronounced and relatively open social class system. Taken together, the three factors have acted with remarkable potency as a focusing and canalizing force in the lives of Soviet families.

The Dimensions of Advantage

Among the majority of the Soviet people there have been few who have been able to make reports of their possessions like the following, by an army officer: "Sufficient material security, a good position in my work and the chance to provide well for my family and to ensure my children's education" (136 B 2). Though the officer had his problems, food, clothing, and housing for his family were not among them. Other refugees also reported satisfactory living standards while living in the USSR, and their testimony provides a brief listing of the types of personnel the Soviet regime has found indispensable, as well as conveying an idea of the psychological meaning of pronounced social differentiation in a land where the average man faces poverty. In addition to military officers, there were technical experts, such as this newsreel cameraman: "I was, or rather belonged, to the category of the 'privileged' and highly paid specialists of the Soviet Union, the number of which was small, and therefore economically I was more securely provided for. Furthermore, my assignments made me travel a great deal, and this enabled me to purchase certain items by *blat* [informal connections]" (49 B 2). A girl describes how for her family it was the "best life": "I have to explain about my family life. I had a very good life, because my father was a singer and my mother was a pianist. Artists have it very good, not as in America or Europe, but for the Russians it is the best life. We had an apartment of five rooms, a bath and everything. We had a piano and a very nice home" (258 A 8). Another group of the favored were the all-important directors of enterprises, such as one described by a government employee: "Let's make a comparison. I had one single room. Ninety per cent of the population live this way, and even that room was hard to get. The director of my office had three excellent rooms, one bathroom, a balcony, and flowers on the balcony. He was a party member. But the rank and file of the party members do not live so well; but still, they can get an apartment. People like cleaning women and workers in offices, they simply lived in cellars" (14 A 29).

In the countryside another Soviet elite is made up of the chairmen of collective farms, state-farm directors, bookkeepers, agronomists, doctors, and the highly placed personnel of rural industrial enterprises.

Even in the labor camps the administrators have found it possible to live well.

A complete description of the advantages of high class position would move far beyond food, housing, and clothing, though these are always close to the center of concern in the USSR. The privilege of travel — for recreation, for visiting, and for shopping — is theirs, as is a regular change of scenery. A government official tells of his family's summer activities: "We had four young people and children and we considered it an absolute necessity to get out of Moscow, to the country. We rented our dacha each year for 3–3½ months" (131 B 4). The army officer with whose comments this section started notes that "I usually spent my summer in a sanitarium, at a health resort" (136 B 3).

A highly paid job also brought another privilege, as shown by an army colonel's evaluation of his family life: "I can't say we were different from other families. Yes, one thing only. I worked and my wife, mother, and my daughter were alone at home and busied themselves with housework and raising our daughter, the typical bourgeois family. This is unusual. Usually the wife and the husband have to work. There are not so many individuals who can support a whole family only with their own job" (72 B 3). Such is one measure of the apogee of success in the USSR.

Another privilege is continued contact with and services for relatives. This, like the earlier examples, is connected with the effort to preserve tradition and represents an accomplishment that the less fortunate often could not enjoy. The army officer reports the following relations with his kinfolk: "My mother came periodically to visit us and stayed for weeks or months each year. She brought sympathy and helped in our domestic chores . . . From 1938 to 40 my wife's brother lived with us. He had tuberculosis and was not able to work, a very young man of 22 to 25 years. He was difficult because of his illness. He had to be isolated from other members of the family because of his illness. He died in 1940 . . . I systematically gave economic help to my mother and sister. Sometimes my elder brother borrowed from me" (136 B 3).

In terms of the future, it was possible to reserve some benefits to a certain degree. Although private ownership of productive property was long ago declared illegal, there are savings accounts in the USSR, and inheritance is fully legal. This, too — some financial security for self and children — is a benefit available to the upper strata. It must be added, however, that inflation and the occasional arbitrary fiscal manipulations by the regime, as in the currency reform of 1947 and the extension of maturity dates of government savings bonds in 1958, have rendered the accumulation of money less attractive. Our army officer says: "First of all it made no sense to save money since one could never be sure that money will retain its value and second, the living expenses consumed all the earnings" (136 B 3).

A complete analysis of the Soviet attitude toward saving for the future would include other aspects of the question. "Saving" often has a special meaning, and is not so much a matter of security as of budgeting. An economist tells us, "To buy some articles of clothing one had to save for some months because one could not buy them out of one month's pay" (134 B 2). A further consideration, corresponding to the official propaganda image, stresses the facts that there is no unemployment in the USSR and that medical care is free. A school teacher denies the necessity for monetary savings: "What for? I was secure in my work. I got my salary every month. If I was sick there was the hospital" (428 B 3).

Finally, there is some evidence in the traditional culture pattern of a certain aversion to saving, a tendency toward free-spending as a symbol of the proper orientation to life — spontaneous, carefree, generous. One side of ideological bolshevism also is hardly favorable, as demonstrated by the fate of the kulaks' "savings" and the general marxist aversion to money as a thing of contamination and corruption. Here, however, as in other parts of the Soviet scene, the ideology is out of phase with developments in both the Soviet institutional structure and popular motivation.

More than monetary savings, future security in the USSR has become associated in the public mind with education. As one young man put it: "In the USSR there is no capital except education. If a person does not want to become a collective farmer or just a charwoman, the only means you have to get something is through education" (74 A 25). Though for much of the Soviet era education has been formally free, the Soviet people are aware that the underlying reality is not so easily described; even though no tuition was required in the years before 1940 and after 1956, it has always been much easier for the children of the better-off classes to get an education. Much of the desire and hope for future security became linked within the family with an ever more salient goal — to educate the children — but the chances of success in this area were directly related to the parents' class level, revealing another very substantial advantage accruing to the upper parts of the Soviet social class order. This fact, and its psychological enhancement by the contrast of the less well-off, are clear in the following response of a student to the question, Was it easy for you to study? "I had no difficulties. My father had a good position. He was a minor employee in the city soviet. It was easier for us to get food and clothing than for the simple worker. At the same time I saw that the children of workers, or of collective farmers, that it was much more difficult for them to buy books and other material" (125 A 9).

As any reader of the Soviet press is aware, the privileges, and temptations, of upper class social position in the USSR are often buttressed by high political office. There are frequent complaints about government and party officials who use their influence to make special purchases, get their sons and daughters admitted to universities, and otherwise obtain exceptions to rules and favorable personal treatment. Not rarely, we may suppose, a good part of the pressure upon them comes from their families. The case of Sergei, a high official in the party and district executive committee is a good example. In the course of a short period, his wife or his mother made the following specific requests of him: (1) speak to the director of the agricultural experimental station about buying some currants that were bigger, firmer, available in thick clusters, and cheaper than those bought through the usual channels; (2) telephone the manager of a store about the purchase of a wool blouse for his wife, to avoid the "frightful queue"; (3) telephone the director of the theater for the favor of seats without previous purchase of tickets; (4) arrange an exception to the hospital rule so his wife could stay there with their sick daughter. Some of these requests were granted by Sergei, others refused, but at the cost of vigorous reproaches from his wife: "I am not inciting you to crime, after all!" or "You're no father, you're a walking moral code! Prude!" How, wonders this model Communist, can he explain to his wife that "a high official has less of a moral right than anyone else to use his official position, even in trivial matters?" [6]

All these things are important in themselves, but they also add up to more than their sum. The Soviet upper classes, like upper status groups everywhere (and perhaps even to a greater extent because so many of them are the families of self-made men), have the feelings of distinction and prestige that accompany high social rank. As always, the separateness of leadership is hard to distinguish from that of social snobbery.

The social self-image of one young army officer is described this way: "He counted himself among the upper class, partly because of his origin, mostly, however, because of his rapid career. He found that as a member of the upper class one had to set an example and he condemned people of his class who let themselves go outwardly or inwardly" (Bi 172). The other side of class consciousness is also visible from time to time in the contempt felt by the haves for the have-nots. A story in a Soviet newspaper titled "Who Are Your Neighbors?" says: "Many families live in one house — under one roof. What are their interrelations? This question does not always interest us. But it should . . . Some people . . . sometimes, proceeding only on the basis of the interests of their own little world, . . . poison the life of their neighbors. Take Lt. Col. Perederi in *Belaia Tserkov*. For 1½ years he has been poisoning the life of his neighbors, and the family of the worker of the furniture factory, Naumov. 'How can this be, that he, a lieutenant colonel, should live under the same roof with a former sergeant, now an ordinary worker?' " [7]

This is a rare specimen, for class consciousness is considered in official circles to be one of the more odious survivals of capitalism, and such open-and-shut cases do not often appear in print. Yet from time to time the fact becomes exceedingly visible, as in novelist Konstantin Paustovsky's fierce exposure of the "thousands of Soviet Drozdovs": "In our country there exists — unmolested and even to some extent prospering — an entirely new social stratum, a new caste of *petit bourgeois*. This is a new group of acquisitive carnivores, a group which has nothing in common either with the Revolution, or with our regime, or with socialism . . . They are cynics, black obscurantists, the same people who . . . without any embarrassment or fear, quite openly carried on anti-semitic talk of a kind worthy of pogrom-makers." [8] When these rare outbursts come to the attention of the casual observer, he is often startled by their contrast with the bland official portraits of class harmony in Soviet society, though, of course, he would not be if he were more familiar with the unpublished side of Soviet life.

The Poor

For most persons in the West, it is more difficult to imagine the dimensions of Soviet poverty than it is to comprehend the living conditions of the advantaged. If even the Soviet rich are poor by Western standards, then the life of the Soviet poor approaches the incalculable. Food consists largely of black bread, clothing is the simplest and most ragged, and living space consists of a few square meters in a mud hut, a cellar, a wooden shack, or, as was the case with a Donbass coal miner, "a cave, two meters by two meters." [9] The occupations of the poor reveal the functions that the Soviet regime, for one reason or another, values less highly. This knowledge has by now become a commonplace to the Soviet people. As shown by a worker's description of one who lived poorly because he had committed the ultimate crime against the Soviet law of material welfare — he had no special skill: "This man had no specialty. He had been a simple peasant before collectivization. . . . He had to find some way to live and he became a hauler. . . . The chief principle upon which his poverty was based is that his wage did not correspond to his work. He worked very hard, but was paid very little" (284 A 36, 37). Above all, there are those who have suffered most from want, that part of the population upon whose backs the Soviet system has laid the main burden of paying for industrialization, the proletarians of the countryside. The plaintive words of a simple collective farmer are eloquent: "The Power did not let us live. We were covered by shortages. We had no brightness in our lives" (176 B 2).

To the bare home, ragged clothing, and the never completely full belly must be added the other privations of poverty: the lack of variety in other than the most primitive types of experience and stimulation, the inability to cope with the everyday demands which among other families and in past time were taken for granted, and often the loss of hope for any improvement. Not only the advantages, but the basic dignities and securities are denied. The Soviet poor have been great in number and, in contrast to the well-off, they have not been able to think of travel, savings, the luxury of a wife who does not work, or generosity toward relatives.

Often the poor have not found within their reach the *sine qua non* of contemporary Soviet family life — the education of the children. This was especially true during the hardest years, 1940–1956, when institutions of higher learning and the upper classes of the ten-year schools required tuition payments. Not only was the monetary cost of tuition and books prohibitive, but poverty influenced study effort unfavorably. A young working-class man from a lower white-collar background discussed this problem: "I should have studied more, I should have concentrated more on school work. But, you know, children never care about studying in the first classes. Oh, I remember my childhood, how we used to go to school hungry. They'd give us soup at school and I'd bring a piece of bread home and hide it, so that I had something to eat later. Well, those children whose fathers were specialists were better off. They studied better because they didn't have to worry about anything else, they didn't have to waste time looking around for food and such things. Then, in school they'd always get parcels from home with everything they needed. That's the people who were not workers' sons" (7 A 21, 26).

The lives of the poor, then, provide evidence for another side of Soviet family life. In the view from the lower portions of the scale of social differentiation, not only is the degree of poverty relevant, but also important is the factor of how the Soviet people experience it. A question asked of the refugees in the Harvard Project on the Soviet Social System sought to establish the subjective and relative material welfare of each respondent: "What were your material conditions during the last years of your life in the USSR? In comparison with the majority, were you better or worse off?" [10] The pattern of responses exhibited in Table 2

TABLE 2. Self-evaluated material welfare by income and occupation.

Disposable ruble income in family, per capita	Per cent "better off" than majority	Occupation of family head	Per cent "better off" than majority
7800 and more	85 (46)[a]	Professional-administrative	72 (399)[a]
6600–7799	87 (24)	Semiprofessional	48 (163)
5400–6599	85 (34)	White-collar employee	42 (247)
4200–5399	50 (54)	Skilled worker	33 (189)
3000–4199	53 (123)	Semiskilled worker	16 (378)
1800–2999	25 (251)	Unskilled worker	10 (105)
900–1799	19 (290)	Peasant	8 (266)

Source: Adapted from Inkeles and Bauer, p. 121, based upon information from the Harvard Project on the Soviet Social System, 1950–1951.

[a] Figures in parentheses indicate total number of respondents.

shows an extremely high correlation between both occupational and income level of the head of family and family, respectively, and the tendency to see oneself as having been better off than the majority. I interpret this to mean a very high degree of class awareness in the USSR, and consider it a significant factor in analyzing Soviet family life.

On the Move

The great dislocations associated with civil and world war, famine, forced resettlement, political repression, and the collectivization of agriculture have combined with those huge, and in the USSR telescoped, developments of the modern era — industrialization and urbanization — to move great masses of Soviet people from one place to another. Some of the movement has been forced, some of it voluntary; some productive to both regime and people, some of little use to either. For instance, the wages and living conditions of the lower echelons of industrial labor have been so depressed that a kind of "worker hobo" psychology has developed as great numbers of the unskilled and partially skilled have drifted from place to place, seeking to better themselves but finding little permanent advantage. To the individual worker, often just out of peasant life, the situation seemed uninviting: "If I have my own [farm property] I can do this and that. I can repair that little thing [respondent points]. But if I work in production I might say, 'Oh, how little they pay me. I want to transfer to another factory'" (279 B 44). For the efficient functioning of the economy excessive labor turnover is a serious fault, of course, and Stalin put an arbitrary end to most of such flitting in 1940. The labor discipline laws made it illegal to change jobs without consent of the work superior and tightened things up in other ways. These laws were repealed in 1956, with the result that excessive labor turnover has again become a problem in the Soviet economy.

Geographical mobility has also been increased by special campaigns to persuade people to settle in Siberia, or in the Far North, or to live and work in the virgin lands of Kazakhstan, and by various more routine devices used by the regime to allocate labor and skill where needed. Engineers, medical doctors, agronomists, in general, all technical experts and specialists who receive a higher education, are required to serve a temporary term, usually three years, in places designated by the ministry in whose institution they have received their training. For the students, working on the land to get out the harvest or employment in factory, office, or field to get "practical experience" during the summer vacation period have been typical patterns.

We shall shortly return to geographical movement, and to its social psychological consequences, but mobility in the sense of traveling through social space is even more important. In between the two extremes of the Soviet class structure, which might be termed the relatively rich and the absolutely poor, is a large middle group of families. Their most typical characteristic is that they have been socially mobile. Some have, by comparison with earlier times, moved downward, but many more have risen, and a very substantial number have left extreme poverty behind to live a better life.

Two broad varieties of such upward social mobility reflect the human side of the process by which the regime has achieved its two main goals, political control and economic advance. The first form derives from the Revolution itself, from the overturn of the tsarist order and the vacating by force and fiat of the positions of power and responsibility occupied by the old ruling classes and from the resulting mass movement upward of the favored proletarians. A well-known early example of the bolshevik drive to recruit new people for a new society is the "Lenin Draft" of 1924 by which some 250,000 workers were taken into the party at one time. One of the most prominent social types to emerge in the early days was the *vydvizhenets* — a person quite literally "moved up" by the party. Such political mobility, if it may be so termed, is still available in the form of the party career. It is also available more generally in that the political attitude — loyalty, militancy, public subscription to the party line — plays an important role in the distribution of many forms of profit and advancement. For instance, admission to Soviet institutions of higher learning is supposed to be given only to those with positive recommendations from Komsomol and trade-union organizations.

The second major, and more purely economic, form of upward social mobility is the social correlate of rapid industrialization. In the space of a few years millions of families have changed residence, occupational pursuit, and an entire way of life, forsaking the land and the collective farm for more desirable jobs in the cities or dropping a job in one place for something better elsewhere. The experience of moving from one major social group to another, from peasantry to working class and from manual work (both rural and urban) to nonmanual, has been a common one in the lifetime of many families. Intergeneration mobility has been even more common.

Some idea of the dimensions of this fact can be gained from statistics. The movement of the peasants into cities is reflected in a net migration from rural to urban areas between 1926 and 1939 of around 23,000,000 persons. By 1959, census figures revealed that almost half of the population was living in towns.[11] The transformation of a backward agricultural country into the world's second industrial power implies also a tremendous social transformation whereby "going into factory work," as the common phrase has it, became a way of life. This experience, so common in the past decades, reveals an interesting paradox: At the same time that the living standards declined in both urban and rural areas, millions of families were able to improve their material circumstances. The improvement offered by the urban job and environment seemed very great, even while real wages were declining, to the impoverished and reluctantly collectivized peasantry.[12] Not only the pull of the city, but the push from the country also counted. The authors of the study of Viriatino put it this way: "Until recently a certain per cent of the village youth have been leaving the village to go into factory work in the city . . . There were two reasons for it: (1) the desire to acquire a particular speciality and qualification and become a part of urban culture, and (2) defects which existed until recently in the kolkhoz in the organization of work and the system of pay" (Ku 259).

While social movement from peasant to working class has been more frequent, mobility from peasantry to nonmanual occupations has also been quite common. Sometimes the peasant's channel to success has become almost a social stereotype, as is the case with the officer personnel in the Soviet army. Nor should we lose sight of the fact that the past decades have brought a rather special kind of social mobility, the mass migration of Soviet women into the occupational system, often to jobs of considerable skill, responsibility, and high compensation. All in all, this side of Soviet life presents an aura of expansion, growth, opportunity, and the steady harnessing of a whole people into the framework of a great industrial and political power. Clearly, the waste of human resources so striking in the political realm must be juxtaposed with the remarkable range of utilization of the occupational and educational potential of the Soviet people. If the former elicits a sense of aversion, the latter excites admiration among the population that has lived through it.

The regime has naturally taken considerable pains to underline the already impressive fact by stressing that the Soviet social order has opened wide the doors of opportunity for study and work. This theme is central in the Constitution and permeates the image of Soviet society that the regime seeks to disseminate at home and abroad. A young refugee tells that at every step he heard how "the Soviet power had opened the roads of opportunity to people . . . in the school, in the Pioneer organization, in the theatre, in the movies, everywhere and always" (110 A 103–104). There is considerable evidence that this image of the USSR as the land of opportunity has become ever more salient in Soviet popular culture. Indeed, no impartial investigation of Soviet daily life can fail to reveal the extent to which this belief has been accepted by the people, with reservations by the older generation, but usually quite completely and unquestioningly by the youth. The key themes of political attitude and technical preparation are apparent in the answer of this young worker to the question, What sort of person gets ahead in the Soviet Union? "Those who follow honestly the communist idea. And those who abuse this communist idea in order to achieve a position. Those who received a good education and who can speak. Even if a man is a simple worker, if he is a good worker, if he shows a good attitude towards his work, he will be promoted although he has little education. He will become a brigadier, a foreman, and he can be sent to an engineering school" (378 A 59–60).

Odd Jobs, Garden Plots, and Other Sidelines

The lure of new opportunity and the sharpness of economic need have affected the Soviet family in many ways. In a life surrounded with material shortages, with a government claiming to improve material conditions, visible differences in living standards among different families, and substantial social mobility, the opinion arises that although life is hard, it is also possible to improve it. The desire for improvement, which becomes desperate need in the lowest stratum, leads to a willingness to change the traditional ways of life — or to maintain them — whichever brings greater economic advantage. In the long run the matter is usually seen as fundamentally a question of social mobility through self or children. As we have seen, this is important, for if nothing more substantial is forthcoming, at least hope can furnish spiritual nourishment. But short-run pressures are also great, and there are immediate shortages to overcome.

A forty-nine-year-old mechanic with a wife and three children employed by the Kharkov district hospital from 1935 to 1943 tells how he was able to supplement his family's income: "I had a free dwelling, one room and kitchen, on the hospital grounds. This was compensation for the fact that I did not work fixed hours, but often had to work at night, i.e., on the central heating, without additional pay. In the hospital itself I had no additional income, but with my boss's consent in my free time, evenings or days off, I was occasionally able to earn money as a mechanic outside the hospital. For instance, I repaired the heating and plumbing in the neighboring schools, the water distillation apparatus in the pharmacy, etc. This was no fixed amount in my budget. In addition, we had a small vegetable garden, which was important to our family diet" (1654 A 6).

Several typical patterns are revealed in this comment. Free housing has been widely used for some categories of occupation which are in short supply — for example, managers, engineers, and technicians — as a hidden supplement to income and thus as an extra incentive. Odd jobbing in spare time is also common for men as well as women, and the small family vegetable garden, considered indispensable among the poor, is also highly regarded by middle-stratum families.

For peasant families on collective farms the proceeds from sale of vegetables, fruit, poultry, and dairy products in the urban free markets have been a main source of cash. In general, in the economic life of the peasant family the private plot of the peasantry has been all-important. In the cities the need to supplement money wages and the deficiencies in the retail trade system have made garden plots also very desirable to the less well-off working-class families. Quite typically the mobile peasant family has settled in the outskirts of urban areas, where it can continue life on a mixed economy basis. The disadvantage of an excessive amount of travel time back and forth to work in the city is offset by the produce and also by the chance for more space and sometimes better housing than could be obtained closer to the city. A man from such a family background tells how his family fared economically: "We lived better than other families because we had our own little house from 1924 to 1939. My father was a hardworking man and kept a small garden. We didn't grow anything to sell, but it was enough for ourselves. My mother clung to some peasant habits so she kept some pigs and we killed a couple each year. Besides that, my mother did washing and other such things which she could do in the house to earn some extra money. My father worked in a technicum. Despite the fact that he was illiterate, he was an instructor in a repair school. Such things can happen in the Soviet Union" (29 A 59). A bookkeeper reveals the economic base of his continuing contact with the village in his explanation of why his family was better off than others. "In the first place I had a vegetable garden outside of the city. Secondly, as I lived in a large city it was possible for me to get clothing and shoes, though not in sufficient quantities; these I could send to my relatives who lived in a village, and they, in turn, sent me additional food items, such as butter, lard and so forth" (114 B 2).

The more resourceful have been able to keep the wolf from the door in a number of ways. The main social pressure to take the initiative falls upon the head of the family, in the best circumstances, the husband and father. Though many Soviet mothers work, the primary responsibilities are quite clear-cut. A worker states: "The husband should materially provide for his family, and the wife should preserve the 'hearth' and bring up the children" (26 B 5).

In the face of the situation we have outlined, the man's responsibility tends to become inflated to the point where extra-occupational activity assumes a normative cast: "All the good husbands sought extra work after their basic work, or took overtime so they could improve the beggar-like conditions of their families" (8 B 4).

Beggarly conditions lead also to illegal activity. As the suffering of loved ones becomes intolerable, petty thieving, graft, and small-scale speculation become commonplace. They also tend to be quite blatant, as revealed in the comments of a forty-year-old communications worker: "However, best of all lived the speculators. They had money reserves. I knew the director of a small trust in Moscow. He was a speculator in furniture by profession and also a party member. Outwardly, he was poor. He lived in only one room with his wife, but he built houses for fourteen relatives near Moscow. Later, he was caught and arrested" (359 A 43).

Illegal economic activity in Soviet families is very widespread and creates a certain snowball effect. Illegal earnings were reported for 58 per cent of the families observed by Bischoff's German observers in the postwar years. It was found primarily in the great middle group of families, for in the upper classes, where monthly family income is adequate, illegal additions are not needed, and the least well-off families are fearful and lack the necessary shrewdness. Those who are best able to profit are the men who act as foremen and officials of enterprises that deal with building materials, clothing, and other consumption items. This is one reason why jobs in the retail-trade network are so highly regarded by many Soviet people, and why retail-trade employees figure so prominently in the frequent Soviet newspaper accounts of graft and corruption.

Although illegal earnings are primarily a masculine specialty, the women also have taken a hand. In the period when abortions were illegal, 1935–1956, such clandestine operations were a typical source of extra earnings for the medical doctors, 75 per cent of whom are women, and for medical assistants, nurses, and village midwives who were willing to perform the service and take the risk. But the most widespread form of such illicit earnings among women is the illegal though very remunerative occupation of home sewing. In some cases Soviet women in possession of the "capital equipment," a sewing machine, can double or triple the salaries earned by their husbands.

It is also notable that there seems to be little association between illegal economic activity and political attitudes. Party members and individuals who in other respects are quite "pro-Soviet" seem to engage in it just as much as the rank and file.[13] Soviet breadwinners have been under great pressure somehow to make their way, and in matters of ethical conflict the family has often come first. A good example is provided in the life of a worker in the rope factory of a village near Voronezh. He had a wife and three children, and, according to the observer, earned six hundred rubles per month in his regular job, eight hundred to nine hundred extra in summer season work, and four hundred or five hundred more through various kinds of illegal speculative activities. The general outlook in the family is revealed by the fact that the parents were "very economical" and "very modest in respect to their own need for food, but the children ate better in the things they took to school with them." Indeed, "the entire marriage was based on the children and on their social ascent, and the parents sacrificed themselves for that." Furthermore, "the father was basically an honest and upright man, but he broke the law without hesitation whenever the requirements of providing for his family dictated it. He did not read newspapers, because they were too expensive for him; he considered them a luxury" (Bi 209).

It seems quite clear that the external circumstances confronted by Soviet families have had a galvanizing effect. Aspirations have soared, as has the expenditure of effort. Much of the latter has been directed toward mobility through legitimate channels, but much also through illegitimate ones. The endemic shortages and the regime's rigid marxist posture toward the role of middlemen have afforded many loopholes.

As a result, it has been relatively easy for the population to adopt a tolerant attitude toward such activities — indeed, to draw a sharp distinction between private property, which is not eligible, and socialist property, which is fair game for all. An unskilled worker reports: "Everything was so expensive, and workers had little money. In the Soviet Union here's the way it was. When I worked in a storehouse it was accepted to steal something to take it to the market to sell it and then divide it up with the manager" (279 B 23).

Such activity is so common, and punitive retribution necessarily so fitful, that it tends to be illegal in name only. Considering the morally justifiable usage to which the proceeds are put — enhancement of the family's welfare — when punishment does come it is experienced more as fate than as justice. And those who are apprehended and sentenced are more likely to be seen as victims than as criminals by their families as well as by their neighbors, friends, and kinsmen.

There is occasional evidence of guilt feelings among those who do further themselves illegally, of course, and the informal cultural interpretation of honesty is two-valued. Personal probity is usually both a social issue and a personal problem. Soviet parents are very anxious for their children to be "honest," but on the other hand, a coexisting formulation has it that "one cannot be honest in Russia." In terms of family relationships the ambivalence is also seen. Apparently, societal repression of a member of the family for illegal economic activity is less likely to unify those remaining in the family than is repression based on political considerations. In the former case, the motive of the "criminal" becomes the most significant factor, whereas in cases of political repression the motive of the victim is usually patently irrelevant. He is a "victim," no more and no less.[14]

The Family's Living Standard, A Sensitive Issue

With the terms in our statement now almost completely enumerated, we can approach our goal of assessing the relationship between them and family life. The over-all living standard has been low, often in a state of decline; the regime has claimed the opposite, thus misleading many; social differentiation is great; and mobility, geographical and social, is widely prevalent. Furthermore, the population on the whole looks upon social mobility as a distinct and real possibility.

One additional factor is the extent to which the pronounced differences in living standards are matters of general knowledge rather than concealed by social segregation of the families from different levels. Here again the Soviet experience is unique. In the USSR today social awareness of differences in material living standards is understandably extreme: there is extraordinary consciousness among the poor of the welfare of the better-off, and the latter's awareness of the conditions of the poor is similarly striking.

Social and geographic mobility involves both individual persons and individual families, but even when the old folks, brothers and sisters, and other relatives, remain behind, the ties of kin and community of origin, although attenuated, continue. The mobile person, even if ties and contact with his people are superficial, can forget neither them nor his humbler past. Neither can the humble ones forget the example of the one who made good; it stands in front of them as a goal for their own emulation. Furthermore, the sense of class difference is emphasized, paradoxically, by an aura of status equality. As the doors of hereditary status in the old society were violently broken down, economic and political position come to depend upon individual achievement, furthered by both the Revolution and modern industrialism. Moreover, much of the atmosphere of interpersonal relations among Soviet citizens is permeated with equalitarianism. Consciousness of status differences, snobbery, segregation by status level — voluntary as well as involuntary — continue to exist, but they are minimal and tend to be seen as illegitimate. Worker, peasant, and intelligentsia sit side by side in the theater as well as in the bus. Although they may find little in common to talk about, they cannot avoid being aware of each other's presence.

Perhaps the most important factor inducing social class visibility is the scarcity of residential privacy and the relative lack of ecological segregation of the sort so common in American and West European cities. Along the main Soviet thoroughfares one finds modern apartment houses with towers, balconies, and central heating, but immediately behind them it is usual to find the dark decrepitude of the slums. Even more frequently, a single large house will contain quite heterogeneous households, with the poorest families living in the cellars, corridors, and upper floors. The upper floors are not usually desirable because of the absence of elevators and adequate water pressure. Mixing of social levels also originates in the exceptionally low vacancy rate, which does not permit the luxury of choosing one's neighborhood.[15]

As a result the Soviet family has become extraordinarily dependent upon its class position, and extraordinarily subject to influence by intense feelings of well-being or dissatisfaction. Those feelings, in turn are determined by how its members see themselves in relation to others. In those families with more or better food, housing, and other necessities the atmosphere is pervaded with a sense of well-being. A photo journalist says: "The district in which we lived was inhabited by workers. The latter received a fairly low pay and, having for the greater part large families, were always suffering from great poverty" (49 B 3). In addition to sympathy, we can anticipate a sense of relative gratification, which is indeed apparent in other comments made by this respondent. In this respect the Soviet upper class is a grateful one, for those who belong are very aware of the extent to which they are favored. It is also quite self-satisfied, because its members often assume that they are where they are by dint of special merits which set them off from the masses.

Objectively, the upper classes are best off, but they are not alone in the sense of subjective satisfaction. The other large group of Soviet families in which a sense of contentment can be found is the socially mobile, those whose present standards, though modest, constitute a marked improvement over their own recent past and over their kin and neighbors. A sports instructor says: "When I was working as an iron worker in the metallurgical factory, my family was in no way different from other families who lived in the Soviet Union. But after I took up sport and received money toward training and for performances, my family and I began to live much better comparatively than the other workers' families" (435 B 2). A worker explains how he rose from the peasantry and how he feels about his mobility: "When I did not yet have my skill [kvalifikatsiia] I wanted to educate myself and get a skill. You have to have a skill. If you don't, you are hungry. So I did, and I stopped herding and became a polisher. The work was easier and I got more for it" (213 B 23).

Significant aspects of social mobility include not only better job, higher pay, and new cultural opportunity, but, above all, better chances for the children. A worker says: "While living in a city my children could have attained much more than I, who was born and grew up in a village" (499 B 9). A schoolteacher also refers to his own background: "I am from a simple worker's family. I got what I got with my own labor without support from parents. My children were sons of intelligentsia. I could help them with what I got" (428 B 7).

An extraordinarily large proportion of the Soviet population, much larger than the objective differences over time in their own life conditions would warrant, seem to feel a sense of improvement, of personal better-ment. In the sample of families observed by the German prisoners of war this feeling was common enough for Bischoff to conclude that at least 50 per cent of the general population share it.[16] In many instances, occupational promotions, even if no more could be bought with any increment of wages, seem responsible. A man who started his career as a state-farm worker reports: "I started to work as an accountant, increased my qualifications, advanced in my knowledge, and advanced in position" (499 B 5). To such people relatively small advantages sometimes seem to have bred a disproportionate sense of satisfaction with self, with society, and with family. The establishment of a modest standard of minimum economic security for carrying on a normal family life was buttressed by the comparisons, constantly forced upon the adequately provided for, with those who struggled with poverty. The poor and the hopeless were close neighbors — in the same apartment block, just around the corner, or at the other end of a letter from home.

Thus the USSR became an extreme open-class society in which the experience of upward social mobility became common in many families. At the same time an even greater number of Soviet families have been brought to extreme awareness of social levels, a stronger desire for a better life, and an eagerness to do whatever was needed to achieve it. And it has become almost standard form within the family for parents to desire their children to do better than they themselves have done.

If success comes frequently and to many, its absence should be felt as a special hardship. This, too, seems to be the case, and the strength of the disappointment is magnified by the objective circumstances. Soviet hardship is both subjective and objective.

The frustration, therefore, as well as the satisfaction of living in such a society appears to be magnified. Although at the top of the hier-archy one finds relative gratification that tends to flow out and cover other sides of life with a rosy hue, in the lower portions of the Soviet socio-economic structure family life is often dominated by a pervasive sense of dissatisfaction. A worker reports: "My life was such as any man of the lower strata had. From my school bench on, it was difficult to look at the lives of others who had more than we did . . . I found nothing to my liking in my life when I compared it with the others who had a better life — not too good, but when compared with ours, still a little better" (614 B 2, 3).

As we might expect in a revolutionary society run quite openly and completely by a single political party, the economically underprivileged sometimes merge their economic and political resentments: "The privileged families were those of the members of the Communist Party; they lived under much better conditions . . . The struggle for daily bread got simply tiresome. Other families in my sourroundings were almost in the same situation, and the hatred of the privileged communistic families grew from day to day" (42 B 2). It is not common to find such emphasis on the privileges of party membership; most Soviet citizens are at least equally conscious of the party member's often very demanding responsibilities.

At times the feeling of frustration was turned inward, loosened upon the family, where it became a cause of dissension. Sometimes the situation was redefined, and the family looked upon itself as a negatively privileged one, suffering through no fault of its own.

To those with handicaps of this kind, social mobility lost some of its attractiveness, because it often increased the fear of exposure. A secret police employee denies that he was ambitious to move up in his profession: "No. Both my wife and I had one opinion on that. To raise one's position means more responsibility. The greater the responsibility, the nearer the unmasking. To sit at the bottom was safer" (147 B 5). Often, too, the desire for political safety merged into a general reluctance, often serving as a rationalization for underlying inability to assume the burden of responsibility: "He [plant director] was well off only materially, not morally . . . I was a simple worker, while he was a director, and so he had many headaches. God only knows what could have happened to him" (302 A 25).

To summarize, the contemporary Soviet population is stratified mainly along the axis of the individual's ability to contribute to the needs of a complex, bureaucratically organized economy, and the family's standard of living is closely dependent upon his occupational performance. Occupational mobility is common, and much of the family's attention is directed toward preparation for specialized and skilled work activity on the part of its members. If the Soviet situation is in any way unique among modern societies in this respect, that can be explained by the recent and rapid entry of the USSR into the modern era, by the protracted period of consumer-goods shortages amid claims to the contrary, by the rising levels of expectation, and by the forces making social differentiation so visible to the whole population.

Those factors have produced a heightened awareness of the mutability of the fate shared by the Soviet individual citizen and his family, along with a general increase in the intention to improve one's lot or, when the way is obstructed, feelings of frustration for a hard lot. Far from being a land of equality or a workers' paradise, the Soviet Union, as judged by the aspirations and behavior of its people, shares such features with the United States, a society often adjudged too acquisitive and individualistic by its critics.

SEVEN | THE SIZE AND ORGANIZATION
OF THE FAMILY

THE MODERN AGE has moved the Soviet family along in directions quite familiar to observers of life in other lands. The family has become smaller in size, many of the functions it used to perform have been relinquished or taken over by larger economic and social organizations, and certain role dilemmas connected with the separation of workplace and home have sharpened. Such social trends as these can be found almost everywhere in the modern era of factory, office, and city life, of course, and they were in evidence in Russia before October 1917. The Revolution has in a broad way hurried the trend, though at the same time, along with other peculiarities of the Soviet social order, it left its own unique stamp. Moreover, the shift from a traditional to a modern family is very much a change "in process," which helps explain why the variety in the patterns of organization of the Soviet family is so great.[1] Like much of the rest of the USSR and like other aspects of family life itself, one finds great contrasts.

Size and Composition of the Household

In the 1959 census the Soviet family was defined as those persons living together under a common budget and united by kinship or marriage. As of that year the average (arithmetic mean) size was 3.7. The rural-urban difference was small, and so were the differences among the three main social groups. Village families had a mean size of 3.9 and urban families of 3.5; of the socioeconomic groupings, collective farmers had the largest families, 3.9, urban workers showed a mean of 3.6, and the white collar group 3.4.

Both urban and rural families became smaller in the twenty-year period separating the last two censuses, but the latter changed more, declining from a 4.3 average in 1939 to 3.9 in 1959 whereas the former fell only from 3.6 to 3.5. Another way to put it is in terms of the number of persons in the modal family, which fell from four to two persons from 1939 to 1959 in the villages but remained at three for urban families. Probably the chief reason for this is the lower sex ratio in the villages and the greater proportion of small families headed by women. In general, wartime losses, the drop in Soviet fertility, increased longevity, and the tendency for newly married couples to seek residence separate from their parents are all responsible for the decline in family size, in cities as well as in villages.[2]

The social disorders, rapid change, and economic hardships of Soviet history have left a strong imprint on the membership composition of the Soviet family. Normal families — husband, wife, and minor children — live side by side with many broken families. Of course, the broken family as such is a peculiarly composed one, but in the long run it can be as much an experience as a permanent state, and the survivors may subsequently enter into new marriages or be absorbed into another conjugal family. However, since there has been a striking shortage of men for some time, millions of Soviet women have remained single or, in the case of widows and divorcées, have not remarried. The ratio of males of all ages per 100 females declined from near 100 at the turn of the century to 93.5 in 1926, 91.9 in 1939, to the low point of 74.3 in 1946. The sex ratio has climbed slowly upward since then, but will not become normal until the next century.[3] As of 1959 about 24,000,000 women in the age range twenty to fifty-nine had no husbands.[4] Since a large proportion of these unmarried women have dependent children to support, and since running a family household under Soviet conditions is difficult in any case, overwork, with considerable physical and mental strain has become a major problem for the female heads of many Soviet families. As a result, health problems have been exacerbated and the disability rate among Soviet women has grown high.[5]

Furthermore, in spite of all their efforts many Soviet women have been unable to provide proper supervision and guidance for their children. The substantial amount of juvenile crime in postwar Russia can be traced partly to this. Soviet research investigations invariably point to fatherless and functionally motherless families as a social problem.

In brief, Soviet women in great numbers have been forced by fate to do their best to be workers, heads of families, and childrearers simultaneously. Without doubt, many aspects of Soviet sex roles are thereby made likely to exhibit permanent change. Once the routines of established customs cannot be followed, the way is open for the development of new ones. For example, in Viriatino it is reported that the old patterns of allocation of household chores are breaking down. Many women are taking over entirely such tasks as giving fodder to the stock, which used to be the peasant husband's job. Such changes, we are told, occur because the collective farm wives are less busy in the general kolkhoz work than their husbands, but also because there are "so many widows who have to do all the work themselves." [6]

A second peculiarity of the composition of the Soviet family has been the extent to which the three-generation or extended family, fitted by tradition more to rural than to urban life, has found as much, perhaps even more, reason to persist in Soviet cities than in the villages. Were the Soviet government to release comprehensive statistical information on the relation between residence and socio-economic level on the one hand and family composition on the other, I should expect to find as many or more grandparents, especially grandmothers (for feminine longevity is seven years higher than masculine), in city families as in village families. I also suspect that there might well be a direct relationship between the socio-economic level and the proportion of three-generation families.

My suspicion that this might be so was raised by the prominence of such a pattern among the urban families of the Harvard Project refugee sample[7] and also by certain aspects of the relation between domestic chores and economic advantage in Soviet family life. The most adequate statistical corroboration available from a Soviet source was published in 1964. In a summary of the composition by generations of families studied in various parts of the USSR (Table 3) four of the groups represent families from collective farm villages and only one refers to an urban family system. It is significant, however, that the latter, referring to the working class, has a higher proportion of three-generation families than three out of four rural family averages.

Working Wives and Mothers

One of the most distinctive and significant facets of the modern Soviet family is the extraordinarily high employment rate of its women. In striking contrast with the American family, and with the American occupational world, a heavy majority of Soviet wives and mothers leave the home every morning for a job and return to the family late in the afternoon or evening. As Table 4 shows, the proportion at work in the USSR is roughly twice as high as that in America.

The table also reveals another important fact — namely, that women

TABLE 3. Number of generations in family, five areas of the USSR.
(in per cent)

	Generations			
Area	One	Two	Three	Other[a]
Viriatino Village, RSFSR	19.3	60.3	20.0	0.4
Villages of Transcarpathian Ukraine	6.6	64.2	24.2	5.0
Villages in Lithuanian SSR	13.6	65.3	13.0	8.1
Darkhan Village, Kirgiz SSR	—	55.1	21.7	—
Leningrad working-class families	17.0	53.0	24.0	6.0

Source: Adapted from sources cited and data presented in Kharchev, *Brak i semia*, p. 231. The time periods vary from 1953 to 1963. Percentages total 100 horizontally.

[a] This category includes, at least for Leningrad, "spouses living together with a brother, sister, or other relatives of one of them."

have been working throughout the Soviet period. Of course, the composition of the occupations has changed greatly, and although approximately half the women in the Soviet labor force still work in agriculture, mainly on collective farms as field workers and livestock tenders, the USSR has gained world renown for the number of its women professionals. As of the 1959 census year 32 per cent of Soviet engineers and

TABLE 4. Women in the labor force, percentage of age groups, USSR, 1926, 1959, United States, 1960.

	USSR		USA
Age group	1926	1959	1960
20–24	93	81	45
25–29	75	80	33
30–34	75	78	36
35–39	77	77	40
40–44	77	76	45
45–49	77	75	47
50–54	72	69	46

Source: Dodge, pp. 35, 37; United States, Department of Commerce, Bureau of the Census, *United States Census of Population, 1960: Detailed Characteristics* (Washington, 1963), p. 487.

79 per cent of its medical doctors were women.[8] However, the important fact for our analysis is the constancy of the pattern since the 1920's. To look at the picture from the vantage point of the labor force itself, there has been no "trend to work" such as that in the United States, where the percentage of women in the labor force grew from 20 per cent in 1920 to 34 per cent in 1962. In the USSR the corresponding figure has always been close to 50 per cent.

Table 4 also is suggestive of life-cycle patterns typical for one country but not the other. There is no sharp decline in the USSR in the ages of maximum fertility such as that found in the United States, where the employment rate drops from 45 per cent in the age group 20–24 to 35 per cent in the 25–29 group. In the USSR this pattern seems gradually to have been pushed aside. On the other hand, in the USSR there is a direct, though small, correlation between age and the tendency to leave employment during productive years, a pattern which is reversed in the United States where after the initial stage of childbearing women become increasingly involved in work outside the home.

Among married women living with their husbands, difference in employment level between those without preschool children and those with is not a great one. Of the three means of estimating this figure that are at hand, the first one, the data in Table 4, shows no apparent tendency at all for women in the most fertile years to withdraw in substantial numbers from the labor force. The second means, however, taken from the budget study of the Harvard Project and referring to the year 1940, revealed a difference of sixteen percentage points between per cent employed of women without children (84 per cent) and those with young children (68 per cent).[9] The third source consists of recent Soviet budget studies, which show that in 53 per cent of families with children up to age sixteen, both parents were employed.[10] All three sources show high rates of employment for women, but without more detailed evidence a sound conclusion about the direction of the trend is not possible.

On the basis of the sparse amount of information available, mainly from the Harvard Project refugee sample, the relation between employment of women and social class level of the families appears to be rather complex. Apparently there is more variation inside families on a particular level than there is between them and other levels. On the collective farms, of course, the issue does not present itself so sharply, because the separation of home and workplace is not so pronounced, there is more work for the women in and around house and private plot, and the subsistence level of living permits little choice — one does what is necessary to get more bread, boots, and clothing. With the move into urban factory work, however, the break with traditional role responsibilities and family organization, if not cushioned by a partial solution, halfway between village and city, becomes more problematic. In working-class families the proportion of unemployed wives seems to be a direct function of the intraclass socio-economic level of the husband, and I have the impression that there is as much opposition in the families of skilled workers and foremen to working wives as in any other type of Soviet family.

A large portion of such opposition may be a result of the kind of work performed in urban-type jobs by women with little educational training or skill to offer. Women have been prominent in street cleaning, road repair, heavy construction work, and other occupations considered in Western countries suitable only for men. This has been so common in working-class families that feminine employment in general may often have received a bad name. For example, an army officer, up from the peasantry, asserted that he was against work by women: "Because a woman in the USSR is used as a slave and is forced to labor beyond her strength. In the Stalin Constitution of the Soviet Union woman has an equal right, to work as a man. But that work is heavy, beyond her woman's strength. I consider that heavy labor is not for women. I consider that forcing women to work as it is done in the Soviet Union is slavery, not freedom" (175 B 5). If such attitudes are at all prevalent, any substantial rise in income level in working-class families may eventuate in the desire to rescue the wife from heavy manual labor.

Pious and even indignant sentiments against heavy work for women are to be heard from time to time in official quarters, and the Soviet labor code lists prohibited occupations and provides definite norms (maximum weight to be lifted, and so forth) restricting such activity. Nevertheless, the toiling, sweating women, including some working in coal mines, are still in evidence. One of the most striking examples of contrast between official claims and expressed intentions and the hard reality of Soviet labor policy is provided by a report delivered in 1958 by the head of the Komsomol, in which he revealed with apparent pride that 40,000 boys and girls had been sent off to perform underground work in the mines of the Donbas, Kuzbas, Kuznetsk, Karaganda, and the suburban Moscow coal basin.[11]

Returning to the relation between feminine employment and social class, within the nonmanual group the association between intraclass occupational level of husband and proportion of employed wives moves in the opposite direction, up to a point. The higher the husband's skill, responsibility, and pay, the more likely is his wife to be employed. In the very top brackets, however, among the Soviet elite, the wife is again less likely to work — a reversal that may be linked with the greater average age of such women, the high status of their families, and the often formidable difficulty of matching their skills and abilities with occupations that are socially appropriate.

It has long been official policy to state directly or to hint that all able-bodied Soviet citizens, including women with young children, should be at work building communism. Moreover, work for women is said to bring about sex equality and is also seen as conducive to the desired communist upbringing of children in state-sponsored childcare institutions. Opportunities in the educational system are plentiful; equal pay and treatment plus generous provisions for rest leave, medical care, and the nursing connected with maternity are accorded on the job; the national need for labor power has always been great; and the daily pressure of agitation and propaganda is very strong.

Yet the main liabilities for family life of the employment of wife and mother are familiar ones. A woman tells us that though she worked, "I did not want to hold a job because my home suffered from it. It was very difficult for me to combine my job and housework" (178 B 6). An army colonel tells why his wife did not work: "According to Soviet standards I was sufficiently well provided for and did not want my wife to work. There was enough work for my wife in the household. Besides, she had the main care of bringing up our daughter" (219 B 5).

Many Soviet men, and women too, still share the sentiment expressed by the old saying: "A house without a housewife is an orphan." Statistically, as we have noted, it is clear that the majority of Soviet women do indeed work. But it is also important to emphasize that many could who do not. A Soviet sociologist calculates that in 1959 there were not fewer than 10,000,000 Soviet women devoting themselves exclusively to housework, and S. G. Strumilin notes that "household work in our country consumes no less than 100,000,000,000 man hours a year, because almost one-third of the women who are far from advanced age have this as their sole occupation." [12]

What presents itself as an economic loss to the Soviet leaders, and perhaps really does retard maximum growth of the gross national product, is to the individual persons concerned a desirable organization of family life. In the agricultural-rural past the wife and mother could both work and be at home, tending field and garden, cooking, caring for the house, and rearing the children. With urbanization and industrialization the workplace became drastically separated from the family home, and household tasks began to go unattended. A strong sense of separation and loss derives from the actual day-long physical absence of the woman and, more than the question of work, lies at the base of the peasant saying about the house without a housewife. Not a few Soviet families have been able to cherish the thought that they have maintained their families intact, even if at the cost of lower living standards or some strain on the part of the husband. These attitudes are apparent in the words of a construction engineer whose wife was not employed: "Even though my extra earning forced me to greater effort, it freed both my wife and daughter from the necessity of work and . . . I did not envy other people. I was happy that my wife and I were able to create a small but harmonious family. [Did your wife ever want to work?] She did want to work in order to help me, but I preferred to strain myself and to keep the family intact. In my opinion, the family becomes deformed if the wife works on the outside, and especially the 'outside' of Soviet reality" (159 B 2, 5).

Thus, some at least in the population draw a conclusion contrary to that proposed by the classical marxist view that social production for women is a progressive step. In such families, when the wife does work, both men and women are very conscious of making a sacrifice in the way of comfort, domestic order, and above all by their inability to give a proper upbringing to their children. The governing opinion is expressed by a mathematics instructor whose wife was also an instructor in an institute. He reports that his wife worked: "Because in the beginning, my earnings alone were not enough for a decent life. But of late, we thought about her leaving work in order to devote full time to the upbringing of our daughter" (181 B 6).

Among the families in which the wife is not employed, the sense of satisfaction is not usually expressed publicly, for it has never been quite legitimate for a woman to be "just a housewife." Since the official position of the regime is that a good wife and mother will work, a large proportion of published materials about women and the family gives publicity and praise to those who do. Especially valued are women who perform heroic feats both at work, becoming Heroes of Soviet Labor, and at home, bearing and raising many children.

Conversely, a markedly negative image is often generated of those Soviet women who do not work, especially if there are no children or only one child. The most scathing tone is reserved for those who receive a higher or technical education at state expense but lose all interest in work as soon as they marry. When such bad examples are pilloried in the daily press, some pains are usually taken to show that the woman in question is irresponsible and parasitic in general, not merely in her attitude toward work. Thus, one young woman left her job the day she registered her marriage, even though she lived with her mother, who acted as housekeeper. The story continues: "Soon Ala became pregnant and somehow she got a job only in order to receive compensation for the statutory leave. After the birth of the child she did not return to work. At home her mother does everything for her . . . One simply marvels at how a young, healthy woman can satisfy herself with such a life." [13] In another case study a "spoiled, only daughter of well-to-do parents" not only failed to finish her education or work but exhibited other faults. At first she refused to go along with her husband, an army officer assigned to the Far East. Once there, she "nagged and reproached him for taking her 'to such a hole,'" complained that her child's nurse was "not diligent enough," demanded that her husband get himself reassigned to Moscow, and finally packed up and left for Moscow without him, to stay with her father.[14]

However frequently such feminine villains are to be found in real life, the intent of such portraits is to convey strongly the idea that work is a prime social duty, that women who could but do not perform are shirkers, and that they are likely to be morally corrupt in other ways as well. It should be stressed, though, that in fact the motivation of a large percentage of unemployed women falls into two other, hardly corrupt, categories. First, and probably greatest in number, are those who are responding to a pattern of ideal urban family life widely shared in the informal culture, well illustrated by the words Ivan spoke to his fellow factory worker, Vera, shortly after their marriage: "Verochka, why should you work, get up early? The work is dirty, heavy, and my pay is enough to maintain the family." [15] Though the intent of the *Pravda* article is to ridicule Ivan and Vera, presenting their case as an example of philistine backwardness, it is likely that the portrait aroused as much sympathy as opprobrium in fellow citizens who read it. The second group of unemployed married women, also very large, consists of those who prefer to work but who are unable to make suitable arrangements for the care of their young children. It is this latter category that keeps the economic planners and the party busy seeking ways to "rationalize" housework and childcare to the point where these women can enter the labor force.

It has never become appropriate for the party and government to exert legal pressure upon all married women to go to work, primarily because the economic resources have never been earmarked in amounts adequate to provide the auxiliary services needed to release women from their domestic tasks. To be sure, as a matter of principle it has been indisputable that public catering and social rearing for children are better, should be provided, and would be accepted by Soviet wives and mothers. It has further been the official view that the latter would then all march gladly to work. In fact, however, Soviet reality in this respect has been far from the image erected by principle.

The truth is that the provision of preschool institutions has lagged behind the needs, and even the promised construction schedules, for virtually all of Soviet history; that there are places available for only a small proportion of children in the relevant age group; and that most Soviet families — including a good many in which the wife is employed — have had to make their own private arrangements for the care of their preschool children. The number of public dining establishments, calculated to save women from wasting time slaving in the kitchen, shows only a modest growth from 1935 to 1961. Similarly, facilities for dry cleaning and laundry services exist only in the larger cities, and even there they are in short supply.

A pitiable tone is found in the people's side of much of the discussion about Soviet services auxiliary to the family. Mothers have been complaining for decades that there is no room for their children in the crèche or kindergarten. There has also been some doubt that the use of those public dining establishments that are functioning does in fact save time for most diners, since delays and queues result from distance, inadequate transportation, and crowded conditions. In addition, investigations of complaints about public dining halls usually have revealed that prices are high and quality low.

When these facts are studied in conjunction with the sparse and poorly organized retail-trade apparatus and the great shortages, until quite recently, of household durables such as refrigerators, washers, and vacuum sweepers, it becomes clear that running a home and organizing family life continue to be very demanding activities in the USSR. Indeed, the estimate, made in 1964, that only about 5 per cent of the household work of Soviet women is done by service enterprises and institutions stimulates some amazement that the proportion of employed women has been as high as it is. The situation can be summed up as follows: "The trouble is not only that we still have few such enterprises and institutions. It should not be forgotten that all these services are still very expensive, and many women 'prefer' to spend their own time." [16]

If large numbers of women still participate as regular members of the labor force under such unpromising circumstances, it is in full knowledge of the fact that they must also somehow see to it that food is brought, meals prepared, dishes washed, house cleaned, laundry taken care of, children looked after, and so on. As Lenin pointed out, it would be fair and desirable if Soviet husbands were to lend a hand, but, unfortunately, Soviet men have been slow to take up dishpan and diaper. An observer of the prewar scene states that housework done by men "is rarely seen. Almost all the housework lies on the shoulders of women. I never saw a man wash clothing or wash dishes. A husband can only chop and carry wood. But all the rest is done by the woman" (67 B(s) 19). A 1960 letter published in the Moscow daily *Sovetskaia Rossiia* makes the same point. Four angry factory worker wives and mothers complain that in the factory: "We work like our husbands often in the same shop . . . But in the home the duties are unequally divided . . . And when you ask a husband to help, the answer is always the same: 'Do you want me to do a woman's work? Why, the neighbors would laugh at me'." [17]

Recent Soviet studies of patterns of household activity have analyzed time budgets of husbands and wives. Comparisons made with studies done in the 1920's of worker families show that in redistribution of household tasks some of the childcare and shopping, in particular, are being gradually shifted to the husbands of employed wives.[18] The process is very slow, however, and such analyses invariably report that men still are sleeping longer and enjoying more free time than women.

A sociological study of Leningrad working-class couples in which both spouses are employed does not give an encouraging picture. Out of the sample of 160 families the housework is done by an older mother or mother-in-law in 26, by the wife with the help of the husband in 48, by the wife with the help of children or some other family member in 17, and by the wife alone in 69 of the families.[19] Thus, when the working wife is chiefly responsible for the housework (with no older female relative present), the cases in which no assistance is offered outnumber those in which it is. From the analysis of several such studies in the years preceding 1961 the following generalizations emerged: A woman with a family who also has a job will be busy for three more hours per day than the fulltime housewife, will have two hours per day less time for self-education, reading, entertainment and rest, and one and one-half hours less sleep.[20]

Within this context the motives for working expressed by Soviet wives and mothers are so various and complex that exhaustive detailing of all of them is not feasible. However, a distinctively Soviet pattern can perhaps be established. To begin, a forty-six-year-old cashier in a savings bank explains that she worked because: "I had to . . . I was forced to work because the rate of pay of my husband was insufficient" (442 B 4, 5). If economic need finds no rival for first place, a strong second would be occupied by career interest, or what might better be called the intrinsic satisfaction of work. A schoolteacher tells of her life: "Having completed my course, I immediately started to work and worked all the time . . . [How did your husband look upon the fact that you worked?] He approved. [Why?] He liked to have me work. Money was needed. [If you had had enough money would you also have worked?] Yes. Just the same. I can't live without work" (627 B 4, 5).

Career interest is often accompanied by distaste for housework, but the latter is so prominent a factor in the thinking of Soviet women that it should be counted a separate motive. A woman who was a teacher doubtless expresses what is on the minds of a good many of the 52 per cent of Soviet professional workers who are women: "I wanted to get away from the hard, thankless work at home. With my pay I could have been able to hire a house worker" (483 B 4). Sometimes Soviet husbands are sympathetic: "I approved. I consider that the state of affairs when a woman is only a wife and housewife is past. There is even something humiliating in the idea of a woman being just a wife" (131 B 8). But sometimes they are not; an engineer recounts an extreme case of difference in views between himself and wife: "She was really more interested in the work outside the home, since she did not like housework. Also, in opposition to my attitude, she loved to engage in the unpaid Soviet political work and to frequent the obligatory meetings that each industry scheduled almost every other day after work, while I tried to get out of them" (430 B 7).

The first three themes may be termed "material interest," "career interest," and "dislike of housework," and the fourth may be called "service to society." The daughter of an engineer and husband of a film operator says: "I wanted to be of some use to society, and I did not wish to close myself only within the interests of the family" (116 B 4). This motivational theme corresponds to the officially desired reason for work, and by all reports is widely shared, especially in the younger generations.

The fifth and final basic motive is the desire for personal independence and security. "You know that you cannot count on marrying and living on the earnings of the husband. You saw how insecure a man's position was. He could be arrested at any time, and therefore every woman wanted to get a profession besides getting married" (501 A 5). Even the well-to-do had to consider this problem. An army colonel says that though he liked his "bourgeois family life," it also made him uneasy: "I felt that earning everything and having my wife earn nothing made her exceptionally and completely dependent upon me for her material welfare. She did not work and had no special skill. What would she have done without me? What job could she have gotten?" (72 B 5)

The distribution of these motivational themes by social class level provides insight into the spirit with which different families contemplate feminine employment. The first is by far the most common reason advanced by working-class women. In their greater need and eagerness to earn, they think little about the interest of the work, being of use to society, and so on. Of course, the nature of the work which they do may also have a hand in this reaction. Refugee responses to a question about job satisfaction while in the USSR showed that women with professional or other skills were generally much more satisfied with their work than those who had unskilled or semi-skilled jobs.[21] Probably both the job specifications and a status aspect are important. In the words of a thirty-year-old semiskilled factory worker, "for a woman in general, it is better to work in an office as an employee [sluzhashchi] than in a factory" (93 A 36).

In the upper-status group women work mainly because of career interest, service to society, and dislike of housework, while in the middle class of Soviet society, where the husbands are lower white-collar and upper-level skilled workers, none of these themes seems salient. This is one of the reasons for reasonably suspecting that women in the middle class are least likely to be employed outside the home. Their material need is only moderate, and they lack the educational training and background to develop strong vocational interests.

Reproduction and Childcare Institutions

The decline in the Soviet birth rate has been drastic, one of the most rapid in history, dropping from 44.3 per thousand in 1928 to 24.9 in 1960. In a country with a bare half of the population living in urban areas the most recent crude birth rate has been lower than that of the much more heavily urbanized United States. Important regional and residential differences in themselves suggest the extent to which the family is in tune with the conditions furnished by the larger social order; the birth rate in cities is lower than in the countryside — in 1962 20.0 compared with a rural rate of 24.9 — and there are significant differences among the union republics, with the Baltic republics low, Kazakhstan, Central Asian and Transcaucasian republics high, and the Belorussian, Ukrainian, and Russian (RSFSR) republics in between but somewhat below the national average.[22] The most outstanding fact by far, however, has been the over-all downward tendency of Soviet fertility.

TABLE 5. Births per thousand by age group, 1938–39, 1960–61.

Age group	Births per thousand	
	1938–39	1960–61
15–24	121.4	119.1
25–29	230.6	160.7
30–34	183.5	110.0
35–39	131.7	60.7
40–44	68.1	23.5
45–49	19.0	4.8

Source: Central Statistical Office of USSR, as reported in United Nations, *Provisional Report*, p. 189.

Table 5 reveals the basic pattern. The rate for the youngest age group has changed little from the prewar years, but among women past twenty-four it has fallen drastically. For women thirty and more in 1960 the difference is a result partly of the lowered sex ratio associated with the war and the fact that many women have had no husbands. For the age group 15–29, however, it would seem that another factor is at work, namely, the tendency to have fewer babies, and to have them earlier.

Behind the over-all trend stand two important factors: first, the huge population losses and the breakup or separation of families suffered during the mankilling crises and frenetic mobility of the Soviet era; and second, the countless individual decisions to restrict births made by the husbands and wives of intact families. Circumstance, an involuntary factor, and voluntary birth restriction have worked together, and it is hard to separate the relative influence of each. Clearly, though, the small family of one or two children has become a strongly entrenched cultural ideal in the Soviet urban environment and is well on its way to acceptance in the villages as well.

One of the most eloquent statements of this ideal, printed in the USSR in the mid-1920's, is by one Nina Velt, who wrote an "open letter to Comrade Smidovich" in connection with the latter's opinions about the proper norms of sexual behavior and childbirth: "When the new base is laid, then the relations of the sexes will be wonderful. That is true. But what do you say one ought to do while waiting for the 'new base'? . . . Frequent abortions cripple the woman. Perfectly incontestable. But what do frequent births do to women? Look around you, and you will understand us. Further. The average monthly wage of a worker is 50–60 rubles. On that sum he can rear one child well, or two worse. Following the advice of Smidovich our worker would have had four after the Revolution. Half a hundred is enough for that family not to die from hunger, but it is not enough to live on. It will give weak, sick, good-for-nothing children . . . instead of two workers the Soviet country will get four invalids. And with four children a woman simply cannot work." [23] Since urban living standards were to decline even more during the subsequent twenty-five years, one can appreciate why the views of Nina Velt were to become ever more widespread.

In the countryside the trend was in the same direction. The peasant masses, called upon by Stalin to bear the heavy cost of rapid industrialization, were forced to the very margin of existence. Among them, and among the unskilled laborers whose lot was scarcely better, the source of a decline in fertility was very obvious. An unskilled worker tells of his life: "We did not have enough food and clothing . . . I went to work hungry and returned hungry and at home there was nothing to eat, but the children don't understand and beg for something to eat" (299 B 2).

Hardship is a relative matter, of course, and as one rises in the social class hierarchy, it merges with such factors as new conceptions of a proper living standard, the contradiction between a woman's occupational interests and childbearing, and higher aspirations for the children themselves. Soviet husbands and wives are quite ready with explanations of why they have small families. A worker compares what he lived through as a child with what he wanted: "We had seen what kind of a life our parents had with a large family and so did not want one ourselves" (614 B 8). An engineer, forty-six, risen from the peasantry and married to a woman with a higher education, observes: "Well, the families with many children, as it used to be, are not possible any more. We cannot tear the woman away from politics, from the cultural and productive role. She must have a choice" (26 A 52). A bookkeeper stresses the importance, and the difficulty, of assuring children a proper start in life: "I would have liked one more, but in Soviet reality it would be too great a luxury. I was afraid that I would not be able to provide acceptable upbringing and education" (8 B 9).

Along with these main themes — hardship, the new opportunities for women, and higher aspirations for the children themselves — a minor though still important factor is the housing shortage. It serves to restrict not only births but marriages, as seen through the eyes of a young engineer from a peasant background: "I knew that I could not get married because my pay was too low to allow for the creation of a new family. Anyway, I knew I would not be able to find an apartment" (29 A 61).

Under some conditions hardship and insecurity can lead to the desire for more rather than fewer children. Even though the trend toward fewer children is striking, and the change from the old pattern rapid, there are still large families in Soviet Russia, although not so many as in the United States. At the beginning of World War II, for instance, the annual number of fifth-order or higher births was in the neighborhood of 200,000, smaller by 43 per cent than in the United States.[24]

Soviet policy on the birth rate has varied greatly over the years. Until 1935 it was determined by the ideology of freedom and equality for women, by open recognition of difficult material living conditions, and by the hope that the state would somehow be able to take over child-rearing. After 1935 the desire to halt the downward trend in the birth rate and the decision to rehabilitate the legitimacy of parenthood and family life became important. Since the general orientations and policy of the regime have already been discussed, here we shall focus upon the details and upon how the people have reacted. Two main issues will be discussed: the extent to which direct benefits and indirect auxiliary institutions have been influential in changing intentions, and the patterns by which the people have practiced birth restriction.

According to the 1936 law, monetary benefits to mothers began only with the birth of the seventh child. Since six is a large number of children to have before receiving any compensation, this is best interpreted as a welfare measure rather than as an incentive to bear more children. The law of 1944 went much further, and even though the original scale of benefits was reduced by 50 per cent in 1947, the payments are still substantial. They begin with a lump sum of 20 rubles upon the birth of the third child and increase with the birth of each subsequent child up to 250 rubles, which is paid for the birth of the eleventh and all additional children. There are also monthly payments ranging from 4 rubles for the fourth child to 15 rubles per month for the eleventh and each subsequent child. These monthly payments are given to the mother from the first birthday of the child to the fifth, a period of four years. State assistance to unmarried mothers is more generous and is paid until the child reaches twelve years of age.

The monetary increment brought to a married mother by the arrival of an extra child is not inconsequential when seen in terms of the average annual wage. From 1944 to 1947, in fact, if family allowances are taken together with exemptions from income and the bachelors' and small-family taxes, grants for the fourth child amounted to 30 per cent of the average annual wage and for the eleventh child, 98 per cent. Since such mothers probably have additional young children for whom they are receiving grants at the same time, the awards could easily have come to more than the mother could have earned in outside employment.[25]

After 1947, when the benefits were reduced by 50 per cent, and in subsequent years as the annual wage level continued to rise, the significance of such grants as a birth incentive declined. In addition, tax reductions already made or in prospect for those who have fewer than three children further reduce the effect upon the incentive to bear children intended by the tax structure set up during World War II. In addition to direct grants and tax preference, employed women who have raised five or more children to the age of eight are entitled to earlier retirement with pension. Similarly, large families receive reductions in nursery-school and kindergarten fees. For families with four or more children the latter are reduced by 50 per cent, for families with three children and income of less than eight hundred rubles by 35 per cent, and so on.[26]

Moreover, for whatever importance it may have, Soviet women with large numbers of children continue to receive favorable publicity and medals for their performance. These latter range from the Medal of Motherhood, Second Degree, for bearing and raising five children, to the Mother Heroine medal awarded for bearing and rearing ten. The awards are given when the last child reaches eighteen. In the period from July 1944 through 1960, the Medal of Motherhood was won by 3,466,000 women, and the title and medal Mother Heroine by 65,000 Soviet women. The average number per year has fallen, however, from one decade to the next. In the period from July 1944 through 1949 there was an average of 260,727 mothers per year who became holders of the Medal of Motherhood and 5,636 Mother Heroines, while in the eleven years from 1950 through 1960 the corresponding yearly averages fell to 184,727 and 3,091.[27] These figures reflect the falling birth rate discussed earlier.

Although there is no way to disentangle the incentive effect of Soviet natal policy from the other factors influencing fertility, the incentive has probably been too small to alter substantially the plans of urban families. For the peasantry, who have traditionally been paid in kind on the collective farms and have therefore often needed money badly, the policy may sometimes have served as an effective inducement.

To the extent that childbearing is a planned activity, Soviet parents are also likely to take account of the extent and adequacy of facilities for daytime child care. The crèche or nursery [iaslia] cares for infants of two months to the age of three years and the kindergarten [detski sad] for children from three to seven years of age. In 1959 it was decided to unify the two into a combined form, to be called nursery-kinder-gartens [iasli-sady], but of course it will be some time before the change-over is completed. In the villages nurseries tend usually to be organized on a seasonal basis, providing child care during the busy summer months. Summer playgrounds are also important in the countryside.

For school-age children relatively recent innovations are the boarding school [*shkola internat*] and the prolonged-day school, introduced in 1956 and 1960 respectively. As the name suggests, the children live at the former on a virtual full-time basis and have a visiting relationship with their parents. Children from broken, inadequate, or very large families with insufficient means have received priority and predominate in the boarding schools. In the prolonged-day schools the children rejoin their parents at home for the evening.

These institutions, corresponding closely to the official ideal of public or collectivist childrearing, are widely advertised as benefiting both child and parents, especially working mothers, and there is some evidence that they are gaining acceptance, if not popularity, among the population. The younger generation of Soviet parents, in particular, seem to favor the idea; as one observer reports, there are long waiting lists for every available space.[28] On the other hand, there is still considerable doubt about the more radical innovation, the boarding school. Hindus, a seasoned observer, states that "except for mothers of large families who are poor and live in crowded quarters, women, whether shop workers or college graduates, do not speak well of the plan. Overwhelmingly they do not want to be separated from their sons and daughters at the age of seven, even if they come home for the weekends and holidays." [29]

Under the existing admission priority policy it is likely that many Soviet parents are influenced by dislike of the disturbed, low-status nature of many members of the student bodies in the boarding schools, which would reinforce resistance based on the traditional feeling that children should be reared at home. Thus, the simpler, less ambitious, and less expensive prolonged-day school will probably become an ever more serious rival of the boarding school, and perhaps eventuate as the standard solution to the problems of busy Soviet parents.

Until the present time the most important fact for our purposes about such childcare institutions, for both school-age and preschool groups, is their relatively small number. At the height of their development in the prewar period there were facilities for only some 800,00 or 900,000 children in permanent nurseries and slightly over 1,000,000 children in kindergartens. In the early postwar years the number that could be served in such facilities dropped markedly, but by the early 1950's the prewar level had been recovered. In recent years the number has increased at a steady rate, but as of 1960, preschool institutions enrolled no more than about 14 per cent of the eligible age group on a permanent basis, with another 8 per cent or 9 per cent in the summer season. Data corroborating this fact, and showing the trend downward and back up during the 1940–1960 period are shown in Table 6.

That such institutions have been in short supply is suggested by scholarly studies, by recurrent complaints of employed mothers, and by the priorities accorded among applicants. One of these priorities has been family composition, with mothers without husbands receiving first choice. It is also likely that the imposition of financial charges for use of nurseries, kindergartens, and similar institutions has been dictated in part by the discrepancy between the small supply and heavy demand.

In any case, it has not been possible for prospective Soviet parents to feel assured that the state would without question support and rear any children they might produce, and the great majority of Soviet children are still brought up at home, by their mothers and grandmothers. Thus, childcare facilities have not yet, at least, proved themselves as an effective device for the liberation of the working mother from the responsibility of child care and probably have not exerted any significant influence on the birth rate.

All the evidence points to the likelihood that two other aspects of Soviet natal policy have been much more important, the supply and quality of contraceptive devices and contraceptive information and the situation in respect to abortion. Both the regime and the majority of the population have been ambivalent about those factors. Contraceptive devices have been manufactured and sold since the 1920's, but both the quantity and quality have been inadequate. In 1928, for instance, it was reported that the average value of the monthly sale of them came to only 1,700 rubles.[30] Thirty years later, the Ministry of Public Health of the USSR asserted that Soviet contraceptives were lacking in variety, reliability, and quantity. So far as can be ascertained, only two devices have been put into mass production, condoms and vaginal suppositories, and it is likely that the latter were first brought out in the post-World War II years. However, perhaps in connection with the re-legalization of abortion in 1955, official interest in contraceptives now seems to be increasing. A campaign has been undertaken to encourage the use of contraception as a substitute for abortion, the first All-Union Conference on Contraception was held in 1959, and considerable research is said to be under way.[31]

Though new devices may be introduced in the future, in the past

TABLE 6. Soviet childcare facilities auxiliary to the family.

Facility	Eligible ages (years)	Number accommodated or enrolled (thousands)			Number in eligible age group, 1960[a] (thousands)	Percentage accommodated, 1960
		1940	1950	1960		
Permanent nurseries	0–2.9[b]	859.5	776.7	1402.2[c]	14,500[d]	9.8
Kindergartens	3–6.9	1171.5	1168.8	2973.1[c]	19,100	15.6
Combined nursery-kindergartens	0–6.9[b]	—	—	359.0	33,600[d]	1.1
Boarding schools	7–17.9	—	—	540.0	39,100	1.4
Extended school-day programs	7–14.9	—	—	525.0	32,700	1.6
Seasonal nurseries	0–2.9[b]	4049.1	1813.1	1228.5[e]	14,500[d]	8.5
Summer playgrounds	3–6.9?	1175.1	983.6	1771.5[f]	19,100	9.3
Pioneer camps	7–17.9	—	2409.9	3571.0	39,100	9.1

Source: Ts. S. U., *Zhenshchiny i deti v USSR*, pp. 157, 158, 163, 207, 208; Bureau of the Census, *Projections*, p. 9; *Pravda*, December 21, 1960, as cited in Dodge, p. 90; DeWitt, p. 74.

a The 1961 figures are used because the year-by-year estimates are for January 1 and the enrollment figures usually refer to the year end.

b Begins with age two months.

c The figure given in Ts. S. U., *Zhenshchiny i deti v USSR* for number accommodated in kindergartens in 1960 (3,115,100) includes the 359,000 reported in combined nursery-kindergartens. Of these 359,000 children, 142,000 were under three. I have therefore added 142,000 to the figure given in that source for nurseries (1,260,200) and subtracted 142,000 from the figure for kindergartens.

d I subtracted 800,000 (my estimate of the number of children under two months) from the figure given in Ts. S. U., *Zhenshchiny i deti v USSR*.

e An estimate derived by subtracting the estimated number accommodated in summer playgrounds (1,771,500) from the total number of children accommodated in summer playgrounds and seasonal nurseries (3,000,000) as given in Ts. S. U., *Zhenshchiny i deti v USSR*.

f An estimate derived by adding to the figure cited in Ts. S. U., *Zhenshchiny i deti v USSR* for 1959 (1,553,700) the increase from 1958 to 1959 (217,800).

it appears that the Soviet people have had to rely heavily on *coitus interruptus,* douching, a variety of homemade devices, and, of course, abortion.[32]

Although abortion was declared illegal from 1936 to 1955, it continued to be performed, as it is elsewhere, by less scrupulous medical personnel in the cities and by the peasant midwives in the villages: "In the village the abortions were performed by the simple village women thrusting a cobbler's needle into the womb and by other primitive methods" (422 B 9).

Since 1955 abortions have been legal in the USSR, costing nothing if certified for therapeutic reasons and a small fee if they are "artificial" — that is, performed simply because the pregnant woman requests them. When approached by Western visitors, Soviet doctors are inclined to claim that abortion rates have fallen in the years since 1955, that the "overwhelming majority" of applicants are married women who already have several children, that abortion outside hospitals has been virtually eliminated, and that abortions are greatly outnumbered by live births (the Maces being told, for instance, that in one Kiev hospital there were 800 abortions compared to 3,500 live births in 1959).[33]

In fact, however, it is likely that none of these assertions is entirely true, a position which finds mild support in some Soviet publications on the subject. One study, published in 1963, cites abortion rates for women of productive age as 106 per 1,000 for those working and 42 for those not employed — a level high enough to persuade a Western analyst that the number of abortions must be roughly equivalent to the number of live births.[34] In another Soviet publication abortion figures by age groups were released by the Leningrad City Health Department for the year 1958. Approximately 20 per cent in the group receiving abortions were twenty-four years old or less, and most of these were not married, which suggests (as the Soviet writer wishes to stress) that numerous seekers of abortion are unmarried women without any children.[35] Finally, from time to time it is reported in the Soviet press that it is still considered shameful to conceive outside marriage, especially when marriage is not likely.[36] Since hospital abortions are likely to be much more a matter of common knowledge, it is not improbable that illegal abortions will continue to be sought by Soviet unmarried women who cherish their reputations.

Of all activities sexual intercourse is furthest removed from official control. Many of the attitudes that influence it stem from deep religious and sex-role attitudes. The peasantry still reveal a strong tendency to look upon the arrival of children as natural or as the will of God and to repeat the dictum, "God gives children, God will give wherewith to keep them." Hence they have neither interest in nor knowledge of contraception, and abortion is seen as an even greater transgression against God's will.[37] There is also some indication of a relatively strong emphasis on exclusively feminine responsibility in these matters. "It is purely the woman's concern," seems to be a widespread view among Soviet men.[38] The heavy dependence on abortion as a means of birth control is probably determined as much by this cultural factor as by the inadequacy of manufactured contraceptive devices.

Many of these attitudes persist in the countryside, and also among the recent immigrants into the cities. The difference in viewpoint is stressed by a worker who was himself a recent arrival: "The peasants are ignorant and uneducated people and they seldom knew what measures one should take to have fewer children. The peasant considers that if you sleep with your wife then you must have a child. But the town dweller knew what to undertake in such cases" (299 B 11). The general trend toward more awareness and sophistication — as well as several other themes — is clear in the account of a working-class woman who was married in 1935 at the age of twenty-three: "We could buy them [contraceptive devices] in the drug store. [Could you always get them there?] Yes. Always. I don't know about later, after we left [1943]. [Were they expensive?] No. [Then poor people could buy them?] Yes. But there were some people who did not even know that there were such things. One of our neighbors did not even know that there were such things. She was a little older than I was. Now of course all the young people know, but sometimes the older people did not. I think that now everyone knows. Everything was so free before. Now, even the children must know. [What kind of contraceptives were used?] Made of rubber, for men. Of course, some people may not know about them or not know where to get them or they may be ashamed to ask for them. It makes you uncomfortable to let someone else know about such things" (49 B 40–41).

On the other hand, the account furnished by a German participant-observer of a mine inspector in a workers settlement in the Donbass and his three young children throws doubt upon the idea that "everyone knows" and also suggests the helpless feeling many in the population must share: "The husband would have been happy not to have had any children. He sought information from the observer about the possibilities of contraception, a matter of which he was largely ignorant. For example, he thought that the blowing of air into the vagina with an air pump was the surest method. Abortion was too expensive for him" (Bi 204). When it is illegal, abortion is more expensive and therefore less accessible to those families who are likely to need it most. Conceivably the legalization of abortion in 1955, like the abolition of tuition charges for secondary and higher education, was in part directed toward the elimination of this patent class discrimination.

Social-class differences in the USSR in rates of reproduction parallel the experience of other countries: the higher the class level of the family, the fewer the children; Table 7 furnishes some official corroboration. The

TABLE 7. Number of children in family, by socio-economic group.
(in per cent)

| Socio-economic group | Number of children | | | |
	One	Two	Three	Four or more
White collar employees	52	38	8	2
Industrial workers	48	38	11	3
Collective farmers	43	32	17	8

Source: Ts. S. U., Zhenshchiny i deti v USSR, p. 88. The data are from budget studies from a sample of families having children under sixteen, as of June 1960. Percentages total 100 horizontally.

differences are not large, which may in part be the result of the nature of the sample, but they do indicate the extent to which birth limitation and the small family have become prevalent in the villages. The typical Soviet family, it appears, includes only one child. The class differences are the result of a great number of factors: later age at marriage, the presence of goals that children would hinder the parents in achieving, differences in emotional discipline, and the better chances of the higher status group to engage in birth control. In the refugee family sample, for instance, one member of the Soviet intelligentsia reported that his wife used a diaphragm of the "best foreign manufacture." A class difference in the conditions facilitating effective contraception is also suggested by the only technique which was more prominently reported in nonmanual than in working-class families, vaginal douching.[39] Both the privacy and the water supply were privileges of their class position.

Shaping the Family to Meet the New Conditions

Economic needs have exerted a weighty influence upon the composition of the Soviet family. As industrial urbanism came to Russia, the great mobility of the individual and the small family pattern favored by the modern industrial order have made it difficult to maintain the traditional kinship associations of the peasant way of life. The separation of relatives has been further increased by war, political misfortune, and various legal devices whose effect, if not intent, has been to further the emergence of a family centered in the work responsibilities of the main wage or salary earner. The new order has clashed most strikingly with the cultures of the Kazakhs and certain of the Central Asian peoples whose traditional way of life was organized in the patriarchal clan system. Correspondingly, their resistance to individual and small family mobility — the breaking of residential ties with kin — has been strongest and census data show that they still have the largest families.

Among the Slavs there has never been a solidary and corporate kin group but, rather, that loose assemblage known to ethnographers as the bilateral kindred. The consciousness of solidarity and the sense of group identity, for this reason, have long been centered mainly upon the families with which each individual has been immediately concerned in his daily life, his parental family and his conjugal family. Consequently, the coming of individual geographical mobility has not been particularly upsetting to the great majority of the population.

In addition, the severity of economic conditions in the nineteenth century and the traditional concentration of loyalty as much upon the household work group as upon the family proper prepared the people for the new arrangements which were inaugurated under the Soviet system. Moreover, moving away from kinfolk has become associated with education, interesting work with good pay, a generally better and more enlightened way of life. Even in the village it has come to be accepted as normal. A young collective farmer and soldier says: "Most of the children already try to make a better life for themselves. They don't go along the old track but live in their own way. They don't know any other way" (514 A). Furthermore, while mobility is great, some ties with relatives are usually retained.[40]

Nonetheless, among those who remain behind in the village, according to the older residents of Viriatino, ties among kinfolk are weaker and more narrowly defined today than they were in the past. For example, second- and even third-degree relatives formerly were invited to participate in weddings, whereas today the circle of kin is much more narrow, and a greater proportion of those involved are not even kinfolk, but work associates from the kolkhoz.[41]

The radical change in the organization of land ownership and work on the kolkhoz has induced other patterns which invite comparison with those of the past. In pre-collectivization days patrilocal residence was the preferred form in most of Russia. One of the sons of the family — usually the youngest, although the rule was not strict — lived with and took care of the aged parents.[42] Patrilocal residence was one of the strongest supports of the traditional male sex preference, for sons were a clear asset and daughters a liability. As an old peasant said: "The family of the daughter is another family. But with a son, that is one and the same family, with one and the same name" (624 B 5).

The residence pattern today, now that the economic basis for patrilocality has disappeared, is much more a question of expediency. As the comments of one old worker-peasant suggest, a primary factor is the tendency of young men from the kolkhozes to lack interest in staying around the village. He explained where the children live when they grow up: "Whoever can find a place lives separately, and if he can find no other place then he lives together with the parents. [Is there any such custom today as there was before collectivization?] No. None. The children grow up and fly away in all directions, like birds. There are cases when neither son wants to stay. So they both fly away" (279 B 17–18, 20). Living separately is often desirable to young couples, but tradition remains strong, and in Viriatino it is typical that a married couple lives with parents, almost always the husband's. In 1955 in Viriatino 77 daughters-in-law resided with the husbands' families, but only 4 out of the total of 456 families included sons-in-law, and 3 of these involved widows who were listed in the village soviet as heads of families. However, it is considered a new phenomenon to take in the widowed mother of the wife.[43]

Thus, traces of the past exist as well as changes. Another example of the former is found today in the fact that among the peasantry a widowed daughter-in-law almost never lives with her husband's parents. After her husband's death she usually returns to her own parents, just as in pre-Soviet times, a reflection of her inferior position in the family of her husband: "The daughter-in-law was always an alien for the family and continued to maintain close ties with her own parents, especially with the mother." [44] In standard practice of former times the patrilocal residence pattern brought the young bride into an already functioning household where she was assigned the most menial and unskilled tasks. The mother-in-law, for example, always prepared the food, and the daughter-in-law was the cleaner of the floor. The young wife could easily come under the oppression as well as the supervision of her husband's mother. Her dependent, helpless position is expressed well by the advice offered in a Viriatino proverb: "Do the work you're told to do; eat what you're given to eat." [45]

Similarly, the title "head-of-family" continues to exist, though Soviet law recognizes only the concept "head of kolkhoz household," a position restricted to an active worker who represents the family in the kolkhoz council. In thirty-two of thirty-four families in Viriatino with an old father present, although no longer the organizer of economic activities or dispenser of property, and not even an effective worker, he was looked upon as head of the family. All are aware that his title is merely a formality; the peasants state that the father's position as "head," even if very old and entirely unable to work, is maintained "out of respect for the old man, out of desire to avoid hurting him." [46]

As noted, the predominant trend among the collective farm population is toward smaller families. The pace of change has been augmented by the policy of allocating a special plot of land for personal use to each kolkhoz household. Such plots have been badly needed and much cherished, and consequently, the policy serves as a strong incentive to divide up into separate households. In effect, the fewer kin-related adults in a given household, the more land the kinsman can dispose of, and the more land the better their economic situation. In Viriatino, the widow of the combat soldier T. M. Kalmykovski, lives separately from her old father, a kolkhoz worker, but they work jointly the two plots allocated to them, maintain a cow together, and receive their workday proceeds from the kolkhoz in common. In this case it is likely that the households are divided only in the sense that the widow and her father live in separate places (and thus are entitled to two plots), and it also seems likely that receiving entitlement to the extra plot was a major factor in their decision to live separately. The ethnographers report many examples of this kind of arrangement in Viriatino[47] but do not explain whether the people in such households also take meals separately and otherwise carry on as individual households.

An unusual case of a seasonally alternating household pattern is furnished by another Viriatino family: "In the family of stable hand B, with many children, his mother-in-law, an old woman, has her own house and plot and is considered an independent proprietress. For the winter she lives with her daughter's family, helping with the household work and in looking after the children. In the summer, since she must work her garden plot, she moves to her own house" (Ku 209).

In the urban family the main problem has been the organization of family life to maximize income and also maintain a reasonably adequate home. The two types of household organization which seem most uniquely Soviet are essentially responses to this same requirement. Though the two patterns are quite different, both permit husband and wife to remain at work without undue discomfort. In the first type the "loss of functions" is maximized, and there is, for instance, virtually no cooking done. Many childless couples are included in this category, but even some families with children take the main meal of the day at places of work or school in the early afternoon, as is the Soviet custom. In such cases breakfast is usually a frugal one, at home, and supper is more frequently eaten by the family as a group in public restaurants.

In the second pattern the traditional functions are retained, but they are performed by someone other than the wife. Of these additions to the family, the most usual is the grandmother, in the villages more often the husband's mother and in the cities either the husband's or the wife's mother. A government official tells that in his family of six, with three employed, it was his mother-in-law who did the cooking, had charge of the money, and chased after the food. The arduous nature of the last task is suggested by the fact that all were involved in some measure: "This important and thankless duty lay mostly upon my wife's mother, but all members of the family tried to show initiative and cleverness — to buy as cheaply as possible, or to get something by *blat* [informal connections and mutual favors]" (131 B 3). Another typical case is described by an engineer: "With me lived only my wife's mother. She was most useful. She educated the children. She taught her daughter things, that is, how to behave and do things better" (381 B 2). In the present kolkhoz family, when there are old folks present, a similar division of labor is found. In Viriatino, if the grandfather and grandmother are able they are also likely to have full responsibility for the individual plot.[48]

Between the two types of urban households already described lie many other varieties of arrangement. Many upper-class families utilize the services of full- or part-time domestic help. As we have noted, in many families all the adults are women. Of course, many couples with and without children live alone — without grandmothers, aunts, or village-girl servants. If preschool children are present they are cared for by the mother if she does not work, or during working hours by a crèche or nursery school.

In addition to the needs and welfare of the conjugal family, with or without children, another factor has contributed to the shaping of the Soviet family. In a society where hardship has been common, the aged have been particularly vulnerable. Until quite recently old-age-security benefits have been minimal and "homes" for the old few and meager. Here is one description of a low point, by an eye witness: "The position of the old people is desperate. No one wants them, there is no one to take care of them. Until 1937, there was no old people's home in Kherson. Old people went around like beggars, and they died like flies. Finally the municipal administration organized a home which had places for forty old people, but this is just a drop in the bucket as it takes care of only a tiny part of those who need help" (1705 A 39–40).

In the face of such conditions, the younger generation often simply had no choice; either the old folks had to be taken in or let starve. Historically the fate of the aged has varied directly with the living standard as a whole. It is understandable that old age in Soviet Russia became a time of great psychological anxiety. One man, a sixty-five-year-old white-collar worker, stated that in prewar times the thought of old age and loss of work capacity "filled us with horror." He continued: "We could not count on our son, because we thought that he might himself have a family which he would be barely able to support. The pension which people receive after so many years of work may suffice only for 2 or 3 weeks' existence in a semistarved condition, possibly one month, but it does not assure a living minimum" (71 B 6).

More frequently, perhaps, parents were optimistic about the supportive ability of their children, especially if they had more than one child. An unskilled worker's joy in his children is clearly linked with his fears for the future, an association which suggests a strong element of continuity with the peasant patterns of the past. His feelings also furnish a reason why the Soviet birth rate has not fallen even more precipitously: "It was a great joy to us that we had two of our own, a daughter born in 1921 and a son born in 1923. We had great hopes that they would take care of us when we would not be able to work any more" (124 B 7).

The main burden of the support of the aged, in consequence, has lain primarily upon the individual offspring and his family. This legal responsibility has been reinforced by the traditional cultural pattern. As a worker observed, "A mother is a mother. She fed us; we should feed her" (213 B 17) — but, unfortunately, the children's ability has not always corresponded with the natural desire and the legal liability. The lot of the aged has been a particularly unhappy one among the more deprived strata of the population; they have suffered from want and neglect, even while their children stood by in despair, unable to help them. An unskilled worker commented: "Some of them want to help but they marry and get children. They want to help, but they can't. They may weep; they want to help their father and mother, but they cannot. There is no way to do it" (270 B 21).

Among urban and semiurban families the shortage of housing space has often contributed an additional obstacle to the discharge of this obligation. It is among this sector of the Soviet people, too, that legal responsibility for the support of aged parents becomes a live force. The judgment of a son with a family of his own to support as to how much he can afford toward the maintenance of parents is likely to be of uncertain reliability, especially if the distance separating them diminishes the sense of urgency. A worker speaking of his own family in the late 1930's explained why his brother refused to contribute to their aged mother's support: "He lived far away, and he was a little stuck on himself, but she brought him into court and so we all paid, but he lived far away and he only paid when he saw her. We lived closer to her and we often brought her things. She called him a bastard [sukin syn]. [The respondent got a big laugh out of this.] She brought him into court, and the judge asked her, 'How many sons do you [ty] have?' 'Six,' she answered. Then he said, 'Then that will be 25 rubles from each of them. Is that enough for you [tebia]?' She said, 'Why must you do that to all of them?' The judge said, 'Well, if one of them won't pay you, maybe the others won't. So each must pay you 25 rubles a month' "

(213 B 16–17). To this relatively fortunate woman, whose sons were overtaken by Soviet justice, must be compared an unknown number of the less fortunate, who have sons both less dutiful and more elusive.

Such phenomena are now probably a thing of the past for that portion of the Soviet population falling within the social security system. The official Soviet concept of social security is expressed in article 120 of the 1936 Constitution: "Citizens of the Union of Soviet Socialist Republics have the right to maintenance in old age and also in the case of sickness or disability. This right is ensured by the extensive development of social insurance of industrial, office, and professional workers at state expense, free medical service for the working people, and the provision of a wide network of health resorts for the use of the working people."

Until 1956 this "right to maintenance" was essentially a dead issue, or at best a supplement rather than a source of support. In 1956, with considerable fanfare, the Soviet government made a virtue out of what had been a most pressing need by revising the pension system. The new statutory minimum was 300 rubles per month, a figure that at least approached what was needed to carry on an independent life. The maximum was 1,200, considerably higher than the current average wage. How inadequate the benefit rates had become before this revision is shown in the official statement that the 1956 law raised the minimum level sixfold. It was, in fact, the first change in minimum or maximum (previously 50 and 300 rubles, respectively) since 1932,[49] despite the fact that the intervening period was one of constant inflation. For virtually the first time in Soviet history, some of the occupationally retired aged received the chance to live separately and without aid from their children's families.

It should be borne in mind, however, that the social security system covers only about half the population, and, of course, only those who have worked in the economy for extended periods. As of 1959 only 6,843,000, or 38 per cent of the 18,000,000 women in the USSR over the legal retirement age of fifty-five were receiving pensions. On the other hand, a *Pravda* article claimed in 1962 that the average magnitude of old-age pensions was 60 per cent of the average wage, considerably higher than that in other countries.[50] Collective farmers have been excluded from the national pension system and forced to depend on the mutual aid funds and practices of their particular kolkhoz. The extent of benefits for this large group of the population is likely to vary considerably from one kolkhoz to another.

The power to establish separate households and live independently has in recent years enabled Soviet old people to exercise more choice in how they spend their last years, and the evidence is that not a few are choosing to live separately. On the other hand, when pregnancy occurs, and if the mother or mother-in-law of one of the spouses is available, the rule seems to be that she will move in and help with the children. As a Moscow university student put it recently: "Soon my girl and I will be married, and we could count on a place of our own in four years, if I get the job I want. Then we would send for my mother and start the children." [51]

Thus, in the past, at least from the Revolution until the strengthening of the pension system, one of the most noteworthy characteristics of the Soviet family has been the extent to which a three-generation, extended form has been an effective adaptation to Soviet conditions. In the marketplace of mutually desired services it has been a good bargain; in exchange for a home, the aged have taken over, according to capacity, the functions left undone by the working wife and mother. In past years this arrangement has been such standard practice that it was defined as desirable. In the words of a worker: "It is good when both spouses work and have someone to do the laundry and cooking, etc." (43 B 9). All benefit from this arrangement, including the Soviet regime itself, which saved itself the expense for many years of becoming a true welfare state.

Perhaps Engels would not have approved, but the fact is that in the transition period the old folks took over in the Soviet family the functions that he felt were properly those of the socialist state, and the Soviet family often took over a function that he somehow completely overlooked, the care of the aged.

Fighting the Shortages

Whether "justifiable" in order to build communism or "outrageous," whether seen as permanent or as temporary — and all combinations of such views are found among the Soviet people — there is agreement that life has been economically hard, and hardship has long been a major orienting factor in family life. At a certain point the conditions which sustain and nourish the family became reduced to the simplest of categories — food, clothing, living space, and free time. Privation has been great in all these dimensions, but the latter two are particularly important because of their close connection with the chances for privacy, a social condition without which family life is crippled.

If the supply of dwellings is an important index of the people's prosperity, as Soviet writers sometimes claim, then it is no wonder that the housing problem has always ranked high in the list of reasons for lack of prosperity among the Soviet people. The figures in Table 8

TABLE 8. Urban population and living space.

Year	Urban population at end of year (in millions)	Total living space (in millions of sq. meters)	Per capita living space (in sq. meters)	Persons per room
1926	26.3	153.8	5.85	2.71
1940	59.2	242.1	4.09	3.91
1950	71.4	333.4	4.67	3.43
1960	108.3	622.7	5.75	2.78

Source: Adapted from Sosnovy, pp. 331–332. In 1960, United States per capita living space was nearly 18.6 square meters (200 square feet) and average density per room was about 0.60 persons.

are evidence that as millions of peasants moved into the cities, and as the drive for intensive economic development got under way, the attention given to housing lagged. The ratio of expenditures for housing construction to total capital investment during the period 1929–1950 was only about half of what it had been from 1918 to 1928. The trend in the 1930's toward deterioration and hardship was greatly accentuated by the massive destruction of the Second World War.

In consequence, most of the Soviet era has seen a steady decline in per capita living space in the cities, a trend that was reversed only toward 1950. Since then a higher rate of expenditure for construction of new housing has brought very slow improvement. It is most significant, however, that housing conditions in Soviet cities around the year 1960 were probably much the same as they were around 1926. In that year 65 per cent of Soviet urban families lived in one room or a part of one room and only 23.5 per cent had separate kitchens at their disposition. Thus, we may assume that throughout the Soviet period the typical Soviet urban family has lived in a single room and shared a kitchen.[52]

Moreover, it has become a byword that the Soviet people are busy. To the hours of the regular work week must be added those spent in extra-jobbing, obligatory meetings, travel back and forth from place of work, work in the garden after hours, and the daily chores of living. The last-named frequently assumes awesome proportions. Daily shopping, queueing for a turn in a communally shared kitchen, bringing up water from the basement, courtyard, or (in smaller towns) from a central well or water tower, searching for and hauling firewood or coal — all of these have been typical daily chores for Soviet families. Indeed, as indicated in Table 9, most families have had to do without

TABLE 9. Percentage of urban residents provided with municipal utilities.

	Year		
Utility	1927	1939	1956
Electric lighting	40.7	84.8	89.3
Running water	25.9	38.7	34.0
Plumbing	17.5	28.1	31.4
Central heating	na	11.1	22.4
Gas	na	na	15.6
Bath	na	7.5	8.9
Hot water	na	.7	2.2

Source: Adapted from Sosnovy, p. 337.

plumbing and running water, to say nothing of washing machines. Thus, bathing and the family laundry become major enterprises requiring much effort and time. Recent budget studies, moreover, have suggested that shopping in 1960 was taking up just as much time as it did in the year 1922.[53]

Although complaints about being constantly busy and overtired — giving a sense of perpetual harassment — were common among the refugees interviewed by the Harvard Project group, some of this stemmed from political insecurity. Although the political atmosphere has improved enormously since the death of Stalin, propaganda, agitation, and frequent campaigns have continued the pressure to build communism, both at work and during off hours. That the response from the people is not always positive is quite obvious, and not infrequently it is referred to in Soviet published sources. A good example is furnished by an anonymous letter writer, expressing what the reporting journalist calls "the philistine view of life": "I read articles. Old and constantly new problems about manliness, conscience, honor. Calls for public participation, to social duty! Indeed, what obligations are not placed upon tiny man . . . The fate of busy people is not a joyous one. Heroes are found more often in books than in life. Leave me the right to live in peace." [54]

It is in this light that the various decrees of the post-Stalin period shortening the workday must be seen. For example, in 1960 the Supreme Soviet adopted a law providing for a seven-hour (shorter in some categories such as underground mining) workday, which brought most Soviet workers close to a forty-hour workweek.[55] Such legislation is doubtless in great part a response to the great need long felt by members of Soviet families to give more attention to their daily needs, though a large number of inhibited needs are still to be met. One of the most important is the increasing amount of attention paid to children: although the time spent preparing food dropped from 1922 to 1960, the extra minutes released were spent on the care of children.[56]

These shortages have made the atmosphere of Soviet family life less attractive, both to those living in a family and to those contemplating it. For instance, some families that could have been formed have not been. A librarian from Kharkov whose husband died in 1927 explained: "The fact that I had a room to myself was one of the reasons I did not remarry, as I could not face the prospect of not being by myself at any time" (1106 A 22). A Ukrainian worker living in Kiev tells of the quarters of his family — himself, his wife, and two daughters: "[In 1939] we had one room and in this four people lived. In addition, our room was a hallway being used by people entering the room next to ours. This was the worst of all things in the Soviet Union — lodging. Everyone scolded and argued with each other because of these things. As a result of our living conditions the morale was extremely bad. Everyone feared for the children. Work for me was a relaxation. That was nothing. The difficulty was at home" (646 A 17).

Because of such crowding, the Soviet home, especially among the middle and working class, has not furnished the space to become the place for relaxation and easy freedom, that haven from the pressures of society and source of new strength which the modern family home has afforded in other lands. Extreme cases of the means (housing) becoming the end and the end (marriage) becoming a means are a part of the folklore of Soviet daily life: "The apartment situation often forced people into marriage — that is, girls married men with a suitable room and vice-versa. They could then divorce and claim a part of the room they had married. It could often be heard said that someone had married a 20 square meter room. Then after two weeks or a month of marriage, the person concerned would divorce. The room would then remain in the possession of the least scrupulous one with the strongest nerves. He or she would proceed to organize parties every night in his or her section of the room. These parties would usually be very noisy, smoky and drink-filled. As a final recourse, if his ex-wife had by that time not yet decided to move out, the man would bring in women. The ex-owner of the room would then attempt to find another man with a suitable room and the cycle would begin all over again" (1069 A 43).

But the paradoxes of family life are many, and time and space shortages have regularly been converted from obstacles into goals in family life, along rather class-specific lines. The rank and file of the peasantry are too concerned about food and clothing to be overly pre-occupied with housing and are also better supplied with both space and time. Though they are extremely busy in the summer months, time often hangs heavy in the winter. Among the upper classes, who are best provided for on the material side, the main aim has become finding hours to be together. Free time for recreation and a full vacation period have apparently become central aims.[57]

Among the Soviet middle classes poor housing is probably psychologically most painful. Families on this level are badly housed and yet far enough up in the class system to see the possibility of something better. For them "busyness" has an immediate and high-prized goal — better housing — and they tend to be less likely to feel their family life impoverished by shortage of time. Their beliefs are often like that of the young engineer who observed: "In the Soviet Union you have to work and you have to study, and there is no time for anything else" (190 A 22). In this same class, however, one occasionally finds traces of the tendency to avoid the treadmill psychology of desiring that which one would in any case not enjoy. A party official, earning 1,000 rubles a month, told the writer in 1958 that a single room was big enough for himself and wife, both of whom were working. A similar lowering of expectations is quite explicitly expressed by a white-collar worker, father of a family: "Under our conditions, housing is the least important problem. Today's man is outside of his home all day. First, he must go to work. After work there's always a meeting, or some entertainment, then a short stroll in the streets and it's late, time for bed. After a full day, you're exhausted. You throw yourself into bed and nothing can disturb you. In the morning you get up, and it begins all over again" (Nov 31). One doubts that most Soviet urbanites find it so easy to make a virtue of necessity, but it is undeniable that this man's attitude is conducive to a certain peace of mind as well as reflective of the extent to which the concept of home can become a residual one.

If more time together is of central importance in the upper class, and better housing in the middle class, in the lower working class of the Soviet cities the picture is less monothematic. Family life among the workers seems to split into three subpatterns along these dimensions. At the lowest level life is typically little more than an extension of the routine and tradition of the village. Often living on the outskirts of cities, the husband is a factory worker and the wife may still be a collective farmer, in any case still close to the chickens, cow, and vegetable plot. In this category just as in the collective farm family, life is busy but horizon, aspiration, and dissatisfaction are all limited.

The top level of working-class family is similar in organization and spirit and merges readily with the middle class; better housing is a crucial goal. In between is the group from which comes the Soviet version of the proletarian family of nineteenth-century capitalism. Like the English workers described by Engels, they live in the most primitive urban housing, have little expectation of doing better in the foreseeable future (because of lack of skills, advancing age, poor political or work records, and so forth) and tend "to have only two pleasures." Some of the other traits characteristic of such families are revealed in the Moscow family of the spinner, O, her husband, a drinker, and two children. The family had just moved from its old quarters, where roaches, fleas, and mice had added to the human disorder, into a spacious room in a communal house, with a window into the garden. "But," continues the observer, "as before there was no bed clothing." Furthermore: "The nourishment schedule of O leaves much to be desired . . . Their household is run in a slovenly, disorganized, and inefficient way. On holidays and after pay day they eat a lot, even quite plentifully, but their money does not hold out until the next pay day and by that time they are on a starvation diet" (Ka 32–34).

The preceding sections have shown that family life is often highly organized in terms of the membership composition and domestic division of labor. Shortages of time, space, and facilities also impose this characteristic upon the Soviet family as well as upon the Soviet person as an individual. Living together must satisfy simultaneously the need for a life of one's own and the need to adapt to the requirements of others. Floor space, for instance, tends to be strictly defined and well respected, just as do places in closets, shelves, and cabinets that have to be shared. All sorts of devices are used to give more usable space and greater measure of privacy. Bricks or other supports are placed under bedposts for storage areas, dressers serve as tables, and cloth, paper, pieces of furniture, and wood partitions are used to separate families and individuals within families.

At its best, enforced proximity creates new cultural norms of cooperative living: avoidance of unnecessary noise, restraint of impetuous children, civility if not closeness, and a general sense of reciprocity and tolerance. Not only space but time tends to be highly organized, with rights and duties made explicit. The author of a recent book tells of his friend's chagrin that the norms of communal living interfered with his desire to extend hospitality: "I was going to invite you to watch a TV program which begins now. But our neighbor K. is still sleeping behind this partition. He works on the night shift. Sorry we can't watch it. Shall we go for a walk?" (Nov 19) It is not improbable that Soviet housing conditions have done more than the ideology of collectivism to lead the Soviet people to a new level of respect for the rights of others and to a sharp concentration of interest in propriety and decency. One might even speak of a certain "cult of politeness," within the family and without, which finds its expression in the much-noted Soviet concern for everyday *kultura*.

Indeed the human gift for adaptive cultural inventiveness can do much to preserve events and relationships that external conditions render difficult of attainment. So it is with the most intimate side of family life. A Moscow nurse, twenty-five, mentions this context: "You must understand that a human being can get used to anything, if he has to, and if he wants to. You can get accustomed to ignoring others just as they become accustomed to ignoring you. You'll learn the great art of becoming indifferent to the problems of the people around you . . . But you'll also learn tact and tolerance of others, just as they learn to be tactful in their dealings with you. You will learn to turn around so as not to disturb their private actions. You will pretend you are asleep in order not to frighten away a moment of love experienced by the people behind the partition" (Nov 31). However, the chance and obligation to develop such finer sensitivity imposes a burden of its own, and the end result is often that the individual is pushed out of the house into the outside world.

As a recent observer concludes, "Soviet man spends very little time at home or with his family." [58] Where, then, aside from at work, does he spend it? Paradoxically, in two rather extremely distinct ways. First in a context which tends to be, again, highly organized, but this time officially sponsored. In these he usually participates as an individual. Much of it is an appendage of his workplace: "There are many kinds of social meetings which are developed, clubs of all sorts, and evening meetings and parties in the enterprises where you work, and people have to pay a little bit for them . . . A person will not invite anyone. He goes there, eats, listens to music, and dances, so it is not necessary to invite people to his home. In the Soviet Union every factory has its club, every trade union has its club, and every supporting society has its club. So people meet together there, in the club" (67 B 27). At the other extreme the Soviet individual and indeed the Soviet family, too, avoid too many people and too much organization. This can be done in the anonymity of nature, the movie house, the city park, the crowds, and the streets of the large city. The city streets and strolling play very special roles in the lives of Soviet families and also in the lives of Soviet young people. A young student of physics is explaining her insistence on "going for a walk": "If we were to see each other in my house, we would never be alone. We'd either disturb somebody or somebody would disturb us. If we go to a restaurant, there would be all kinds of people milling around and staring at us. If we go to the theatre or the movies, then we can't even talk to each other. But on the street we are alone, completely alone, don't you see? We are lost in the crowd, they don't bother us, and we don't bother with them" (Nov 40).

In all of this the individual takes the lead. He, and less often the small family, leaves the home to seek out the activities sponsored by the regime, the privacy of the great outdoors, or less respectable pursuits such as a bottle of vodka. The chief casualty, perhaps, is not the family itself, which is bound by more than the categories of time and space, but the informal social clique, the group of friends and friendly families who like to visit informally in each other's homes and company. To visit in homes is quite rare, and to "go out" in company is very difficult except among the highest-level families who can command the space and service of public facilities.

A version of this trend plays down the role of the housing shortage and finds the source of the trend in changing patterns of leisure. "Meetings in cafeterias and restaurants have created a serious threat to such a form of family leisure as going visiting and receiving guests. The ways to spend leisure time and the tastes connected with it have become more and more differentiated, which has made the organization of leisure time inside the family more difficult even in those situations where it continued to be necessary. In short, the family has gradually lost this function, although in individual cases it also tries to resist the growing competition of public diversions." [59] In any case, the transfer of activities and interests outside the family leads not to a more pronounced informal social structure, but to the opposite. One feels that there is little of substance between that large part of the individual's life that is organized for him in a group context and the much smaller part that is still reserved to the family. Society on one side and a great mass of relatively isolated and sparsely fleshed families on the other, with little else between, make up Soviet social life.

In its changing modes of size and organization and its loss of functions with concomitant increase of concentration of family members' energies in the activities of the outer society, the Soviet family bears strong resemblance to those patterns of change in the family in modern society which have increasingly come to be recognized as standard. Nonetheless, every social system, every culture, and every historical era show their distinctive features, and some of these leave their mark upon the family.

In the Soviet case the standard patterns of change in family life seem magnified. The decline of the birth rate, the transfer from farm to factory, the rate of participation of women in the labor market, the appearance of an old-age problem of support and security — these have all come quite quickly to the Soviet scene. Moreover, certain unique traits can be found, such as the frequent reshuffling of membership composition for economic purposes, the out-of-dwelling recreation pattern, the great number of families headed by women, which reflect more specifically Soviet conditions of stress. As responses to stress, however, they are reminiscent of similar patterns elsewhere, such as the lower-class American Negro family adaptation to the deprivational pressures of the

American scene. A third general trait is the effort to orient and adjust by innovation — making the best of things in various ingenious and novel ways — such as, the nearly institutionalized separation of the biological and social aspects of the mother role.

In brief, this chapter has revealed a family pressed hard by outer circumstances and expending some effort to reorganize. Along with the changes, even though these may seem inevitable or even desirable to the individual in terms of his personal goals, there is often a perceptible sense of regret, of loss and even harassment, as if the individual has come to feel that his family does not quite fit into the larger pattern of life in the USSR, or at best as if the changes have come too rapidly for comfort.

IV
HUSBANDS
AND WIVES

Soviet women have become more educated, more involved in the labor force, and more active politically and have received the right to own personal property and to choose freely their own marriage partners. Official salesmen offer Soviet marriage as one of the truly superior products of the Revolution, claiming that the end of capitalist exploitation and legal, political, and economic equality in the larger society bring equality in the relations between husband and wife and that equality brings love.

In fact, however, Stalin has proved that exploitation can indeed occur in a society without private ownership of productive property, and in one sense Soviet women are far from equality because they are ascribed the responsibilities of housewives and mothers in addition to being offered positions in the larger society. Thus, propaganda claims diverge markedly from reality. Soviet accounts of the relationships of men and women in marriage usually are unsatisfyingly schematic or unrealistically positive. Therefore it is of interest to look closely at particular types of marriage relations, the interplay of personality and social trends, and the typical patterns in the different social classes.

Chapter 8 concerns the two ideal patterns of Soviet marriage, one inherited from the peasant past and one taken from the recommended practice of today; it then inspects the predominant or modal marriage pattern of today, which also reveals the trend of change; and, finally, considers some of the variations found in between. Chapter 9 presents some glimpses of a special Soviet social type, the "nichevo man," and of his role in the family life and in the family policy of the Soviet State.

EIGHT | ELEMENTS AND TYPES
IN SOVIET MARRIAGE

"THERE IS NO LOVE so ardent that it will not be cooled by marriage," says a traditional proverb. Some idea of the distance Soviet men and women have been invited to travel since the Revolution can be obtained by contrasting the sense of the proverb with the marxist notion that no marriage is valid *unless* it is bonded by love. As we know, the Soviet regime under Stalin felt obliged to compromise with the marxist ideal and urged husbands and wives to seek, at least in the transition period, other sources of bondedness in addition to that individual sex love so praised by Engels. Nonetheless, the record suggests that many in the population have found the ideal marriage pattern not only desirable but attainable. These two positions can be regarded as the extremes of the Soviet continuum of marriage types.

The Peasant Pattern

A peasant woman described the proper position of husband and wife in marriage as follows: "In the majority of good families the wife subordinates herself to the husband. Now, with us, when my son comes home my daughter-in-law takes off his boots, cleans them for him, and you see how it is. She is obedient and devoted to her husband. There is no other way" (275 B 31). Subordination, obedience, and a slavish devotion comprise the duties of the wife; the husband is the ruler. Anyone who has visited in a traditional Russian peasant household knows the deferential quality of the wife's demeanor. She guards her silence when her husband speaks, serves the food for husband and guest, and remains standing while they eat. If differences arise between the couple, it is the wife who is expected always to give in. A young collective farm wife says: "If my husband shouted at me because of the children I just remained silent, so there would be no quarrels" (288 B 14).

Traditionally, one of the most symbolic of the relative positions of the two sexes has been wife-beating. There are still families to be found in which this male prerogative is practiced. To the women "Christ is the Head of the Church, the husband of his wife," and often the blows are accepted as in the past, submissively and dumbly, as another aspect of a hard fate.

Love is customarily a muted or entirely missing sentiment. In general, emotional involvement in peasant marriage seems to be minimal, with familiarity constituting the chief source of attraction between husband and wife. The men and women who live in these marriages can rarely describe the details of the relationship; usually the most they can say is that relations are "good" or "bad." The outside observer finds description easier. A fifty-year-old forester is described as religious, patriarchal, and moody. Occasionally he beat his wife. The relation was not a bad one, however, for "in spite of the lack of emotional ties, relations between the spouses were relaxed and always cheerful. He ruled the family with strict, but good-humored patriarchalism" (Bi 144). The label "tension-free but superficial" seems apt for the good times, and when the husband is angry, his emotions emerge in spontaneous, full form. The wife then usually forgives him quickly, for it is in the nature of men, she thinks, to be hot-tempered [*spilchivy*], and her husband is proud of this trait.

Positive feelings between the spouses are held more in check, however. There is a taboo upon overt, certainly upon conspicuous and public, display of affection. Kissing or taking the wife's arm on the street is looked upon as abnormally affectionate and unmasculine.

The relative unimportance of strong positive regard, of love, is seen clearly in mate selection. In the past the custom was for the parents of the prospective couple to take the lead in making the match. In Viriatino the older respondents asserted that there were cases of brides and grooms who had not known each other at all before marriage.[1] A somewhat different aspect, but leading to the same conclusion, is presented by the Viriatino family in which the mother protested against the daughter's intention to marry, "because in the family there were older sisters not yet married" (Ku 226).

Even now that the choice is mainly an individual one, the way in which it is made is revealing. A young man, returning to Viriatino after army service, had resolved to marry a village girl with whom he had been friendly before his army days. On his return he found that she had married someone else.[2] He then found another to his liking, a medical student, but she refused, saying she wanted to continue her higher education. He proceeded to quickly decide on another who caught his fancy. He sat down next to her in the club and after about three days asked her to marry. Such dispatch is apparently typical. Another young kolkhoznik says: "We don't look for a great friendship. You like the girl, so you marry her" (Ku 226).

It all seems quite casual and matter-of-fact. To the man it seems that "any wife will do" and to the woman that "men are all alike," or at most can be divided into two classes, good men and bad men, those who drink too much vodka and beat them and those who do not. But the formula "any wife will do" is, of course, an exaggeration, and young peasant men prefer wives who are attractive and friendly, good cooks and housekeepers, sensible, and so on. Yet there is some truth in the epigram, and to this extent it fits in with the opposition to divorce. Peasant custom, for instance, does not take kindly to incompatibility as a reason for divorce. One peasant admits that it seems he made a mistake in choosing his wife: "She was a cross one, like a fire. It was hard to get along with her . . . If I had known it I might not have married her, but if I wanted to divorce, my father would not have permitted it, and I respected my father. [Why would your father not have permitted it?] Because he was religious and did not want people to divorce. 'Marry once,' he always said, 'even if she's an onion and your tears flow.' Thus, he would not permit it" (296 B 15–16). If "any wife will do," then it is obviously inappropriate to divorce.

In the peasant marriage sexuality is seen as a need and prerogative of the man, and sexual relations are usually suffered more than enjoyed by the wife. Marital fidelity on the part of the husband is not considered important — "men are like that" — but both virginity before marriage and fidelity after marriage are expected of the wife. Not only in sexual behavior, but also in other realms of impulse release, the double standard is very strong. Drinking, smoking, fighting, swearing are all prerogatives and symbols of masculinity and are denied to the proper peasant wife. She is expected to obey and to please her husband as best she can, and if he fails to reciprocate with wisdom and kindness, that, too, even though it is resented, is to be expected from men. The chief solace to the wife in an unhappy marriage is the church and her children.

In sexual relations the peasant woman is expected to be innocent, passive, and relatively uninterested. The man takes full initiative, looking upon sexual intimacy as a right which a wife can under no circumstances deny him. To a considerable extent his positive feeling for his wife is linked directly to her sexual desirability; as a consequence, the

Soviet peasant husband sees the first period in his marriage as most enjoyable by far — the high point in his relation with his wife. After the initial excitement furnished by novelty, the relations with his wife settle down to a routine form both sexually and in more general terms. A young peasant girl says: "Of course your first year is the best. Your husband treats you better the first year. After that the children — after three or four years" (288 B 14).

In the past such a marriage was embedded in a larger, usually patri-local, extended family, and the tie between the young spouses was only one of the factors to be considered. Central, for instance, was her capacity to adapt to the already established routines of her husband's family of orientation. The submissiveness of the wife was supported by the residence custom, in which she was literally given away by her parents to become a member of another family and thus became economically dependent upon her new family. The real ruler of the family in those days was the old man, the husband's father. The wielding of power was determined primarily by age and sex, the order of precedence being from husband's father to husband's mother to husband. For the newly married husband and wife this worked well in the beginning of their marriage, giving them a chance to get used to each other without the immediate responsibility of exercising power, though by tradition the young wife was "always a stranger in the household of her husband."

These patterns have gradually crumbled, because the economic and legal basis for the aged father's authority has ended. On the kolkhoz, for example, work and payment are assigned and made to the individual, not by the head of household, and the new opportunities and outer status of women make the role of dependent daughter-in-law quite un-attractive. Today, when a new wife feels uncomfortable with her parents-in-law she and her husband quickly decide to live by them-selves. As noted in the previous chapter, there are definite advantages to living separately, but the responsibility for maintaining the marriage is thrown directly upon the participants' shoulders. Unfortunately, in the countryside, love — in the sense of that institutionalized expectation of permanent romantic attachment which elsewhere is important as a binding factor — is usually present, if at all, only in the early stages. Thus, it offers little support.

Village custom, religious opposition to divorce, dependency of wife and children on continuation of the marriage, and official divorce policy have all continued to exert some pressure. Sometimes when a peasant wife feels ill-treated and threatens to leave her husband, he uses naked threat of bodily harm, and she stays because she is afraid of what he will do to her. To some degree the traditionally low expectation of what peasant marriage provides helps to maintain it. If "a wife is only dear twice — when brought into the house and when carried out in her coffin," then the peasant husband is not too disappointed about it. Nevertheless, in a time of rapid economic and social changes all these forces have lost some of their sustaining capacity, and Soviet peasant marriage has become more and more unstable with the passing of time.

Equal Rights with Love

This pattern corresponds to the relations deemed proper by modern urban populations around the world. Both spouses share power by conscious agreement and deliberate effort. Sharing does not mean an absence of friction over the question, but when power is abused by one or the other of the sides, usually the husband, it is the wife's right to demand her say. Nor are the spouses required to perform in other respects in any set manner.

In many of the marriages observed the question seems to have been solved without great difficulty. The social unrest and uncertainties in the larger society seem to have combined with the challenging tasks offered by Soviet daily routine to make many Soviet husbands and wives only too glad to share rather than monopolize responsibility and power. The pattern seems often to involve a very rational alternation between two spouses, with an attitude of easy permissiveness for the most qualified to exercise influence, as in a Stalingrad working-class marriage. "In their partnership he predominated at times, and sometimes she did. He then gladly acceded to her guidance" (Bi 179).

Often the husband, especially if he is at all "coopted" by his occupation, is content if the wife takes full charge of running the family household. This is a common factor to the equal-rights pattern. The wife of the busy Moscow factory director, for instance, did not work on the outside, but did take full charge of the furnishing of their luxurious five-room modern apartment near the Kremlin and of planning how to spend the couple's free time.[3] Such spouses often seem quite highly specialized in their marital roles. In the relationship of a research chemist and his wife, also a trained chemist and serving as his assistant at work, the specialization by sex is muted but still noticeable. Their personalities and relationship are described this way: "He was quiet, controlled, serious and reserved; she was the same. He was very active in his work, but as a person more passive. With her it was somewhat the other way around. While at work she was under him; at home she was really somewhat more the leader. Added together, this led to complete equality of rights between them. All problems were dealt with in common with complete calm" (Bi 177). Other equal-rights marriages seem more tense, and apparently much effort has to go into the preservation of the equal status of the spouses. It seems that underlying, less conscious needs press the husband and occasionally the wife in a direction that diverges markedly from their conscious ideal of equality. This situation is especially common in younger families, where idealism is stronger, when husband and wife are still adjusting to each other, and where the limits of each other's desires and capabilities are not clearly understood.

Sometimes, perhaps as frequently as the wife, it is the husband who most seeks this kind of relationship. A young man from Viriatino, a recent version of the "progressive Komsomol youth of the 1920's with its uncompromising view of religion as a class-alien ideology, and with its urge to break with the routine of family life," married a young peasant girl with whom he wanted to establish an equal-rights relation. He became quite a proselytizer, taking his wife to the cinema and Komsomol meetings, reading to her aloud, and "insisting on a baby sitter on evenings when meetings or some other activities were going on in the village club" (Ku 206). Another example is a young marriage between a twenty-six-year-old military officer and the daughter of a university professor: "Relations between them were very affectionate, and they did a lot of things together, though she did not share his occupational life. Surprisingly, he was more for equal rights in the marriage than she, who preferred to be somewhat subordinate and made no use of the liberties he was ready to extend to her" (Bi 172). The affective bond in this kind of marriage is a deep sense of intimacy and sharing of all aspects of the self. The partners see each other as unique and look upon their relationship as irreplaceable. There is considerable self-control exercised, with the mood swings so typical among the peasantry occurring only rarely. Love is expected and spoken about, the partners are self- and relationship-conscious.

To be sure, mutual understanding and aid are also stressed, as is respect. When referring to the spouse in talk with an outsider (such as an interviewer), a respondent is apt to refer to his spouse as a "friend," or "life comrade" as well as a wife or husband. In general, such spouses seem decidedly more conscious of each other as separate personalities than is the case in the preceding pattern, and also more consciously dependent upon each other. Research into the personalities of Great Russians has repeatedly furnished evidence that dependency and affiliative needs are strong.[4] Marriage is an obvious form for their satisfaction and seems to be the more strengthened by the presence of these needs, provided that they can be integrated with a pattern of distributing power that makes it possible to express them.

As a matter of fact, successful marriages that follow the equal-rights-with-love formula impress one with not only the conscious recognition but the considerable degree of enjoyment afforded by satisfying dependency and affiliative needs. A white-collar worker, age sixty-five, says: "It is easier to meet all life's problems when one has a close friend, when one can be of assistance to one another. In that sense I consider my wife as a source of life-giving energy, which enables me to have the strength to meet the struggle for life" (71 B 12). In the case of the factory director and his wife, "If he came home from work exhausted, she cheered him up, so that he became visibly transformed — more cheerful and relaxed . . . The link between them as two human beings was extremely deep" (Bi 176). If peasant-style marriage ranges from relatively unfeeling familiarity at best to savage oppression at worst, those at the opposite extreme range in terms of the typical emotional experience from reasonably sympathetic at worst to impressively rich at best. The capacity to enter into a full, intimate relation seems great; perhaps there is an unusual reservoir of stored emotion in the Russian psyche. A Stalingrad couple has an almost idyllic relationship: "They cared for each other not only in the usual sense of marriage, but took an interest in each other's work. Thus she visited him on her free days at his construction site. They also shared the same values and opinions . . . when they had nothing to do, they sat together in front of the door of the house, the wife played the balalaika and the family sang, or the husband and wife played chess" (Bi 178–179).

Attitudes and practice in mate selection and divorce correspond to the elements of the expected nature of the marriage. Love and comradely sympathy are paramount, and the sharing of interests, values, and general philosophy is a secondary criterion for deciding whether and whom to marry. When eight hundred couples newly married in Leningrad were asked in 1962, "What in your opinion is the chief condition for a stable and happy marriage?" love, it is reported, together with "common views, faith, sincerity, friendship, and such" accounted for 76.2 per cent of the responses.[5] In this kind of marriage divorce is disapproved of in principle but accepted as a necessary evil, for: "If people torment each other, why should they stay together?"

Sexual life is valued by the husband and wife as their personal property, not to be soiled by promiscuity. There is a single standard of fidelity after marriage. Consider the Stalingrad worker, a forty-two-year-old construction trust painter. His wife is forty, a factory worker, and they have two sons, ages eight and nine. Both spouses are of working-class background and live in very modest circumstances in a small wooden house, one and one-half rooms, on the Volga. The husband has a number of the personal traits most valued in the traditional culture: he is lively, fond of singing, courageous, sympathetic, big-hearted, frank, and even outspoken—"whenever necessary, he delivered his opinions point-blank to his work superiors." Also, "he liked the company of women, and liked to joke with them, but never anything serious, for he esteemed his wife too much" (Bi 178).

To the observer of such marriages it seems that the two partners are held together mainly by love. Nevertheless, a closer acquaintance often reveals a broader scope in which harmony prevails — in mutual work interests, for example — and in which personal regard looks almost like a by-product. In the case of a scientist and his wife joint occupational achievement was evidently both the goal and symbol of a happy marriage: "Both had studied chemistry in Moscow, and had also met each other, married, and worked together there. Now they were working together in a project which he was directing, on problems of the decomposition of uranium; she served as his personal assistant . . . Both lived for their professions and for their duty. Everything was subordinated to it . . . Their life goal seemed to be the Stalin prize" (Bi 176–177). A factory director lives in a different style. Summers are spent in the Caucasus and in the Crimea. Otherwise, in free time the two read, listen to the radio, and like to ice-skate. The observer reports that they love each other. Further: "He was proud of his good-looking wife — she adapted well to managerial circles. She was proud of him because of his achievements. He also impressed her as a man, and there was probably also a certain material factor influencing her . . . Moreover, they agreed in opinions and values on all matters, and had great trust in each other" (Bi 176). All in all, it appears that their love contributes to and is enriched by being in tune with the outer society. Their strong sense of mutuality of fate, and the privileges that go with it, brings them even closer to each other.

The Trend of Change

Even in rural areas the old days, when the reins were firmly in the hands of the oldest male, have gone. A saying that until recently the men liked to repeat — "woman has long hair and a short wit" — has ceased to be true or amusing, and the unequal terms of address — by which the patriarchal male was likely to address his wife with the familiar *ty*, while she in speaking to her husband was well advised to use his name, patronym, and the formal *vy* — have been long since replaced by the familiar form. The patriarchal pattern, both as an ideal form for peasant family life as a whole and as an implicit ordering principle for absolute male dominion in marriage, has undergone a gradual and uneven weakening. The process has been under way for some time. Urbanization, education, the emancipation of women — these worldwide trends have had their effect in Russia as elsewhere, and the Revolution has greatly accelerated them.

All sources agree that Soviet marital life is tending toward more equality between husband and wife. The changing pattern of relative age of the two spouses is one particularly significant symptom of the degree to which this is so. Table 10 is based on a sampling of three thousand marriage registration records for the three years, 1920, 1940, and 1960, for two urban districts and one rural district in the Leningrad region. If the decline in age disparity indicated by these data is typical for the whole country, the change is a striking one indeed.

Male dominance is still frequent in the peasant marriage, especially in the older generations. Yet even those who still subscribe to the pattern in their own lives express a presentiment of change. A peasant woman says of the new pattern she observes around her: "I am your wife. You say, 'You will not go there. I don't want you to go there.' But I say, 'You have no right. I'll go where I please. The husband does not have the right to tell his wife what to do.' There is a law . . . they call it equality of rights. The wife may want to go into the Komsomol or do something, and she does what she wants, not what her husband wants" (275 B 30). In many worker and peasant marriages the confrontation of the old pattern by the new equality brings considerable malaise. As in the above case, there is a tendency for some lower-class women to see the legal equality of woman as extending to family relations as well as economic and political life. Another wife, from a working-class marriage, says, "In the Soviet Union the husband had no say about his wife's working or about his adult children" (100 B 4).

TABLE 10. Relative age at marriage of spouses, Leningrad region, 1920, 1940, 1960.

Location of registry office and year	Relative age of spouses			
	Same or groom younger (per cent)	Groom 1–6 years older (per cent)	Groom 7 or more years older (per cent)	Total (per cent)
Urban				
1920	19.0	49.5	31.5	100.0
1940	32.5	51.0	16.5	100.0
1960	40.0	46.5	13.5	100.0
Rural				
1920	17.5	46.0	36.5	100.0
1940	26.5	50.5	23.0	100.0
1960	41.0	48.0	11.0	100.0

Source: Adapted from Kharchev, *Brak i semia*, p. 190. The rural sample numbered 1,500 and was taken from Mginski district, Leningrad region. The urban sample also consisted of 1,500 cases, taken from Kirov and Kuibyshev districts, Leningrad city.

Most peasant men have been unwilling to grant such a radical shift in power so quickly, and most of their wives, I believe, have not wanted it either. The transition from the old order has been slow and often painful. Even where the man has remained dominant, however, the nature of his relationship with his wife has been different. Consultation and mutual agreement about important decisions have become prescriptive. A young collective farm wife is asked who makes the decisions in her family. She says, "My husband, of course. Of course he talks it over with me, asks whether I agree. But he is the husband, he decides mostly. Because he understands more" (288 B 9). While the old order involved absolute and irrational hegemony, the new male supremacy is more temperate. Frequently, as in the case above, it is rationalized as "he understands more." Another peasant, who became a tractor driver, presents a different rationalization: "Of course a man should be head of the family. Because I can earn more than my wife. If I get anything my wife has it too" (299 B 5).

Actually, in many peasant families today there is a characteristic arrangement, by which the husband is the ruler "in principle," while it is the wife who often makes important decisions and wields considerable influence in other ways. The distinction between public appearance and private reality is more apparent, I suspect, to the wives than to the husbands. An old collective farm woman says: "The husband is the boss, but it's I who tell him 'Father, we need such and such a thing.' I know the needs of everyone in the family better than he does. I wash their clothing and can see better than he who needs something" (Ku 214).

The contradiction between the still lively cultural norm of masculine dominance and the observed behavior of such partners leads to a kind of ritual patriarchalism which can easily be misinterpreted by the casual observer who sees only the outer form and concludes that masculine dominance is more thoroughgoing than is actually the case. A Soviet ethnographer described (perhaps with some exaggeration) the new situation in the families on a *Kazakh* kolkhoz: "In the overwhelming majority of families in the absence of outsiders the wife has an equal position with the husband, and at times in some families even is the ruler. But in the presence of outsiders, by tradition she must exhibit her supposed submissive position . . . [for example,] when visiting she does not sit in the place of honor [*tör*]." [6]

This is probably close to the situation today in the typical Soviet marriage (taking typical to mean modal with respect to the entire population). Masculine dominance, while still present, has become more moderate, and humane, tending gradually toward acceptance of full equality for the wife, though there is still a long way to go among the peasantry. A study of three hundred Leningrad working-class families conducted in 1961 offers some good evidence in support. Two types of marital relationships are distinguished, both of which involve masculine predominance — "by tradition the overwhelming majority of women name the husband head of the family." In the first the personal power of the husband is conserved, but it is said to be based not upon constraint but upon "the moral authority of the husband with more or less voluntary submission on the part of the rest of the members of the family to this authority." In the second type the predominance of the husband is merely formal and masks a *de facto* equality of rights in deciding basic intrafamilial questions. Of course, it may be significant, as the researcher claims (but does not support with evidence), that these are all families in which the wife is employed. In any case, the second type, in which the masculine dominance is merely a formal one, is the majority pattern, found in 60 per cent of the sample.[7]

Marital patterns change much more slowly than behavior in public contexts. To the Russian man surrender of power over his wife — a right extended by God, customary law, tradition, and superiority of physical strength — however justifiable in a rational sense and on a conscious level, nonetheless gnaws at his self-esteem. For this reason the outer form so often remains patriarchal even while things are more equal in private and even if feelings of affection and love may have become strongly influential. Thus the typical marriage today combines, in friendly coexistence, male dominance and tender affection, attitudes which do not merge well when they are found in extreme forms. A good example is given by the marriage of a thirty-five-year-old construction foreman from Kiev. His wife is twenty-eight, and they are described as in love: "They met before the war during their student days at a dance, and were married at the time he was drafted . . . Both expected a mildly patriarchal marriage, and conducted their marriage accordingly. He led the way, but in a gentle and less absolute way than had been the case in the marriage of her parents, his father-in-law . . . The main influence on both their attitudes was that of their parents' home, mellowed by the advances made by the society which surrounded them" (Bi 147).

In addition to ritual patriarchalism with love, there are other signs of what is happening in Soviet marriage. Patterns of the future as well as the past are found in the changing nature of the association between social relations and ceremony. It is usual in Viriatino to go through two wedding ceremonies, one in the Civil Registry or ZAGS office and a second, traditional, service in the home of the husband's parents. Significantly, it is reported that sexual relations often are initiated after the first of the two, though the girl continues to live with her own parents until the second ceremony has been completed.[8]

It seems that the link between the girl's continued residence in her parents' home and the traditional wedding ceremony in her husband's parents' home is furnished by the larger circle of persons, mainly kinsmen, who are in some way involved with the young couple. Moving out only after the traditional wedding symbolizes their continuing willingness to see their marriage as contingent upon the larger community, specifically the two parental families, and, perhaps, their desire to express respect for the traditions of their peasant heritage.

The association between the official Soviet agency and their sexual intimacy is also important, the connecting link here being their marriage itself. The initiation of sexual relations before the girl moves out of her parents' home, but only after a trip to the ZAGS office, suggests that the couple sees the Soviet order as supportive of their right to live a separate and independent life as a married couple, and in particular to behave in a fashion independent of and different from that of their parents. However, they assert this right unobtrusively, in terms of the most private aspect of their life together, sexual relations, so as not to offend too greatly against their relatives' or their own sense of respect for tradition.

Such behavior patterns reveal social change in process and the extent to which cultural malintegration is creatively adjusted to by the partners of individual marriages. It is also not without significance that sexual intimacy, perhaps love too, between spouses seems to find its defender in the new Soviet order, whereas the traditional way of life appears to uphold the more repressive, less spontaneous aspect of marriage, namely, the power of the community to influence the young couple's life together.

Of course, this trend toward more individualism in marriage is by no means novel. The shift of solidarity priority from the larger kin group to the marital pair is shown by changes in other patterns of peasant life. In the old days the relationship of man and wife was influenced by the general assumption of male superiority, in connection with which the women were subjected to discrimination and segregation in various guises. The older folks in Viriatino still remember when the mealtime seating order at table in the peasant cottage required the men to sit on one side and the women on the other. But, they report, married couples had begun to sit together before the turn of the twentieth century.[9]

To conclude this portion of the discussion, it is worthwhile to stress several facts about the most typical of Soviet marriages, that which is in transition between the peasant pattern and the pattern of equal-rights-with-love. Transitional forms are compromises, and, as we shall become aware in the next chapter, they do not always work too well. In this marriage not only are power and affection governed by contradictory forces, but often so are other aspects of married life, such as the spouses' religious and political views. Consequently, the continuity from one generation to another is not great, there is a certain fitful unrest to the marriage, as if elemental spontaneity and conscious self-control are vying for supremacy, and very often the spouses work out their uncertainties on their children. In a highly sublimated form of this unrest, husband and wife divert attention from themselves and their own relationship and focus their conscious thoughts and goals upon their children. Such seems to have happened in the case of the happily married Stalingrad couple already referred to: "The children were the purpose of the family. They were to get a better education. He carefully supervised their school work. And when they won prizes for good work he was very proud of them. Their social intercourse was also controlled; the children were not allowed to play with the children of Volga River workers . . . The family was passively religious, and the children were so reared and they crossed themselves" (Bi 179).

Underground Archtypes

1. The vestigial marriage. Turning now to a characterization of marriage types that are out of correspondence with any cultural pattern but of frequent enough occurrence to merit attention, I have chosen to label the first "vestigial," since its most typical trait is an absence of content. Other appropriate descriptions would be "casual," "ad hoc," or "empty shell." External circumstances rather than love, tradition, or community control predominate as the binding factor. Often forces beyond the control of the individuals concerned bring them together in ways that preclude full commitment to each other and they live in what they both seem to accept as a union likely to be only temporary. This was so in the case of a forty-five-year-old horse driver for a Donbas construction trust. As a former prisoner of war he had been sentenced by the Soviet Government to stay in that region, not his original home, and at the time of observation in 1948 had not seen his first wife and three children since 1941. He carried on correspondence with this wife, however, tried to exert some influence over their children in letters, and counted on returning eventually to them. His present *de facto* marriage is described by the observer with eloquent brevity: "He lived in K. with a widow and her son in relations akin to those of marriage. The widow tolerated his connection with his family. With her he did not play the dominant role very much, for he felt more like a guest; moreover, the widow was more independent and active than his own wife" (Bi 194). Mobility, both involuntary, in connection with the wars, collectivization, resettlement, and so forth, and voluntary, has been very common. It has brought frequent and long separations between spouses, with temporary *de facto* marriages serving as a substitute.

Moreover, the confusion and disorganization of Soviet history works in a vicious circle, in which deaths, arrests, occupational demotions, divorces, and separations in prior experiences reduce the individual's chances in subsequent marriages. There are many in the population with damaged identity. A construction director, aged sixty-four, is married to a thirty-two-year-old woman with whom his relations are not especially close. He had been a party member since 1916 and of fairly high rank, but, like the wife, had some liabilities in his past: "After 1945 he was expelled, because he was complaining, wanting to see fulfilled the promises he had had to make to the people in his wartime speeches" (Bi 239). Thereafter he lived in S. and followed his original profession of carpenter but as a foreman. His first marriage ended in divorce; his wife had grown too old for him. The second marriage took place in 1946. The wife was 32 years younger, parentless, and had been raised in an orphanage. She had been previously married and divorced and brought a child from that marriage into this one. Because of negatively valued personal traits these two partners have little chance to establish a better marriage, they realize it, and they accept the present setup as the best that circumstances can provide.

Deep involvement in one's spouse is lacking in these marriages, and personal convenience seems the main return from marriage. Sexual gratification, regular meals, and a place to live seem central as binding factors, as in this example: "He is interested in his wife only insofar as she cares for the house and the children and affords him a certain comfort. The marriage is for this reason only a physical togetherness; inner feelings are quite absent. From this it is evident why the husband took up with other women and girls from time to time. This is of little importance to his wife who feels, on the contrary: if he has other women sometimes, at least I have some rest from him . . . Nevertheless the marriage is not bad, nor is the family's integrity endangered" (Bi 302). In other cases, the marriage is even more bereft of mutual esteem, and bare sexual satisfaction alone seems salient.

Interestingly, the distribution and exercise of power is not ordinarily problematic, being solved by social distance between the spouses, a grandparent who takes over, or simply indifference. To the casual observer the spouses seem quite equal. An army lieutenant's marriage to a peasant girl in 1945 was described as having the following aims: to help him lead a more orderly life, to gain access to more food products through her kin, who lived on a kolkhoz, and to get sexual satisfaction. The pattern of authority and its background is further described thus: "The two have just about equal rights in the marriage, but he is still somewhat the leader. Basically, however, they lived together without any relationship; each followed his own interests. Just as before [the marriage], he spends much time with his comrades, and she takes care of the small household and chats with the other officers' wives. The partners were together solely at mealtimes and at night. In addition, there are regular visits to her relatives which however, serve mainly as an opportunity for them to eat their fill. They do not think about the future nor eventual children, because each of the two partners is happy and satisfied in his situation" (Bi 174).[10]

As suggested by the preceding case, the interests of the two partners are essentially individual, or, as the observer put it, "narrow" rather than shared. For the man it is almost like a bachelor's life. Such was explicitly admitted in an interview with a newspaper reporter. He continued his "bachelor-like existence" after his marriage — a pattern aided by work assignments requiring frequent travel. When asked to compare his tie with his wife with that between his own mother and father, who were peasants, he replied, "My wife and I were completely independent of one another, whereas my parents' relations toward one another possessed a patriarchal character" (67 B 7). Such a relationship he found pleasing, and, as one can imagine, it was greatly facilitated by the fact that his mother "ran the house" (67 B 3).

2. *The mother-wife and the son-husband.* In some marriages the usual roles in wielding power are reversed, and the weaker sex produces the paradoxical phenomenon, in a land of patriarchal tradition, of the strong woman.[11] The most visible characteristic of the wife, as well as

of the marriage, is a certain feminine sustaining capacity. The wife is a person of stability and bountifulness. In such marriages the makeup of the wife often tends to take on the shape of the mother role. The observer is inclined to describe the wife's feeling for the husband as one of kindness rather than love. The husband's feeling is harder to characterize, since the relationship, being somewhat illegitimate, and foreign to the conscious masculine self-image, is for him more primitive, ambivalent, and oscillatory.

A description of the interplay of behavior and feeling in this type is taken from a Soviet film. The character traits of the grandmother and her relationship with the grandfather are being described. She has strength, charm, generosity, peace of mind, a calm conscience. Furthermore: "This old woman seems to represent the matter-of-factness of the earth, the self-evident strength of the flesh, and the native stoutness of the heart . . . [She is] even nursing the wailing grandfather along . . . she lets the senile old man beat her, simply going down on her knees as if he had actually been strong enough to push her down . . . 'he is my husband,' she says . . . This woman seems to know no law but that of giving; no principles except the complete trust in her own inner endurance . . . She accepts the passions of men as she accepts . . . fire: both are external if unavoidable evils. It is as if she had lived long before passions had made men ambitious, greedy, and, in turn, childishly repentant, and as if she expected to outlast it all . . . The grandmother takes him into her arms, almost her lap. She calms him . . . He collapses on her in foolish fondness, only to rally suddenly and to knock her down in a rage of jealousy." [12] Although the grandfather is obviously getting on in years, the senility serves to accentuate the underlying forces that have been there all along.

The pattern itself is in its grosser form quite unmistakable, even though both partners might subscribe in principle to the traditional propriety of masculine superiority. A construction worker, in his mid-forties, of Russian background but living with his wife and two children in a village in Lithuania, earned about five hundred rubles a month and thrice-yearly bonuses of about one thousand rubles each time. Relations came to a focus around the spending of his earnings: "The wife controlled the money; she took it from him immediately. If he wanted to have a drink, he had to borrow money . . . He did not worry about the household—that was her job—but she was somewhat involved in his job. She sent him off to work punctually, and if he did not come right home after work, she went to get him, because she was afraid he would go somewhere to drink" (Bi 187). The observer adds that while the wife commanded in the marriage, both were convinced that the man should rule, and "externally and also in relation to the children . . . he had again at times to fulfill the patriarchal role" (Bi 188). In such a ritual patriarchalism the ritual is very hollow indeed. In fact, in terms of behavior the patriarchal roles are turned upside down. The woman is as much a mother as a wife, while the man is as much a boy, in this case obviously a bad boy, as a husband.

Seemingly, such marriages have been in existence for quite some time. Even in a time when tradition, Church, and Tsarist law produced a picture of a strongly patriarchal way of life in Russia, the outward appearance of male dominance was often mellowed by an inner permissiveness, the external paraphernalia of the patriarchal way balanced by the superior personal resources of a woman who had her say behind the scenes. Vladimir Polunin, for instance, tells how his grandfather, a wholesale fish merchant in Kursk in the 1840's, "never abused his power —indeed not infrequently, though unwillingly, he surrendered to grandmother's more forceful character." [13]

An old peasant man whom I interviewed in 1950 tells how it is important to take the intelligence of one's wife into account in arriving at a proper disposition of authority: "The law of God says 'the wife must submit to the husband,' but he should also not insult her. Thus, if it is a wise wife, seek her counsel. But if it is a stupid wife, there is no use to. [How was it in your family?] If you have a wife, like mine, who believes in God like I do—thus, I had to share with her. But with a bad wife, why seek her counsel? She will spend money foolishly and the husband will suffer" (624 B 4). Thus the patriarchal principle, mellowed by the allowance of this important qualification to masculine predominance, has for some time been sufficiently flexible, when the need exists, to permit the wife a considerable increment of power which she exercises mainly in a motherly way. Apparently in fairly bargained exchange the husband surrenders power to his wife and receives extraorinary succor, as if from his mother, in return.

In addition to the sex-typical character structure formed by pre-Soviet tradition this variety of marriage reflects some of the more unique aspects of recent Soviet social history. A result in later married life of the insecure and aimless life of the homeless child, so common in the early years, is seen in a marriage between a store official and his wife in

White Russia. Although younger than her husband, she is looked up to by him and seems to combine the role of wife and mother quite handily: "The husband, thirty, had been at times a homeless child, and had learned to read, write and count only as an adult, taught partly by his wife, twenty-five, a nurse. The wife always had the deciding word in the marriage, but he was very attached to her and showed her genuine affection" (Bi 241). The turmoil of Soviet history and the shortage of men have brought a considerable number of unequal partners together, especially since many of the men who died prematurely were the more vigorous and courageous specimens. For example, a woman from a Leningrad middle-class background, by profession a medical doctor, was married to a construction-trust official from a lower-class background with considerably less educational experience. She was described as of higher social origin, more intelligent, and less passive. The observer conjectures that the marriage, in 1942, occurred mainly because she wanted to escape the misery of being alone somewhere in the middle of a primitive forest in the Urals. She had been evacuated from Leningrad in mid-winter and "no one but him took any trouble over the crying and abandoned girl" (Bi 181). Subsequently, she came to be much more the leader in the marriage than he.

This pattern bears considerable resemblance to the "mother-centered" family, which has come to be associated with the family life of groups under stress, lower-class families generally, and particularly the lower-class Negro family in American society. The Soviet version under discussion differs from that in two ways. The husband is present rather than in-and-out or entirely missing, and he accepts the dominant position of his wife rather easily. In fact, both partners seem quite comfortable about it, much more so than the extent of deviation from the two ideal patterns of Soviet culture would suggest.

3. *The new Soviet woman's marriage.* The two types described to this point seem reasonably successful as marriages. Though deviant from the cultural norms and social modes, they fit the needs of the partners. Two additional types constitute less happy examples. One of them seems extremely common, has probably played a central role in the unfolding of Soviet family policy, and is discussed at length in the next chapter. The other is another type of marriage in which the wife is the controlling influence. There seem to be two varieties of strong women marriage in the USSR. The first is a mother in wifely semblance; the second is a newer product, shaped by bolshevik, industrial, and cul-

tural revolutions of recent times, newly-won economic independence, rising levels of self-regard, and the woman's new determination to exercise her will in marriage.

The key facter in these marriages is the wife's forceful personality. Often she is a Komsomol activist and party member. In the marriage of a forty-five-year-old political police lieutenant from a village near Vologda, both spouses are party members. They differ strikingly in personality traits. The wife, "though short and small-limbed, had a very lively personality, sanguinely vivacious, talkative and impulsive. She was also dogmatic and very ambitious . . . of above average intelligence, with her own ideas, and with backbone. Thus she was even able, in resolute fashion, to get her own way with the political police wherever it was necessary. She was sociable and liked to laugh. In relations with others she was self-confident and authoritative . . . As a personality she was an individual of strong feelings whose impulsiveness was compensated for and controlled by a strong will. In this she was aided by the party ideals, in which she believed completely, and which were the guiding principle in her behavior . . . Quite as a matter of course she demanded and received not only equality of rights but also the leadership of the family" (Bi 184–185). The forceful and colorful personality of this woman contrasts remarkably with that of her husband. "He was small, serious, and somewhat shy. Over-all, as a person and a personality, he made a colorless impression. He was of barely average intelligence, and in addition quite passive and phlegmatic . . . His bearing was always unassuming; to his wife he was even somewhat humble" (Bi 184).

Most likely this type of Soviet marriage is composed of three elements: a forceful woman; a retiring, passive husband; some kind of socially recognized superiority — in class background, intelligence, job level, political commitment — which serves as a factor legitimizing her predominance in the eyes of all concerned. In a marriage of similar nature, an energetic young hospital laboratory assistant lived with a man of singularly contrasting personality. He served as an administrative employee of the same hospital: "He was quite passive and lazy, seldom thought things over, and let himself be led. He was superficial in his feelings. He yielded to his wife, and had no rebellious feelings about his inferior position in the marriage" (Bi 242). This sounds like an easy and close marriage, yet the observer also notes that the wife, of strong personality, quick and impetuous in temperament, consistent, scrupulous, and duty-oriented, was in addition a party member, although her husband was not. Morever, she was "tyrannical and dogmatic by nature . . . always eager to convince others." Not too surprisingly, she sought also "to convince her husband and to drive him out of his [political] indifference. Occasionally they fought about it. All of their conversation had a political tinge to it" (Bi 242).

All in all, these marriages usually manifest a serious flaw in the extent to which the positions of the two partners are reversed in terms of sex role expectations. The wife's leadership is often a result of obvious weakness on the part of the husband, leadership by default rather than preference. Sometimes, of course, the situation is what she needs and enjoys, but more often, probably, she is forced to assume more of the role than she would like. A young construction foreman from Stalingrad is described this way: "Energetic, but somewhat on the fat and chubby side, the husband looked like a big adolescent. And basically, he was one also. He was jolly, affable and good-hearted, not a bad person at all but quite a decent one" (Bi 186). However, as a "big adolescent" he was also immature, and in consequence his wife, a "charming and pretty girl, friendly, lively and jolly, but much more solid and sensible than he" had to take an uncomfortable measure of initiative. "By nature, she was inclined toward subordination to her husband, but since he failed to take this cue, she had to be the leader in the marriage much more than she really wished" (Bi 186).

Or, on the other hand, the wife may insist too conscientiously on her equality, to the point where it divests her of her femininity. This seems to have occurred in the life of the secret police lieutenant: "Since at that time these [party] ideals left little room for femininity, she sought very much to suppress her femininity. She always wore a uniform. When once she was seen in a dress and afterwards received compliments about it, she never put on a dress again, though compliments obviously did not displease her" (Bi 184). Bischoff reports the interesting fact that wife-dominated marriages lead to family atmospheres that are more ideological than most. In the older generation such families tend to be very religious; in the younger they tend to be very bolshevik in outlook.[14] Perhaps this is one of the ways in which the wife struggles with her feelings of doubt and guilt for not following more closely the traditional sex-role pattern.

Quite probably the marriage arrangement of the new Soviet woman is an overly extended form of a general theme in the Soviet feminine character. I suspect that a psychological conflict in which a conscious desire for sex equality struggles with a less conscious drive for a dependent and submissive role is typical for many Soviet women. If so, it must almost inevitably affect the relationship with her husband, who, even though he may be eager, is hard put to give her what she wants. A young daughter of a postal worker seems to fit this pattern. She describes her husband as charming, kind, attentive, unobtrusive, and with a "complacent" temperament. Further, she states that in the relationship between husband and wife "both should have equal authority." Yet, she seems uneasy about her husband's failure to play the traditional role and also feels that "the husband should be the head of the family." Her contradictory yearnings are suggested in her full statement: "The husband should be the head of the family, yet his relation to his wife should be of the closest, as to himself; he should be her friend, her helper, and should consider her opinion" (41 B 6).

4. The predominance of the personal factor. Up to this point we have inspected the two extremes of Soviet marriage that correspond with the two ideal patterns, peasant and equal-rights-with-love, have discussed the transitional form that falls between those extremes, and, finally, have inspected some "underground" variations. In social-class terms the most noticeable distinction is between peasant and urban marriages. Most of the former seem to fall into the transitional category, leaning toward the more purely peasant pattern. Probably most urban marriages also are transitional — masculine dominance going together with love — but tending more in the other direction, that of equal rights. Once outside the influence of peasant traditionalism, marriage patterns seem to fan out, presenting a varied assortment to the choice of the individual, but are not correlated in any discernible way with urban social classes (except in the manner to be described in the next chapter).

The breadth of the variation is in itself important, for it contributes, along with the two competing cultural patterns, to what sociologists call anomie, a situation in which important actions have to be taken without a normative standard to provide guidance. From one point of view this generates confusion and uncertainty. From another it suggests greater freedom for the individual couple to attend to its own preferences without too much concern for what others will think.

It is my strong impression that in matters of love and authority in Soviet marriage today there is an extraordinary tolerance and permissiveness among the people, if not in the regime. Not only do individual needs and personality differences play a great role, but many Soviet citizens feel that it is quite proper that they should. For instance, in regard to the proper locus of authority, many would oppose any standardized pattern and would feel, as one respondent suggested to me, that "authority should be enjoyed by the spouse who is better able to organize a family life" (67 B 4). Indeed, it is possible to see a parallel between the role of "personal gifts" in determining eligibility for re-election to political posts at the top level in the Soviet Union[15] and the role of the same factor at the bottom level in determining eligibility to wield power in marriage.

An interesting corroboration of the importance of personal character is found in the lack of any discernible statistical correlation between political commitment and the authority pattern found in a given marriage. Although the official line favors equal rights, party members are no more likely to manifest this relationship with their wives than are nonmembers. A likely explanation is that as a rule only the most able and energetic men join the party. Such men would tend to assume leadership in marriage because they are usually highly endowed with the trait of dominance, which would nullify in practice their inclination to grant equal rights to their wives on ideological grounds. The solution to the conflict of determining principles involved is exemplified in the words of an army colonel, also a party member. In our interview the question of reasons for divorce came up. Would, for example, having a politically reactionary wife be a valid reason for a party member to divorce her? "No. If I would say I want to get a divorce because my wife is apolitical, they would throw the blame on me. 'What kind of a communist are you, when you can't influence your wife? . . . What? You, an organizer of the masses, can't even convince your wife?' " (72 B 30)

NINE | MARITAL DISCORD
AND DIVORCE

THE LESS ATTRACTIVE, more disorganized aspects of Soviet life are in the main quite thoroughly camouflaged by official policy and cant. Statistical information about crime, suicide, divorce, and similar problems is either withheld completely as a state secret or released in fragmentary form for the practical needs and guidance of law-enforcement agencies or for propaganda effect. Legal, journalistic, and social scientific writing is also infused with didactic purpose and all too often can serve only to document or hint at facts that are commonplaces of knowledge in most countries and to most of the Soviet people themselves.

Thus Soviet publications explain that a "certain portion" of Soviet youth is not seldom wayward, that there are Soviet women who engage in prostitution but who cannot be punished because prostitution is not a crime[1] (as in the case of unemployment, there are no "objective grounds" for its existence), that various "survivals of the past" in family life such as wife-beating still persist, that Soviet university youth seldom take kindly to having Engels and Lenin as recommended authorities on the topic of love and marriage, and so on. Questions of frequency and incidence by sociological subcategories are, however, rarely touched upon.

Marital unhappiness can certainly be found in Soviet Russia, just as in any country, but its peculiar sources, types and patterns of distribution, and consequences are largely unknown, even though more information has been made available in the past five years than in the three decades preceding. This chapter describes, on the basis of piecemeal evidence, what I believe to constitute an important, and to Soviet leaders very disturbing, social problem — marital disharmony and family disorganization on a scale at least as great as that known in any Western country.

The Nichevo Man and His Marriage

Usually a love triangle is thought to involve a surfeit of affection in that two men love the same woman. They are jealous and may fight over her. In Soviet family life another kind of triangle has been common, one in which there is too little affection, and the role of third party is played by Soviet society in some authoritative guise.

One Soviet social type is in many ways the mirror opposite of the new Soviet man, his closest parallel perhaps being the damaged personality of the lower-class Negro male of recent American history. Although he is partly a product of the valued masculine traits of the traditional culture, which tend in the Dionysian direction, the heavy traumas wrought by the Stalin era must be held mainly accountable. In most respects the major traumas of Soviet life have fallen more heavily upon men than upon women. Counterrevolutionaries, spies, traitors, and enemies of the people — the executed, exiled, and persecuted of the Soviet past — have been predominantly men. For example, 90 per cent of the inmates of Stalin's slave-labor camps and most of the victims of the purges were men. Even those men not directly harmed themselves were confronted by their consciousness of the fate of others, which served as a most distressing threat to their own security and self-respect.

Then, too, economic support of the family has continued to be primarily the man's task. Many Soviet men have been steadily frustrated by the inadequate Soviet living standard in the discharge of this, their main responsibility to their families. At the top and upper-middle levels, and for the socially mobile, success has been noticeable and even relatively sweet. I have already shown that for the rest lack of success has been especially bitter, and failure, like success, has been made the more visible by Soviet conditions of daily life. Among that half or more of the population of men that has felt no improvement as the years have passed, disappointment and desperate need have sometimes led to antisocial, often criminal, activities.

Although less sharply than political and occupational deprivation, Soviet man has also suffered cultural deprivation in the constant reminder that his traits and values are not up to par — that he lacks the persistence, discipline, work devotion, and self-restraint so extolled in the ideal portrait of the new Soviet man. Even inside the family his sense of failure and frustration has often been heightened by the rising status of his wife and children, who, supported by the regime outside, have more and more asked him to relinquish traditional prerogatives and respect as a man and head of household.

As a result of these blows, a common masculine social type has appeared on the scene. Life seems too much for him. He lacks hope. His feelings and behavior are primitive, determined mainly by resentment and rebelliousness. In his best moments he is good-natured, generous, sociable, even jolly. But he has many bad moments, and then his lack of self-restraint leads him to damaging behavior. Bischoff coined the term "nichevo man" for the man who has lost his confidence and sense of mastery, and who has become interested primarily in pleasures of alcohol and sex in an orgiastic and promiscuous way. Psychologically, he is addicted to self-indulgence and driven by feelings of guilt and fear of punishment. As the vicious circle grows deeper, the seriousness of the deviant behavior grows greater and sooner or later leads to crime or other open conflict with society. The end is prison or labor camp. The man is well aware of his problem but cannot help himself; *nichevo* — so what? — he says.[2]

The most vivid examples of this style of pathology in human behavior seem to have come from the stalinist labor camps. For example, a house painter of a Moscow working-class background was released from a camp in 1952. The observer reports that this personality showed deterioration in several ways: "He was a volatile, impulsive, hot-blooded person — ready with his fists and clever but also obstinate and impatient. His personality bore the clear stamp of his ten years in the camp. He could probably have become a fairly decent person, but he had by now turned into an irresponsible and egoistic pleasure-seeker, who no longer believed in nor had respect for anything . . . As long as he was in the camp he was carefully and cleanly dressed, but afterwards he began letting himself go and soon had gone to the dogs. Similarly, while in camp he read books (historical novels), but later he stopped reading" (Bi 163–164).

However, the nichevo man includes a much broader category. Even outside the punishment camps Soviet life has been severe, political indignities have been many, job demands have been too great and rewards too few. The self-indulgence is primitive and self-defeating, but it is more than simply the soldier's search for easy pleasure in anticipation of battle and death. It is probably also determined by an unconscious and convulsive effort at self-assertion, to recapture, even for a moment, the image of the self as a proud, patriarchal male, master of his land, his women, and his fate.

As can be imagined, such men make unreliable husbands. They function on a very superficial relational level, aptly described by the phrase, "looking upon women as things rather than persons," a survival of the past in the official lexicon. Thus the house painter referred to above "had the old Russian attitude toward women, felt superior to them and regarded them merely as a source of sensual satisfaction. The motivation for the marriage on both sides was primarily sexual need. She was the first woman that he met after his release; indeed, he met her during the formalities which accompanied it. For him the marriage was a cheap source of support and sexual pleasure" (Bi 163–164). A Stalingrad construction foreman, described as not unintelligent but, rather, simply immature and completely unable to cope with the duties of his new job, became a nichevo man. He lost interest in his work and "retreated into an unbridled search for pleasure." It affected his marriage in much the way it affected his life as a whole: "He himself had the feeling that he would come to a bad end, and he also knew that his way of life was leading to the destruction of his marriage. Yet both these considerations only caused him to become even more unrestrained. At times, when his wife reproached him, he was most ashamed of himself, but then like a young boy, would react with even more obstinacy" (Bi 186).

When the nichevo man enters into marriage in the patterns designated peasant or transitional in the preceding chapter, the effect is often disastrous. A distinguishing trait of peasant marriage is the relative absence of close ties of affection. The same is often true in the transitional pattern, where the peasant style is no longer accepted fully and the time has been too short to assimilate the new equal-rights-with-love style of marriage.

The self-oriented motivation of the nichevo man, in collaboration with the weak emotional ties and lack of community support or control, gives added strength to the divisive tendencies between husband and wife. By pushing forward the crumbling of the patriarchal tradition, the gradual development of such tendencies has set the stage for the fundamental pattern of disturbance in Soviet married life. In the family of Russian tradition a patriarch was a responsible autocrat. He controlled the work routines, the patterns and style of consumption, purchases and sales, the rearing of children, relations with the neighbors and the rest of the village, disposition of family land and property, and choice of mates for his children — in general, all the major dimensions of the activity and experiences of the other family members. Their duty was to listen and obey the word of the patriarch, which was law.

Such a structure did not necessarily imply tyranny, for the patriarch was also supposed to be responsible for the physical and spiritual welfare of the family. The ideal pattern was the *Domostroi,* a sixteenth-century collection of rules for conduct in religious, public, and especially family affairs which accord full dominion to the head of the family. The effect was to isolate fully the family from the rest of the world. An ascetic religious aspect prescribed that the rescue of the soul should take place inside the family through the help and leadership of the husband, who was at the same time the single necessary connection of the family with the outer world. Women and children were on the same level — subordinate to the husband who was "fully responsible for them (and their soul's welfare) before the worldly and heavenly court." [3] The long tradition of power bred in the Russian male, as a sovereign ruler, the psychological liabilities inherent in the position of autocrat: love of power, egotism, and rigidity of principle. In the modern era, such are still present, but both his ability and his desire to exercise the qualities of responsibility — moderation, prudence, foresight, generosity, and especially compromise — have diminished greatly.

In brief, the Soviet man, just emerging from a patriarchal family tradition, has tended to retain his rights but to allow his duties to go by the board. The post-revolutionary family policy of the party and central government unwittingly reinforced the tendency. The promise of legal, economic, and other features of equality for women and assertions of the state's willingness and desire to take over household maintenance and childrearing, in line with classic marxism, if at first taken by the Soviet man as an unwelcome intrusion into his family relations, have later been interpreted as an invitation to forsake his own responsibilities toward his wife and children. At the same time his other difficulties and status losses and the scanty bonding force of his marital tie have made him want desperately to hold on to the traditional prerogative that most forcefully set him off as a man — namely, the right to behave in a free and self-serving way in sexual life, drinking, and other matters. Two additional factors — the great amount of moving about inside the USSR and the man scarcity — have underscored the ability of the man to behave, if he wishes, according to his instincts rather than the requirements of a stable marriage. The theme of the deserted and helpless peasant or working-class wife has been a constant one for decades. In a story from the mid-twenties, for example, a peasant left his family behind in the village to go to the city and find work in a factory. At first he lived alone, but then:

In the absence of his wife he took up with another young woman, who moved into his room. For two years he failed to send his wife any money, leaving her to get along as best she could with her poor peasant's household. Not receiving any answer to her complaints and requests, she came unexpectedly to Moscow with four of the children. The two women engaged in a desperate brawl. The neighbors were able to separate the two of them, all bloodied up, only with difficulty. The young wife, having gathered her things together, left the dwelling. But the old wife demanded that she return the things that were bought with the husband's money. The event greatly excited all the workers living in the house. They gathered together in court. They decreed that the husband was to live once more with his old wife and children and to hand over his wages to them. Household goods such as the samovar and the washtub were to be taken from the young wife and to be given back to the old one. Clothing bought for the young wife was to be left to her. The next day the workers themselves went to the dwelling of the young wife and triumphantly bore back the samovar and washtub. The same evening, with drink and accordion, they celebrated the reconciliation of the husband with his old wife and the triumph of righteousness. The wife and children remained in Moscow. But after two weeks the husband went off to the young wife and did not return. This event in all its aspects was discussed in every corner of the house. In the B. family the sympathy of all, including B. himself, was with the woman who had grown old early, and who had ragged and sick children on her hands. (Ka 52–53.)

The drama seems quite a usual one, and the fierce but in the end unavailing effort of the first wife to reclaim her husband as well as to dispense folk justice presents a good example of the typical triangle. The workers in the house represented the nascent force of societal authority.

Twenty years later the scene and actors have changed a little, but the story of a forty-year-old truck driver from Vologda is familiar:

He was interested only in his stomach and his pleasures — women and vodka. They were things which should be subject to a man's will, he thought, existing only for him and his enjoyment. Only when drunk could he be affectionate . . . In the two years of observation [1945–1947] he married (that is, registered with) four different wives, but after a time divorced them again and took his first wife back. He threw each of the women out if she did not accomplish her duties precisely, if she began to bore him, or if he became interested in another woman. During the entire period that he would live with a new wife, his very first wife, together with their two-year-old child, would sleep on the very threshold of his room and wait patiently until he threw the new wife out. Then she would return, without ever showing any jealousy. (Bi 152.)

Such marriages are reported with enough frequency[4] and seem so likely on theoretical grounds that they probably make up a major type of Soviet marriage. The most prominent features are the primitivized, self-oriented, often cynical personality of the husband and a helpless wife who usually must silently accept the husband's activities, objecting if at all only in a feeble or spasmodic manner. She may be old, unattractive, unskilled, with a major worry being how to feed her children and herself if not through the wages of her husband. The partners are held together by purely circumstantial forces; there is no semblance of sharing of power or love.

Patterns of Discord and Adjustment

To an extent the reaction of the wife to masculine behavior of the kind described here can be correlated with the main marriage types discussed in Chapter 8. If the peasant husband is a nichevo man and the peasant pattern (masculine dominance, minimal love between spouses, and the like) is otherwise adhered to, the wife has little alternative than to submit and tolerate. In the relations of a forty-seven-year-old janitor and his peasant wife such is the case: "He really only looked upon her as a beast of burden that had to work and earn money for him. About twice a month he used to whip her and, if he was quite drunk, the rest of the family, too . . . In the marriage he monopolized all the rights; there were none left to her, but she tolerated this without visible resistance . . . He was quite often unfaithful; he was carrying on, among others, an affair with his own stepdaughter (age 16) . . . The wife showed no sign of jealousy about his infidelity — as a man, this was something permitted him" (Bi 150). One item in the observer's description of this family is dissonant: he reports quarreling about money, especially that earned by the wife, "most of which he drank up." Quarreling already presupposes an increment of leverage for the wife, and the family is thereby moved in the direction of the transitional type.

But there is not yet visible the capacity of the wife to enter fully into marital combat. Another example, in the mixed nature of its component elements, definitely lies on the continuum between peasant and transitional types. A fireman by profession was a patriarch-drinker in his home life. When he spent large sums for vodka, his wife "rebelled, but only with a bad conscience and the feeling of playing a role which did not suit her. When things really went badly in their quarrels, she had to give in . . . She went to church as often as time allowed, hoping for some consolation for her personal unhappiness" (Bi 153).

In marriages where equal-rights-with-love is predominant the power positions of the two spouses are relatively equal and behavior akin to that of the nichevo man is less likely to be tolerated. Love is more closely implicated, both as the central issue and in the role of a social control factor. The description of the marriage of a political police officer, thirty-two, decorated as a "Hero of the Soviet Union," with a woman of Austrian birth and rearing, twenty-eight, gives interesting insight into upper-status attitudes toward this subject, as well as into the masculine character in which, even on this social level, traces of the nichevo man are present. Both partners are described as intelligent and able. She was more sensitive than he but also "more dogmatic in her adherence to communist ideas." Both were party members, and they were well off materially.

Inside him various principles seemed to be in conflict: in part he was duty-oriented, in part pleasure-oriented; in part he lived according to strictly rational principles based on tradition, ideology and his rearing, in part he followed impulses from his subconscious, unrestrained and uncontrolled by self-discipline. Thus he loved his wife very much, knew that she gave him much stability; but nevertheless he deceived her when he could do it without danger. In some ways he expected an equal rights relationship with his wife, in other ways he expected patriarchal submissiveness . . . In spite of everything he remained somewhat of an old Russian in his outlook. Since manly pride did not permit him to be submissive, and since he could be impulsive and unbridled, from time to time he took liberties. She on the other hand fully insisted on partnership and equality of rights . . . To outer appearances, however, she wisely allowed him the feeling that he was directing their marriage . . . One day he deceived her with a woman doctor who was engaged to a lieutenant. He and the lieutenant started a shooting match about it, but were separated by the camp guard. His wife straightened out the whole affair, though she manifestly was very hurt and in the days of the crisis visibly suffered because of his infidelity. The engaged couple was reunited, and the lieutenant was transferred. The wife, however, had threatened in all earnestness to divorce her husband and agreed to continue the marriage only after his very contrite and comprehensive promises. (Bi 161–162.)

Several important points are apparent in this example: the husband's indecision over his wife's rights, the presence and importance of love on both sides, the expectation of fidelity, and the threat of divorce as a means of inducing change in the husband's adulterous behavior.

To be sure, means other than the threat of divorce are also used. In all Soviet marriages traditional sex roles call for wives more often than husbands to take the initiative in avoiding open quarrels. As the wife of a lecturer in a polytechnical institute put it: "Very often I gave in to my husband in argument and thus helped maintain family peace and unity. Without giving in one cannot keep peace. I have tested it in my own case. If I did not give in to my husband we would have had frequent misunderstandings. I tried to be diplomatic and preserve peace" (178 B 7). Here again, however, feminine adaptation as a mechanism by which family harmony is maintained suggests that conflict resolution follows the pattern of ritual patriarchalism characteristic of the transitional family. The outer appearance of masculine predominance, "a price which the wife pays," to use terminology that would have pleased Engels, has been granted in return for a substantial increment in *de facto* influence for the wife. This arrangement usually remains in the background as part of the private understanding of husband and wife and consequently is markedly less visible to the outside observer.

Equally distinctive of the Soviet scene is the degree to which external forces have induced pressures for change in male and female sex roles so rapidly that there has not been enough time to assimilate them; consequently, conflicts have appeared in more raw and insoluble form. When the spouses occupy positions in which the wife has lost her allegiance to the peasant pattern and the husband is unwilling to grant an equal-rights relationship, frequent and explosive conflicts arise.

Vodka, it is clear, plays an important part in the lives of Soviet men. Whatever may be the weights of the various sources, and these are both historical and functional (to escape boredom, compensate for loss of male prestige, and so forth), there is no doubt that drunkenness is a focal point in Soviet marital conflict. Another vice, adultery, seems to be common but less important, its significance varying somewhat according to social level. Drunkenness and adultery are at once expressions of would-be masculine privilege and ways to injure the wife's interests. But in many worker and peasant families where money is scarce and need is great, money spent for vodka can wreck the family completely, and the husband's control over expenditures becomes a condition easily lending itself to abuse. This situation did not occur in the peasant family of the past, nor is it the case in many collective farm families of the present, where much of the needed wherewithal for support of children and household is "in kind."

On the other hand, in lower-class marriages, where the double standard hangs on tenaciously, worker and peasant wives who fight fiercely to prevent the biweekly wages from going into vodka will usually look upon the adulterous behavior of their husbands with equanimity: "As a man he is permitted that." In middle- and upper-class families, since economic means are not so limited, continual drunkenness brings consequences that are hardly benign but are at least not immediately disastrous. In the equal-rights marriage, however, adultery is a serious matter because sex behavior is more closely linked with romantic love, the expectation of a unique and intimate relationship with only one person.

With the passage of time the question of sexual fidelity and infidelity is becoming more important for Soviet transition marriages, especially those of workers. As a male privilege, sexual access to other women is easier for a city worker than it is for a villager, and the working-class wife, usually more emancipated than her peasant counterpart, is more likely to be an adherent of sex equality and to demand equal rights. Often her demand takes the form of vigorous opposition to extramarital sex indulgence by her husband precisely at a time when his opportunities are greatest.

There is some evidence not only that adultery is strongly associated with a struggle for dominance within marriages that are in a stage of transition from patriarchalism to equality of rights, but also that it is less sex-specific in such marriages. Apparently one way to get equal rights is to take them, a process that is not difficult in regard to extramarital sexual indulgence. In fact, simply because it has been episodic and less damaging to the masculine self-image of the husband in a face-to-face sense, adultery has seemed an intrinsically appropriate form of feminine revolt in a land with strong vestiges of patriarchalism. It has great significance to the individual concerned, but little influence on the day-to-day functioning of the family. Correspondingly, in those families in Bischoff's sample where the pattern of spouse dominance was under contention, about one-third of the wives were known to be unfaithful during the periods of observation. In the families where a pattern of masculine dominance, equal rights, or feminine dominance was clearly prevalent, there were only two known cases of adultery on the part of the wife.[5]

Of course, sources and expressions of marital conflict take many directions, and most, like these two, are simply variations on themes found in family life in any modern society. In contrast, for many years after the Revolution a distinctively Soviet theme of marital conflict was quarreling over politics and religion. The study published in 1923 by Leon Trotsky, based on discussions held at a Moscow conference on Soviet family life, described as typical a marriage between a communist husband and a religious, nonparty wife in which quarrels over the rightful place of religion were said to be frequent. It is still typical for wives to be more religious than husbands,[6] but the sharpness of any such conflict about religion that may persist has apparently subsided, so that by the 1960's religious differences probably play no more important a role in disturbed Soviet marriages than in marriages elsewhere.

If there is today any core source and syndrome of marital discord relatively unique in Soviet Russia it is to be found, one feels, in the unstable psyches of so many Russian men, as discussed in the first section of the present chapter. There are some signs of subsidence of the turmoil and disorder of the past, however, and as political and economic security become more firm, as sex ratios become more normal, and as less traumatized and resentful generations of Soviet men take over, Soviet marriages will doubtless be less troubled by nichevo men.

Analysis of the nature and sources of marital cohesion and conflict, as well as the available statistical evidence, suggest that the distribution of levels of tension and solidarity is in good measure a function of social class level. The Soviet era has been seriously disturbing to lower-class families, though the extreme of class differences in marital tension and instability was probably reached in the time before World War II, the period when all the sources of tension and cohesion combined to make worker and peasant families least stable and white-collar, especially intelligentsia families, most cohesive. Dekulakization, extreme material hardship, extensive mobility, and the destruction of traditional ways in general all conspired to destroy marriages in the lower classes, while the forces of political terror and relative material advantage had a greater, and opposite, effect on the upper classes.

Equally important is the subcultural difference already noted — the greater need and capacity for a strong bond of love and dependency in upper-class marriages and the scant emotional bonding of marriage among the peasant and worker. This difference, very striking in the USSR, accounts for the different effect of external obstacles and difficulties: the lower the class level, the more dependent is the marriage on outer circumstances; the higher the class, the more it is held together by love and mutual respect, and the more impervious it is to ill turns of fate from the outer society. The very bottom of the status hierarchy, marriage partners from peasant areas with little education and only minimally influenced by the new Soviet era, may be an exception to this pattern. The most accurate estimate of the pattern of distribution among social classes of solidary marriages, then, would place them in the following order: (1) intelligentsia, (2) white-collar and the traditionalistic, least assimilated peasantry, and (3) workers and those peasant families into which the new patterns have been able to penetrate. In terms of the types described in the preceding chapter, the least cohesive is a transitional marriage, which is often transitional in residence and occupation — from rural to urban and farm to factory — as well as in authority pattern, emotional relations, and spiritual atmosphere.

Since one of the functions of normative culture is to restore and bond social relations that are disrupted or disruptive, it is worthwhile to note that the ideal patterns and virtues of Soviet men, women, and marriage stand in a systematic relation to the most likely sources of failure. In worker and peasant marriage, where the transitional type is so frequent, the main cultural norms focus on what not to do. Excessive drinking, for instance, seems to be so much a lower-class pattern that it dominates the role prescriptions of adult male among worker and peasants. An old peasant, describing his son-in-law, a sovkhoz worker, says simply: "He was good. He didn't drink vodka" (624 B 10). The need for control of physical aggression is also more frequently mentioned by workers and peasants. Being gentle (*tikhi*) and not having a hard temperament (*tverdyi kharakter*) is not likely to be such a salient part of the role expectations of a white-collar or intelligentsia man. A woman from a peasant background describes her husband, from a worker background, as she saw him at the beginning of their married life: "Tall and dark, attractive and attentive. He was calm, loved children, never quarreled with people, did not get into arguments or fights, did not drink" (97 B 4). A worker describes the temperament of his peasant father: "It was very mild [*miagki*]. It was . . . good. He never beat anyone" (213 B 20). Sobriety, control of aggression, honesty, marital fidelity, not kindness perhaps so much as the absence of its opposite — these are typically the most-stressed expectations of worker and peasant husbands. Women in these families are grateful for what seem like commonplace virtues to the equal-rights-with-love marriages found on higher social levels. A worker wife, for example, notes with approval that her husband worked and "brought all the money home to me" (98 B 2).

In the role of wife much the same order of differences can be observed. Sexual promiscuity is a cause for much concern in the lower class. A socially mobile respondent, one who progressed from peasant to worker, explains why divorces occur: "That is a serious question. Sometimes young people, 18 or 17, marry and they don't yet understand life. They do not yet understand character. You see a pretty face but no head, so you marry her and when family life comes she has no interest in it so they divorce; or the husband starts to run around, or the wife starts to run around. So they divorce" (213 B 39). The image carries over into his relationship with his own wife. He describes his marriage proposal: "I asked her, 'Do you want to marry me?' She said, 'Yes,' and I then said, 'Will you deceive me?' She said, 'No,' and then I said, 'All right, we'll continue.' [When was that?] In 1934, and in 1935 I married" (213 B 32). Even when some of the positive virtues are mentioned, it is characteristic that respect (*uvazhenie*) instead of love (*liubov*) is the type of marital bond desired. An army officer from the peasantry says that for a happy marriage between two spouses: "One should respect the other, help the other. Seek advice from the other, and not deceive the other" (175 A 20).

In general, the normative culture of Soviet marriage stresses taboos among workers and peasants and imperatives among the nonmanual sectors of the population. Injunctions to refrain from drinking, fighting, wifebeating, adultery, and other objectionable practices occupy the center of attention among the lower-status groups. In the upper-status family such behavioral restraint is taken for granted, and role expectations focus on the possession of especially notable and rewarded traits and accomplishments and on the essential and unique quality of the reciprocal personal feelings.

A Major Social Problem

There has almost certainly been a great amount of marital discord in the USSR, perhaps even of disaster-like proportions. It is likely, moreover, that as the decades have passed, marital conflict has become more rather than less troublesome. In Chapter 3 I examined some of the evidence indicating that the 1920's were turbulent in this respect. As a recent Soviet survey of the history of Soviet family life puts it, after the revolution moral decline and "psychological excesses" developed which "further deepened the disorganization of the family brought about by the mass destruction of the male population . . . and economic hardships," and in marital-family relations "Soviet society had to start off at an even lower level than that which existed in Tsarist Russia." [7]

The 1930's saw additional economic, political, and demographic convulsions which reached deep into the traditional ways of life of the peasantry, bringing millions of them precipitously into hastily expanded or newly contrived cities, dwellings, and jobs. Collectivization, the Five Year Plans, and Stalin's ever more closed and oppressively ruled society formed the outer façade; but behind the scenes, although Stalin's taboo permitted practically nothing to be written or even said about it at the time, there was great disorder in interpersonal relations. The official line until 1935 was that easy divorce was a way to guarantee sex equality — no woman need remain married to a man she did not love — and that marital and family affairs were a part of private life in which state, party, and society had no right to interfere. Thus, party policy and supporting legislation contributed to the toll of marital disruption already made heavy by more fundamental social and psychological forces.

Among the peasants and workers the right of divorce was often used or regarded as a lever that could spoil traditional modes of relatedness, with much attendant distress. A thirty-eight-year-old railroad worker from a peasant background says, "The Soviet regime gave the right of divorce . . . The wife, feeling strong from the legal viewpoint is not afraid; she is not respectful; and she does not trust her husband" (304 A 24). Freedom to divorce, remarry, and engage in extramarital sexual activity probably never reached the proportion in the villages that it did in the cities. In the larger cities particularly, and in some parts of the population, it was evidently stylish to change spouses frequently, and, so to speak, leave the care of the family to the former partner and the state. A boy tells of the behavior of his father, an engineer and university professor: "The years 1929 to 1932 were the unhappiest period for my family. At that time there were many cases of divorce. Many of our acquaintances got divorced. It was like an epidemic. My father was in the dangerous years — he was 39 or 40 years of age then — years in which he was looking for someone else. In general in the Soviet Union that was the kind of time it was. It cost nothing and it was very easy to get divorced. My mother held old opinions. For example, she thought that when you got married, you were married for all of your life" (14 A 54–55). It is not unusual to meet people in the Soviet Union who have been married and divorced fifteen times during the course of their lives,[8] just as one can find Soviet women who have had twenty abortions. If Soviet society was collectivist in official philosophy, and becoming more so in the formal aspects of its social structure, it often seemed quite dedicated to egoistic self-seeking in the informal relations of everyday life. A reportorial investigation of the situation in early 1936 in a Moscow civil registry office lists a number of "reasons why people divorce," noting, for example, that "there are many cases of instantaneous divorce as soon as 'he' learns that 'she' expects a baby." [9]

In the years from 1917 to 1936 divorce was legally easier to bring about than marriage in the USSR, for the consent of two was required for marriage, whereas one partner could divorce the other without the latter's consent and without any court process, at least from 1926 to 1936. It is now the generally accepted view inside the USSR, as it always has been in the outer world, that such a policy is a seriously disruptive influence on the stability of marriage. This assumption is probably true, but the cautionary possibility that the contrary may have been the case should at least be noted; the easy divorce policy and the spectacular excesses of some who used it may have aroused widespread indignation in the large majority of the population. A forty-two-year-old engineer, speaking of the pre-war period, says: "In the Soviet Union, marriages are conducted anywhere, with anyone one takes a fancy to, and no one is ever punished because the government allows it and punishes no one no matter which side is to blame" (615 B 10). Such indignation may well have served as an alerting device, often contributing to stronger marriages by bringing constantly to a person's mind the thought that his own particular marriage could be endangered if the excesses were not met by corresponding preventive measures. For instance, one Harvard Project respondent, a forty-one-year-old artist, said his most important goal in family life was "not to allow the family to fall apart under the influence of the domestic policy that was directed against it" (263 B 3). Presumably it became very clear that spouses had to make a special effort to be understanding and forebearing and to come to mutual agreement about such matters. A bookkeeper tells how a husband and wife must enjoy "complete mutual respect and trust, and mutual help," and that "all this is especially necessary in the USSR" (8 B 7).

In general, it has been easy for those interested in this problem to exaggerate the influence of party propaganda and the legal measures simply because these are the most explicit and visible causes. It is my impression, however, that urbanization, social mobility, and basic changes in the patterns of daily routine and relations inside the family such as those discussed in the two preceding sections have been much more important.

The best indicator of the extent of marital discord is divorce, but national divorce rates have been published only in the most recent years. In consequence, the argument that Soviet marital discord became increasingly serious with the passing of time must be supported in the main by an even more tenuous connecting link — swings in party policy and supporting legislation.

Divorce was free and easy from 1917 to 1935. In 1936 a new code was issued which required a graduated set of fees for divorce: 50 rubles for the first, 150 for the second, and 300 for the third and any subsequent divorces. Since average monthly earnings of workers and employees amounted to 238 rubles in 1936,[10] it is obvious that these fees must have acted as a powerful deterrent to registration of more than one divorce, at the least, and to any registration of divorce, particularly among the peasants, at most. Also, both parties were henceforth required to appear at the registry office, and the divorce was to be registered in the personal passport. Even though no court procedure was required, a continuing campaign of agitation and propaganda was waged against thoughtless marriage, frivolous divorce, foolish girls, and licentious rakes.

Toward the last years of World War II the now famous "law of 1944" was promulgated, introducing not a single but a double court procedure. It imposed a fee of 500 to 2,000 rubles for those couples who wanted a divorce badly enough, could get judicial approval, and had enough money to pay the cost. In addition to the fee, payable upon issuance of the divorce decree, applicants had to pay 100 rubles to the court when filing for divorce and to pay a similar sum for the publication in the local newspaper of the intention to seek a divorce. The lower or people's court then could hear the case, but all such courts were instructed to do everything in their power to reconcile the couples, a mission fortified by the code's failure to provide a specific list of grounds for divorce. Although the lower court was empowered to conduct a thorough investigation, the divorce itself could be granted only if reconciliation failed and another application was made to a higher, city or regional court.

It is evident without further details[11] that the new procedure was indeed a radical change from the past, a departure from the socialist attitude toward divorce, and an extremely tough divorce policy. Its intention was made maximally clear by the further proviso that no legal claim or right was to be extended to a wife or children resulting from an unregistered marriage, thus introducing for the first time since the Revolution an officially sponsored concept of the illegitimate child. Furthermore, "the decree was directed primarily at women; it said to them, 'If you wish to establish a sound and stable family and if you wish your interests and the interests of your children to be protected, do not be casual about intimate relations.'" [12] Such a pattern — an increasingly restrictive policy and law of divorce — serves as prima facie evidence that the social relations that it was designated to control and change have been distressingly unsettled, especially since socialist tradition and Soviet ideology had been so much in favor of easy divorce; Lenin himself is on record with a forceful declaration in favor of "complete freedom of divorce." [13]

There have been several results of this pattern. First, after the issuance of the 1936 law, dated June 27, 1936, the number of divorces in Moscow dropped from 2,214 in June to 215 in July, and the number in Leningrad registered for the January through June period dropped from 10,313 in 1936 to 3,860 in 1937.[14] By any standards, the previous Moscow rate had been a high one, in the neighborhood of one divorce for every 2.1 marriages in 1936.[15] Similar declines occurred after the passage of the 1944 law. For example, in the Uzbek Republic there were 52,700 marriages and 9,617 divorces registered in 1939, whereas in 1946 there were a similar number of marriages, 48,000, but only 653 divorces. In more urbanized areas rates remained relatively higher, but the decline after 1944 took on a similar pattern. In three districts of Kiev in 1939 there were 7,458 marriages and 2,063 divorces, while in the same districts in 1949 there were 6,592 marriages and 824 divorces.[16]

A second result of the restrictive divorce policy has been considerable variation from court to court and from year to year in the strictness with which the injunction to reconcile rather than divorce unhappy couples was followed. Some courts have been extremely reluctant to grant divorces, sometimes to the point where judges are caricatured as deaf to the needs for justice and humanity, holding rigidly and mechanically to the formula, "Reconcile the couple. We are against divorces." [17] In other courts, at least in the period from 1944 to 1949, it was common to grant divorces simply on the basis of mutual consent of the parties without even considering the validity of the grounds for divorce. A decree of the USSR Supreme Court Plenum of September 16, 1949, put an end to this, however, and supplied some further guidelines which in general required grounds to be serious indeed before divorce could be granted. A review of court practice reveals four types of such proper reasons: (1) absence of and inability to have children; (2) marriage originally contracted under pressure, threat, or deceit, including concealment of a serious illness; (3) conduct which "sharply violates the rules of socialist society," including gross mistreatment of spouse or children and adultery; and (4) actual long-term dissolution of the marriage.[18]

One of the variables to consider in the evaluation of Soviet divorce is the rate of refusal, which apparently has been declining. The Moscow City Court's refusals declined from a peak of 10 per cent in the years before 1956 to 4 per cent in that year, and in the Kiev Regional Court the decline was from 11.3 per cent in 1947 to 7.6 per cent in 1953 to 2.2 per cent in 1959. Probably these figures represent a more lenient court practice in the post-Stalin years as well as increasing reluctance on the part of the people to go to the expense and trouble of filing with a weak case.[19]

A third result of the 1944 law and attendant difficult divorce has been frequent abuse. The law which was "directed mainly at the women" has been taken advantage of by the men, chiefly, it seems, by those who would enjoy the pleasures of family life while they will and then move on to further experiences. This is revealed by a dramatic case published in 1963, concerning Rita and her unregistered husband, Nikolai: "He flung the door open and walked into the room, and even the visor of his cap, pulled down over his eyes, attested to his resolve. He pronounced these words in one breath, as if he had learned them by heart: 'I don't want to live with you, I won't give any money for the child. And try to prove he is mine. Nothing is registered.'" [20] On the other hand, there has also arisen the tendency to mistake the form of the law for the content, creating in Soviet family life a situation that would have appalled Marx, Engels, and Lenin. In a 1956 version: "Under cover of the law, which is intended to strengthen the family, bigots and hypocrites have crawled out of obscure crevices. These people, in essence, want a man to have a mistress without divorcing his wife, and a woman to betray her husband secretly, but, God forbid, not to leave openly to join the man without whom she cannot live." [21] All in all, in spite of its good intentions, the 1944 law has in fact subserved masculine irresponsibility, and for the past ten years the Soviet press has been filled with complaints about nichevo-like husbands and fathers who seek, and frequently have been able, to evade the law in avoiding their duties to support their families and raise their children.

A fourth result, which has become apparent only in the most recent years, is a crude divorce rate that has been surprisingly high. In 1960 the Soviet crude divorce rate was 1.3 per 1,000, not too far from that in America, 2.2, and much higher than England, France, and Germany, with rates of 0.5, 0.6, and 0.8 respectively.[22] Such a fact, in a land where it is claimed that objective conditions make for happy marriage and the law is supposed to take care of contrary tendencies arising out of subjective factors, permitted one commentator to state that the "rather complicated and expensive procedure" established in law for obtaining a divorce has not exerted any great influence: "Couples who have firmly decided to obtain a divorce are not deterred by the complexity of the divorce procedure." [23] Actually this comment is very misleading on two counts. In the years when the courts were enforcing the law with all strictness, there were indeed many couples whose firm decisions were completely ignored. Even in recent years the high cost of the fees has been an important deterrent, and the crude divorce rate of the USSR might well have been twice or three times as high if there had been no such "complicated and expensive procedure."

Perhaps most important of all, this chapter of Soviet social experience is entirely reminiscent of the ill-fated American experience with prohibition. For the fact is that the divorce rate reveals only a fractional part of the story; millions of Soviet couples have lived and are living in a state of unregistered or *de facto* marriage. No one knows, of course, exactly how many there are. A reporter wrote in 1956, "I have not been able to find statistical data anywhere on the number of families which have dissolved their marriages without going to court at all. As a matter of fact, no one is responsible for this matter, and I had to investigate it on my own." [24]

The reporter's investigations were conducted in villages, since he was told that "it is exceptional for inhabitants of rural areas to sue for divorce in the people's courts, and that there are hardly any cases of marriage dissolution in the villages." [25] He cited two examples. In the village of Pashkova, Byshev District, Kiev Province, there had not been a single divorce action among the 580 families, but seven had broken up without going to court and ten families were composed of men and women whose marriage had never been registered. A similar situation was found in the village of Stavishche, Brusilov District, Zhitomir Province. There were no divorce cases, but four collective farmers had left their wives and both the husbands and the wives had started new families without any formal registration.

Such examples, states the author, are typical. This is probably an understatement, for it is most likely that many have been ostensibly registered by misrepresentation, by altering or forging passports so as to hide previous marriages, and by changing city of residence. It has, indeed, become common knowledge in the USSR, and even something of a national scandal, that a good proportion of the population has been evading the law. For instance, a jurist pointed out in 1958 that "the existing divorce procedure . . . results in a situation in which many registered marriages exist on paper only. The fact is that the parties to such marriages have long since entered into so-called common-law marital relations with other mates, relations they are unable to formalize because of the unduly complex divorce procedure." [26] A Leningrad school teacher asked in 1960, "Do we not know many families in which the father and mother live together and everything seems fine, but the child's papers [birth certificate] contain a blank [instead of the name of the father]? What does such a child think, how does he explain to himself his unusual 'position in society'?" [27]

If *de facto* marriages are indeed "one of the chief sources of such 'illegitimate' children" [28] it is of some importance to know how many of the latter there are in the USSR. The school teacher from Leningrad, who has taught at least four classes, 150 pupils, per year for ten years, asserts that on the average one-fifth of a class has a blank after the word "father" on the birth certificate. A good many of these, of course, are the children of genuinely unmarried mothers and are regarded as truly illegitimate by the man on the street. But a good many of the rest are children of *de facto* marriages. A Soviet legal specialist estimated that there were 11,000,000 illegitimate children in the USSR in 1947, a year in which 3,312,000 unmarried mothers were receiving grants for support of their children.[29] The analysis cannot be carried further because additional information about ages, number of children per unmarried mother, and the like cannot be obtained and because it is probable that some proportion of the so-called unmarried mothers are actually living in wedlock but remain unregistered in order to be able to collect the generous state benefits for unmarried mothers. In any case, the huge number of illegitimate children is surely composed of a great many who are so only in name, by virtue of the difficulty experienced by one or both of their parents in getting a divorce.

If further evidence is needed, it can be furnished by the analysis of the 7,640 divorces granted by the Leningrad City Court in 1959. Of these, 20 per cent involved cases where one or both of the contestants were already living in another, *de facto,* marriage and had had children. If in half of the 20 per cent both spouses were in such a situation, and not members of the same divorce cohort, then 30 per cent of 7,640 or 2,292 *de facto* marriages, could be substantiated for Leningrad on this basis alone.[30]

To sum up, it would seem that a large amount of socially induced conflict in Soviet marriage has led to an official divorce rate reasonably high in comparative perspective and extraordinarily high in terms of legal obstacles to a divorce. A policy that denies divorce except on the most weighty grounds, whatever its attendant social advantages, is certain to be manipulated. "Sometimes, by prior agreement, husband and wife slander one another because they know that the court will not grant a divorce without serious accusations." [31] It has also led, we may be sure, to two further consequences. First, it has created a situation in which many persons must remain married only in a formal sense — "where only the common residence of a man and a woman remains, without love, without respect, without common interests and regard for each other — that is, without the basic elements that constitute a marriage." [32] Some of these couples remain together for the children's sake, or for personal, material, professional, or residential (for example, to retain the right to occupy a desirable residence, to be able to live in Moscow) reasons; other estranged couples may separate but remain married. In both cases, in addition to the usual problems when children are present of custody and rearing, payment of alimony, and so on, both partners are prevented by the law from seeking new partners in legal marriage. It is understandable that the bolder and less scrupulous in the population are often led to misrepresent their identities and to assume new family lives with falsified documents and new areas of residence.

A second consequence has already been discussed: a large number of unhappy Soviet marriages end with *de facto* divorce and *de facto* remarriage. Often couples do not even bother to seek a legal divorce because of the high cost; they simply move away and start new families, facing a life together in which both their legal and social status is shaky. The *de facto* marriage has become so common that by sheer force of numbers and mutual sympathy it has won a measure of social acceptance, though there are still traces of a depreciatory attitude toward it.

Matters become even more serious in the event that a *de facto* marriage fails. The estranged wife has only a tenuous legal basis for support[33] and the children are likely to become not only illegitimate but also hungry, ragged, and unsupervised, good candidates for juvenile delinquency. Soviet writers point with unexceptional regularity to absence of one or both parents as an important cause of delinquency. One discussion notes that a frequently violated norm of Soviet socialist morality is gross violation of the requirement to support children and that this is usually found where there are children from an unregistered marriage in which the partners are estranged. Furthermore, while public opinion and various collectives can play some role in obliging the father or, more rarely, the mother to support the child, they are no substitutes for legal compulsion.[34]

It is not often that analysis of Soviet published sources permits the demonstration of a serious but publicly unadmitted social problem which derives in good part from a Soviet law. This has been the case with the 1944 law, however, for throughout the entire decade after the death of Stalin the defects of the 1944 legislation on marriage and the family have been the most widely aired topic of Soviet family life. Writers have repeatedly pointed out the sore consequences of *de facto* marriage and urged a return to the divorce policy of Lenin. One vigorous proponent of reform claimed that he talked with "dozens of judges, lawyers, officials of the prosecutor's office, engineers, doctors, workers, and collective farmers, people of various ages and educational backgrounds, and not one of them — not one! — approved of the situation that has developed in our divorce practice. Everyone — absolutely everyone! — felt that this situation has to be changed."[35] In the same year, 1956, four of the country's most famous intellectuals published a critical letter pointing out that not only childhood but motherhood was taking both legitimate and illegitimate forms, and urging that the Supreme Soviet "repeal legally what life itself rejects."[36] In 1960 a well-known writer declared that it had been fifteen years since the law was passed, that many complaints had been published, that judges have to act against their consciences, and that soon the children will begin to object, too. "Why is nothing done?" he protested.[37]

Although the theme is muted in the Soviet published sources, it seems quite apparent that a situation had developed through the regime's own action which merits the label "anomic." A commonly shared goal — the attainment of a happy marriage through, if necessary, divorce from the partner of an unhappy one — was made inaccessible to many, as a result of which illegal or deviant means of reaching it became common. In the words of one observer, "the government states that everyone has the right to divorce while simultaneously making it extremely difficult for most persons to utilize this 'right.' "[38]

The wheels of justice, it is known, turn slowly, but by 1964 a Supreme Soviet subcommittee of thirty-four members had prepared a new draft law on marriage and the family which, it was announced, would eliminate the most objectionable flaws of the 1944 law. The law was passed as a decree of the Presidium of the USSR Supreme Soviet on December 10, 1965, and ratified in August 1966.[39]

In respect to the preceding decade, the effort to repeal the law came about as close as conceivable in the USSR to a ground-swell of public opinion, a genuine popular campaign by the people, and reform from below. Intellectuals, jurists, and evidently a good percentage of the rank and file proved to be against a situation in which it was necessary for large numbers of people to employ illegal means — evasion of the law on marriage and divorce — in order to reach a commonly desired and approved goal — establishment of a happy marital relationship. The whole episode showed, in the words of a Soviet commentator, that: "People's family and marriage relationships lend themselves less than any others to direct regulation by legal norms. Legislation undoubtedly influences these relationships indirectly. But the influence of legal standards is beneficial only provided that they take into account the actual, existing relationships."[40] Soviet marriages will not all become notoriously happy thereby, but it is not insignificant that with the passage of a new law the Soviet people will have won a small victory in their struggle to live as happy a life as their material and social circumstances permit.

V

PARENTS
AND CHILDREN

Although a great deal is known about officially recommended patterns of childrearing in the USSR, very little information is available about the actual behavior and feelings of Soviet parents and even less about those of their children. Apart from the general absence of a tradition of social scientific research, there seem to be three main reasons for the lack of information. One is the fact that much interest, both inside and outside the country, has been focused upon state-sponsored institutions for childcare and the handling of children by public agencies. These have constituted a departure in modern societies from the focus on the role of home and parent, but the departure has been primarily a matter of principle only, for, as we have seen in Chapter 7, the great majority of Soviet children continue to be raised at home by their parents and grandmothers. Secondly, there are some very pronounced social class differences in childrearing, as in most other aspects of informal patterning in Soviet society. The eliciting, study, and publication of such contrasts would constitute a large step toward the portrait of a society with major subcultural cleavages along the socioeconomic dimension, which would not be to the taste of the Soviet rulers. A third explanation stresses the major theme of Soviet social history, namely, the fact that it has been a time of immensely rapid social change. Social change, it appears, is reflected most poignantly in the relations between parents and children and has often resulted in considerable and unwelcome parent-youth conflict.

In Chapters 10 and 11 social class differences will be prominently discussed. The first of the two chapters looks at Soviet parents in the earlier stages, and the second shows them in later years, confronted by children who sometimes think differently, especially about such important matters as religion and politics.

A SURVEY OF the family life of Moscow workers in the 1920's states that care for children rather than "individual sex love" was often the basic link uniting the members of the worker family. A textbook published in 1964 asserts that childrearing is the family's "most important spiritual function." The generalizations highlight a glaring shortcoming in the marxist theory of the family: children are seen mainly as a millstone around the neck of a would-be productive worker, their mother, and public childrearing is preferred not only to give the mother freedom but for other reasons as well.

For almost two decades the party and the Soviet State offered little encouragement to parents; they were temporarily holding the line until better arrangements could be made for their children. Subsequently, as the policy shifted, the family became a legitimate socialist family, childrearing came to be its main social responsibility, and a home-grown, very un-marxist, social worker and pedagogue, Makarenko, in fact if not by conscious intent filled in the lacuna left by Marx, Engels, and Lenin. But these are all part of high policy rather than the real Soviet family and its children, which can be discovered only if we copy Makarenko's example in our own way by eschewing theory and dealing with life itself. How, then, are Soviet children treated, reared, thought about by their parents? Some of the latter do indeed accept and follow Makarenko, seeking, for instance, in their own lives to carry out the formula: "Confront the child with maximum demands and accord him maximum respect." But many others, as we shall see, do not; official family policy, Makarenko's theories, and recommended practices are all submerged in a sea of tradition, social class differences, and the difficulties offered by Soviet social conditions.

The State Takes Over

Some Soviet children are reared not in families but in public institutions. The Soviet land has always had more than its share of orphans, and to their number may be added many more semi-orphans, most typically children with mothers but no fathers. There are, in addition, places in homes for babies, children's homes, and boarding schools where children are reared on a relatively full-time basis for parents who wish to relinquish them and can establish good reasons for doing so.

Full orphans are sometimes cared for by relatives, but during hard times it has often been easier to take advantage of the state's facilities. The law of 1944 carried as one of its provisions the chance for mothers without mates to allow their children to be reared by the state if they wished, and apparently large numbers of them have taken advantage of the right. It was reported in 1959 that of the seventeen children's homes located in the Saratov Region a majority of the children had a father or mother and that some even have both parents living. In the Svishchevka Children's Home fifty-three out of ninety-one children and in the Pugachev Children's Home sixty-two out of one hundred twenty-two children had at least one parent.[1] Thus, it is not entirely accurate to think of the children's homes as orphanages, although historically it is probably true that the majority of charges have been orphaned by death or desertion.

There are also circumstances in which the authority of the Soviet Government is used to divest the parents or parent of their legal rights. For example, in 1962 *Pravda* reported the case of a mother who was giving her daughters an unsuitable rearing. After becoming a convert to a religious sect, she had prevented the children from wearing the badge of the Young Pioneer, forbidden them to attend meetings, forced them to learn prayers, and (somewhat illogically, it strikes the reader) left them without supervision. The mother was divested of her rights as a parent in a court process and her children were taken from her, the older two being sent to boarding school and the younger daughters placed in a children's home.[2] This case illustrates the Soviet official prejudice against religion, as well as displaying the state's power to interfere in the personal life of its citizens. Against parents, however, this power is probably invoked more frequently for abuse and lack of support than for giving religious instruction. A sensational and tragic episode is furnished by the case of Tatyana Tarasova, a construction worker from a populated settlement of Khabarovsk who, it is reported, "abused her nine-year-old son, Kolya, and beat him for no reason." Kolya was also poorly looked after, running around ragged, hungry, and dirty. Finally, in November 1955 he ran away, hid in a haystack, and eventually had to have both of his frostbitten feet amputated. His mother had not only to forfeit her parental rights for this, but also to start serving a six-year sentence of "deprivation of freedom." [3] Kolya, we may suppose, benefited considerably from the change.

The provisions governing Soviet children's homes allow parents to give up their children voluntarily, if they have a legitimate reason. Some reasons are temporary, such as incapacity to act in the role of parent caused by sickness, trips and expeditions connected with occupational life, and severe hardship of any sort that would make it difficult to give proper attention to the child. An article of 1961 states that one often sees the "so-called 'student children' " in the infants' homes (*dom rebenka*); the student parents are out in the field getting their practical training, or living in a dormitory finishing work for a degree.[4] Relatively permanent disability may be based on family situations that are not easily remedied. For instance, in 1956 the Gorelov family of Moscow was in a difficult situation: Mrs. Gorelov was seeking to support by herself five small children and two old women unable to work. The Soviet version of social workers, representatives from the "Children's Room" in the Ninth Precinct of the Moscow militia (police), helped Mrs. Gorelov by alerting the equivalent of the Parent-Teachers Association — the Parents Committee at the local school — who extended aid. The police also helped Mrs. Gorelov place three of her children in a children's home.[5]

Probably the most troublesome aspect of the operation of children's homes lies in those cases where parents have the capacity to rear their children but lack the will. It is often easy to find excuses that qualify as legitimate in the official regulations — crowded housing conditions, frequent travel assignments, and the like. Soviet press reports, as well as accounts by several parents in the sample of families discussed by Bischoff, suggest another facet of the problem, the ready availability of a complex of convenient beliefs. Made up of a biased selection from the official ideology about such matters, these beliefs include the notion that producing a child in itself represents full discharge of the main duty to the state, that the state is in principle responsible for the rearing of the children, and that while caring for children is socially useful labor it is done more effectively by specialists.

In recent years these attitudes have been criticized by the regime. The parents have been accused of social parasitism and callousness, and suggestions have been made that they contribute to the support of their children even if the latter are in children's homes. Several varieties of injustice are at stake here. The children frequently suffer from the knowledge that they have parents who have "abandoned them to the care of strangers";[6] there is no chance for legal adoption by another couple because the parents are required by law to give consent and usually refuse to do so; and (as a suggested explanation of the last point) from time to time such parents turn up in their old age to claim that right to support by children which the code of law on marriage and the family accords them. There is also some inconsistency in the policy followed by the boarding schools, where parents must, in contrast to the situation in the children's home, pay partial support for their children. This inconsistency is doubtless one reason for the decision announced in 1959 to convert some of the children's homes into boarding schools.[7]

In any case, the statistics show that neither children's homes nor the newer boarding schools have as yet taken care of many children. The figures cited for number accommodated in children's homes, youth colonies, homes for delinquent children, and boarding schools for physically handicapped children are not very high — 324,200 in 1940, 635,900 in 1950, and 375,000 in 1958.[8] Since, as noted in a preceding chapter, in 1960 there were some 525,000 children in the boarding schools, most Soviet parents are at best, to repeat a point also made earlier, assisted rather than replaced by public childrearing agencies.

A detailed picture of what happens in Soviet childrearing institutions would be revealing. The philosophy and approach is distinctive enough to make comparisons with other countries worthwhile. A systematic study of the effects of rearing children in public institutions in the USSR would also be helpful: the whole question of institutional childrearing has become more and more controversial since the death of Stalin, and it is entirely possible that the climate of official opinion and policy is swinging away from it. In any case, after this brief survey of some of the patterns and problems connected with childrearing by the Soviet state, it is best to leave the minority and turn to the majority of Soviet children, reared by their parents much as in years past in Russia and in other lands today.

"Natural" Childrearing

In a large proportion of Soviet families children are conceived, born, and reared with relatively little concern, guidance, or attention from their parents. The sense of parental responsibility does not go far beyond the most primitive demands of nature, and children are "just there," taken as a natural result of married life and accepted quite casually, almost with indifference. The attitudes of the parents and their relations with the six children in the family of a store manager in a Donbass city are described as follows: "The children were hardly a burden, they were simply there, but did not strengthen the marriage. He had little interest in them, the wife somewhat more. She guided their upbringing somewhat more than he, but the school was first and foremost in this. The tone between the mother and the children was harsh, but not without affection; he did not concern himself with them at all. The children grew up quite wild; for example, they fed themselves partly by garbage from the street [1950–1953], and had a rather neglected look to them. This was due to the mother's lack of time. [She did not work, but was often away for the purpose of "providing" for them.] The children themselves treated each other quite inconsiderately and in an unfeeling way. The number of children was not planned; they simply came" (Bi 199).

In another family many of the same features are found. B is an assistant manager of a large dump for a city in the Urals. He has three children:

Neither Mr. B nor his wife were particularly concerned with their children's upbringing. Mr. B. occasionally insisted that the school work be done. But otherwise the children were throughout the day left to their own devices and they wandered around in the area. That the oldest, a daughter not yet 15, already was carrying on a love affair was a matter of indifference to the mother, and looked upon even with a certain pride by the father. Relations between parents and children varied; at times they were overwhelmingly affectionate and at times astoundingly coarse. The children themselves behaved in general quite apathetically, but in some ways were very ill-bred. The father had the greater influence. What he demanded was for the most part done, even if unwillingly. In contrast the mother was at times even tormented by them, treatment which she accepted without any counter measures, for "the kids don't mean any harm by it . . ." The mother received some help from the oldest daughter, and would rapturously praise her for it, the daughter accepting the praise half vainly, half forgivingly. [Bi 200.]

A third example, in which the circumstances are even more casual, is the family of a metalworker in the Komi Autonomous Republic where there are eighteen people, including seven children: "The children were growing up amidst it all just like the pigs, who themselves lived together with the family. They experienced everything possible and became accustomed to everything at an early age. No one worried especially about them nor took any special interest in them. The parents were not unloving toward them, but supervised them little, so that all the children had a somewhat neglected look. In the summer, for example, they ran around clad only in little shirts. Some of the children were already going to school, but this had little influence upon them . . . The births were not planned; the children simply came. A birth meant only a short interruption in sexual intercourse . . . The children were not punished; they were only shouted at" (Bi 200).

These and similar cases, which represent a common pattern for the peasant and part of the worker sectors of the population, present eight typical features:

(1) There is little or no birth planning or systematic use of contraceptive techniques. Intercourse, pregnancy, and birth tend to be accepted as natural and inevitable. Abortion, often under primitive conditions, is the major means for restricting the size of the family if this is deemed desirable.

(2) There are strong traces of a male sex preference — more joy at the birth of a son than a daughter. This view is doubtless at present linked to the presumed greater capacity of a son to earn and provide a household for haven in old age. However, it is also a cultural value, good for its own sake. In the words of a peasant woman: "[Did you want to have a son or a daughter?] A son. [Why?] It is always better to have a son first and then the second one can be a daughter. [Why is it better?] It is considered better. It's a real mother [thrusts out her chest, stresses word "real"] who bore a son, but she's not so much of a mother if she has a daughter. And the father is more satisfied with a son" (275 B 37). As might be expected, these families also show relatively strong traces of the traditional patriarchal influence in husband-wife relations.[9]

(3) Babies are breast fed, on demand as a rule. A forty-eight-year-

old peasant says: "When he begins to cry it means he is hungry. It is a law" (296 B 24). Peasant babies are also often tightly swaddled in long strips of cloth for the first nine months or year. The old-fashioned pacifier (*soska*), in which the mother first chews grain or bread, then puts it into a small cloth bag, and thence into the baby's mouth, is often used.

(4) As the children grow older, little attention is paid them and little expected of them. They are not punished physically, at least not regularly or often, but rather are controlled primarily by scolding, threats, and shouts. The father tends to look upon the younger children as playthings, but as they grow older he seems relatively uninterested in them. There is much less display of affection from the father and less spiritual closeness between him and the children than between the mother and the children.

(5) The children run free and even wild at an early age, often clad only in a little shirt, as was the peasant custom in earlier times. To the observer from an urban area or higher class level they seem unkempt, prematurely exposed to the world, and generally neglected. By the time the children grow into adolescence, they are often quite independent of parental surveillance. A young man from a worker family tells of his youth: "In Russia it is this way with us. I had many friends, and sometimes I didn't come home for the whole summer, especially I and my older brother. For three months I didn't come home; we used to travel on freight trains. There were many like this . . . in poor families they don't pay any attention to the children. Very little boys often play cards, and do whatever they want . . . As soon as the weather got warm we were rarely found at home. Only mama and papa lived peacefully" (521 A 39, 40).

(6) Social relations between parents and children and among the children themselves have a spontaneous or natural air. Emotional variability rather than evenness is characteristic. As in one of the preceding cases the parent-child tie is at times "overwhelmingly affectionate and at times astoundingly coarse." [10] The use of physical punishment as a means of discipline, when it does occur, is often haphazard or *pro forma,* more an expression of parental feelings than a tactic deliberately used to socialize. Unless the beatings are especially severe or frequent, which rarely is the case, the children accept them with marked casualness. Another youth from a worker family explains his lack of attendance at the obligatory meetings connected with his school: "On these

occasions the teacher would visit my parents and my parents beat me a little, but nothing else in particular happened" (539 A 4).

(7) The children's education and control, insofar as possible, is given over rather completely to the school, often with an air of gratitude and even relief, as if the parents realize that their own capacities are limited. Because of the lack of a suitable home atmosphere in relation to learning and education and the general family indifference toward the children, however, school experiences are not always happy ones. The children are likely to have a more or less unpleasant or meaningless experience at school and grow up to be adults without much attachment to the idea of education.[11] In this respect, too, these families perpetuate tradition.[12]

(8) The chief meaning of the children in the lives of their parents other than as "natural members" of the family is as a future source of security. The attitudes of B, the assistant dump manager, are typical: "The children were for B not a decisive factor in maintaining this marriage. He was attached to them rather as to a toy from which one derives his pleasure. From the other side, he also wants them to be able to earn good money, so that when he is old they can support him . . . Mrs. B also . . . thought that later, when she would not be able to work, she would be able to live with one of her children, so that, with the aid of the otherwise inadequate social security benefits, she could then live better" (Bi 199–200).

In general this kind of family, the most traditional, contrasts most strikingly with the officially proscribed patterns against which the greatest part of Soviet official efforts at reform have been directed and in which the process of change is occasionally most clearly to be observed. There are several issues at stake, the most important, perhaps, being sanitation. In Viriatino at present there are no peasant midwives, though there were until recently. Births, which take place in the home, are "always with a *feldsher* [medical technician] present." However, pregnant women "especially the younger ones, do not divulge the fact, and this makes the work of the medical personnel difficult." Furthermore, continues the account, "With the older women it is sometimes necessary to struggle, in particular to insist that they give birth in a bed, since, they, by tradition, want to give birth in the bath or on straw upon the floor" (Ku 222). Similar problems are faced after the birth of the child. The continuing practice of chewing bread to give to the baby has been cited by ethnographers as proof of how slowly the more deeply rooted family customs die out: "Such a custom is followed even in families where the mothers follow medical advice and the care for the children in other respects is completely hygienic" (Ku 222).

Many of the basic norms of the officially recommended pattern of childrearing can best be understood as the contrary of the behavior that is most typical in this group of families. For instance, though Soviet literature and propaganda have long urged that mothers discard the practice of tight swaddling, it persists stubbornly and is rationalized in a variety of ways. One is described by a forty-six-year-old skilled worker: "They still do it. It was done with my children and it is done in the Soviet Union. They say it is because if you don't do it the feet of the children will be crooked" (167 A 16). For another example, scheduled rather than demand feeding is strongly recommended. The future and the past are both to be seen in Viriatino: "Young women carefully observe the feeding of the child according to schedule, in which it is often necessary to skirmish with older women in the family (with the mother-in-law, with the old mother), who suffer sharply with each cry of the child and demand immediate feeding" (Ku 222).

Since the early 1930's the precepts of Anton Makarenko have been accorded special prominence as models for Soviet childrearing practice. One of the most important of them applies to a great range of behavior over and above the feeding of infants and is ordinarily absent in this first group of families — a careful daily scheduling and systematic organization of the children's time and activities.[13] Similarly, parents are persuaded to love their children in a rational, demanding, or conditional way. One wartime example is unusually strong, leaving no doubt about the principle: "The true love of a mother is bound up with the demands she has upon her children . . . Thus the maternal heart cannot fail to turn away from a son who shows cowardice in battle." [14]

Although few mothers would be inclined to formulate conditional love this way, in many respects a good number in the population seem to have accepted the official views as their own. This is particularly true of patterns that are prejudicial to the health of children. A young worker, up from the peasantry, describing the behavior of his parents and his sister, still a peasant, is obviously quite displeased: "Our parents did it thus: a child is born and the mother feeds him for nine months. Then he chews a pacifier. And then he does not cry, but gets a great big belly and rickets comes from it. It is just black bread. I did not do that with my child. My sister did and I bawled her out for it. She even did under the Soviet power. She said, 'It's all the same. We have a lot of them. If they die, let them die.' . . . It was a sorry situation with her. [Were there any other differences?] Of course. They were as free as the wind, always running around, and she sat at home while they were outside. They were barefoot and only clad in a little shirt. In the wintertime they ran about undressed" (213 B 45).

It is understandable that the children of such parents grow up to be relatively independent and often unruly. The lack of consistency and attention to matters of discipline in the earliest years creates its own special problems later. In such families the parents' attention is usually focused more on avoiding trouble than on inculcating the more positive virtues. The most salient norms of childbearing, like those in marriage, therefore tend in this group to be proscriptive rather than prescriptive, taboos rather than imperatives. One young man from a worker family comments: "My mother was illiterate. She only said, 'Do not lie, do not steal' " (121 A 12). Other salient norms in these families are similar. Parents see themselves responsible for efforts to "keep the children off the street," to "raise them as well-behaved, not vulgar people," and to prevent them from becoming "hooligans."

The biggest problem for such parents, from the children's earliest years, is control, particularly the role of physical punishment, to which there is a long tradition of official opposition. In the past, if a complaint was entered, parents who beat their children could be rebuked, fined,[15] publicly shamed, or otherwise brought to account. As one young peasant reported, "In 1939, for instance, if you beat your child, the child could go to the village soviet and report it, and the father would be fined twenty-five rubles" (432 A 30). The official viewpoint on physical punishment is well expressed by Lenin's widow, who wrote in 1930: "Earlier it was so: if a father thrashed his little son with a strap, nobody would say anything. It is 'his' son. If a mother pulls the hair of her adolescent daughter, they see it and say nothing. It is 'her' daughter. Our house is on a different territory. Children are the 'live property' of parents. This cannot be tolerated any longer. It must be made clear that every person who beats a child is a partisan of the old slave faith, a partisan of the old slave views, a partisan of the power of the landowners and capitalists, although they might not even be conscious of it." [16] By and large the Soviet population of parents seems receptive to this taboo. Even in worker and peasant families the use of physical punishment, although it does occur from time to time, is hardly a frequent trait,[17] and many Soviet refugees expressed considerable indignation at what they saw in the German family. One reports: "They beat children oftener in Germany. The simplest people in the Soviet Union do not beat their children. [Not even the peasants?] No, it is done much less than it is here. I was amazed to see how a mother would hit her child in the face in Germany. It's a horror" (618 B 8). A pre-Soviet cultural pattern may be involved here, for apparently physical punishment was never widely used in childrearing in traditional Russian peasant life.[18]

In any event, whether cultural tradition or official Soviet pressure has been the predominant reason, there is no doubt of the existence of a rather strong taboo concerning the use of physical force against children. Both this taboo and a norm previously mentioned are described by a university professor: "One must be able to anticipate the children's naughtiness, and never punish them by spanking; they should be brought up according to a schedule, with meals, outdoor exercises and work at set times" (454 B 10). The interesting question here is, if there is both a strong taboo and a general disinclination against physical punishment, what kind of influence takes its place? The recommended techniques include conditional love, deprivation of pleasure or privilege, rational argument, and setting a good example. All of these, however, require a level of effort, articulateness, and self-restraint that is rarely found among peasant and working-class parents. Many such parents, consequently, are markedly unable to do much in the way of influencing their children. It often seems to them a question of letting the children run free and wild or backsliding into the use of physical punishment. The fact that the latter is a distinct possibility is implied by the liveliness and salience of the no-beating norm itself. A working class boy, for example, makes a typical comment: "I always had good relations with my father. He never beat me" (153 A 31).

Apparently, at issue is more than a matter of beating, a term that implies an undue level of severity, the use of a strap, welts on the back, and so on. That is to say, the proscription is not a matter of degree but an absolute. As such it applies not only to the presumably stronger and more violent father but also to the mother, who is responsible for the children in their younger years. In this respect there is some evidence of a historical reversal in the younger families, of a structurally imposed difference in the attitudes of mother and father, in which the father rather than the mother plays the role of protector. Mothers seem more inclined to use physical coercion and also more likely to be rebuked for it by their husbands. A worker tells: "I did not like it when they beat a little child so it hurt. [Who did that?] My wife. You can threaten him a little, but you should not beat him. I came home from the factory and he showed me his little red bottom. I bawled her out properly for that, and also for not looking after him" (213 B). The women, closer to the everyday tasks of childrearing, are more likely to surrender to the temptation to use force, and the men, it seems, are more idealistic about the treatment of the child.[19]

However, the main conclusion to which one is led by a survey of the control and punishment problem in these families is that a good part of it is simply relinquished — given over to the school, the youth organizations, and the street. That influence which the parents do exert is usually sporadic, expressive rather than purposive, and ultimately ineffective.

Child-centered Families

In some families the children are the pride and joy of the parents, and a good part of family life is oriented, sometimes quite exclusively, toward their welfare. The contrast with the preceding group is striking. Rather than the casual and even indifferent attitude described previously, these mothers and fathers are much concerned from the beginning. A nurse, married to a university lecturer, reports: "Because we had a dearly loved only child, we lived and worked for him. He was the main aim of our life. My husband and I wanted to make him a decent, honest, and diligent man" (178 B 2). Time, attention, and interest all tend to become focused upon children, family, and home, often to the extent that the advent of a child changes the entire daily life routine, as in the case of this worker from Moscow: "His striving was in the direction of his family and upon his and its well-being . . . He was very interested in his house and household, for he made many things for his home at his place of work . . . His free time was important to him; if he could, he finished work on the dot, for he wanted to go home to his family life. While on leave he stayed at home and journeyed to the Moskva [River] with his wife and children to go swimming . . . He was interested in the child and often went walking with him" (Bi 298).

For these children, life is quite different. They are, in the first place, likely to be part of a small family and have a mother and father by whom they are consciously desired and eagerly awaited. Most of the traditional patterns of childrearing are not to be seen. They have been replaced by new ones, more rational and scientific and more self-conscious. As one man, himself reared in a peasant family, reported about the recommended method of feeding infants: "She fed them by the clock. At first every two hours and always until the child was full, i.e. until the child let go of the breast by himself" (102 B 7). Another, also himself reared in a peasant family, notes that: "Our child was fed according to a definite schedule, regardless of whether she was crying or not" (67 B 9). However, backsliding seems to be frequent. A worker notes that: "My wife nursed the baby according to a schedule, but if he cried she fed him" (34 B 7).

Questions of control and discipline are discussed and solved deliberately. The parents tend to be conscientious and often demand high standards of behavior of themselves. Setting a good example is an important role, quite in the pattern advocated by Makarenko. A white-collar worker states: "First of all the parents themselves must be disciplined, and show their children an example. Only then can they later on require the same from the children" (71 B 8). In contrast to the practice among parents from peasant and worker background, considerable stress is placed upon the use of rational argument. However, it is true that such patterns cross the boundaries of the social group where they are modal. An older worker from the peasantry recommends this approach: "Talk to them, influence them with stories and examples: 'Look how that girl does and how people laugh at her, but look at this one. See how smart she is.' That is the way to influence her and that will be good" (279 B 51). When punishment is needed, these mothers and fathers usually try to follow the officially recommended technique — deprivation of some prized activity or pleasure. Among the very young, restraint of free movement is common. The wife of a mechanic tells that when her child misbehaved: "I set him on a chair in the middle of the room" (43 B 6). Conditional love is also a consciously used technique in many families. An engineer and his wife punished their son by "denying him our affection and ignoring him until he came to apologize" (255 B 7). All these practices, of course, are much more closely aligned with the approach recommended by official agencies and literature than is the case in the preceding group.

Again in contrast with the modal pattern in the first group, those in which childrearing is "natural," these children are neither neglected nor are they given great freedom. They are never allowed to run wild. Social relations and behavior between parents and children in this group are markedly more even, less expressive emotionally. On the parental side this corresponds to a greater ability to plan ahead, to control impulses in other ways,[20] and sometimes even to undergo considerable sacrifice for the sake of the children. In the family of a transportation worker from a rope factory near Voronezh, at the time of observation (1950), the parents were setting aside 150 rubles per month to be used to further the children's schooling. Further: "The parents were very modest in respect to their own needs for food, but the children ate better in the things they took to school with them. The entire marriage was based on the children and on their social ascent, and the parents sacrificed themselves for that" (Bi 208).

As in the first group, the parents' thoughts for the future are tied up with their present attitude toward the children. However, it is less a question of material security for themselves than a matter of ambition and probably vicarious satisfaction to be derived from the successful lives of their offspring. Social mobility for the children is often the most important goal of the family. Correspondingly, the attention of the parents and consequently also of the children is concentrated upon the main pathway to social mobility — superior performance in the system of formal education. The contrast with the recent past, in fact often the childhood experience of the parents themselves, makes the goal of educational achievement on the part of their children all the more important. A young worker, up from the peasantry, is explaining the contrast between his aim as a parent and the way in which his own parents saw things: "I wanted my son to be educated, so he would know, so he would be an engineer. Higher education. But our parents — we grow up and they look at you and say, 'Can you work?' and so to work. That is the difference" (213 B 47).

It is hard to exaggerate the importance attached by this group of contemporary Soviet parents to educational achievement. The attitude is found on all class levels, including the collective farm peasantry. Of course, the expressed reasons for such great stress on education vary by social class. Collective farm and worker parents tend to see education more exclusively as a means to a better job. A young working-class girl displays this attitude: "[Why is it good to get an education?] So I could get a job. So I could live better . . . [Are there any other advantages to education besides getting a good job?] You can get a better job. You can get a good job . . . [Are there any other advantages to getting more education?] Yes, a better job. [I mean beside that?] No. I don't know of any other advantages" (93 A 39).

Although white-collar parents do connect educational training with a well-paid, interesting, or high-status job, they also see it as a means of self-development or as simply a value in itself. For example, the daughter of a school teacher explains the attitude of her parents: "[How did your parents feel about your education?] They always wanted me to get a good education, and Mama always saw to it that I did my lessons. Mama always said that the most important thing is to study, and the rest will take care of itself. All I had to do was to look out for my education. If I did not do my lessons, she would find out about it and I was not allowed to go to the movies" (438 A 12). Of course, the perceived rewards of education are partly a matter of attitudinal salience. The more educated parent tends in the Soviet Union to look upon an extended period of education and a well-paid job for his children as a matter of course, and hence both he and his children tend to find the corollary advantages or fringe benefits most worthy of attention.

The deification of educational achievement and occupational mobility has several sources. First, perhaps, it is simply the correlate, inside the family, of a rapidly industrializing society with a virtually open class system. To an extent, too, there is the influence of the official propaganda line — youth-centered humanism. The welfare of children is a serious, even a sacred, matter in an ideology that portrays a better future. An excerpt from the official line on "why Soviet parents should love and care for their children" explains: "Children are our future, our joy and happiness. Our first thoughts are about them. Theirs must be a life of smiles. For their sake are we fighting and working. Our children are destined to live in a communist society and in the Soviet Union everything is being done to give them a happy life so that they should grow up to be healthy, vivacious citizens of the state, its future masters." [21]

There are other reasons for the elevated position of children in these child-centered families. The substantial effort of the state to accord special privileges to children, to make them an "upper class" — "best clothed, best fed, best entertained, best everything" — as a Western visitor describes it,[22] has an aura of expiation about it. The happy children of today easily call to mind the less happy past. The memory of homeless waifs — ragged, hungry, often criminal — the product of wars, collectivization, the chaos of the early years — is probably still vivid at the top level. Similarly, individual Soviet mothers and fathers remember the deprivations of their own lives with the determination that they not be repeated in the lives of their children. The president of the RSFSR Academy of Pedagogical Sciences reported in 1961 that "we still have parents who think their children must in no way put themselves out. These adults figure that they worked hard enough in life, and have even seen a great deal of sorrow. 'Let our children live easily and lightheartedly,' they say." [23] Apparently, for many in the contemporary generation of adults, childhood has few happy memories. In the minds of such parents, children are redemptive instruments; they bring new hope into the ruins of the parents' own lives. The son of a Ukrainian peasant-worker family says: "You had to study further if you wanted to get through with the middle school. I clearly saw that as my father gathered his last kopecks so that we should finish school. They could not even afford to buy themselves clothing. They only wanted us to get an education. Mother said that her life was gone anyway, and that she would work for the sake of her children, so that maybe her children would live better" (520 A 40).

Much the same sentiment is portrayed by the novelist Leonov in his interesting character sketch of a "new Soviet man" of 1930. Uvadiev is a "dedicated priest of the dictatorship of the proletariat." "He fled tenderness." Smoking and drinking are banished because they are "against regulations." Love is a necessary evil, annoyingly interfering with the exacting demands of his work. Yet this man, "intolerant of happiness and inhuman in his contempt for the pleasanter amenities of living," is at heart a lonely, almost tragic figure. His humanity breaks forth in his feelings for his mother and in his desire to be a father: "He wanted a child, not so much for the conventional reasons, but as a kind of justification of the bitter self-sacrifices of his life; a child who would grow up to enjoy, or whose progeny would enjoy, the fruits of everything he had labored to accomplish." [24]

Often the sense of personal failure, disappointed hopes, and frustration of occupational ambition plays a role. In a society where opportunities have been plentiful, an attitude tends to emerge in many worker and peasant families which calls to mind the relation of the American immigrant father to his son. A respondent, telling of his working-class father's hopes for him, said: "My father always insisted that I should change my profession and not be a worker. All this he insisted on even when I was still in school" (614 B 6).

Finally, a central element in the personal lives of Soviet parents since the earliest days has been the conflict between old and new. The traditions of the past have clashed with the new way of life; the spirit of education, science, and progress with the security of the tried and familiar. In addition to its good sides, rapid social change brings uncertainty and confusion in values. Not only personal values, but shared values within the family often issue into a void. Many Soviet families have turned their backs on religious ideas, and have found marxism an unsatisfactory substitute. Secular learning, occupational achievement, and social mobility have taken the center of the stage in many cases, but these orientations, although intensely important in the younger years when it seems that all choices are open, tend to lose force in later years. Elderly Soviet parents often find themselves faced with an uncomfortable lack of purpose. Sometimes the sense of family life has been found in the relationship between man and wife, but frequently something more has been needed.

Often the destiny of their child supplies a goal and gives meaning to the parents' lives. Identification with children thus affords continuity and stability to the parents' own personalities. Possibly there is even a trace of the proprietary instinct in such families. "There is no capital but education," observed one young man, illustrating that education is considered a possession of the children. By extension, involvement in the fate of one's children is for many a bridge to more positive feelings for the larger society and for the regime itself. For instance, pride in the educational achievements and future prospects of children easily generalizes to confidence in the school system. Gratitude for opportunities made available to children easily leads to a stronger emotional bond to the entire Soviet order.

In fact, child-centered parents are influenced in many ways by the very influences acting upon their children. Insofar as the slogan of parents is, indeed, "everything for the children," [25] the children tend to serve as the agents of introduction of new ideas and patterns inside the family, and these latter are often accepted by the parents.

The peculiar problems of this kind of family derive from the combination of an intense concentration of parental affection and interest upon the child and the great importance attached to educational achievement as career preparation. In the early years of the child's life such parents often are unable to bring themselves to exercise sufficient control over their beloved children. This is not, of course, for the same reason that was typical in the first type of family, that favoring natural childrearing, and the result is more often not a neglected child but a spoiled child. Out of the most tender motives, too much is given and too little required. It is "another, concealed, kind of neglect, brought about by some parents' blind love for their children. Such parents satisfy their children's every whim indiscriminately." Further, an objective evaluation of the results of such a parental attitude is blocked by some of the factors mentioned above. In newspaper terms: "They are greatly insulted if someone tries to open their eyes to the behavior of their 'beloved offspring.' " [26] Soviet writers regularly take a dim view of what is apparently a widespread tendency toward parental overindulgence and refer sarcastically to a "happy childhood" in which the child is spoiled by having no demands made upon him and turns out to be a "social parasite."

Early spoiling is very likely to be linked with a pattern appearing in late adolescence, one which has received attention in the Soviet press for over a score of years. It has been called the overmotivation factor, and it refers to a situation in which a child, encouraged or pushed by his parents, develops levels of educational and occupational ambition that transcend his real opportunities. He also shows disinclination toward the less rewarding jobs, more specifically, toward manual labor occupations. As early as the Tenth Congress of the Komsomol in 1936 it was noted that many youths were avoiding factory work.[27] Since then the problem has not been solved, in spite of numerous epithetic references to idlers and *beloruchki* (people with delicate, white hands), who shrink from the hard, often dirty, work necessary to "create material values for the people." [28]

While such an attitude can be traced most directly to the structure of wages and salaries in the Soviet economy, the role of the parent is also crucial. Indeed, in this type of family, educational achievement and occupational mobility for the children are so central as goals that it sometimes seems as if the main criterion of parental adequacy is the mark received for school work by the children. In the following exchange with a young respondent about a more general topic such is clearly his view: "[What, for example, do you consider to be the best traits of character?] First, one should study and get a good job so that one does not become a simple worker. [What other desirable traits of character are there?] The father should teach his children many things. He should reward the children who are the best students, who get the best grades, by treating them on holidays and giving them the best presents" (360 A 21). Naturally, marks depend on intelligence as well as on application, and in not a few examples of this type of family children develop aspiration levels too high for their intellectual capacity. Where innate capacity is high, however, a family background of this kind produces strongly motivated and presumably very capable members of Soviet society.

There is perhaps another, more rare, variety of overmotivation to be found in Soviet family life. A teacher, married to an engineer, speaks critically of the way she herself reared her only daughter: "I brought her up in a manner removed from the daily practical life. Too many outside interests, too many demands on life, toward others and herself, and because of this — a feeling of disappointment" (493 B 6).

Pattern of the Future?

The third type of Soviet childrearing milieu shares some of the characteristics of the natural approach and some of those from the child-centered family. It deserves to be treated as a separate type, however, because it fits so well both with the current officially desired pattern of family life and with the probable modal pattern of the future and because many of its defining features are associated with the distinctive social role of the Soviet woman. There are several main themes. First, although often quite highly organized, home, family, and the life of the children all tend to assume a less central place in the thoughts of the husband and wife than is true in the child-centered family. Both parents are career-oriented and busy. There is often a certain instrumental orientation manifested toward the family, as in the case of a university professor who says: "I loved the family circle, my home, and all such things as served to prepare me for my subsequent pedagogical and scholarly work" (454 B 2). In another instance, the implication is even more apparent. A forty-seven-year-old professional officer married to a newspaper reporter discusses his daily routine. He states that he regularly spent twelve to fourteen hours a day working, an hour going back and forth to work, six to eight hours sleeping, one to two hours eating, and also engaged in reading, meeting with friends, and attending the cinema and theater. His wife, he notes, "led the same kind of life." Almost as an afterthought he remarks: "Her mother was occupied by the children" (136 B 3).

The second theme, implicit in the first, has to do with the meaning and role of children born into the lives of a married couple who typically have acquired considerable educational training and occupational skill, have developed a variety of cultural and social interests, and have already committed themselves heavily to their occupations. A child is able to displace these concerns to some extent, but they carry considerable inertia of their own. A child in such a family is neither accepted casually nor does he become the center of the family's existence. Rather, his relationship with the parents tends to be seen as one of several relationships and values that ought to be supported and cultivated.

The main goal that the parents seem to seek in their childrearing activity can be summed up in the words, "mature independence." The qualities most desired in the child are capacity for autonomy, social adjustment, and self-expression. In terms of early personal independence, the child in this kind of family perhaps most closely resembles the product of the milieu described in the section on natural childrearing. But the quality of the independence is different, being more consciously fashioned by the parents and less spontaneous and rebellious in nature. It seems as if these parents are instead in a hurry for their children to grow up and apparently also able, for a variety of reasons, to do a reasonably good job of enabling the children to do that.

In a more detailed fashion, having and rearing children is likely to be regarded by this kind of parent with some concern, if not reluctance. A typical response to the question, "Did you consider that in order to have children you had to make a special sacrifice in any way?" is given by a forty-three-year-old medical researcher, whose wife is a scientific worker: "Yes, we had to sacrifice our freedom and free time and our amusements. We had to work more, and harder" (353 M 8).

Children are anticipated as a burden and experienced as a conscious but worthwhile sacrifice. In contrast to the natural approach, in which children are seldom planned, in this kind of marriage family planning is almost always present. Birth-control techniques tend to be more advanced and probably more reliable, and the husband and wife are less likely to show a male sex preference than in the two preceding family types.

After the birth of the child the patterns of childcare adopted resemble those used in the child-centered family — close scheduling of feeding and other activities, careful attention to high standards of sanitation, and frequent consultations with medical authorities. The comment of the respondent quoted above is typical: "My wife fed the child strictly on schedule according to the direction of the child's doctor" (353 B 8). Swaddling is completely absent in these families, but breast feeding continues, at least for the early months. Discipline is similar to that followed in the child-centered families — consistent and purposeful, with the imputed needs of the child receiving maximum attention and the spontaneous expression of the parents' feelings consciously suppressed. The ideal of a model parent in this kind of family is suggested by a forty-seven-year-old army officer, who notes that he made two types of mistakes in rearing his children: "I sometimes used physical punishment, boxing the ears, a cuff, spanking. I put demands on my child which depended upon my mood at that moment" (136 B 9).

An important distinguishing feature is the frequency with which there is present in the family an auxiliary in the tasks of childrearing, often a parental surrogate. It is very common for the older feminine relatives of the marital pair to take over a good share of the care of the child. Grandmothers, in particular, are likely to be present. If there is no grandmother, aunt, or other relative, a servant is usually employed. In the case of the medical research worker and his scientist wife, both kinds of assistance were at hand. He states, "Our child was brought up by a servant [a peasant girl], and only partially by his mother and grandmother" (353 B 8). Patronage of the crèches and nurseries, it appears, tends to be at a low level in this kind of family. The need is less sharp, for parental surrogates are more apt to be present and the parents are apt to see disadvantages in these public institutions that are not so visible to parents of the types described previously. The army officer referred to above states that his children, born in 1929, 1937, and 1939, were never in a crèche, and gives three reasons: absence of care and attention in the institution, mingling of children of different families and manners of upbringing, and exposure to infectious diseases.

When the children are ready for school, the mother and father expect as a matter of course that they will like it and do well there. They do not usually place emphasis on the need for special effort in doing school assignments and for receiving good marks; rather, they tend to see both as occurring without great strain on the part of anyone, and without giving rise to a great sense of accomplishment. Such accomplishment is seen as natural and normal to a great extent. Indeed, when such parents are asked what they are most proud of in their child, they usually mention qualities and achievements quite independent of the school. For instance, the medical researcher says of his son: "I was proud of the fact that he never told any falsehood, that he is a fine sportsman, that a feeling of fair play is well developed in him, and that he has good manners" (353 B 9). The physics professor touches upon academic achievement, but says nothing about marks and also mentions other qualities not usually found in the two preceding types of family. He was proud of his children: "for their health, and their progress — My daughter learned to speak German and English, and knew music — and for their exceptional attachment to one another, and their parents" (454 B 10).

Social relations in these families are more even and controlled than in the families adopting the natural approach, but perhaps on the average not quite so emotionally intimate as in the child-centered families. The modal pattern of relations is affectionate but distant, a result mainly of the heavy involvement of both parents in extrafamilial affairs. Of course, the situation is highly variable, depending a lot on the personality and interpersonal competence of the individual parent.

Little or no thought is given to the economic side of the children's future. Children are virtually never seen as a future source of material security, and parents are likely to envisage living separately from their children when the latter are grown. In general, however, the far future is not a major concern, and an inquiry about old-age arrangements often brings the response: "I never thought about that."

An important distinguishing element in this third type of childrearing is the extent to which the parents are aware of the sources, extent, and significance of outside influences on the lives of their children. Reactions differ, but the common factors are awareness and concern. Three points seem to be at issue. First, all these parents, like most in the child-centered group, agree on the potentially corrupting influence of bad companions and the street and do what they can to protect their children from them.

Secondly, these fathers and mothers seem to show a high degree of consciousness, sophistication, and relativism in their approach to such issues as politics, religion, and moral values. There is less interest in strong expression of religious and political ideas and values and more awareness of the link between them and the later welfare of the child. To some extent, they see religion and politics as realms to be consciously segregated from other affairs or even manipulated for personal benefit. This attitude contrasts with the other family types where political and religious ideas play a more absolute and pervasive role. Often, the parents stress only those values that they feel will be helpful to their children's personal adjustment and ability to get along in Soviet society and omit or play down those that would handicap them, even if this contradicts their own feelings. A fifty-nine-year-old woman, manager of a research laboratory in the public health department of a large city and the mother of three children, observes that one of her special aims in family life was: "To discuss politics as little as possible in the presence of the children. I endeavored to avoid rousing contradictory feelings in the souls of my children. This was the reason, for example, why I never mentioned religion to them" (373 B 2).

Finally, it is significant that these Soviet fathers and mothers are keenly aware of the massiveness and rapidity of the changes taking place in their own era. Of course, no Soviet citizen can be completely unaware of the fact, as the woman quoted above said, that "we lived during wars and revolutions" (373 B 7). The significant difference is that in this type of childrearing the consciousness of change plays a major role in dealings with the children, and to some extent sets the tone for family life. As noted above, personal reaction styles differ; the important common factor is the awareness of change. One version of this attitude, considerably exaggerated, is expressed by an army officer: "The education of children who grew up before the Revolution was very different. Then the basic influence upon the children was that of their parents, while in the USSR it is that of school, Pioneer, and Komsomol organizations" (136 B 8).

The most common problems in this type of parental pattern stem from the same factors that make it a distinctive type of family — the heavy involvement in career of both parents, their active pursuit of a variety of interests, and the consequent likelihood that in some way the child will be given short shift. The parents themselves tend to define their typical problem as one of a time shortage. A woman teacher complains: "I was forever occupied and devoted little time to my child" (627 B 8). The professor of physics quoted above considers that one of the mistakes made in rearing his children was "too little time that my wife and I could give the children" (454 B 10). Of course, time is one aspect, but almost certainly energy, attentiveness, and interest are also depleted by the number and intensity of extrafamilial demands upon the parents.

The best solution to the problem of these parents is to find someone to help with the children, and apparently a suitable arrangement is often available, especially when the wife's or husband's mother is able to take over. In general, this seems a very significant factor in the family life of the Soviet upper class. However, success is not always complete. For one thing, assistance cannot always be had and, if it can, is not always satisfactory. In the life of the director of a research laboratory the following incidents occurred. In the case of her daughter, born in 1926, she "was very fond of our maid, who had lived with us for 25 years. She was deeply religious, and even went to church. Only later I found out that she talked on religious subjects with my youngest daughter. When my little girl went to school she heard anti-religious talks. One day, after one of such talks to which she had listened, my little girl stood up, blessed herself with the sign of the cross, and said, 'Lord forgive her, for she knows not what she does.' The children reported the incident to the headmaster" (373 B 12). In the case of her son, born in 1919, the same essential difficulty became manifest in a different way: "Unfortunately . . . my husband was very busy with his scientific work, and when our boy reached the age of 15 or 16 he was left to himself, and for this reason came under the bad influence of some schoolmates" (373 B 10).

In addition to occasional failures there often seems to be a nagging feeling of guilt and malaise about their lack of involvement in the parental role. Sometimes this feeling is suggested by a typical upper-class view, which is in part true, in part exaggeration. The physics professor observes that in regard to rearing children: "It was impossible to apply any desirable strictness in the conditions of Soviet reality, full of undisciplined morals existing among grown-ups and children." He also asserts that the "typical Soviet family," which his closely resembles, is "merely a splinter of a real family, for it has been superseded by the club, the school, and the street" (454 B 11, 14).

In the relationship between the mother and father themselves, the big problem often comes to a focus in terms of the proper allocation of ultimate responsibility for discipline and the exertion of parental authority. The mother usually continues with her job, even when the children are in the preschool years, and the father is unable or unwilling to balance her withdrawal by contributing more to the tasks of childrearing. The director of a research laboratory indicates that she frequently rebuked her husband "for his not taking part in the upbringing of the children. His scientific work came first, and he had no time left for the children. True, the load he carried at work was great" (373 B 7). Her dissatisfaction with her husband is also suggested in another context. Asked to describe unpleasantness or contradictions in her family, she comments: "In the upbringing of our children my husband was much softer than I. Therefore, whenever it was necessary to show parental authority, it was lacking. On these grounds we had arguments, and even quarrels" (373 B 2).

This discussion describes the modern family in the USSR in its most sharply defined form. The relationship between husband and wife tends to be quite equalitarian, and family life as a whole quite stable. Although the rearing of the child tends to be seen as more problematical than in the other types of families encountered, this does not mean that the solutions found are less adequate or desirable. In fact, sometimes they seem appropriate modes of adjustment to contemporary Soviet life and even strike the observer as the most likely pattern of the future. At present, however, because of the relative shortage and inadequacy of preschool institutions, the shortage of grandmothers, and the still lively cultural pattern of full parental involvement in childrearing, there is often found a rather temporary, over-organized, and at times tense atmosphere in such families. In others, relatives or servants fill roles similar to those of the governesses, tutors, and servants of prerevolutionary times, and the life of the family flows quite smoothly.

Some Comparisons and Trends

Several of the contrasts among the three patterns discussed serve to bring the main features of each into sharper focus. Parents in the first group, that following the natural approach, seem to lack definite and strong goals for their children. In the child-centered family the goal is usually quite precise and strong — educational achievement and occupational success. In the third, the pattern of the future, the goals set for children are more conscious and more easily articulated than in the first group, but more abstract than in the second group, and often expressed in the form of desirable character traits. Emotional maturity, social adjustment, and the development of individuality are important.

The families also differ in the extent to which childrearing and family life in general are organized. The degree of organization is lowest in the first, highest in the second, and most varied in the last of the three types. In the third group there is usually a great need for the daily round of life to be well organized, in view of the demands pressing upon the parents. Yet they themselves are often unable to do the necessary planning and supervision. A case in point is furnished by the physics professor who recommended, as part of the proper approach to rearing children, setting a "definite direction" for them, "anticipating their mischief," and bringing them up "according to a schedule, with meals, outdoor exercise, and work at set times." Unfortunately, he himself was too occupied with other affairs to be able to carry out the recommendation in his own family.

The question of exerting parental influence over children in opposition or contrast to influence from outside is relatively less problematic in the first two types of family. In the natural family the issue often fails to come up at all, and in the child-centered family the parents exert careful supervision and control. In the third pattern the question is most sharply posed, but the actual outcome is to a great degree dependent on the parents' success in acquiring assistance in the form of parental substitutes.

It is perhaps also helpful to think of these three approaches in terms of the force or factor that elicits their most visible and distinctive traits and in terms of their typical social class affiliations. In the first type it is the traditional culture that influences most strongly, and it is in the Soviet peasantry that it is most often found. Natural childrearing is a relic of the past, or of the rural present, of the more stable and traditional life preceding the modern era. In these families life is traditionalistic in other respects. The old-style wedding ceremonies are still practiced; the marital relation is more frequently patriarchal; religion is more important; and so on.

In the child-centered family occupational opportunity and the lure of increments of material benefit constitute the chief mobilizing force and the dominant theme of family life. These families are characteristically skilled-worker and lower white-collar in the social scale, and their outlook is in large part an alert response to the demands of a rapidly expanding modern economy.

The pattern of the future is found almost entirely in upper-class families. Upper-class persons in the USSR are most conscious of the nature and trends of life in the larger society, and their outlook is also strongly influenced by their own status and interests. Of the three types they are most sensitive to the advantages of adapting values to meet current expectations and opportunities. Their way of taking these external factors into account in discharging their responsibilities as parents is to strive to foster personal autonomy and social adjustment and to develop the urge for self-expression in their children.

At the approximate midpoint of the time period covered by this study, 1940, natural childbearing and rearing was probably the most prevalent of the three patterns, and the pattern of the future was found in probably less than 10 per cent of the population of Soviet families. There is of course no doubt about the direction in which these patterns have been shifting, but even though the natural approach is giving way to the other two varieties, it will be common in the USSR for some time to come.[29]

ELEVEN | OLD PARENTS
AND NEW CHILDREN

THE SOVIET FAMILY, in comparison with society as a whole, has changed quite slowly. With good reason the party leaders have looked upon the family as a conservative institution, and, also with good reason, members of Soviet families have felt dubious about many of the campaigns and enactments of their leaders. However, in an era when an increasing portion of the Soviet citizen's time is taken up by life in the outer world, developments there can scarcely be ignored inside the family.

Indeed, as if in echo of the larger disparity, inside the home the family members are typically out of step with each other. The most striking manifestation is a result of age differences, of the conflict between parents matured in an older tradition and young people freshly turned out by the new society in accordance with new specifications. Mothers and fathers, sons and daughters, are bound together by the closest of ties and live in intimate daily contact, but they are also different. Even while they continue to live together as parents and children, their relationship is colored, occasionally dominated, by their differences. These appear in the first place in the form of controversy, which activates forces subsequently leading to other processes and social structures. In identifying and tracing these processes and structures one appreciates why large-scale social change sometimes strikes modern man as a Pandora's box.

A large part of the material in this chapter comes from interviews with former Soviet citizens who were themselves children and parents in the USSR under Stalin. Thus, not only the family in a changing society is presented, but also an unusual opportunity to analyze the broader problem of indoctrination or political socialization in the USSR in its most totalitarian phase. Because of the importance of the topic, the nature of the sample, and the fact that these have indeed been the most controversial of subjects inside the Soviet family, religious and general political attitudes are given particular attention in the pages following.

Controversial Themes

Sources of trouble between parents and children are legion. They become most relevant for our purposes only when the position of either side reflects the changing circumstances of the total society. For instance, when a Soviet father complains that he and his son were at odds because "my son often spent time with some of those who had a bad influence on him, taught him to smoke" (499 B 9), we can sympathize with him. But this problem is universal, unlikely to be dispelled in even the most stable societies. However, when controversy about a child's friends focuses on their political views, as in the case of a working-class boy who tells how "my mother sometimes would try to get me to give up a friend whom she considered too communistic" (110 A 107), the case is relevant to this analysis because the mother's efforts signify the peculiar role of politics in Soviet social change.

Four issues are grist for the mill of Soviet family controversy and reflect larger social changes as well: education, job choice, religion, and attitude toward the Soviet order. In earlier times going to school was by no means the important goal it is today. Many of the present generation remember when most of the population looked upon prolonged formal education with indifference. A young man, who eventually became a bookkeeper, tells how his illiterate parents gave him little encouragement: "They could not give me any guidance, in the sense, for example, of education. The beginning school was very difficult for me, and I left when I was only nine years old, having finished the fourth class. I remember when I left, my mother said to me, 'That's enough education already anyway' " (18 A 35). In the matter of choice of job, too, tradition dies hard, and even while opportunities for social advance were rapidly multiplying in the 1930's many peasant youngsters found that their parents assumed without question that sons and daughters would follow in their footsteps: "My father wanted me to stay at home and to follow in his footsteps and to take up farming . . . But I didn't like that sort of thing and so I decided that I was going to leave home as soon as I could" (339 A 29–30).

In most families religious feelings and political attitudes are correlated in the minds of the parents and tend to play complementary roles in the childrearing process. At one extreme we find families in which the parents are active in the party and, quite consistently, antireligious, providing a model Lenin himself would have praised. Such is the case of a young worker: "I was not baptized. My mother never had ikons and my father was a complete atheist. My father helped me in my anti-religious Komsomol activity and none of the three children was ever baptized" (417 A 19). At the other extreme, a court official reports of himself: "I am a very religious man, and influenced my children in that way as much as I possibly could" (42 B 10). Also, an engineer's son asserts that: "The strongest influences in my life were those of my mother, my father, and my grandmother. All of them were always opposed to the Soviet government, and I, of course, was raised in such opposition" (1578 A 33).

In the former group are found Soviet parents who have volunteered as shock-workers and joined the League of Militant Atheists. The Soviet regime has found a supporting hand in the relations of these parents with the younger generation, and they have served as a direct means of transmitting the new values to their children. Rather than controversy, argument, and conflict over political questions, feelings of mutual confidence and pride are usually present.

In the latter group of parents, a very much larger group during past years, controversy has been characteristic. As one young man saw the situation from the perspective of an interview some years after: "In the Soviet Union there are two sides of life: the official line which is taught in school and unofficial home education. In my home they taught me the old Russian ways" (310 A 15). Although the contest of forces seems equal — parent versus school — in the majority of such families the circumstances are similar to this young man's account of the in-effectiveness of his father's criticisms of the Soviet regime: "I was corrected at home, but I still believed what they told me in school. I believed that my father was old, and did not know about living condi-tions, that he was bourgeois and did not like the Soviet regime. I be-lieved that everything was good, everything was correct in the re-gime" (623 A 30).

The case above is merely a mild example; quite often political views of youngsters in Soviet families took on the fanatic coloring of a literal internalization of the official propaganda. A young man, whose parents considered themselves Stalin's enemies, tells how, as a ten-year-old at the time of the great purge: "I admired Stalin extremely and when he conducted the trials against the older communists, Bukharin and so on, I was happy about it and I even did the following thing. I had an album with portraits of communist leaders. As soon as one leader was tried and shot I took the photo out of the album, nailed it on a door and shot this photo myself" (114 A 93). Such was the tragic reality of the time — impressionable youth being molded into unquestioning loyalty even at the height of Stalin's purges.

Consequently, in the working-out of relations between parents and their patriot-children can be seen a most vivid expression of the inner turmoil wrought by contemporary events. Past experiences, greater awareness, perhaps age itself led to conflict between Soviet parent and Soviet child. Indoctrination of youth led in one direction; the violent social changes and coercive policies of the regime led many, perhaps most, parents in the other direction.

Conflict or Conformity: The Dilemma of the Parent

Intense controversy takes various behavioral forms. One is conflict, either in the shape of physical violence or, more frequently, in verbal exchanges and outbursts: "My mother would often say, 'We have nothing and we never will. During tsarist times we lived better.' Sometimes we got fed up with her raving and told her to keep quiet . . . She would say, 'Our comrades! What have they done for us? We have gotten nothing good from them.' She would say this every day and she would always cry. My mother felt that she had lived better before. Then she often had arguments with my brother over religion, too" (452 A 33). In general, harsh words and mutual animosity are not unusual in the Soviet family, but political dissension has been concentrated in the parent-child relationship. Pavlik Morozov, who denounced his own father to the village soviet, symbolizes the regime in the conflict of generations that probably reached a zenith in the 1930's when stalinist oppression drove parents furthest in one direction, and indoctrination with great falsehoods led children most decisively in the other.

In those years Soviet mothers and fathers had often to face extremely distasteful eventualities inside their families as well as outside. In attempts to do something, besides carrying on small civil wars, about what was happening to their children, parents developed three further

patterns of response. All of them diminished, avoided, or ended conflict with the children, but all required moral compromise on the part of
the parent.

The avoidance pattern involves parents who differ with their children
but maintain their distance in order to preserve peace. A young man
from a working-class family describes how his mother, "a very devout
woman, . . . did not force me to pray, because, although she prayed
all the time, she figured it would be useless to make me pray. She went
to church every Sunday, even when the churches were forbidden"
(452 A 25). Although little effort is made to force or influence a child
to follow his parents' preferences, these preferences must at least remain visible to the children. They, in turn, are aware that their parents
and the outer society are at variance. Thus, the conflict in views between parent and child remains open, but the parents adopt an attitude
of resignation.

Another mode of response is more ambitious and more difficult to
carry out. In this case parents seek to develop ideas in their children
that permit each side to carry on to maximum personal advantage.
These ideas consist of explicit recognition of a dual standard of right
and wrong — "two truths but in different places." A young girl was
bothered by the contradiction between school and family: "I often did
not understand about religion. They said that there was no God. It
was not pleasant, because at home they said that there was a God. I
asked Mama and she said that what they say in school is necessary.
That is what is said for [other] people, but at home, do not forget that
God exists" (438 A 66). The most concrete distinction made under
these circumstances is usually between at home and at school, and children are warned to treat the two as separate situations calling for contrasting behavior. In particular, opinions about political affairs and
expressions of religious faith must be carefully concealed: "At home
we spoke quite freely on many political subjects. We children were told
not to speak of the family to anyone, because family affairs should not
go beyond the threshold of our home" (1467 A 27). Such norms govern
the children effectively when two further conditions obtain: if the
family is also openly stigmatized, severely disadvantaged, relative to
other families, and if the number of alienated persons in communication with one another is somehow enlarged so that additional social
support is given. When both these conditions are present a genuine
though limited antiregime subculture develops and the parents are

most successful in passing on not only models of concrete behavior appropriate to specific situations, but their own values as well. If either or both are lacking, the children, under cross-pressure, are likely to count the number on each side of the opposing sources of information — "I got the impression that only my parents told me it was good under the Tsarist regime. All others said it was bad." (189 A 79) — add them up, and reject their parents' values. This same young man was at first quite troubled about the contradiction: "But at the same time I felt that my parents did not want to deceive me. Finally I decided: 'Well, suppose it was so, as they said, so what? That is the past.' Or rather, I did not decide it, but it just came so, I just forgot it, stopped thinking about it. The more so as my parents did not say it specifically to me, just said it to me in occasional talks. They did not insist and did not argue with me about it" (189 A 78–79). Whether he suspended judgment about the relative worth of Soviet and tsarist living or finally rejected his parents' view, his problem seems similar, as a psychological one, to that faced by the Soviet family as a social group living in a society often unfriendly. And the pragmatic solution suggested by his "Well, suppose it was so, . . . so what?" is quite similar to yet another kind of reaction of alienated Soviet parents.

This pattern appears to coincide with what many observers see as a general impoverishment of man's autonomous spirit in modern life. Dwarfed by the society towering over him, the individual's main goal often seems one of survival by conformity. In the Soviet version, conformity takes especially sharp form, for it is political and in the USSR politics has been made all-embracing. Thus, disaffected though they were, many Soviet parents adapted to the situation much as did an elderly doctor interviewed. She and her husband "were both strongly against the Soviet power." Nevertheless, she continues, "in raising our son we immediately faced the question: 'Should we raise him in the spirit of the Soviet Union or not?'" (139 B 5). The question was answered in the affirmative; conflict with their son was avoided by compromise and conformity on the part of the parents. Another mother, a scientist, reports of her children: "We tried to introduce communist ideas for them. What can I say about the education of our children? It was of a different sort than I would have preferred, but I didn't object" (373 A 38).

An important factor in parent reactions is the substantial differences among Soviet social classes. The first two of the four parental responses discussed, both involving overt expression of alienated attitudes on the part of the parents, are found more in worker and peasant families. The latter two are more common in the Soviet middle and upper classes. There are several reasons for the distinctions. Worker and peasant parents tend to be more religious and also more hostile to the Soviet regime.[1] They also share a more general lower-class personality trait — greater spontaneity in the expression of feelings, leading to a willingness to tell about the past, to speak out directly about anything. Employee and intelligentsia parents in their own thoughts have been less strongly religious, often manifesting what one respondent termed an old-Russian atheism. They are also less violently hostile to the regime. Similarly, in the past lack of enthusiasm toward education has been largely a trait of working-class and peasant culture, and the new opportunities offered by the Soviet order have not always been keenly welcomed. But higher-status parents are very conscious of these opportunities and of the political attitudes needed to take advantage of them.

Disputes about occupational choice, like serious disagreement on the question of how much or what kind of education, tend also to occur mainly in worker and peasant families. Occupational choices, of course, may be quite relevant to the political feelings of parents. For example, posts in the Red Army and in the political police, as well as in the Communist Party, have furnished attractive career opportunities to many a peasant and worker youth. But occupational choices for many children on this social class level ordinarily have to be made while the children are still minors. Indeed, since worker and peasant children are less likely to continue their education beyond the secondary school, the question of job choice comes up while it is still at least somewhat legitimate for their parents to try to influence them. In middle- and upper-class families, on the other hand, the question of job choice is not so sharply posed, for it is linked more closely to educational careers, and almost any job is defined as a good one if entry into it requires higher education. Thus, once a certain status level is attained, job choice in the Soviet family ceases to be much of an issue, being defined as a matter of individual taste and ability, hence not within the province of parental influence.

The question of parental prerogatives also contributes to parental response. Among the peasantry in the old days paternal authority was a cultural absolute. An older peasant says: "We obeyed father. Such was our upbringing. What father said was law" (624 A 7). In such a family system the very idea of major differences in political and religious views between parents and children has come as more of a shock and a trial than in the middle and upper classes, for whom urbanization and associated influences have had more chance to serve as a training ground. Younger workers and peasants are therefore more likely than middle- and upper-class youth to consider their parental family relations unsatisfactory — more disturbed, cold, distant.[2]

Finally, there is the influence of education itself. With more knowledge, verbal ability, and sophistication, intelligentsia parents sometimes express their true feelings in a devious way, perhaps by simply maintaining a discreet silence in the presence of the propaganda slogans brought home by their children. Worker and peasant parents are less accustomed to the fine points of belief systems and perhaps less sensitive to the needs and abilities of their children. Their techniques of influence are cruder, and as a result have tended to take extreme directions, disregarding the possibility of a compromise position. A worker, upwardly mobile from the peasantry, reports: "I'll tell you. They [parents] want to teach the children to believe in God, but the Soviet regime does not want them to believe in God. There is much disagreement on this. The old people are very religious, but a father cannot say to a child, 'The Soviet power is bad.' He cannot say that . . . Under the Soviet law it was impossible to do it the way you could under the Tsar. You teach the Soviet system. If you teach any other system they exile you to a concentration camp for ten years" (213 B 50–51, 59).

Parental Roles: A Link Between Past and Future

A close scrutiny of parental influence shows that Soviet mothers and fathers often differ on their conceptions of their roles. When such differences occur, the mother is likely to be concerned with moral issues, with religious training, for example, and the father with the practical side of things, such as occupational choice and political affairs. For example: "My mother was a very religious woman. My father did not believe at all, or at least he never said anything about religion in the house. We used to keep icons in our home and my father often scolded my mother on this account. He said that he did not care about religion itself one way or another, but he was afraid that having the icons in the home would cause him difficulties, that he might even lose his job" (85 A 17). The father's concern is symptomatic; he has experienced and understood the outer society more than his wife. The mother, on the other hand, is often impressed mainly by the immorality of Soviet society. To the father religion itself does not matter; it is his job that counts. Each parent also defends his own conception of his role in supporting the interests of his children. In the case following, told by the young son of a construction foreman, religion is a too-expensive luxury: "My mother kept icons in the house and frequently prayed. My father always told her she should not make her children cripples. He said she should let her children be like everybody else, not handicap them by making them religious. He understood that a person could not carry out his religion in Soviet conditions" (305 A 36).

Sometimes parents who cannot reconcile or hide their differences specialize in relations with their children. A typical case from the early years involved the family of a nonparty lithographer whose eleven-year-old son complained to the interviewer: "Mother forces me to say prayers, and father forces me not to say prayers" (Ka 219). A similar case is that of a metalworker with two children, a son and daughter: "The father is raising the son in the communist spirit; the mother is raising the daughter in a religious spirit" (Ka 219). If the question comes up of leaving home to engage more fully in the life outside, and the parents disagree on the decision, again it is typically the father who favors and the mother who opposes, each according to his differential sensitivity and receptivity to the new currents. A kolkhoz worker recalls the situation with her parents: "My father had a great influence on me, much more so than my mother, and when Komsomolsk was being constructed in 1935, I wanted to go there and help in the construction of the city . . . I just wanted to. I was caught up in this trend or current. My mother was opposed to my going, but my father said 'Let her go. The youth are all like that'" (Ro p. 326). Even the home's interior decoration can be symptomatic, as described by a young truck driver. "My mother was religious. She had icons . . . Father had pictures — of Stalin, Karl Marx, Engels, Voroshilov, Budenny" (138 A 33).

As Soviet parents differ with each other and specialize by sex in transmitting values to their children, Soviet children develop typical images of their parents. These images are indicative of how sex roles have served in a rapidly changing society. There are two important patterns at issue. First, it seems likely that there is a prototypical and dramatic form of parent-youth conflict in the Soviet family. It is most likely to occur, as we have seen, in the peasant or worker family. The two typical adversaries are the mother and the son, the two who best express in their own life histories the most acute contradictions of the society: "I used to see my mother standing and praying to herself, but I was not interested. She sometimes got angry, and said: 'Why don't you pray to God?' I laughed at her. I knew nothing at all about religion. The history of the Communist Party said that religion is an enemy of communism" (138 A 34). Feelings are strongest and resources of communication and knowledge weakest in such situations. The mother represents the past, the son an idealized society and future, and they fight to defend their different interests.

On the other hand, it is possible for the actors in this drama to stand for larger entities and images even while emotional ties remained close. An active young Soviet patriot tells us that he and his mother differed politically and argued, but that: "These arguments did not, however, change the relationships of our family. I continued to love my mother, and after 1936, when I went to Stalino to study, my mother would welcome me as a mother would welcome her son, whenever I came home for a holiday. Of course, we considered my mother to be a reactionary in comparison with us [laughs], but whenever she interfered in my private affairs, I told her that I was an independent person and that my joining the party was my own business. We did have some difficulty over this occasionally but I always loved my mother and she always loved me" (110 A 108–109). Each of the antagonists continued to love the other, but the difference in attitude persisted and the price to be paid involved "some difficulty . . . occasionally" a separation — "to Stalino to study" — and an obvious loss of influence by mother over son.

Such is part of the second prototype image of the parent in Soviet family relations. The mother is loved; tender feelings prevail, and there is no open conflict. But she is not influential in transmitting her core values to the children, with an attitude developing in them similar to this woman's: "I did not want to hurt mother, but always regarded her habit as an old custom and for myself accepted life without God as we had been taught in school" (445 A 28).

Concerning the father, the above analysis already suggests why it is that the Soviet young people in the Harvard Project sample considered their fathers the more influential parent in forming their own views.[3]

Much the same pattern was reported by the survey of worker families in Moscow during the 1920's. It was the father who consistently provided the link between the new way of life and the children's rearing. The influence of school, activity groups, and comrades was united with that of the father; and "therefore, peace with the father and disharmony with the mother" appeared in several of the families, but "most frequently of all, the mother takes care of the household chores and the physical care of the children, and leaves 'all the rest' to the father and to the school" (Ka 219).

In symbolic terms there grew up an association between the father and the new opportunities and rewards of the Soviet order (and political conformity) and an association between the mother and religion, family tradition, and the past in general. The image of the father is thus linked in the thinking of the children with educational striving, self-development, and the reward of upward social mobility outside, while that of the mother is linked more closely with thoughts about the old way of life, stability, and security — in short, with all the traditional family values. By further association the family becomes linked with femininity, a feminine institution, and the Soviet outer life, the Soviet order as a whole, becomes associated with masculinity.

Such mental connections have probably helped slow down the rise in the status of woman. They also encourage Soviet youth to look upon family life with an ambivalent attitude. If mother and family represent the past, and father and outer society symbolize the future, it is a sign of strength and maturity to ally oneself with the latter and to reject the former. In the following account we see a number of such links: "And there are some other children who listened to their parents and had a weaker character. They think that what Mama says must be so, and they believe Mama and hear nothing more. It all depends on the children . . . I think that the child who believed what he heard in school must have more will power, because here he must go against his family, away from the very road that was given to him in his childhood. He must make his own way, and I think he must be stronger than those who listen to Mama and take things as they are. This is what I think, and I know that I had to struggle greatly within myself . . . But not my sister . . . She was not as strong as I. She loved the house and her peace. She didn't want to struggle, she was passive and stayed at home" (258 A 72–73). It therefore comes as no surprise to hear this same

girl announce that although she does not know why she always preferred her father to her mother.

It has been suggested that the Soviet father is best able to display in
his person the demands made by the new outer society and that he
plays an important transitional role inside the family by acting out in his
own life a pattern of adaptive conformity in which practical necessity
is emphasized. Two further points and a qualification should be kept in
mind. First, millions of Soviet children grew up in families without a
father. The fact that a great number of the missing fathers fell in battle
— heroes in the struggle against a foreign invader — is not easily lost
from mind, and we may suppose that pictures and memories of such
fathers often symbolize and vicariously evoke the demanding expectations of the larger society, even though the fathers themselves are
absent.

Secondly, it should not be forgotten that evidence showing substantial marital disharmony is weighty, and that many Soviet men have been
failures as fathers. In fact, in a sense Soviet men have acted in general
as villains as well as heroes in Soviet social history. For this reason,
among others, Bischoff concludes that women have played an important
transitional role in the changing Soviet society. He argues that Soviet
women have both retained the better traits of the past and acquired the
more admirable features of the new social order. Thus, they have
furnished moderation and cultural stability. Perhaps this is so in terms
of socio-cultural change and personal character integration as a whole,
but the evidence for the situation within the family suggests that the
father is more important as a model for the growing child.

The qualification that must be kept in mind is the fact that much of
this discussion enters the realm of speculation. It is true, for instance,
that because of their several role responsibilities as workers, wives and
mothers Soviet women have on the average been busier than Soviet
men. But, of course, that does not in itself make them better candidates
for emulation by children. Perhaps they have been too busy, too tired,
and too worried to serve as good role models. On the other hand, if the
main carrier of social change in the USSR has been the man, it is also
true that Soviet political man exists in the popular mind as an agent of
ethico-moral corruption as well as of strength. In contrast, by her relative political inactivity and her greater faithfulness to religious and
other traditions of the past the image of woman has taken on a certain

moral luster, and she is seen as exhibiting a different order of strength. This was especially the case in the days when the Soviet population was being made so conscious of the evils of the cult of personality. In the words of the poet the idea comes through clearly:

> Everybody weakened. Women didn't —
> Through hunger and sickness, war and drought.
> Silently they rocked the cradles,
> Saving our sons.

> Women were better, were cleaner
> And they betrayed not their virginal dreams
> For bread, for this food here,
> For medals, for new clothes.[4]

If we raise the discussion to a more abstract level, disregarding questions of differences in social class and parental role patterns, we find that neither parent has been able to play a full part in guiding Soviet children. As the image of the mother has been pushed into the background by the more involved, enterprising father, so, too, has the family, both parents included, been pushed aside by new forces, institutions, and organizations in the larger society.

The Decline of Parental Influence

Everyday encounters sometimes illustrate dramatically basic social patterns. The writer Sergei Mikhalkov tells of a Soviet family in which the father was trying to reason with his five-year-old son: "Look how badly you are behaving — you don't obey Mama and Papa. We do everything for you — we show you every concern." The son answers: "It is not you who show concern for me. It is the party and the government that show concern for me." Mikhalkov comments: "He listened to the radio and watched television. And, being a child, he absorbed like a sponge everything he heard and saw." [5]

Probably no generalization about trends in the Soviet family finds more support from all sources than that of a decline in parental influence over children. Among the refugees in the Harvard Project, the younger generations were less influenced by their parents than the latter had been by theirs, even when seeking a model for their own roles as parents.[6] Often the point is made by stressing the new qualities of Soviet youth. The precise adjectives and phrasings used by parents to describe the younger generation vary—"quite fearless," "raised in a new spirit," "more developed," "get about easily by themselves" — but their common meaning is summed up by the word independence. As a Soviet analyst put it in 1964, young people in the USSR have a veritable "greed" for independence, a need which is nourished in part by the tendency of their parents to accord considerable importance to the autonomy of their children's "personal life." [7] However, Soviet parents confronting this pattern display a mixture of feelings, as if they are a little amazed, a little disgusted, a little proud, a little fearful at what they see in their children.

Why have Soviet parents, even those most in opposition to the Revolution and regime, lost so much ground in the shaping and control of their children? A basic point suggested here is the differing pattern of life experiences — harsher treatment of the older generation, greater receptivity to propaganda on the part of youth, and so forth — and the parent-youth conflict that results from it. But conflict need not end in such a lopsided victory for the younger generation as seems to occur. In considering the question, four additional factors are paramount: (1) the official policy and attitude toward the family, (2) new opportunities and benefits offered to the children, (3) circumstantial incapacity to exercise fully the parental role, and (4) loss of parental status inside the family.

1. Official policy and attitude toward the family. Marxist ideas about the family as an institution and the historical developments in official policy are outlined in Parts I and II, earlier in the book. To Soviet parents, this marxist theory often meant little, but there could be no mistaking the intent of the Soviet leaders. Their low opinion of the family came through to the grass-roots level in several ways — first, in the extent to which full Soviet patriotism carried the implication of a downgrading of the importance of family life. In the party the sense of loyalty to the regime, of devotion to the cause, may have made for a larger than average number of bachelors among party ranks. Among those who did marry, the family usually took a back seat. A classic case involves the family of a young truck driver: "My father was a worker; he started to work when he was thirteen. Thus, from the viewpoint of social origin he was the best kind of a person. My parents of course were of peasant stock . . . my father had many advantages because he was of proletarian origin. My father studied in a party school, even took correspondence courses in the Communist University. Even at one time he wore the army uniform and at all times had the right to carry a pistol in order to protect himself. After 1927 he did not have to work physically but devoted 100 per cent of his time to the party and paid very little attention to his family" (417 A 18).

Even though the family was looked on with more favor in 1935 than it had been in the two previous decades, it continued to be an institution of relatively low priority. The more actively involved, successful elements in the population were likely to include in their political orthodoxy the view that society comes before family.[8] They would subscribe, at least in principle, to the assertion of a twenty-nine-year-old sports instructor: "The Soviet Union does not need a closely knit family. It needs people who are ready to part with their life for the goals of the world revolution. In the Russian family you had the authority of the father. In the Soviet family you have the authority of the party" (189 A 44). In families where all subscribe to this view, it has seemed quite proper for parents to entrust the task of childrearing to the state. They are apt to share some of the official contempt toward the family as expressed, for instance, in the continued use of the derogatory term *semeistvenny* (family-like) to describe the illegal informal relations of mutual benefit and protection which tend to develop in Soviet bureaucratic structures.

Even the main responsibility of the Soviet parent recognized in the exhortatory literature — childrearing — is a delegated responsibility. Parental influence is always conditional. First, it is stressed that the leading role in the rearing of children belongs to the school. Secondly, parents are expected to refrain from exerting influence in a direction contrary to the interests of the state. They are strongly urged, or ordered, for example, not to give religious instruction. Furthermore, the whole context of the parent-child relationship is affected by the still lively ideological premise that the future will bring an even greater diminution in the influence of individual parents and a correspondingly greater increase in the influence exerted by special state institutions and society as a whole. Soviet discussions of the family still carry occasional references to that future time when the state will be able to take over all responsibility for childrearing, although the 1961 party Program promises that the ultimate decision is to be made by the parents, not the state. The attitude of the regime is now more moderate than it was between the Revolution and the mid-1930's, but it still upholds the children's position above that of the parents.

Finally, if the Soviet parent's enthusiasm for the Revolution and zeal for communism fail completely, if he stubbornly persists in contradicting the party line in his childrearing practices, he can be reminded of Pavlik Morozov, who had his father arrested. Statues and posters still admonish the Soviet people that no sacrifice is too great for the cause. The Soviets reverse the roles in the Old Testament story of Abraham, who stood ready to offer up his son Isaac as a measure of his love for God, and it is the boy hero-martyr who makes a sacrifice similarly commendable, and whose action is even now recommended as a symbol of proper priorities for a well-trained child.

Pavlik Morozov may serve as a model to Soviet children; to parents he functions as a warning. In fact this epic story has contributed greatly to the popular image of what typically happens in the Soviet parent-child relationship, and what, by inference, could easily happen in one's own family. A girl received the following impression while living in the USSR: "Films and books always showed us these things — that children tore themselves away from their parents and went their own way. But I cannot say that everyone did it. I do not know how many did it, but this was the popular kind — this was what people talked about and this is what we learned" (258 A 72).

The whole question of official policy on the family raised the issue of loyalty to a problematic status within the family. Soviet parents were often deeply concerned about this uncertainty of position. An institute instructor discusses the problem in respect to his son: "I would not say that my son always agreed with me, but he was always loyal to me. Once during the Finnish War, I said in his presence, 'How can one believe that a small country like Finland could attack the USSR?' He spoke up and said that he thought it was entirely possible. Then during the German War, I came home on leave and told my wife and son that the Soviet soldiers did not want to fight for the regime. My son immediately wanted to know how it was possible that soldiers would not fight for their fatherland. I imagine that, had I remained in the USSR, my son and I would have had many sharp conflicts of opinion. And perhaps, like so many of the Soviet youth, he would have left his family and gone to live in a dormitory" (307 A 17).

If feelings became too divisive the two sides could separate. Such a serious step was most likely at a time when not just opinions but a decision about educational career or job choice had to be made. The theme cropped up repeatedly, almost in a matter-of-fact way, as in the case of a young woman whose occupational choice differed, just as did her political and religious outlook, from that of her father and mother. They had arguments, she reports, but: "I always won the arguments because I knew my parents could not do anything about it. I had my own passport and the full right to leave my parents if I wished" (85 A 16).

At times Soviet parents played a role in the minds of their children similar to the one they often seemed to play in the eyes of the Soviet leaders. They were simply obstacles to progress. Inasmuch as home and a good life were in direct opposition, leaving home became a prerequisite for personal advancement. A young worker narrates his feelings at age fourteen: "My primary intention was to become a cultured man. As a boy I was afraid of factory work. When I looked at my brother, who was still young but already disgusted with life, I always intended to run away from home and to get to school. I was convinced that school was the only means of elbowing my way into life" (1582 A 29). In consequence, leaving home also became a special weapon for Soviet youth, and another echo in youthful behavior of the official policy of urging young people to leave home in spirit.

However, even children too young to leave home exerted a disproportionate influence. Alongside the air of self-righteous independence and vigilance so encouraged in the school was a trait that appeared to parents as political naïveté. One of the most salient norms of parental behavior during the Stalin era, when there was maximum antagonism between regime and people, called for the exercise of great care in expressing political sentiment openly in front of young children. A girl tells us: "Everyone was afraid of his children. A small child can betray his parents unwittingly and therefore my parents were always careful in what they said before me and my brother" (1684 A 14). A doctor and administrator reports that: "A father couldn't be free with his son. I never spoke against Stalin to my own boy. After the story of Pavlik Morozov you were afraid to drop any kind of unguarded word, even before your own son, because he might inadvertently tell it in school, the directorate would report it, saying to the boy, 'Where did you hear this?' and the boy would answer, 'Papa says so and Papa is always right,' and before you know it you would be in serious trouble" (40 A 15–16).

We may conclude that feelings of helplessness and alarm were common among Soviet parents. They conformed to the dictates of the regime's policy, especially while their children were young, because they felt they could not do otherwise, even if they wished, for fear of punitive sanction. These feelings corresponded to the regime's policy toward the family, especially toward the role of parent, and explain why the policies were successful in persuading parents to reduce the extent of their influence over their children.

2. *New opportunities for children.* In the meantime there developed opportunities for children which their parents could not give them on their own. First came school and associated extra-curricular activities. As the country advanced, education became more and more important, and the state had a monopoly on its control. Even the most rabidly anti-Soviet of parents were faced with this fact. As an old Cossack said of his children and their attitude toward school: "Since the upbringing at home in the family circle differed greatly from a moral standpoint, they could not feel any special love for the school, but they had to study" (626 B 12). From their earliest years, Soviet children are impressed by the widely publicized (though not always true) assertion that: "There is no dependency of the son on father's position and on father's ability to pay for his education out of his wage" (136 B 9, 7). This claim applies to chances for occupational success as well as education. As a consequence a political police officer-father believes that responsibility, not only for education in a narrow sense, but for the whole "upbringing of a child and a young man" rests with the school, the Komsomol, and the party: "The family influence is not predominant because the parents, due to the existing atmosphere, try to bring up their children in the spirit of the school and of the party. The parents are really the supporters of the Komsomol education, maybe not always according to their own wishes but because they have no other choice. The choice of a profession, of an activity depends more on the party. There might be a sudden campaign on. Young men are needed for military schools . . . After that a son would not listen to his father. He would say, 'Papa, you are old-fashioned, I shall attend a military school.' There could be campaigns for other professions as well" (136 B 9, 7).

Many interesting and useful side activities were organized in the context of school life and youth organizations. "I used to go on vacation every year, and spent either a few weeks or all summer in a Pioneer camp, where I did not see my parents for all summer. There we used to eat very well, and we played games and swam in the water and sang songs. They were very interested in the children" (111 A 76). Some parents did not want their children in the parapolitical youth groups, but as the children usually wanted to join, they let them. A young man describes his joining the Pioneers: "I kept asking her and after some time she finally said, 'If you really want it, go ahead.' I was ten years old at this time when I joined the Pioneers . . . I was very happy that they took me. I had to memorize the answers to a lot of questions, such as what the star means, and why the tie is red. I had to say, 'Because it stands for the blood that was shed by the workers in the Revolution.' Or they would ask why the star has five points, and I would say, 'Because it stands for the five continents of the earth.' We had to take an examination of this sort. Then we had to raise our hand and vow that we would fight for Lenin. There was a big ceremony when they first put the red tie on me. It was one of the great happinesses of my life" (111 A 78–79). Youth activities are by general agreement among the most popular aspects of the Soviet social order. After-school activities, summer camps, and the often elegant buildings for children's affairs are widely praised.

Extracurricular organizations and activities are for many parents the best alternative available. They themselves are simply unable to spend time with their children, and the main substitute for officially supervised after-school interests is not attractive: "The street has a great influence on children in the Soviet Union and, in the case of parents who are always so busy, they are glad to have their children go into the Pioneers, because it keeps them off the streets, out of the movies and out of the market" (139 B 74). School, Pioneer group, and summer camp act as parental substitute; their extensive development helps to explain why many Soviet parents willingly grant their children independence early in life. Class differences evident in this attitude show that, roughly, the lower the class level the more likely the parents are to want to turn over their responsibilities, to see the school as a major aid in childrearing rather than solely as a source of learning.[9]

An additional factor is the close link between political views and career success. In order not to handicap children in their educational and occupational careers, therefore, parents frequently must avoid transmitting to their children their own values. As one young man said: "At home we did not discuss religion and they did not force us to study it. They felt that religion might be very harmful to us" (398 A 11).

Not only to help their children get along in school and work, but to make life better for them in all ways, Soviet parents feel that they are doing the best thing they can for them by rearing them as Soviet children. A man tells of his mother, anti-Soviet in her own opinions: "My mother never tried to convince me of the rightness of her ideas. She was extremely cultured and knew I had to live my own life, that I had to live in Soviet society, and she did not wish to make it difficult for me" (534 A 30).

3. Circumstantial incapacity. Some features of Soviet family life foster the trend toward early juvenile independence. Foremost is the large number of incomplete families, in which the guiding hand of a parent is missing because there is no father and the mother has to earn a living. Even in complete families it is hard to be a good parent. Although indulgent and careless mothers receive some attention in Soviet writings on the subject of childrearing, complaints about fathers are more frequent. Too often fathers are not properly concerned about their children and their own responsibilities as a parent, a fact that has given rise to the view that not only manifest but covert fatherlessness (*skrytaia bezotzsovshchina*) is a major problem in the life of Soviet families.[10] Moreover Soviet mothers and fathers often have higher expectations of their own behavior than they are able to fulfill. The sharpest tension seems to be present in parents preoccupied by their work. An army colonel reports: "I and my wife worked and we were always busy at our place of work and we were seldom together as a family. This was a cause of mutual reproaches and I could not give enough attention to the upbringing of my children" (1 B 2). Lack of adequate housing space makes carrying out parental responsibilities difficult and causes parents to search for outside help in childrearing.

These circumstances result in the development of a pattern previously mentioned, the grandmother who is assigned the role of mother. A striking example is reported by the young son of an army officer and party member. He declares that the most important person in his life as a child was *babushka,* grandma: "I spent my whole day with my grandmother. In fact, I called her 'Mother.' She was always the one who asked where I went and why I went. She took the place of my mother. This is very characteristic in Russia. Mothers are usually young, they want to go out and often they want to work. But the grandmother always stays home to take care of the children" (110 A 41–42). But because grandmothers, being older and less vigorous, must relinquish some influence over young children, and because they represent older times and discredited patterns, they rarely take over the mother's role completely. Thus, they tend to exhibit in even more extreme fashion what may be the characteristic emphasis of the mother role in a society rapidly changing, namely, the concentration on physical care with relinquishment of ideas about the outside world to the father or to extrafamilial forces. By contrasting so strongly with the ideal pattern of Soviet man — young, progressive, involved in social production and political work — the image of *babushka,* so prominent in the lives of many Soviet young people, reinforces the idea of a radical split between family and society. The family is a place of intimacy, nurturance, and security, all part of grandma, who is loving but old-fashioned and getting feeble. Challenge, novelty, exciting adventures are part of the world outside, where not only father but often mother, too, spend their time and dedicate their lives.

The typical behavior and belief patterns of these four people — *babushka,* father, mother, and child — as well as the locus and scope of their main responsibilities suggest a dramatic, if fanciful, paradigm in Soviet life. The ontogeny of the child as he grows recapitulates the experiences of Soviet society in recent history. He (Soviet society) is born of his mother (the Revolution). She then returns him to *babushka* (Russian cultural tradition) while she goes off to work (rapid industrialization). In the meantime the father (Communist Party), who was instrumental in the birth, occupies himself with guidance of the child's ideological development, mainly by his own busy example in the outside world where his activities are only vaguely discerned but clearly are very important. As the child grows older the contrast between *babushka* and the father grows stronger and stronger, and the drama ends as the child firmly but tenderly rejects her and follows his father into the future.

4. Loss of parental status. The above allegory, however, has a major inconsistency. Soviet fathers themselves have strong ties with the past, just as *babushkas* do, and in various ways fail to measure up to the highly publicized ideal Soviet man. Instead of being party members many are anticommunist or apathetic in political orientation and some are disorganized or criminal in everyday behavior. In years past many carried the defect of alien social origin. Sometimes their sons reject them as well as their origin. The son of a Ukrainian landowner notes that: "In my youth I wanted to declare myself a homeless child (*bez-prizorny*) to be rid of responsibility for my antiproletarian origin" (102 B 10). Parents who stand officially stigmatized are, of course, the more handicapped in influencing their children if the children suffer for the stigma and blame the parents for it.

In more recent years politically legitimate status has been much less a problem, but many Soviet fathers continue to bear a tarnished image. Social mobility is frequent and educational training and occupational promotions are quite accessible, but not all, nor even a large majority of men, share in these advantages. Sometimes, it seems, the father consciously sets himself up as a negative role model. The son of an un-skilled worker explains his father's desire for him to go to school: "He didn't want me to do unskilled work as he did. He often said that he wanted me not to be like him . . . He used to say that I should study, so that I could get a job which was not with my hands, as he works with his hands. He said if I got a good job I would not have to work so hard. Be a teacher, or an engineer or something like that" (521 A 8, 29). Such an attitude is probably typical for lower-status fathers in dynamic modern societies, as is the voluntary, if partial, surrender of influence, although, of course, urging a son to be different is in itself a mode of influence.

In a very broad sense the status of parent has been diminished by the relative social accomplishments of parents and their children. The younger generation is considerably more educated than the older. In a land where education has a very high prestige, so do the educated. Thus, less well-instructed Soviet parents often seem a little in awe of their well-educated children. A Soviet source reports the "characteristic" answer of one I. Dimitriev, a collective farmer in Yakutia, to a question about the future of his daughter, just out of seven-year school: "She is now her own boss. You see the children know more than we do. They seek out their own fate by themselves" (Ku 232). Similarly, the children themselves are almost forced to respond to the new standards of per-sonal worth by depreciating their parents. It is not, of course, simply a matter of knowledge: in a more complete sense, the old way of life is at issue. Consider this unskilled worker's characterization of the fatal-istic philosophy of his peasant parents-in-law: "Both of them were flabby types (*slabokharakterny*) . . . Such people who are nothing to anybody. They worked very little and then they lived. They never did anything with anyone. No quarrels. They were quiet people and very religious . . . Something today, nothing tomorrow, and it's all right. In every way they give in to life" (279 B 8).

Complete political acceptability, more education, better job chances, and a new, more vigorous outlook on life — in all these ways the younger generation is more distinguished. Clearly, Soviet parents have been demoted by life and by their children, and all the more so if their political views are dissonant. To be an anti-Soviet father often leads to complete rejection, as in the case of a doctor whose son tells this story: "My father was very reactionary; he was a real enemy of the Soviet power. As a child, I could never understand it. [But later] I was more liberal [and I saw that] he was an extreme idealist [and] an extremely moral man. In fact, he was a little too good. For Soviet conditions, he could never be adapted. That was why he was finally killed by the NKVD. When I was a child, I used to fear that I would inherit this in him and that I too would be too idealistic, which is very dangerous in Soviet life. It is impossible to live by these ideas in Soviet society" (25 A 25, 42). The Soviet father must not be reactionary, too idealistic, moral, or too good. To earn the following of his Soviet son he must be the opposite or, in the word of this young man, adapted.

Easing the Strain and Filling the Gap

The process of adjustment to a new pattern takes place slowly in the family. Much of the transfer of influence and power from the hands of the parents is accomplished in a semiconscious way and through gradual redefinitions of the situation. The symbolic linkages between age- and sex-differentiated roles inside the family and larger entities of history and society are important. They are necessarily vague, for if such images were more explicit they could not perform their function, which is to mediate slowly, without too much open conflict, between the forces of change outside and the need of individuals for stable relations and mutual support inside the family.

Still, to a considerable degree the loss of parental influence over children has been experienced by Soviet men and women as a conscious deprivation. Habits and faiths are tenacious, and many Soviet mothers and fathers would like to see more of themselves live on in their children than has been possible. Other developments have served to ease

their feelings, however. Above all, probably, is pride and vicarious gratification in the accomplishments of their children. In addition, some
changes in the nature of parental expectations have appeared which
have made it easier to be satisfied. Four aspects are predominant.

First, Soviet parents have had to lower their standards of acceptable
behavior. The sense of moral compromise has been strong, yet parents
have felt it to be their duty to take Soviet conditions into account and
expect less of their children than their parents expected of them. As
one man put it: "My parents saw to it that I would be a believing man
and would love God and my fellow men. I saw to it that my children
were clothed and fed and that they would not be any worse than others"
(499 B 8). A second shift involves a conscious narrowing of the range
of specific expectations, sometimes to the extent that the sole criterion
for a good child is that he look after his mother and father in their old
age. A young journalist describes his parents' reaction to his youthful
atheism and their general orientation: "When I was ten years old and
entered the Pioneers, I just was not supposed to believe in God, and
I decided that I would not. [How did your parents feel about this?] They
may have been hurt inside, but they were people who felt that a new
era was coming and they were left over from the old era. They did not
know whether the future would be good or not, but they were satisfied
to see their children enter on the new road, so long as we were real
children, fulfilling our filial obligation. They understood that their way
of life was over" (385 A 37).

The third pattern of change is in the level of abstraction of the
normative standards themselves. The sense of diminished control and
some loss of faith in their own values often induces Soviet parents to
reformulate their expectations for their children into the most abstract
form. That is, they have met the pressures for change by placing greater
stress on the inculcation of the most general values, such as personal
happiness and adjustment, being a moral person, and the like, all of
which place minimal emphasis on specific imperatives or taboos of
conduct. A young man notes that in his home: "Religion was not a
topic of discussion. They [parents] thought the children could be religious or atheists as they wanted. They only wanted to develop a highly
moral character in me" (144 A 57). General traits and values have
very elastic content; in this abstractness parents as well as children
more easily find what they wish to find.

A fourth pattern involves only a partial submission. Life has been troublesome under Soviet conditions, often oppressive, and the average Soviet adult has had a deep need to maintain good relations with his close relatives. The main hallmark of social change has been a transfer of power and influence. If social change has also brought a deterioration in personal relations inside the family, it has been to a much smaller degree than would seem likely in view of the sharpness of differing beliefs and interests. Rather than as a war between the ages the Soviet family accommodates the shift in statuses in a different way, namely, by widespread recognition of each of the two well-defined ways of life as legitimate in the informal culture. Such recognition allows parents and children to live in relative peace with each other by maintaining cultural if not social distance. A typical formulation is described by a young Ukrainian girl whose parents were teachers: "Naturally, we children disagreed with our parents. We were always scolded by them for our new-fangled political ideas. We hardly listened to them, talked back, argued. But we were a very closely knit family just the same. None of the arguments within the family circle were ever carried outside. We loved our parents. With years we developed a tolerant attitude toward them, as if they were old-fashioned people who couldn't see the progress" (1354 A).

If "old-fashioned but lovable" characterizes the orientation of youth toward age, then "immoral but still dear" is typical of that of age toward youth. Many Soviet parents see their era as one of moral decline, in which the youth have been corrupted by the regime. This recognition has also helped to maintain closeness. By ascribing vice to the entire younger generation, a total class of persons, the moral decline of the family's own children is more easily tolerated and the children still loved.

Two further subpatterns deserve mention. Tolerance and respect among relatives and friends have become doubly admired virtues, which children are expected to develop as they grow older. Certain topics become ineligible for family discussion. For example, an army officer explains how a young person who has been away from his family and has changed his political and religious opinions should behave when he returns for visits: "Out of respect for his parents and his home, he should not enter into discussion and arguments; he should not try to change their opinion. He could express his views but in a way which would not offend the religious views of his parents. On political problems he could express his disagreement; but both they and he would have a disagreeable feeling afterwards. A rift would certainly form" (136 B9 12). Such norms as these have become important as informal defenses used by the Soviet people to protect themselves and their families from becoming mirror images of a malintegrated total society.

Explicit boundaries, a realm of private life and a realm of public life, have to be erected to preserve human dignity and self-respect. Such boundaries are on the map of Soviet culture today and have to be learned by Soviet children as they grow up. That is, Soviet parents, while giving in to the trend of change, have had to make explicit to their children that religious belief, although perhaps outmoded, is at the same time a sacred matter for some and to be treated accordingly. The youngest son in a prominent intelligentsia family, whose father was a theatrical director and whose mother was an office worker, tells the story of an interesting occurrence from his early years: "The beginnings of communist education which my brother received in school were transmitted to me. He brought from school elementary communist slogans; for example, that religion is the opium of the people . . . Thus once my brother and I arranged an antireligious demonstration. It was his idea. A religious aunt often came to us and she liked to pray before an ikon in our home. We placed Stalin's portrait on this ikon and we enjoyed it very much when we saw her surprised face. Of course we received plenty for this from my mother . . . After that we understood that this may be deeper than just a joke and we never did similar things again" (144 A 57, 91).

Such are some of the patterns by which the strains of transition are managed inside the family. Taking a larger view, such as that from a window in the Kremlin, the decline in the influence of the Soviet parent has helped to shape Soviet youth to the desired mold, but it has brought its own new problems with it. Youthful independence means that some boys and girls will join the Komsomol and become patriotic Soviet citizens, but it also means that some will choose other paths. There is good evidence that juvenile misbehavior is common in the USSR, and it is obvious that Soviet authorities are very concerned about what we might term the "control gap" in which parents have relinquished more responsibility for the conduct of youth than the society as a whole is able to assume. The main official reaction to wayward youth is to blame the family: "It is the family which is most responsible before the state and society for the bad conduct of children." However, many Soviet parents, it seems, feel that society should be held responsible, as in the following report: "When the workers of the Sverdlovsk District Komsomol Committee called Mikhail Goncharov's mother and told her that her son had been drinking for two days in night clubs, she replied angrily, 'You should educate my son!' " [11]

This unexpected feature of the regime's policy probably appears merited. Insulted and neglected by Marx and Engels, rescued too little and too late by Makarenko, and cheated by the Soviet regime, which blames parents when things go wrong and takes credit when they go right, Soviet parents have a pretty good claim to unjust treatment. Soviet leaders themselves are anxious to see Soviet youth continue independent of their parents, but they also want youth compliant to the regime's desires. Heavy reliance is placed on the Komsomol, which since its 1936 Congress has had as its chief mission the indoctrination and control of Soviet youth, but the press is filled with complaints about its failures as an agency of indoctrination and there is evidence that a large proportion of Soviet young people do not take it very seriously.

This attitude has apparently been especially evident in the years since the death of Stalin. There are signs that destalinization brought ideological disillusionment to many Soviet young people. Presumably it particularly influenced those whose political ideals had been most completely shaped under Stalin but who had not yet come under the sobering influence of occupational duties and family life, responsibilities that ordinarily lead to a more realistic attitude. This group would be composed mainly of teen-agers. At the time of the Twentieth Congress of the Komsomol in 1956, when the mistakes of Stalin were discussed, it was the fifteen through nineteen age group among the youth that was reportedly most troubled: "Not having yet learned to think independently, to analyze the complex phenomenon of life, not all of them, naturally, were able to penetrate to the essence of the party's criticism of the cult of personality and its consequences. For some of them this criticism became in the first years the basis for various kinds of serious doubts and disillusionments." [12]

The most likely targets for such doubts and disillusionments have been the men, ideas, and institutions most clearly associated with Stalin himself, namely, the Soviet leaders, communist ideology, the party, and the Komsomol. Here then is one source of the manifestly increasing concern of the Soviet leaders about the younger generation. In a survey conducted in 1961 by the Institute of Public Opinion of the Soviet youth newspaper, a large number of the youthful respondents felt that ideological shortcomings (for example, admiration and imitation of the West, apathy) ranked high among the negative traits of Soviet youth. Some of their elders, outstanding officials and public figures, felt even more strongly about this particular shortcoming.[13]

Indeed, the process of destalinization has elicited a continuing internal controversy in the USSR which is largely focused on problems of ideology and intellectual freedom. The main dialogue has been conducted by spokesmen for party and government on the one side and representatives of the creative intellectual community on the other. Generally speaking, the former tend to be older, and many of them were in positions of power during the reign of Stalin, while the great majority of the latter are younger men who had not yet come to prominence or even come of age under Stalin. In consequence, many observers have visualized the whole affair in terms of a "conflict of generations" or as a modern example of the "fathers and sons" problem, in the manner of the novel by Turgenev, where nihilistic sons collided with the outlook of their fathers. It is important to keep in mind, however, that these expressions are metaphors using the language of family relations to describe a phenomenon that is in the main a political controversy rather than a problem of the internal life of the Soviet family.

The effect upon the inner life of the family of the destalinization process has probably been that, with the abatement of extreme tension between regime and people, problems arising out of political differences between parents and their children have diminished. Insofar as the political attitudes of youngsters tend to emerge as carbon copies of the official ideology, any liberalization in the indoctrination of youth would be reflected inside the family in a more relaxed relationship between the generations.

Thus, the most likely result of destalinization for the Soviet family would be some decline, perhaps temporary, in the prestige and influence of the political leaders, ideals, and institutions of the nation over Soviet youngsters, and some increment, probably permanent, in the levels of agreement and affiliation between parents and children. A modest paradox seems evident, in which the tension between the generations increases in full public view on the national scene at the same time that it declines in the privacy of family life.

From the point of view of the Soviet leaders, of course, the most visible and troubling aspect of their efforts to dislodge the heritage of Stalin has been experienced as a mushrooming youth problem. In trying to deal with the problem of youth become too independent the most radical innovation, introduced under Khrushchev in 1956, is the boarding school, which takes responsibility for the upbringing and control of children almost entirely out of the hands of the parents. The number and capacity of these schools have grown steadily, and they seem intended to become a mass phenomenon in the future. If so, the Soviet Union will have taken a long stride toward the situation envisaged almost a century ago by the ideologues of communism, toward the social rearing of children.

If in the future the children will both study and live in boarding schools, the average Soviet parent worries about what remains for the family to do. In fact, announced goals for construction and accommodation capacity of boarding schools tend to be postponed, official writing on the subject is still tentative and speculative, and it is stressed that time, extensive expenditures by the state, and careful organizational work will be needed before these schools can do their best work. It is expected that traditional ties of love and respect between parent and child will remain and even grow stronger; that there will be meetings between the parents and the workers of the schools to discuss the children's progress; that there will be mail correspondence and evening and week-end visits when possible; and that the parents and children will be able to spend their vacation times together.

It may be, as some have suggested, that the time of extreme stress is past — gone like Stalin and much of stalinism — and that, correspondingly, parental influence in the USSR may well be gaining in importance. If so, perhaps some of the institutional devices intended to correct or supplant the influence of Soviet parents, such as the Komsomol and the boarding school, have already reached their peak of influence. Indeed, perhaps the future of Soviet parents and children will be just as happy but considerably less separate than that anticipated in official characterizations of the communist future. If so, how many keen followers of the marxist orientation toward social institutions will be able to resist the conclusion that such Soviet institutions — youth league and boarding school — have in them more of the superstructure than does the family?

CONCLUSIONS

THE MARXIST THEORY of the family bears many similarities to the marxist theory of capitalist society. Both are seen as ephemeral stages in a historical series; property ownership is a divisive and corrupting influence; social justice is laid low by inequalities of power; and cultural values and established institutions tend to be epiphenomenal, serving mainly to cloak the tawdry character of "real" or economic relations. The specifics could easily be extended. In their iconoclasm, radicalism, claim to scientific status, muted humanism and naturalism, and in the locus of their main errors the two theories are obviously of the same parents. Similarly, both theories have received a like fate in the USSR. The marxist theory of the family, like the theory of capitalist development, has become canonized, and, like the theory of capitalism, has not been susceptible of revision on the basis of research. Finally, as with capitalist society, official policy on the family has over time required adjustments. The label "peaceful but antagonistic coexistence" describes with some accuracy the relations of both capitalism and the family with the Soviet rulers.

This then is the starting point: a theory of increasingly obvious inadequacy which became dogma. There can be no doubt that the leaders of the Bolshevik Revolution subscribed to the main principles of the marxist theory of the family. In evidence we have their written testimony, the radical family legislation of the early years, the speed with which these laws were originally enacted, and the slowness to change them and the policy from which they originated. In the meantime Stalin was driving the USSR toward industrialization, collectivization, urbanization, and political purges. Under the pressure of these great stresses Soviet social life became more disorganized. The seriousness of social problems was magnified. Partly as a response to this fact, and partly for the other reasons described in Chapter 4, Soviet family policy changed.

In a broad sense family policy changed from a radical to a conservative one. Sometimes explicit principles of marxism and corresponding legislation were simply reversed. Engels' principle of the noninterference of society in relations between the sexes, and the principle of absolute freedom of divorce, defended strongly by Marx, Engels, and Lenin, are two important principles that underwent conservative change. Sometimes the same fate overtook the more implicit or derived principles of the early years. Adoption, for example, was in the beginning made illegal, but that law was soon repealed and since the mid-twenties adoption has been more and more encouraged. The concept of illegitimacy was ethically unacceptable to most marxists, and the legislation of the early era on family, marriage, and inheritance in effect did away with the legal basis for the status of illegitimate child. But from 1944 until quite recently the children of unwed mothers have been easily identifiable because the fact that they have had no father was noted on the birth certificate.

In some respects Soviet family policy is of a cyclical nature, oscillating between counterposed forces of relatively equal weight. For example, in 1920 abortion was legalized, in 1936 it was made illegal, and in 1955 it was again made legal. Perhaps there are cyclical tendencies at work also in the policies concerning divorce and illegitimacy. A prohibitive policy on divorce and the stigmatization of the illegitimate child are devices serving to support and enforce the family as an institution. Yet both of them run counter to the spirit and recorded principles of marxism. There is also good evidence that they arouse evasion and some resentment among the population. As with many social problems of modern societies there is no perfect solution, and the tendency of national policy to be unstable may reflect the fact that its connection with the behavior of people in everyday life is distant and imperfectly understood.

In respect to the keystone element in marxist social theory, private property ownership, the Soviet experience suggests that the wholesale abolition of private ownership of the means of production is of debatable benefit to society. Other institutions and conditions, political and economic, seem much more germane to the ultimate fate of man. The same can be said of the relation of property institutions to the family. To be sure, Soviet society has been confronted with a variety of difficult economic and political problems from the start of its existence, and the provision of facilities auxiliary to the welfare of the Soviet family has always been low on the scale of priorities. Moreover, the radical transformation of man's personality in a society divested of antagonisms, if such is to occur, lies in the distant future. Thus, two of the facilitating conditions, or mechanisms, through which the socialization of the means of production was expected to influence the family have not materialized.

For these reasons the Soviet experience to date has not provided a fair test of the central marxist proposition. However, it can be said, contrary to the claims advanced by Soviet philosophers, sociologists, and politicians, that there is no evidence that the Soviet family has become any more stable, solid, or otherwise better than the family in capitalist societies.

By and large, the multiplicity of influences acting on the family and the distance separating personal relations from national ideology and policy are both great, and it is usually extremely difficult to connect particular causes with particular effects. It is likely, however, that those portions of national family policy and corresponding institutions that are relatively unique to the Soviet scene, many of them deriving from marxist theory, have not concretely modified the Soviet family. Other forces, such as urbanization, agricultural collectivization, industrial growth, communist political rule, housing policy, and official discrimination against entire groups and classes of people have been much more influential.

Two observations on the future can be made. First, housing policy is a sure indicator of current policy on the status of the family. To date there is no indication that the individual, small-family dwelling, whether separate house or apartment flat, is not to be the main housing unit for the future. It seems evident that Soviet families in the future will carry on their lives in such housing in much the same way they do now. The main way in which Soviet family life will differ from family life in a modern Western society will lie in a broader and easier acceptance of more active involvement in the life of society on the part of Soviet women and children.

Secondly, on the age-old issue of whether a society can do without the family, the history of the Soviet family does not appear to provide an answer. There was no real Soviet effort to replace the family, because other tasks and demands were so pressing that basic fuctions, child-rearing, food preparation, and the like, could not be sponsored by public agencies on a sufficiently large scale. Consequently, we would be ill-advised to ring down the curtain in the fashion proposed by some observers, who hold that the Soviet rulers "tried to abolish the family but failed, which proves that the family is indispensable." Nothing of the sort, and the question is still a legitimate one.

However, the rulers of the Soviet Union, now and in years ahead, will probably not show any further interest in the problem. Some of the more ill-considered aspects of the marxist theory of the family will continue to be awkward for party policy makers but, as past experience has shown, they can be bypassed or tacitly repudiated without disturbing the reverential aura surrounding their authors. As of the present moment, the view that the family is indispensable has gained much weight in the USSR and is backed by some extensive domestic experience, if not scientific evidence. The backers of this view advance two arguments: (1) constant and relatively invariant parental care is required to produce psychologically normal children, and (2) society is unable to provide adequate substitutes for parents. If and when such an attitude becomes officially accepted, one of the most central of the remaining planks in the marxist program for the family — the social rearing of children — will have been discarded, as have many of the other marxist tenets, from Soviet plan and practice.

A close look at Soviet family life does not reveal a radical variation from the family systems and trends of other societies in comparable stages of development. Although there are special features — the large proportion of employed mothers and wives, the important role of the grandmother, the rapid surge toward independence of the youth, and so forth — most of the patterns found are the same elsewhere. The differences associated with social class, for example, will in the main sound familiar to students of the American family. Attitudes toward education and occupational career, relations of husbands and wives, patterns followed in rearing children all vary in predictable directions.

Two generalizations about Soviet family life should be stressed: (1) the single most striking feature of Soviet family life is the great diversity of patterns and types of individuals found in it, and (2) the question of adapting somehow to change in the outer society is a more prominent feature than is basic change in family life itself.

Social and individual diversity is typical. Along virtually any dimension or characteristic — size, material living conditions, stability, spiritual and political atmosphere, degree of order and organization, quality of affective relations, educational and cultural level — there are many, and crosscutting, variations. There are upper-class families who live in well-furnished flats near the center of the larger cities who enjoy most of the conveniences and pleasures available more widely in the West, even travel abroad. There are also poverty-stricken families who live in caves and have little to eat. There are devoted communist families and there are fiercely hostile ones, religious families and atheistic families, law-abiding families and families whose members break the law regularly. There are very traditional families and very modern ones, broken families and whole families, patriarchal ones and equalitarian ones.

The sources of this pronounced diversity are numerous. The USSR is, of course, a big country, with perhaps a hundred culturally distinct nationalities. At the time of the Revolution, with its manifold political implications, large sections of the population divided on the question of loyalty. With the start of the Plan era the USSR became to an ever increasing extent an open-class society. Consequently, the social class level and mobility pattern of the family and its members became a potent diversifying force. In fact, material circumstances have been throughout the Soviet period a most significant determining force in respect to a variety of specific patterns of family life.

Historical events left a strong imprint on entire groups and categories of the population. Famine, dekulakization, the purges and terror, world war with its suffering and losses left millions of families with inerasable scars, while some families were touched lightly or not at all. There is some doubt, for example, that a large per cent of the Soviet older generation today can ever regain the sense of security and dignity which Stalin took from them. But younger families, whose lives were less blighted by such trauma, are more optimistic and secure. There have been national victories and successes to be celebrated and shared, and these too have affected some more than others, and some perhaps not at all.

These great social processes, structures, and events mold individuals as well as families. Consequently, the traits of the Soviet personality are also among the influences shaping family life. Of these features two stand out, the severely traumatized and deteriorated personality — victim of the purges or the forced-labor camp — and the peculiarly Soviet trait of a marked disjunction between outer appearance and inner reality. The latter trait appears in the individual who, like Soviet society, has two selves, a more private inner one and a more public outer self. There are many ways to describe the situation — as one of "high standards" and "low behavior," or as a clashing between Soviet and traditional values, or as a contradiction between the ethical imperatives of Soviet collectivism and the everyday claims of life itself, leading to a more self- and family-oriented individualism. This syndrome is part of Soviet man today.

Some of these contradictory forces are built into the very nature of the Soviet system. Outer coercion inevitably leads to inner resentment. Unrealistically "high" expectations of behavior — requiring the hungry peasants to subscribe to the state loan, the wife to renounce the arrested husband, the individual to put loyalty to the Soviet state before loyalty to his family — create a type of person who becomes at worst cynical and self-seeking and at best willing in various ways to "fool the Power."

Two other features of the Soviet personality lead to an even greater diversity of patterning in family life. First, there is likely to be unusual motivational complexity behind the simplest of commitments. Second, psychological ambivalence is common. Perhaps these are to be expected in a land where the Revolution is recent and still controversial, and where social change has continued to be rapid and often violent. In any case they make for additional variety in family life.

The main consequence of great diversity in the patterning of family life seems to be a substantial amount of tolerance. Many Soviet persons have come to feel, as a postwar popular song puts it, "In our life anything can happen," and recommended and legal norms as well as the traditions of the past have lost much of their compelling power. As a result, Soviet family behavior seems to be governed to a remarkable extent by individual personality factors — experiences, abilities, and needs which cannot be predicted or controlled ahead of time.

If the first general attribute of the experience of the Soviet family is diversity, then the second is adjustment to change. Life in the outer society has indeed changed remarkably, much more than life inside the family. Social change has occurred there, too, but all sources agree that the family has been the slowest of Soviet social institutions to undergo modification. Such changes as we have noted — fewer children per marriage, an increase in marital equality, more independence of children — have been overshadowed by the struggle to maintain family life intact, and in as much the same form as in the past as possible. This reluctance to change is another proof that the influences serving to alter the Soviet family system have been mainly indirect ones, mediated through the economic, political, and other systems of the outer society.

The very slowness of the family to change, in comparison with other institutions, plays an important role in the life of the individual. Evidence indicates that the family performs for the individual a very significant supportive and rehabilitative function. The hard-pressed, often fearful and exhausted Soviet citizen, long buffeted by arbitrary and oppressive forces from the outer society, has regularly sought in his family a source of stability and permanent values during the chaotic times of modern Soviet history.

The prominence of the adaptive role of the family vis-à-vis society, and its supportive role for the individual lead to two further issues: how the slow-moving family keeps in touch with the more rapidly evolving society and how changes in the family itself can occur without too much damage to the sense of equilibrium and security of the participants.

The family is linked to the larger social system through the various functions that it performs for the society and through those proffered in return. Such a linkage helps to change the values and social organization of the family. The provisions of a social-security system, free medical care, educational opportunities, recreational facilities, and the like, all require that family members come into contact wih persons acting as official representatives of the larger society and with new ideas about truth and falsehood, beauty and ugliness, and good and bad. It is often helpful to think of the family-society link as an exchange relationship. Thus, in 1936 and 1944 the Soviet regime assisted families with many children to perform better the function of providing an adequate living standard, and in return required a greater measure of parental control over children and more stability in marital ties.

Some of the most interesting patterns found in this study can be given a functional interpretation. The politically stigmatized family, of alien social class, of kulak background, or with a history of political arrest, was frequently able, through geographical mobility, securing false documents, or such, to "pass." From the point of view of the Soviet rulers this procedure was ideal for eliminating the previous ruling class and other presumed opposition groups, for the individuals and their families remained at the same time that the classes and groups disappeared. Society as a whole benefited, we may suppose, from the various contributions that live citizens can produce and dead ones cannot, and the individual families benefited by assuming a legitimate new status in the life of the community and an unblemished past to pass on to the children.

Another linkage of family and society comes through the various roles which family members are called upon to play inside the family and out, and which they somehow have to harmonize in their own personalities. The requirement that each person do this is the basic psychological mechanism by which the family and a rapidly moving outer social system remain in contact with each other. The interaction of mutual influence between family and society comes out clearly in the way the meaning of a child in the life of a parent expresses the changing dimensions of the parent's own life, in the manner in which the Soviet school and youth organization work their influence indirectly upon Soviet parents through the new ideas and enthusiasms they generate in school children, and in the fact that changing political values and institutions are often experienced inside the family as controversies between generations.

In the realm of sex roles, there is little doubt that the legal and ideological changes in the status of women outside the family have had their repercussions inside it. As pointed out in Part IV on the differing fates of men and women in the Soviet system, the nichevo man and the strong woman may be the individual expressions of patriarchal degeneration, a process by which the different parts of a traditional cultural complex change at different rates.

In all these respects we find examples of the way in which the great social processes and changes of modern Soviet society are mediated through gradual and semiconscious shifts in the roles of child, parent, husband, wife.

One other major way in which the Soviet family has kept in touch with the larger society and minimized the stress of rapidly changing its own way of life involves a body of ideas shared in the informal culture which are only partly true, in the sense of reflecting the scientifically observable facts. These ideas play a part both in adjusting people to social change and in maintaining their capacity to live together in reasonable harmony. Among such ideas is the feeling that: "Parents are not important in the Soviet Union. The regime brings up the children, not the parents, and they have nothing to say about it." Although this situation is true for only a small minority, the fact that it is a common idea among the people and that many do indeed accept it as acccurate must be reckoned with. Alongside it is the notion that any Soviet child is a potential Pavlik Morozov, or betrayer of his father, and the idea that social mobility is either dangerous or apt to lead to the abandoned wife. All these ideas have some basis in fact, but they are expanded and used to justify what appear to be moral shortcomings when people are judged in terms of traditional values. Similarly, the concept of material hardship has acquired a peculiarly functional role in Soviet family life. Although actual hardship has been considerable, consciousness of it and complaints about it do not always correlate closely with objective measures of it. One can only conclude that the pain of repudiating the patterns of the past has been rationalized, and thus softened, by adopting the idea that life is hard and that one must sacrifice some of the old values in order to gain new ones.

Consequently, husbands and wives practice birth restriction for one reason, but find it more convenient to point to hardship as the responsible factor; men neglect their families to pursue personal glory in the shape of occupational success, but justify it by reference to the alternative hardship which their families would suffer. In brief, to some extent Soviet hardship has been a valid experience, but it has also been seized upon as a convenient justification for deviating from some of the established patterns of family life. The acceptance of these ideas thus serves as an unconscious psychic mechanism which helps people adjust to the difficulties of rapid social change.

The Soviet leaders have come to accept the family, and there is very little talk these days about its withering away. On the other hand, regime-family relations are far from perfect, and on one question in particular the current state of affairs is one of malaise on both sides. Still at issue is the question of where the line should be drawn between public life and private life, of what the limits of personal freedom should be.

There is no doubt that the Soviet people as individuals, from leader hierarchy to peasant, prefer maximum privacy and anonymity in their family lives. For many years it was almost a rule of survival for the average citizen to exert extra effort to obtain this, and even the most loyal and indoctrinated of Soviet citizens, leading party and government officials, have always drawn a sharp line between their public and their personal lives. Yet there has gone on for some thirty years, with little sign of diminishing intensity, a struggle over where the line should be drawn between the legitimate interests of the individual and his family and the legitimate interests of the regime. In the record of public discourse the controversy appears repeatedly. The no-man's-land is the area in which people behave in ways the regime does not approve, but for which legal prosecution is difficult to arrange or inappropriate. Included are greed and philistine-like attitudes toward wealth and material things, snobbish-ness, sexual exploitation and caddishness, following a religious way of life, in short, all those patterns the regime labels "survivals."

The official position has changed little since the mid-thirties. Displays of the old way of life are said to occur most frequently inside the family, and the party organizations are urged to accept the responsibility of ending them. Yet, because the opinion is so widely shared and not infrequently openly expressed that there is a realm of life that ought to remain private, local party organizations and various work and apart-ment house collectives are very reluctant to take any action that intrudes upon this view.

Notwithstanding, the party line remains adament in principle. Two official doctrines are invoked to support it. The first denies any conflict of interest between Soviet society and the Soviet family. The second holds, after Lenin, that "at the basis of communist morality lies the struggle to strengthen and perfect communism." From this it follows that any survival impedes the struggle to build communism, and that therefore any item of behavior or belief in family life which detracts from the public interest is immoral and a possible interference to progress.

There are several reasons why these official doctrines are intellectually weak and self-defeating. The argument that there is no conflict of in-terest between society and family is too manifestly untrue; Soviet social history is filled with grievous violations of the people's interests. Con-cerning the second doctrine; it is quite difficult to show any close and systematic correlation between the various aspects of family life and the goal that lies "at the basis of communist morality." Life is not so simple, and characteristics that seem at first view or in the short run disorganiz-ing or improper may upon closer inspection or in the long run turn out to be beneficial to society. The self-defeating feature of the official line is that by insisting on the principle of no separation between public and private life so tenaciously, the regime simply fosters a more distinct and rigid counter-principle in the informal culture. It repeatedly calls the Soviet citizen's attention to the fact that his private life must be jealously guarded, because both the general principle and its specific applications are constantly thrust in his face. There probably is considerable private sympathy for the social cads and religious believers who are publicily pilloried in the Soviet press, for their exposure also constitutes an implicit threat to the secrets of every family and every individual.

Further, the core of family life is essentially personal and even religious. The main events are the various *rites de passage* and crises of birth, marriage, sickness, and death, which call up deep emotions and require traditional sacred symbols. It is not without significance that after forty-five years of effort to expunge them, religious rituals still play some role in the life of most Soviet families. Moreover, it has not been possible to establish broad acceptance of substitutes in spite of sporadic efforts to compete with the church, organize Komsomol weddings, conduct contests for the development of Soviet rites, and so forth. Religious rites and things sacred cannot be consciously invented or planned for; they must appear spontaneously, out of life itself.

So it is with the social relationships of family life. Intimacy and love are by definition private and personal experiences; they are the source of the deepest, most spontaneous, and most lasting loyalties. Because these natural sentiments are so strong, it is difficult to understand the behavior of the Soviet rulers. For what reason do spokesmen for the Soviet regime still insist that there is a "single, correct viewpoint" from which actions, conduct, every step in public and private life must be evaluated?

The answer, of course, lies in the nature of Soviet totalitarianism itself. The totalitarian mind refuses to recognize that society is pluralistic and that the family is an institution that cannot be shaped or controlled beyond a minimum degree by law, political doctrine, or power. Nevertheless, one also finds open Soviet minds, in which the family, like the church, education, the arts and sciences, works as a slow but effective enemy of totalitarianism. In the long view of history this special mission — to afford to the individual some privacy and protection against totalitarian encroachment — may prove to have been the Soviet family's most important function.

ABBREVIATIONS IN THE BIBLIOGRAPHY

BIBLIOGRAPHY · NOTES · INDEX

ABBREVIATIONS IN THE BIBLIOGRAPHY

CDSP   *Current Digest of the Soviet Press*
Izv.   *Izvestiia* (News)
Kom.   *Kommunist* (The Communist)
Kom. Tadzhik.   *Kommunist Tadzhikistana* (The Communist of Tadzhikistan)
Kras. Nov.   *Krasnaia Nov* (Red virgin soil)
Let. Marks.   *Letopisi Marksizma* (Chronicles of Marxism)
Lit. Gaz.   *Literaturnaia Gazeta* (Literary gazette)
NDVSh. FN   *Nauchnye Doklady Vysshei Shkoly. Filosofskie Nauki* (Scientific reports of the higher school. Philosophical sciences)
Nov. M.   *Novy Mir* (The new world)
Pr.   *Pravda* (Truth)
Pr. Ukr.   *Pravda Ukrainy* (Truth of the Ukraine)
Sov. Bel.   *Sovetskaia Belorussia* (Soviet Belorussia)
Sov. Etnog.   *Sovetskaia Etnografiia* (Soviet ethnography)
Sov. Ped.   *Sovetskaia Pedagogika* (Soviet pedagogy)
Sov. R.   *Sovetskaia Rossiia* (Soviet Russia)
Sov. Gos. i Pr.   *Sovetskoe Gosudarstvo i Pravo* (Soviet state and law)
Tr.   *Trud* (Labor)
Vest. Stat.   *Vestnik Statistiki* (Chronicle of statistics)
Vop. Ekon.   *Voprosy Ekonomiki* (Problems of economics)
Vop. Fil.   *Voprosy Filosofii* (Problems of philosophy)

BIBLIOGRAPHY

Abramzon, S. M., et al. *Byt kolkhoznikov kirgizskikh seleni Darkhan i Chichkan* (Daily life of the collective farmers of the Kirgiz settlements Darkhan and Chichkan). Moscow, 1958.

Akishin, Vladimir. "Origins of a Crime," *CDSP* 9. 13:33–34, from *Kom. Tadzhik.*, March 10, 1956, p. 4.

Barash, M. "Sex Life of Workers of Moscow," *Journal of Social Hygiene*, 12:274–288 (1926).

"Be Equal to the Great Tasks of Building Communism — All-Union Conference on Questions of Ideological Work," *CDSP* 14. 1:5–7, from *Pr.*, Dec. 28, 1961, p. 2.

Bedny, Demian. " 'Vserez i . . . ne nadolgo' ili sovetskaia zhenitba" ("Seriously and . . . for a short time" or the Soviet marriage), pp. 111–124 in *Brak i semia*, 1926.

Belfrage, Sally. *A Room in Moscow.* New York, 1958.

Belyayev, Vadim. "Controversy: The Third Person — An Answer to Writer V. Kaverin," *CDSP* 12. 21:14–15, from *Lit. Gaz.*, May 14, 1960, p. 2.

Berman, Harold J. *Justice in Russia.* Cambridge, Mass., 1950.

———— "Soviet Law Reform — Dateline Moscow 1957," *Yale Law Journal*, 66:1191–1215 (1957).

Bikzhanova, Murshida A. *Semia v kolkhozakh Uzbekistana* (The family on the collective farms of Uzbekistan). Tashkent, 1959.

"Birth of a New Law — Interview with O. P. Kolchinaya, Vice-Chairman of the Legislative Proposals Committee of the USSR Supreme Soviet," *CDSP* 16. 11:10, from *Tr.*, Feb. 16, 1964.

Bischoff, Malte. "Die Struktur und die Wandlung der sowjetischen Familie (um 1950): die Familie in der sowjetischen Gesellschaft" (Structure and change in the Soviet family around 1950: the family in Soviet society), unpubl. diss., Universität Hamburg, 1956.

Black, Cyril E. (ed.) *The Transformation of Russian Society.* Cambridge, Mass., 1960.

Bobryshev, Ivan T. *Melkoburzhuaznye vliiania sredi molodezhi* (Petty bourgeois influences among the youth). Moscow–Leningrad, 1928.

Bogorov, I. I. "Gigiena braka" (The hygiene of marriage), pp. 173–186 in M. I. Lifanov (ed.), *Za zdorovy byt* (For a healthful way of life), Leningrad, 1956.

Bolshaia sovetskaia entsiklopedia (Great Soviet encyclopedia). 2d ed. Moscow, 1954.

Bowen, James. *Soviet Education: Anton Makarenko and the Years of Experiment.* Madison, Wisc., 1962.

Brackett, James W. "Demographic Trends and Population Policy in the Soviet Union," pp. 556–569 in Joint Economic Committee of the U.S.

Congress, 87th Session, *Dimensions of Soviet Economic Power,* Washington, D.C., 1962.

Brak i semia: sbornik statei i materialov (Marriage and the family: a collection of articles and materials). Moscow, 1926.

Bronfenbrenner, Urie. "The Changing Soviet Family." Paper read at a symposium on Soviet women, Bryn Mawr College, April 25, 1964. Part of a volume to be published by Teachers College Press of Columbia University.

Bubekin, V. M. (ed.) *Za liubov i schaste v nashei seme* (For love and happiness in our family). Moscow, 1936.

Bukharin, N. "Vospitanie smeny" (The upbringing of the younger generation), pp. 21–33 in Razin (ed.), *Komsomolski byt,* 1927.

Bureau of the Census, U.S. Department of Commerce. *Projections of the Population of the USSR, by Age and Sex: 1964–1965,* by James W. Brackett. International Population Reports, Series P-91, No. 13. Washington, D.C., 1964.

Bystrianski, Vadim A. *Kommunism, brak i semia* (Communism, marriage and the family). Petersburg, 1921.

Carr, Edward H. *History of Soviet Russia: Socialism in One Country, 1924–1926.* Vol. I. New York, 1958.

Chapman, Janet G. *Real Wages in Soviet Russia Since 1928.* Cambridge, Mass., 1963.

"Chelovek i kollektiv" (Man and the collective), *Pr.,* March 23, 1962.

Chetyrnadtsaty Sezd Vsesoiuznoi Kommunisticheskoi Partii (b), stenograficheski otchet (Fourteenth Congress of the All-Union Communist Party [b], stenographic report). Moscow–Leningrad, 1926.

Chkhikvadze, V. M. "Importance for Soviet Criminal Law of Leninist Views on Crime and Punishment," *CDSP* 9. 40:50, from *Sov. Gos. i Pr.,* No. 11, pp. 130–145 (1957).

Clark, J. Grahame D. "Archeological Theories and Interpretation: Old World," pp. 343–360 in Alfred L. Kroeber, *Anthropology Today,* Chicago, 1953.

Crankshaw, Edward. *Khrushchev's Russia.* Baltimore, Md., 1959.

Cunow, Heinrich. *Die marxsche Geschichts-, Gesellschafts- und Staatstheorie: Grundzüge der marxschen Soziologie* (The Marxist theory of history, society, and the state: characteristics of Marxist sociology). 4th ed. 2 vols. in one. Berlin, 1923.

Curtiss, John S. "Church and State," pp. 405–425 in Black (ed.), *The Transformation of Russian Society,* 1960.

Daniels, Robert V. "Fate and Will in the Marxian Philosophy of History," *Journal of the History of Ideas,* 21:538–552 (1960).

Deaton, Robert B. "Postwar Juvenile Delinquency in the USSR," unpubl. diss., University of Illinois, 1955.

Decree of Presidium of USSR Supreme Soviet: On Changing the Procedure for Hearing Divorce Cases in the Courts, *CDSP* 17. 51:29, trans. from

Vedomosti Verkhovnovo Soveta SSSR (Gazette of the USSR Supreme Soviet), No. 49 (1292), Dec. 15, 1965, p. 1084.

DeWitt, Nicholas. *Education and Employment in the USSR.* Washington, D.C., 1961.

Dodge, Norton T. *Women in the Soviet Economy: Their Role in Economic, Scientific and Technical Development.* Baltimore, 1966.

Dodon, L. L. *Kultura povedeniia sovetskogo molodogo cheloveka* (The etiquette of a young Soviet person). 2d corrected and enlarged ed. Leningrad, 1956.

Dolinina, N. "For the Third Person!" *CDSP* 12. 21:15, from *Lit. Gaz.*, May 28, 1960, p. 6.

Dunham, Vera S. "Eros in Contemporary Russian Poetry," *Social Problems* 7:339–351 (1960).

———— "The Strong-Woman Motif," pp. 459–483 in Black (ed.), *The Transformation of Russian Society*, 1960.

Dunn, Stephen P., and Ethel. "Directed Culture Change in the Soviet Union: Some Soviet Studies," *American Anthropologist* 64:328–339 (1962).

Eliseeva, V. "Pozornoe blagorazumie" (Shameful reasoning), *Lit. Gaz.* Aug. 16, 1956, p. 2.

Engels, Friedrich. *The Condition of the Working Classes in England in 1844.* London, 1892.

———— *Herr Eugen Dühring's Revolution in Science.* Moscow, 1947.

———— *The Origin of the Family, Private Property and the State.* New York, 1942.

———— *Principles of Communism*, trans. by Paul M. Sweezy. New York, 1952.

Entsiklopedicheski slovar (Encyclopedic dictionary). Vol. I. Moscow, 1953.

Erikson, Erik H. *Childhood and Society.* New York, 1950.

Federov, D. "On Bolshaia Bronnaia in Moscow" (Notes on the work of a children's room), *CDSP* 8. 48:18; trans. from *Pr.*, Nov. 30, 1956, p. 6.

Feuer, Lewis S. "Meeting the Philosophers," *Survey* (April 1964), pp. 10–23.

Field, Mark G. "The Re-legalization of Abortion in Soviet Russia," *New England Journal of Medicine*, 255:421–427 (1956).

———— with the assistance of Susan Salser. "Workers (and Mothers): Soviet Women Today." Paper read at a symposium on Soviet women, Bryn Mawr College, April 24, 1964. Part of a volume to be published by Teachers College Press of Columbia University.

Filonovich, Yu. "Popular Literature on Communist Morality," *CDSP* 8. 27:13–14, from *Kom.*, No. 8 (May 1956), pp. 114–123.

Fischer, Markoosha. *My Lives in Russia.* New York, 1944.

Fisher, Ralph T. *Pattern for Soviet Youth.* New York, 1959.

Geiger, H. Kent. "Changing Political Attitudes in Totalitarian Society: A Case Study of the Role of the Family," *World Politics* 8:187–205 (1956); also in Inkeles and Geiger, *Soviet Society*, 1961, pp. 546–558.

———— "Deprivation and Solidarity in the Soviet Urban Family," *American Sociological Review* 20:57–68 (1955).

—— "The Family and Social Change," pp. 447–459 in Black (ed.), *The Transformation of Russian Society*, 1960.

—— "Juvenile Delinquency in Soviet Russia: Statistics of Frequency and Trend." mimeo. 1963. 30 pp.

—— "The Urban Slavic Family and the Soviet System," unpubl. diss., Harvard University, 1955.

Gelman, I. *Polovaia zhizn sovremennoi molodezhi* (The sexual life of contemporary youth). Moscow, 1923.

Gibian, George. "New Trends in the Novel," *Survey*, No. 36 (April–June 1961), pp. 49–55.

Ginsburg, B. S. *Sud nad materiu pokinuvshei svoego rebenka* (Court for the mother who has abandoned her child). Moscow, 1924.

Grushin, B. A. "K problem kachestvennoi reprezentatsii v vyborochnom oprose" (On the problem of qualitative representativeness in the sample survey), pp. 61–107 in G. E. Glezerman and V. G. Afanasev (eds.), *Opyt i metodika konkretnykh sotsiologicheskikh issledovani* (Experience and methods of concrete sociological research), Moscow, 1965.

—— and V. V. Chikin. *Ispoved pokoleniia* (Confession of a generation). Moscow, 1962.

Gsovski, Vladimir. "Family and Inheritance in Soviet Law," *Russian Review* 7:71–87 (1947); also in Inkeles and Geiger, *Soviet Society*, 1961, pp. 530–540.

—— "Separation of Church from State in the Soviet Union," pp. xi–xxxi in Gsovski (ed.), *Church and State Behind the Iron Curtain*, New York, 1955; also in Inkeles and Geiger, *Soviet Society*, 1961, pp. 414–424.

—— *Soviet Civil Law*. 2 vols. Ann Arbor, Mich., 1948.

Hazard, John N. *Law and Social Change in the USSR*. Toronto, 1953.

"Heartless People," *CDSP* 8. 33:16, from *Sov. R.*, July 17, 1956, p. 4.

Hendel, Samuel. *The Soviet Crucible*. Princeton, N.J., 1959.

Hindus, Maurice. *House without a Roof: Russia after Forty-Three Years of Revolution*. Garden City, N.Y., 1961.

Iaroslavski, Emilian (ed.) *Voprosy zhizni i borby* (Problems of life and the struggle). Moscow–Leningrad, 1924.

—— "Predislovie" (Preface), pp. 3–4 in Razin (ed.), *Komsomolski byt*, 1927.

—— "Moral i byt proletariata v perekhodnom periode" (Morality and daily life of the proletariat in the transition period), pp. 34–54 in Razin (ed.), *Komsomolski byt*, 1927.

—— "O komsomolskoi distsipline, kurenii i prochem" (About Komsomol discipline, smoking and other things), pp. 113–115 in Razin (ed.), *Komsomolski byt*, 1927.

—— "Kakoiu dolzhna byt nasha molodezh?" (What should our young people be like?), pp. 144–146 in Razin (ed.), *Komsomolski byt*, 1927.

Inkeles, Alex. "Social Stratification and Mobility in the Soviet Union: 1940–1950," *American Sociological Review* 15:465–479 (1950); also in Inkeles and Geiger, *Soviet Society*, 1961, pp. 558–573.

—— and Raymond A. Bauer. *The Soviet Citizen: Daily Life in a Totalitarian Society.* Cambridge, Mass., 1959.

—— and Kent Geiger (eds.) *Soviet Society: A Book of Readings.* Boston, 1961.

Iurkevich, N. "Za ukreplenie sovetskoi semi" (For the strengthening of the Soviet family), *Sov. Bel.,* April 9, 1958, p. 3.

"Iz otzyvov chitatelei *Pravdy* na statiu Tovarishcha Smidovicha 'o liubvi' " (Some comments from *Pravda* readers on the article "Love," by Comrade Smidovich), pp. 273–278 in Razin (ed.), *Komsomolski byt,* 1927.

Juviler, Peter H. "Communist Morality and Soviet Youth," *Problems of Communism* 10. 3:16–24 (1961).

—— "Marriage and Divorce," *Survey,* No. 48 (July 1963), pp. 104–117.

—— "The Soviet Family — Everything Planned," *The Milwaukee Journal,* Feb. 7, 1965, p. 5.

Kabo, E. O. *Ocherki rabochego byta* (Sketches of the daily life of the workers). Moscow, 1928.

Kalmanson, S. M. (ed.) *Polovoi vopros* (The sex question). Moscow, 1924.

Kantner, John F. "The Population of the Soviet Union," pp. 31–71 in *Comparisons of the United States and Soviet Economics,* Part I (1959), paper submitted to the Subcommittee on Economic Statistics of the Joint Economic Committee, 86th Congress, First Session, Washington, D.C.; also in Inkeles and Geiger, *Soviet Society,* 1961, pp. 15–28.

Kaplun, S. *Sovremennye problemy zhenskogo truda i byta* (Contemporary problems of feminine labor and daily life). Moscow, 1924.

Kassof, Allen. *The Soviet Youth Program: Regimentation and Rebellion.* Cambridge, Mass., 1965.

Kautsky, Karl. *Die materialistische Geschichtsauffassung* (The materialist conception of history). 2 vols. Berlin, 1927.

Kaverin, V. "Witnesses for the Prosecution," *CDSP* 12. 21:13–14, from *Lit. Gaz.,* April 2, 1960, p. 2.

Kharchev, A. G. *Marksizm-Leninizm o brake i seme* (Marxism-Leninism on marriage and the family). Moscow, 1959.

—— "The Nature of the Soviet Family," *The Soviet Review,* 2:3–19 (1961), from *Vop. Fil.,* No. 1 (1961).

—— "O roli semi v kommunisticheskom vospitanii" (On the role of the family in a communist rearing), *Sov. Ped.,* No. 5 (1963), pp. 62–72.

—— "O nekotorykh rezultatov issledovaniia motivov braka v SSSR" (Some results of a study of reasons for marriage in the USSR), *NDVSh. FN,* No. 4 (1963), pp. 47–58.

—— *Brak i semia v SSSR* (Marriage and family in the USSR). Moscow, 1964.

Kingsbury, Susan M., and Mildred Fairchild. *Factory, Family and Women in the Soviet Union.* New York, 1935.

Kiselev, Vlad. "Is There Such a Thing as Love?" *CDSP* 8. 38:10–12, from *Lit. Gaz.,* Sept. 13, 1956.

Klemm, V. O. "Tovarishchu Nine Velt" (To Comrade Nina Velt), pp. 186–192 in Razin (ed.), *Komsomolski byt*, 1927.

Kluckhohn, Clyde. "Studies of Russian National Character," *Human Development Bulletin*, University of Chicago, Feb. 5, 1955, pp. 39–60; also in Inkeles and Geiger, *Soviet Society*, 1961, pp. 607–619.

Kolbanovski, V. N. "Rabochi byt i kommunizm" (The workers' way of life and communism), *Nov. M.*, No. 2 (1961), pp. 276–282.

Kollontai, Aleksandra M. *Semia i kommunisticheskoe gosudarstvo* (The family and the communist state). Moscow, 1919, 1920. Trans. and publ. as *Communism and the Family*. New York, 1920.

—————— *Obshchestvo i materinstvo* (Society and motherhood). Moscow, 1921.

—————— "Dorogu krylatomu Erosu! (Pismo k trudiashcheisia molodezhi)" (Make way for the winged Eros! [Letter to the toiling youth]), *Molodaia Gvardiia* (The Young Guard), No. 3 (1923), pp. 111–124; also in Iaroslavski, *Voprosy zhizni i borby* (1924), pp. 170–182.

Koltsov, Mikhail E. "V zagse" (In the civil registry office), pp. 164–174 in *Feltony i ocherki* (Feuilletons and sketches), Moscow, 1956.

Korbe, O. A. "Kultura i byt kazakhskogo kolkhoznogo aula" (Culture and daily life of the Kazakh collective farm aul [mountain village]), *Sov. Etnog.*, No. 4 (1950), pp. 67–91.

Korolev, Yu. A. "The Integration of Morality and Law in Marital and Family Relations," *CDSP* 16. 11:10–13, from *Vop. Fil.*, No. 11 (1963), pp. 75–85.

Kotovshchikova, A. "Neobychnye deti" (Exceptional children), *Lit. Gaz.*, Oct. 29, 1960, p. 4.

—————— "Esli roditeli zhivy" (If the parents are alive), *Lit. Gaz.*, Jan. 10, 1961.

—————— "O nikh dumaiut mnogie. Eshche o 'neobychnykh detiakh' " (Many are thinking about them. More about 'exceptional' children), *Lit. Gaz.*, July 25, 1961.

Kramer, Richard. "Practical Morality Taught to Soviet Children, as Illustrated in Four Official Soviet Periodicals, 1937–1951," unpubl. diss., Columbia University, 1953.

Krapivenski, S. E. "Po povodu tak nazyvaemoi oshibki Engelsa" (On the so-called mistake of Engels), *NDVSh. FN*, No. 2 (1963), pp. 104–111.

Kriving, P. "Zheny i byt" (Wives and daily life), pp. 278–282 in Razin (ed.), *Komsomolski byt*, 1927.

Krupskaia, Nadezhda K. *O bytovykh voprosakh: sbornik statei* (Problems of daily life: a collection of articles). Moscow, 1930.

—————— "Slovo Starykh Bolshevikov" (A word from Old Bolsheviks), pp. 58–63 in Bubekin (ed.), *Za liubov i schaste v nashei seme*, 1936.

—————— "Krepkaia sovetskaia semia" (The strong Soviet family), pp. 141–147 in Krupskaia (ed.), *Zhenshchina strany sovetov — ravnopravny grazhdanin*, 1938.

—————— (ed.) *Zhenschchina strany sovetov — ravnopravny grazhdanin*

(Woman of the land of Soviets — a citizen with equal rights). Moscow, 1938.

Krylenko, N. "Brak, semia i sovetskoe zakonodatelstvo" (Marriage, family and Soviet legislation), a discussion held in the Polytechnical Museum, Nov. 15, 1925, pp. 91–94 in *Brak i semia,* 1926.

———— "Obyvatel nastupaet" (The philistine advances), pp. 125–131 in *Brak i semia,* 1926.

"Kultura i byt kolkhoznikov Lvovskoi Oblasti" (The culture and daily life of the kolkhozniks of the Lvov Region), *Sov. Etnog.,* No. 4 (1950), pp. 133–149.

Kurski, D. I. "Brak, semia i opeka" (Marriage, family and guardianship), pp. 35–41 in *Brak i semia,* 1926.

Kurylev, S. "In the Interests of the Family," *CDSP* 10. 21:20–21, from *Izv.,* May 22, 1958, p. 2.

Kushner, P. I. "O nekotorykh protsessakh proiskkodiashchikh v sovremennoi kolkhoznoi seme" (Some processes occurring in the contemporary collective farm family), *Sov. Etnog.,* No. 3 (1956), pp. 14–24.

———— (ed.) *Selo Viriatino v proshlom i nastoiashchem* (The village Viriatino in past and present). Moscow, 1958.

Kuzmin, V. "Pismo o novom byte" (A letter about the new way of life), pp. 65–67 in Slepkov (ed.), *Byt i molodezh,* 1926.

———— "O molodoi starosti, asketizme i kazenshchine" (On old age among the youth, asceticism and the conventionalities), pp. 204–214 in Razin (ed.), *Komsomolski byt,* 1927.

Lapin, K. K. *V liubov nado verit: po pismam sovetskikh liudei o druzhbe i liubvi, brake i seme* (You have to believe in love: from the letters of Soviet people dealing with friendship and love, marriage and the family). Moscow, 1957.

Lass, D. I. *Sovremennoe studenchestvo* (Contemporary students). Moscow–Leningrad, 1928.

Lenin, Vladimir Ilich. *Sochineniia* (Works). 30 vols. 2d ed. Moscow–Leningrad, 1926–1932.

Levkov, I. "Brak i semia" (Marriage and family), pp. 151–168 in M. I. Lifanov (ed.), *V cheloveke dolzhno byt vse prekrasno* (Everything in man can be beautiful), Leningrad, 1958.

Levshin, A. *Family and School in the USSR.* Moscow, 1958.

Lilge, Frederic. "Anton Semyonovitch Makarenko: An Analysis of His Educational Ideas in the Context of Soviet Society," *University of California Publications in Education,* Vol. 13, No. 1 (1958).

Lorimer, Frank. *The Population of the Soviet Union.* Geneva, Switzerland, 1946.

Luke, Louise E. "Marxian Woman: Soviet Variants," pp. 27–109 in Simmons (ed.), *Through the Glass of Soviet Literature,* 1953.

Lukin, I. "When Life Is Difficult for a Person," *CDSP* 14. 30:31, from *Pr.* July 25, 1962, p. 3.

Lunacharski, Anatol V. "Moral i svoboda" (Ethics and freedom), *Kras. Nov.*, No. 7 (17), 1923, pp. 130–136.

———— *O byte* (Daily life). Moscow, 1927.

———— "Bolyne storony komsomolskogo byta" (Difficult aspects of komsomol daily life), pp. 112–113 in Razin (ed.), *Komsomolski byt,* 1927.

———— "Kakoiu dolzhna byt nasha molodezh?" (What should our young people be like?), pp. 150–153 in Razin (ed.), *Komsomolski byt,* 1927.

Mace, David, and Vera. *The Soviet Family.* Garden City, N.Y., 1963.

MacMaster, Robert E. "In the Russian Manner: Thought as Incipient Action," pp. 281–300 in Hugh McLean et al. (eds.), *Russian Thought and Politics,* Harvard Slavic Studies, Vol. IV, Cambridge, Mass., 1957.

MacMillan, Benton Y. "Divorce and Its Implications in the Soviet Union Since 1944." Term paper for Sociology 184, University of California at Berkeley, 1963–64.

Madison, Bernice. "The Organization of Welfare Services," pp. 515–540 in Black (ed.), *The Transformation of Russian Society,* 1960.

Makarenko, A. S. *Sochineniia* (Works). Moscow, 1950–1951.

———— *A Book for Parents,* trans. by Robert Daglish. Moscow, 1954.

Marshak, S., G. Speransky, D. Shostakovich, and I. Ehrenburg. "Life Has Rejected It," *CDSP* 8. 38:12, from *Lit. Gaz.,* Oct. 9, 1956, p. 2.

Marx, Karl. *Capital: A Critique of Political Economy,* trans. from the 3d German ed. by S. Moore and E. Aveling. 2 vols. Chicago, 1906.

———— and Friedrich Engels. *The Communist Manifesto.* New York, 1933.

———— ———— *Die deutsche Ideologie.* Berlin, 1953. Parts I and III ed. by R. Pascal and published as *The German Ideology.* New York, 1939.

———— ———— *Sochineniia* (Works). 30 vols. 2d ed. Moscow, 1955.

Mayer, Gustav. *Friedrich Engels, A Biography.* London, 1936.

Mehnert, Klaus. *Stalin versus Marx.* London, 1952.

Metter, I. "Oni ushli iz shkoli" (They quit school), *Lit. Gaz.,* Jan. 13, 1962, p. 4.

Meyer, Alfred G. *Marxism: The Unity of Theory and Practice.* Cambridge, Mass., 1954.

Mironkin, A. "Life and the Marriage Application," *CDSP* 14. 3:28, from *Izv.,* Jan. 17, 1962, p. 3.

Mosely, Philip E. "Moscow Revisited: Moscow Dialogues, 1956," *Foreign Affairs,* 35:72–83 (1956).

Nadezhdina, N. "On the Threshold of Working Life," *CDSP* 16. 4:21–22, from *Tr.,* Jan. 12, 1964, p. 2.

Narinyani, Sem. "A Rake's Progress," *CDSP* 4. 25:25, from *Pr.,* June 21, 1952, p. 2.

———— "Because of a Statistic" (feuilleton), *CDSP* 8. 44:24, from *Pr.,* Oct. 31, 1956, p. 4.

———— "Question for the Judge" (feuilleton), *CDSP* 9. 41:32–33, from *Pr.,* Oct. 2, 1957.

Nash, Edmund. "Recent Trends in Labor Controls in the Soviet Union," pp. 391–407 in Joint Economic Committee of the U.S. Congress, 87th Session, *Dimensions of Soviet Economic Power,* Washington, D.C., 1962.

Newman, Bernard. *Visa to Russia.* London, 1959.

Novak, Joseph. *The Future Is Ours, Comrade: Conversations with the Russians.* New York, 1959.

Oridoroga, M. T. "Grounds for Dissolution of a Marriage," *CDSP* 9. 20:20–24, from *Sov. Gos. i Pr.,* No. 1 (1957), pp. 111–115.

Paustovsky, Konstantin. "The Drozdovs: A Speech," pp. 155–159 in Hugh McLean and Walter N. Vickery (eds.), *The Year of Protest, 1956: An Anthology of Soviet Literary Materials,* New York, 1961.

Petrosyan, G. "On the Rational Use of the Off-Work Time of the Working People," *CDSP* 15. 33:3–7, from *Vop. Ekon.,* No. 6 (June 1963), pp. 32–41.

Pochivalov, L. "Your City," *CDSP* 15. 51:37–38, from *Pr.,* Dec. 19, 1963, p. 6.

Polunin, Vladimir. *Three Generations: Family Life in Russia, 1845–1902,* trans. by A. F. Birch-Jones. London, 1959.

Preobrazhenski, E. A. *O morali i klassovykh normakh* (On ethics and class norms). Moscow, 1923.

Rabinovich, Nadezhda V. "Semeinoe pravo" (Family law), pp. 276–305, Vol. I, and pp. 263–300, Vol. II in O. S. Ioffe (ed.), *Sorok let Sovetskogo prava* (Forty years of Soviet law), 2 vols., Leningrad, 1957.

Razin, I. (ed.) *Komsomolski byt* (Komsomol daily life). Moscow–Leningrad, 1927.

Recht, Carolyn. "The Quantity and Adequacy of Soviet Urban Housing as Viewed by Former Soviet Citizens," mimeographed report of the Harvard Project on the Soviet Social System. Cambridge, Mass., 1953.

Riazanov, D. (Goldendach, David B.) "Marks i Engels o brake i seme" (Marks and Engels on marriage and the family), *Let. Marks.,* No. 3 (1927), pp. 13–35.

———— "Introduction" and "Explanatory Notes" to *The Communist Manifesto,* trans. by Eden and Cedar Paul. London, 1930.

Romashkin, P. "Some Questions of Criminal Legislation," *CDSP* 9. 30:6–7, from *Izv.,* July 27, 1957, p. 2.

Rossi, Alice S. "Generational Differences in the Soviet Union," mimeographed report of the Harvard Project on the Soviet Social System. Cambridge, Mass., 1954. In revised form, unpubl. diss., Columbia University, 1957.

Rostovshchikov, V. "Orphans with Parents," *CDSP* 11. 23:19, from *Izv.,* June 9, 1959, p. 4.

Sabsovich, L. M. *Sotsialisticheskie goroda* (Socialist cities). Moscow, 1930.

Schlesinger, Rudolf (ed.) *The Family in the USSR.* London, 1949.

Schwartz, Harry. *Russia's Soviet Economy.* New York, 1950.

Shimkin, Demitri B. "Current Characteristics and Problems of the Soviet Rural Population," pp. 79–127 in Roy D. Laird (ed.), *Soviet Agricultural and Peasant Affairs,* Lawrence, Kansas, 1963.

———— and Pedro Sanjuan. "Culture and World View: A Method of Analysis Applied to Rural Russia," *American Anthropologist,* 55:329–348 (1953).

Simmons, Ernest J. (ed.) *Through the Glass of Soviet Literature: Views of Russian Society.* New York, 1953.

———— "Review" (of "Part V, Literature, State and Society"), pp. 451–469 in Simmons (ed.), *Continuity and Change in Russian and Soviet Thought,* Cambridge, Mass., 1955.

———— *Russian Fiction and Soviet Ideology: Introduction to Fedin, Leonov, and Sholokhov.* New York, 1958.

Slepkov, A. (ed.) *Byt i molodezh* (Daily life and youth). Moscow, 1926.

———— "Semia i stroitelstvo sotsializma" (The family and the construction of socialism), pp. 52–57 in Slepkov (ed.), *Byt i molodezh,* 1926.

Slepkov, Vladimir. "Komsomolski 'zhargon' i komsomolski obychai" (Komsomol slang and Komsomol custom), pp. 46–48 in A. Slepkov (ed.), *Byt i molodezh,* 1926.

———— "Ne o edinoi politike zhiv komsomolets" (Not by politics alone does a Komsomol member live), pp. 215–219 in Razin (ed.), *Komsomolski byt,* 1927.

Smidovich, S. N. "Molodezh i liubov" (Youth and love), pp. 60–64 in Slepkov (ed.), *Byt i molodezh,* 1926.

———— "O korenkovshchine" (On the Korenkov affair), pp. 132–140 in Razin (ed.), *Komsomolski byt,* 1927.

———— "O davidsonovshchine" (On the Davidson affair), pp. 140–144 in Razin (ed.), *Komsomolski byt,* 1927.

———— "Otvet na pismo komsomolki" Answer to the letter of a Komsomol girl), pp. 176–178 in Razin (ed.), *Komsomolski byt,* 1927.

———— "O liubvi" (On love), pp. 268–273 in Razin (ed.), *Komsomolski byt,* 1927.

———— "O byte" (On daily life), pp. 164–166 in Razin (ed.), *Komsomolski byt,* 1927.

Smith, Jessica. *Woman in Soviet Russia.* New York, 1928.

Solts, A. A. "O revoliutsionnoi zakonnosti" (On revolutionary legality), pp. 89–90 in *Brak i semia,* 1926.

———— "Brak, semia i sovetskoe zakonodatelstvo" (Marriage, family and Soviet legislation), pp. 91–94 in *Brak i semia,* 1926.

———— "Kommunisticheskaia etika" (Communist ethics), pp. 55–70 in Razin (ed.), *Komsomolski byt,* 1927.

———— "Ne nyt, a stroit" (Not to complain, but build), pp. 108–111 in Razin (ed.), *Komsomolski byt,* 1927.

Sosnovski, Lev S. *Bolnye voprosy (Zhenshchina, semia i deti)* (Painful questions [Woman, the family and children]). Leningrad, 1926.

Sosnovy, Timothy. "The Soviet City," pp. 321–345 in Joint Economic Committee of the U.S. Congress, 87th Session, *Dimensions of Soviet Economic Power,* Washington, D.C., 1962.

"Sovetskaia semia" (The Soviet family), *Pr. Ukr.,* Sept. 16, 1959, p. 4.

"Speech by Comrade I. A. Kairov, President of the Russian Republic

Academy of Pedagogy," *CDSP* 14. 3:23–24, from *Pr.*, Oct. 27, 1961, pp. 6–7.

"Statisticheskie materialy: sostav semei po dannym vsesoiuznoi perepisi naseleniia 1959 g." (Statistical data: the composition of families according to figures of the all-union census of the population of 1959), *Vest. Stat.*, No. 11 (1961), pp. 92–95.

Stepanian, Ts. "Semia nashei epokhi" (The family of our era), pp. 35–40 in Bubekin (ed.), *Za liubov i schaste v nashei seme*, 1936.

Stepanov, I. "Problema pola" (The problem of sex), pp. 204–208 in Iaroslavski (ed.), *Voprosy zhizni i borby*, 1924.

Stern, Bernhard J. "Engels on the Family," *Science and Society*, 1:42–64 (1948).

Steward, Julian H. "Evolution and Process," pp. 313–326 in Alfred L. Kroeber (ed.), *Anthropology Today*, Chicago, 1953.

Strumilin, S. "Family and Community in the Society of the Future," *The Soviet Review* 2. 2:3–19, from *Nov. M.*, No. 7 (1960), pp. 204–220.

—— and A. Peremyslov. "Daily Routine and Time," *CDSP* 16. 15:28, from *Izv.*, Apr. 15, 1964, p. 2.

Svetlov, V. "Socialist Society and the Family," pp. 315–347 in Schlesinger (ed.), *The Family in the USSR*, trans. from *Pod Znamenem Marksizma* (Under the banner of Marxism), No. 6 (1936).

—— *Brak i semia pri kapitalizme i sotsializme* (Marriage and the family under capitalism and socialism). Moscow, 1939.

Teitelbaum, S. M. "Parental Authority in the Soviet Union," *American Slavic Review*, 4:54–69 (1945).

Terenteva, L. N. and N. V. Shlygina (eds.), *Semia i byt kolkhoznikov Pribaltiki* (Family and daily life of the collective farmers of the Baltic region). Moscow, 1962.

Timasheff, N. S. *Religion in Soviet Russia: 1917–1942*. New York, 1942.

—— *The Great Retreat*. New York, 1946.

—— "Religion in Russia, 1941–1950," pp. 153–194 in Waldemar Gurian (ed.), *The Soviet Union: Background, Ideology, Reality*, South Bend, Indiana, 1951.

—— "Urbanization, Operation Antireligion and the Decline of Religion in the USSR," *American Slavic Review*, 14:224–238 (1955).

—— "Anti-religious Campaign in the Soviet Union," *Review of Politics*, 17:329–344 (1955).

—— "The Inner Life of the Russian Orthodox Church," pp. 425–437 in Black (ed.), *The Transformation of Russian Society*, 1960.

Time, Events, People. Moscow, no date (probably around 1958), no pagination.

Triska, Jan F. (ed.), *Soviet Communism: Programs and Rules*. San Francisco, 1961.

Trotsky, Leon. *Voprosy byta* (Questions of daily life). 2d revised and enlarged edition. Moscow, 1923. Partly trans. as *Problems of Life*. New York, 1924.

———— *The Revolution Betrayed.* New York, 1937.

Tsentralnoe statisticheskoe upravlenie pri Sovete Ministrov SSSR (Ts. S. U.). *Zhenshchiny i deti v USSR* (Women and children in the USSR). Moscow, 1961.

United Nations, Department of Economic and Social Affairs. *Provisional Report on World Population Prospects, as Assessed in 1963.* New York, 1964.

Vaksberg, Arkadi. "Bigot in a Scholar's Toga," *CDSP* 12. 30:31–32, from *Lit. Gaz.,* July 16, 1960, p. 2.

Velt, Nina. "Otkrytoe pismo tovarishchu Smidovich" (An open letter to Comrade Smidovich), pp. 179–185 in Razin (ed.), *Komsomolski byt,* 1927.

Veselovsky, V., and Yu. Shabarov. "Divorce Announcements," *CDSP* 13. 51:8, from *Izv.,* Dec. 20, 1961, p. 6.

Vinogradskaia, P. "Voprosy morali, pola, byta, i tovarishch Kollontai" (Problems of morality, sex, daily life, and Comrade Kollontai), *Kras. Nov.,* No. 6 (16), 1923, pp. 179–214.

Vladimirov, S. "A Delicate Subject" (feuilleton), *CDSP* 9. 15:30, from *Tr.,* Feb. 17, 1957, p. 4.

Volfson, S. Ia. *Sotsiologiia braka i semi* (Sociology of marriage and the family). Minsk, 1929.

———— "Socialism and the Family," pp. 280–315 in Schlesinger (ed.), *The Family in the USSR,* trans. from *Pod Znamenem Marksizma* (Under the banner of Marxism), No. 6 (1936), pp. 31–64.

Volkov, A. "Incorruptible Conscience" (Short story), *CDSP* 14. 3:30–31, from *Izv.,* Jan. 16, 1962, p. 4.

Vostrikova, A. "Nekotorye dannye o rozhdaemosti v SSSR" (Some data on fertility in the USSR), *Vest. Stat.,* No. 12 (1962), pp. 42–46.

"Voters Meet Candidates for Deputy to USSR Supreme Soviet: In Onega Election District," *CDSP* 14. 12:15–16, from *Pr.,* March 14, 1962, pp. 2–3.

Winter, Ella. *Red Virtue: Human Relations in New Russia.* New York, 1933.

Yanowitch, Murray. "Soviet Patterns of Time Use and Concepts of Leisure." *Soviet Studies,* 15:17–37 (1963).

Zalkind, A. B. *Ocherki kultury revoliutsionnogo vremeni* (Sketches of the culture of the revolutionary period). Moscow, 1924.

———— *Revoliutsiia i molodezh* (Revolution and youth). Moscow, 1924.

———— "Etika, byt i molodezh" (Ethics, daily life, and youth), pp. 70–88 in Razin (ed.), *Komsomolski byt,* 1927.

———— "O byte" (On daily life), pp. 166–168 in Razin (ed.), *Komsomolski byt,* 1927.

———— *Polovoe vospitanie* (Sex education). 2d ed. Moscow, 1930.

Zavadovski, B. "Kakoiu dolzhna byt nasha molodezh?" (What should our young people be like?), pp. 156–159 in Razin (ed.), *Komsomolski byt,* 1927.

Zenzinov, V. *Bezprizornye* (The homeless children). Paris, 1929.

Zetkin, Klara. *Reminiscences of Lenin.* London, 1929.

NOTES

One: The Family from the Armchair of Marx and Engels

1. Explicit inclusion of this last phrase in the title reflects the enthusiasm of Engels for the work of Lewis Henry Morgan, an American evolutionary anthropologist (1818–1881). In it, according to Engels, "a new foundation was laid for the whole of primitive history" (*Origin,* p. 16), a fact which, in his view, had an importance for anthropology corresponding with that of Darwin's theory of evolution for biology and Marx's theory of surplus value for political economy. Parenthetical page references throughout this chapter are to this volume. Quoted by permission of International Publishers Co. Inc. © 1942.

2. This point is an important aid to the refutation of Soviet efforts to cover a basic difficulty in marxist social theory. See the discussion in Chap. 2, below.

3. Riazanov, "Marks i Engels," p. 25. The author of this article further asserts, however, that these "several individual differences" were "significantly harmonized in the process of joint work." This authority is David B. Riazanov (Goldendach), a talented, witty, marxist scholar who joined the party around 1917, after heading a small literary group. He became the party's most distinguished student of Marx and in 1935 published an excellent biography of him. For many years director of the Marx-Engels Institute, he was dismissed in 1931 and is presumed to have perished in Stalin's great purges.

4. *Capital,* I, 536. However, noted Engels, it was Morgan who was able to outline "for the first time" a successful history of the family (*Origin,* p. 16). Moreover, on the basis of Morgan's work Marx changed his mind about exactly when the family put in its appearance upon the stage of history. See n. 50a on p. 298 of Karl Kautsky's edition (*Volksausgabe*) of *Capital* (Berlin, 1914).

5. There were a few reservations about the first stage, based on Engels' conclusion that the evidence was inadequate (pp. 27–32).

6. *Punalua* is a Hawaiian affinal kin term of address, translated by Engels as "intimate companion" or "partner" and used by the members of either sex in this group marriage.

7. Engels noted this fact only by implication. Indeed, he stated explicitly that the development of the family parallels the development of the three "main epochs" of human history constructed by Morgan — savagery, barbarism, and civilization — but that the periods are not so strikingly differentiated (p. 19). It is less likely, then, that the development of the forms of the family could easily be made to parallel closely that of the fivefold typology of social orders. To do so puts considerabe strain upon Marx's and Engels' ideas.

8. Perhaps I am doing Engels some small injustice by neglecting the relevance of the matrilineal gens, now referred to by Western ethnographers as clan. The reader interested in further details of marxist views on institutional classification is invited to inspect the voluminous Russian literature on the subject.

9. I shall show later that a logical contradiction is involved here. Engels invoked another major explanatory principle, "individual sex love," but later in the book, and with the qualification that it plays no role in the emergence of the pairing family. At another place, however, he insisted that there are only two printciples governing family relations, the economic and the "natural" one of true sex love.

10. Steward, p. 313. The presumed temporal priority of matriarchal over other kin patterns is one of the most inadequate of Morgan's conceptions. It was his "proof" of precisely this, ironically, which led Engels to rank him as an equal of Darwin and Marx. For detailed criticism of Morgan, see Robert H. Lowie, *Primitive Society* (New York, 1925) or *The History of Ethnological Theory* (New York, 1937), especially pp. 54–67. It has been suggested that Morgan's stages of history were "cribbed," originating in fact with the Swedish zoologist Sven Nilsson. Clark, pp. 344–345.

11. *Die deutsche Ideologie,* p. 183; hereafter cited as *Ideologie,* or as *Ideology* if the English translation.

12. Engels, *Herr Eugen Dühring's Revolution,* p. 380.

13. See *Ideologie,* p. 183; *Origin,* passim.

14. Engels, *Condition,* pp. 125–126.

15. *Ibid.,* pp. 23, 65 ff., 115–116, 129, 125.

16. *Ibid.,* pp. 129, 142–144, et passim.

17. *Capital,* I, 706.

18. *Condition,* pp. 144–145.

19. *Ideologie,* p. 183.

20. See also *Condition,* p. 126.

21. *Ideologie,* p. 390. See also *Herr Eugen Dühring's Revolution* where Engels speaks of "the rupture of all traditional bonds based on descent of patriarchal subordination" (p. 387).

22. The careful reader may suspect that Engels himself was made uneasy by such contradictions. He devoted relatively little space to description of the proletarian family in *The Origin,* even hinting at one point rather directly that the proletarian as well as the bourgeois family is founded on domestic slavery. At this point both are subsumed under a new concept, the "modern individual family" (pp. 65–66). One marxist exegete sought to dispel the contradiction by introducing a new element. Riazanov asserted that the unhappy portrait of proletarian family life found in Engels' first book appeared because "the worker has not yet become a conscious member of the revolutionary army of labor, and is in submission to the bourgeois social order." Riazanov, "Marks i Engels," p. 21.

23. Engels, *Principles of Communism,* p. 18.

24. Engels, *Herr Eugen Dühring's Revolution,* p. 474.

25. Engels, *Principles of Communism,* p. 18.

26. The women will force them to be monogamous, said Engels, a little too easily.

27. To my knowledge, the only authoritative marxist writing on the subject of housing is by Karl Kautsky in the last chapter of the second part of his *Die Agrarfrage: eine Übersicht über die Tendenzen der modernen Landwirtschaft und die Agrarpolitik der Sozialdemokratie* (Stuttgart, 1899), where he asserts that the disappearance of the individual "economic" household does not mean the end of marriage and the family, but its transformation into a higher form, nor does it mean the end of the individual dwelling. Riazanov hints that Lenin, who edited this work of Kautsky in 1903, approved of this point of view, Riazanov, "Marks i Engels," pp. 31–32.

28. Marx and Engels, *Manifesto,* p. 27.

Two: Historical Materialism and the Family

1. Confusion and controversy on this point have been notorious and will probably continue to be. My own view is that Marx and Engels allocated exclusive reign to economic factors as the moving force of history when they were in their most forceful polemical moods. The dramatic impact of economic determinism is much greater than the watered-down causal eclecticism of their other emphases. In their more sober and reflective moods Marx and Engels were better sociologists. To this extent, I agree with the generous "functionalist" interpretation of Alfred G. Meyer, but I would place more emphasis on their inconsistency. An excellent recent discussion of the problem is available in Daniels.

2. The use of materialistic is meant to extend the notion of *economic* determinism in the spirit with which Marx and Engels wrote about the family — namely, as related to sex and age differences and the act of reproduction. See below for more on this.

3. The word abolition here is a translation of *Aufhebung,* which is also used to refer to what would happen to private property, to the individual household economy, and to the family. See the German edition, *Ideologie,* pp. 25–26.

4. This difficulty is noted by Engels in his discussion of the proletarian family, which is no longer monogamous "in the strict sense" or "in its historical sense." *Origin,* p. 64.

5. For the sake of greater ease in pursuit of my main goal — to understand the structure of marxist thought as a whole — I am usually not pausing to note whether key generalizations or propositions are valid or invalid. However, this particular one is inadequate on at least two counts, the assertion of a rigid historical sequence from matrilineality to patrilineality and the mechanism of transition used by Engels. There has never been any such recognizable war between the sexes. For another example, Engels states that in the possessing classes it is the husband who is obliged

to earn a living and support his family, and that in itself gives him a position of supremacy. *Origin*, pp. 65–66.

6. The language used in *The German Ideology* also supports this interpretation: e.g., a reference is made on p. 9 to the "natural division of labor occurring within the family," of which the division of labor in the first stage of its development — that corresponding to the holding of property in common by the tribe — is no more than "an extension."

7. "Aspects of social activity," "fundamental conditions," "facts of history," "moments," "premises," and still other words are used synonymously.

8. The phrasing of the third premise is cryptic: "men . . . begin to make other men, to propagate their kind: the relation between man and wife, parents and children, the FAMILY." *Ideology*, p. 17. It should be remembered, however, that *The German Ideology* was left in semifinished form and never published during Marx's and Engels' lifetime.

9. The Soviet editors of the 2d edition of Marx's and Engels' *Sochineniia* note that this term was replaced by the term "relations of production" in later works, and assert that the term is meant in fact to refer to a wider range of phenomena, roughly "social institutions" (*obshchestvenno-eko-nomicheskie formatsii*). *Sochineniia*, III, vii.

10. Thus, more than 100 years ago Marx and Engels worked out a scheme of analysis which is still very useful. It was their genius to have seen that premises (1) and (2) are in process of constant change and that they tend constantly to get out of adjustment with the mode of cooperation or social stage.

11. Cunow, p. 141.

12. Kautsky, p. 842. He further speculates that the idea "retreated to the farthest recesses of the consciousness of our master, and only took on new meaning through the researches of Morgan."

13. Lenin, *Sochineniia*, XXVI, 26–35.

14. Krapivenski, p. 106. This writer also asserts that the tendency to see the whole thing as no more than an error was enhanced by the "cult of personality" of Stalin, and helped to exaggerate the latter's "theoretical merits" (p. 110).

15. Fourier, quoted by Marx, in Riazanov, "Marks i Engels," p. 21. See also Engels, *Herr Eugen Dühring's Revolution*, p. 386, and Stern, p. 43.

16. Worldly asceticism is prominent in Engels' valuation of "hard, real work" (*Origin*, p. 43) and in the whole notion of progress through suffering. Poverty is also invested with strong themes of redemption — reminiscent of the biblical promise, Blessed are the poor in spirit: for theirs is the kingdom of heaven.

17. In contrast to the official image, which has Marx as a model family man, there is evidence that his family life was far from ideal in contemporary Soviet terms, and that among other difficulties he had an illegitimate son. See Feuer, p. 22. A biographer writes of Engels' views on marriage: "Neither his convictions nor his sentiments would allow the claim of state and church to legitimize his closest human relationship. But to give one last

pleasure to Lizzy [Burns] he married her on her deathbed." Mayer, p. 226.

18. Note the changed meaning, now positive, of monogamy.

19. In American social thought more attention has been directed toward the other side of the coin, toward patterns which are seen as "needed but absent." See the concept of "cultural lag," made famous by William F. Ogburn, *Social Change* (New York, 1922).

20. "Der heilige Max," as quoted in Riazanov, "Introduction," p. 162.

21. Professor Alfred G. Meyer, in a personal communication, has contributed a qualification of the interpretations in this chapter. He observes that some of the ambiguities and contradictions I have discussed may be "either explained or further complicated" by linking the marxist theory of the family to certain additional features of marxism, such as the concept of alienation of man in modern civilization and the tradition of social Romanticism from which it was derived, and also to "the radical climate of opinion in the middle of the 19th century, where some of their views may have been generally current." He also notes that "there are a number of problems on which close examination leads to the conclusion that Marx and Engels simply voiced the radical clichés of their time, even though these did not fit in with their broad theories."

22. Cunow, p. 141.

23. Kautsky, pp. 844–845. But, of course, Kautsky is, in the Soviet view, a renegade to marxism, so his theory of the family has been in itself a substantial obstacle to any revision by Soviet writers of the theory propounded by Marx and Engels. The Great Soviet Encyclopedia, for example, states that his "counter-revolutionary views" are most clearly expressed in *The Materialist Conception of History,* where his version of the marxist theory of the family is given.

24. There are several allusions to the idea in *The Origin.* In perhaps the most explicit, Engels quotes with approval Charles Fourier's "profound recognition that in all societies which are imperfect and split into antagonisms single families (*les familles incohérentes*) are the economic units" (p. 162; see also pp. 29–30).

Three: Problems of the Transition Period

1. This period never played an important role in the theory of Marx and Engels; it received only a short discussion in Marx's *Critique of the Gotha Program.*

2. For details, see Daniels.

3. Lenin commented to Klara Zetkin: "Perhaps one day I shall speak or write on these questions — but not now. Now all our time and energy must be devoted to other matters." Zetkin, p. 61.

4. Bystrianski, p. 66.

5. A Slepkov, "Semia i stroitelstvo sotsializma," pp. 52, 57. The most thorough discussion of the whole problem is in Volfson, *Sotsiologiia braka*

i semi, pp. 375–450. His position is similar to Slepkov's. At one time or another N. Bukharin, N. Krylenko, Anatol Lunacharski, Trotsky, and Kollontai espoused the idea that the family would wither.

6. Lenin, *Sochineniia*, XXVIII, 161.

7. Zetkin, p. 68.

8. *Ibid.*

9. Kabo, p. 204. "Fifty-eight per cent of a workday," 4.8 hours, was spent solely on preparation of food and care of utensils (p. 149).

10. Sabsovich, p. 33.

11. Strumilin, in Kingsbury and Fairchild, pp. 201–202.

12. Sabsovich, p. 34; Volfson, *Sotsiologiia braka i semi*, p. 387.

13. "It is perfectly obvious that without achieving genuine equality between husband and wife in the family in matters of daily life and morality, one cannot speak seriously of their equality in social production or even of their equality in state politics, because if the woman is chained to the family, to cooking, washing and sewing, then this fact itself strips away the possibility of her influence in governmental life to the final measure." Trotsky, *Voprosy byta*, p. 49.

14. Kollontai, *Obshchestvo i materinstvo*, p. 13.

15. Kingsbury and Fairchild, p. 205.

16. Sabsovich, p. 75.

17. Cited in Krupskaia, *O bytovykh voprosakh*, p. 22.

18. Sabsovich, pp. 131, 49, 48, 32.

19. *Izvestiia*, June 7–8, 1931, as quoted in Winter, p. 268.

20. Krupskaia, *O bytovykh voprosakh*, p. 22.

21. Gsovski, *Soviet Civil Law*, I, 624.

22. Schlesinger, p. 36.

23. Gsovski, *Soviet Civil Law*, I, 627–629.

24. *Ibid.*, 624.

25. Smith, p. 111.

26. Volfson, *Sotsiologiia braka i semi*, p. 396. I cannot accept the author's qualifying phrase, "among the petty bourgeoisie," implying that proletarians were not so affected.

27. Vinogradskaia, p. 191.

28. Kollontai, *Semia i kommunisticheskoe gosudarstvo*, p. 10.

29. The term "anarcho-individualistic disorganization" is from Volfson, *Sotsiologiia braka i semi*, p. 389; Solts, "Braka, semia i sovetskoe zakonodatelstvo," p. 92.

30. Trotsky, *Voprosy byta*, pp. 110–117.

31. Kriving, p. 280.

32. *Ibid.*, p. 281.

33. Bobryshev, p. 57.

34. Bukharin, as quoted in Carr, p. 30.

35. Fisher, p. 64.

36. Zalkind, *Ocherki kultury*, p. 54; "Etika, byt i molodezh," p. 87.

37. Lenin's widow, Krupskaia, was one of the most active opponents of

childbeating. See, for example, pp. 40–47 of *O bytovykh voprosakh,* a collection of articles originally appearing in *Pravda* and other newspapers.

38. Teitelbaum, pp. 57–58.

39. Fisher, pp. 134, 170; K. B. Radek, *Izvestiia,* June 28, 1931.

40. *Bolshaia sovetskaia entsiklopediia,* 1954, XXVIII, 310. See also Teitelbaum, p. 66.

41. Volfson, *Sotsiologiia braka i semi,* pp. 445, 391.

42. Velt, p. 185.

43. Kollontai, *Obshchestvo i materinstvo,* pp. 18–19; Volfson, *Sotsiologiia braka i semi,* p. 445.

44. Solts, "O revoliutsionnoi zakonnosti," p. 89.

45. Carr, p. 32.

46. Observations of "a communist," quoted in Winter, p. 131.

47. Stepanov, p. 208.

48. Iaroslavski, "Moral i byt proletariata," pp. 50–51. This last assertion is doubtful. A good proportion of the remaining 97 per cent were still out roaming the streets as homeless children.

49. Trotsky, *The Revolution Betrayed,* p. 146.

50. Kaplun, p. 79.

51. Winter, p. 270; Smith, p. 155; Trotsky, *The Revolution Betrayed,* pp. 146–147.

52. Klemm, p. 185.

53. Sosnovski, p. 34.

54. Zetkin, pp. 68–69; Preobrazhenski, pp. 96–97; Lunacharski, *O byte,* p. 27; Krupskaia, *O bytovykh voprosakh,* p. 8; Volfson, *Sotsiologiia braka i semi,* p. 383.

55. For the early years, see Kaplun, p. 75. For the thirties, see Kingsbury and Fairchild, pp. 169, 249, 251, et passim.

56. Trotsky, *The Revolution Betrayed,* p. 156.

57. An example cited during the discussion of the 1926 draft code on marriage and family. Smith, p. 118.

58. Vinogradskaia, p. 195.

59. Lunacharski, "Moral i svoboda," pp. 130–134.

60. Volfson, *Sotsiologiia braka i semi,* p. 449.

61. Smidovich, "O korenkovshchine," p. 132.

62. *Ibid.,* p. 140.

63. Lunacharski, "Moral i svoboda," p. 135; *O byte,* p. 8.

64. For example, in the mid-twenties she advocated immediate imposition of a nationwide per capita tax to be used for the construction of crèches and other facilities that would transfer the burden of childrearing from the individual mother to the state.

65. Kollontai, "Dorogu krylatomu Erosu," pp. 176–178.

66. *Ibid.,* pp. 178–180.

67. Preobrazhenski, pp. 110–111.

68. Ravich, "Borba s prostitutsiei" (The struggle with prostitution), *Kommunistka,* No. 1–2, 1920, as quoted in Lass, p. 8.

69. Smidovich, "Molodezh i liubov," p. 63; Vinogradskaia, p. 186; *Brak i semia,* p. 125.

70. *Chetyrnadtsaty Sezd VKP (b),* p. 815; Vladimir Slepkov, "Komsomolski 'zhargon,'" p. 47.

71. Lunacharski, "Kakoiu dolzhna byt nasha molodezh?" p. 152.

72. Lunacharski, *O byte,* p. 45; Vladimir Slepkov, "Ne o edinoi politike," p. 218.

73. Vinogradskaia, p. 187; Bobryshev, p. 121.

74. Lunacharski, "Kakoiu dolzhna byt nasha molodezh?" p. 150.

75. A medical doctor asserted that proletarian youth were most disorderly (Razin, p. 278), and Lunacharski noted that the birth rate had not declined more because the peasantry were "not as yet touched in such degree by 'pseudo-revolutionary' ideas as to reflect them in their family life" (*O byte,* p. 14). But Smidovich asserted that rural youth are "most primitive" of all in their sexual relations. "Molodezh i liubov," pp. 60–61. See also Barash, who reported on the basis of a questionnaire survey that workers start sex life later and are more restrained than peasants and students.

In 1923, Trotsky indicated that there was "some truth" to the reports of the fall of morals among Soviet youth, especially the Komsomol members. *Voprosy byta,* p. 51. See also Iaroslavski, "Moral i byt," p. 48. But see Bobryshev, who in a brochure written in 1927 states that, "the basic portion of our youth, and Komsomol members above all, do not take part in the activities typical of the 'down with shame' circles" (p. 121).

76. Gelman (1923); Lass (1928).

77. Smidovich, "O liubvi," p. 268; "Molodezh i liubov," p. 62. See also the assertion by L. A. and L. M. Vasilevski that "the opinion is widely spread that sexual abstinence, especially for the man, is connected with nervous disturbances, with the development of bad blood, with the decline of physical powers, etc." Kalmanson, p. 64.

78. Kharchev, *Marksizm-Leninizm o brake i seme,* p. 19; Vinogradskaia, p. 187.

79. Volfson, *Sotsiologiia braka i semi,* p. 397; Lass, p. 209.

80. Lunacharski, *O byte,* p. 69. See also Kuzmin, "Pismo o novom byte," pp. 65–67, who satirizes this theory and others such as the condemnation of ties, attractive clothing, and handshaking as customs of the bourgeois and the pope and as unsanitary.

81. Lunacharski, "Bolnye storony komsomolskogo byta," p. 113; Lass, pp. 198–199.

82. Smidovich, "Molodezh i liubov," p. 61. Lunacharski is a prominent example of the exaltation of natural man, especially in his early writing.

83. Lass, p. 12.

84. Lass's 1928 study showed a decreasing tendency for male students to visit prostitutes for their first sexual experience (14 per cent) in contrast with a 1914 Moscow survey (42 per cent) and an earlier post-revolutionary study by Gelman (28 per cent). He attributed this tendency to the "growth of revolutionary consciousness." Lass, p. 113.

85. Smidovich, "Molodezh i liubov," p. 62.

86. Lass, p. 44.

87. Lunacharski, *O byte*, pp. 15–16.

88. Kharchev, *Marksizm-Leninizm o brake i seme*, p. 20.

89. Lass, p. 203; Iaroslavski, "Moral i byt," p. 50. Iaroslavski ascribes this phrasing to Oscar Wilde.

90. Klemm, p. 189.

91. A. Slepkov, "Semia i stroitelstvo sotsializma," p. 52.

92. Smidovich, "Molodezh i liubov," p. 62; Zavadovski, p. 157. The latter, a professor, coined an indignant slogan: "Away with references to ideological principles as a pretense for the lust of the male!"

93. Lunacharski, *O byte*, p. 68.

94. Volfson, *Sotsiologiia braka i semi*, p. 381. Reports of such exploits reached massive proportions in the Soviet press in 1935 and 1936.

95. As quoted in Stepanov, pp. 205–206.

96. Lass, pp. 148–149, 197–213; Volfson, *Sotsiologiia braka i semi*, pp. 427–428; L. A. and L. M. Vasilevski, in Kalmanson, pp. 39–40; Smidovich, "Molodezh i liubov," pp. 62–63.

97. Iaroslavski, "Moral i byt," p. 51; Lunacharski, *O byte*, pp. 28–42.

98. Volfson, *Sotsiologiia braka i semi*, p. 381.

99. V. Zenzinov, *Deserted* (London, 1931), pp. 27–29, as quoted in Teitelbaum, p. 57, originally appearing in *O vospitanii detstva* (Moscow, 1922), p. 3.

100. Carr, p. 34; Stepanov, p. 207; Sosnovski, p. 11; Krupskaia, *O bytovykh voprosakh*, pp. 13, 48.

101. Smith, pp. 177–178.

102. Iaroslavski, *Pravda*, Oct. 9, 1924, in Carr, p. 33; Vinogradskaia, p. 201; Smidovich, "Molodezh i liubov," p. 61.

103. Lunacharski, *O byte*, p. 14. In fact, the birth rate was to decline sharply among the peasantry, too, but whether the presence amongst them, as among urban dwellers, of such "pseudo-revolutionary ideas" was an important reason is doubtful. Larger social trends and processes are more important. See below, Chap. 7.

104. Lebedeva, in Ginsburg, p. 5.

105. The estimate of 9,000,000 for 1922 was made by Lunacharski in 1928. In 1923 Krupskaia made an estimate for the same year, 1922, of 7,000,000. The *Great Soviet Encyclopedia* gave a figure of 334,000 for 1927, and other "official" figures are even lower. Zenzinov, pp. 111–120, has a good discussion of the official and unofficial estimates. See the table, Zenzinov, pp. 116–117, for different estimates for various years.

106. Smidovich, "Molodezh i liubov," p. 61.

107. A. Slepkov, "Semia i stroitelstvo sotsializma," p. 55.

108. "Kommunisticheskaia etika," p. 65.

109. Sosnovski, pp. 10–11.

110. Kingsbury and Fairchild, p. 154; Smith, pp. 185–188.

Four: New Thoughts and Policies

1. Smidovich, "O liubvi," pp. 268–273; Carr, pp. 36–37.
2. Sosnovski, p. 3.
3. Lunacharski, *O byte*, p. 67; Iaroslavski, *Voprosy zhizni i borby*, p. iii; Iaroslavski, "Moral i byt," p. 44.
4. Volfson, *Sotsiologiia braka i semi*, p. 440; Trotsky, *Voprosy byta*, pp. 125, 123.
5. Velt, pp. 179–180.
6. Trotsky, *Voprosy byta*, p. 83.
7. Smidovich, "Molodezh i liubov," p. 60.
8. Bystrianski, p. 4; Riazanov, "Marks i Engels," pp. 25, 28. See also Smidovich, who uses the following identity: "polygamy or, better, disorderly sexual relations, characteristic of primitive communism." "O liubvi," pp. 271–272.
9. Riazanov, "Marks i Engels," pp. 18–20, 30.
10. *Ibid.*, p. 31.
11. Bukharin, p. 25, for example.
12. Iaroslavski, "Kakoiu dolzhna byt nasha molodezh?" p. 146.
13. As quoted in Kaplun, p. 81.
14. Iaroslavski, "Moral i byt," p. 50.
15. Zalkind, *Revoliutsiia i molodezh*, p. 56; Preobrazhenski, pp. 51–52.
16. Stepanov, p. 208; Solts, "O revoliutsionnoi zakonnosti," p. 89.
17. Lunacharski, *O byte*, p. 21.
18. *Ibid.*, pp. 34, 36, 76.
19. Smidovich, "Otvet na pismo komsomolki," p. 176.
20. Slepkov, *Byt i molodezh*, p. 4; Smidovich, "Molodezh i liubov," p. 61; Bobryshev, p. 58.
21. Krylenko, "Obyvatel nastupaet," p. 129.
22. Vinogradskaia, pp. 181, 189.
23. *Krasnaia Nov*, No. 7 (17), December 1923, p. 306.
24. Riazanov, "Marks i Engels," p. 26.
25. Preobrazhenski, pp. 97–98.
26. Modern scientific knowledge was also a legitimate authority. For instance, the advice of medical authorities and scholars was from time to time sought on the question of whether sexual satisfaction was necessary to maintenance of health. Some authorities claimed that sexual abstinence was not harmful, and some, often relying on the ideas of Freud, avowed that it was.
27. Zetkin, pp. 52, 55.
28. Iaroslavski, "Predislovie," in *Komosomolski byt*, p. 3.
29. Lunacharski, "Moral i svoboda," p. 134.
30. Preobrazhenski, pp. 97, 98, 102; Kalmanson, pp. 85–86.

31. Zetkin, pp. 57, 60, 58.

32. Zalkind, *Revoliutsiia i molodezh*, p. 91.

33. Zalkind, *Polovoe vospitanie*, pp. 243, 247.

34. *Ibid.*, pp. 249, 248; Kollontai, "Dorogu krylatomu Erosu!"

35. In other respects Zalkind was hardly a serious Freudian. For instance: "Real sex life only starts at 22–23 years for men and 20–22 for women" (*Polovoe vospitanie*, p. 253). Freud, wrote Zalkind, was not "sociologically" correct in his thinking (*ibid.*, p. 281).

36. *Ibid.*, p. 282.

37. *Ibid.*, pp. 287, 319.

38. *Ibid.*, p. 229.

39. As quoted in Volfson, *Sotsiologiia braka i semi*, p. 282.

40. Zalkind, *Polovoe vospitanie*, p. 331.

41. Iaroslavski, "Moral i byt," p. 49.

42. Zalkind, *Revoliutsiia i molodezh*, p. 72.

43. Speech at Third Russian Congress of the Young Communist League, Oct. 2, 1920, as quoted in Hendel, p. 175.

44. This is the gist of thoughts expressed by Iaroslavski, "Moral i byt," p. 44.

45. Bowen, p. 126.

46. Makarenko, *A Book for Parents*, p. 7, as quoted in Bowen, p. 174.

47. *Ibid.*, p. 51, as quoted in Bowen, p. 176.

48. "Their intolerance was directed against a specifically Russian intelligentsia whom they reproached for excessive reasoning and theorizing, for denying the possibility of a true revolution, and above all for being separated from the masses." Lilge, p. 11.

49. Timasheff, *The Great Retreat*, pp. 197, 202; Kramer, pp. 134–138; Schlesinger, pp. 333–335.

50. Teitelbaum, p. 60.

51. Decree of Council of Peoples' Commissars of July 6, 1935, in Luke, p. 101.

52. Luke, p. 97.

53. For some time it was even possible in the Ukraine for a marriage to be registered by only one of the parties concerned. Naturally some consternation resulted, for it was possible to travel in the Ukraine, become married, and depart without even knowing about it. Smith, p. 133.

54. Luke, p. 77.

55. However, registration of a bigamous marriage was a punishable offense. Berman, *Justice in Russia*, p. 243.

56. Hazard, p. 124.

57. Winter, p. 28.

58. May 28, 1936, as quoted in Gsovski, *Soviet Civil Law*, p. 129.

59. Smidovich, "Otvet na pismo komsomolki," p. 176; Iaroslavski, "Moral i byt," p. 47.

60. Luke, p. 78; Simmons, *Russian Fiction*, p. 106. In another of Leonov's

novels of this period, *Skutarevski* (1932), there is a similar type, Cherimov, who "had never been able to spend more than half an hour a month for love" (Simmons, *Russian Fiction*, p. 117).

61. Kramer, p. 131.

62. Svetlov, *Brak i semia*, p. 144; Timasheff, *The Great Retreat*, p. 200. See also, below, Chap. 9.

63. Until the mid-1950's the Soviet government published only scattered figures on divorces as well as on marriages. Such data as became available were published primarily for internal consumption, were largely for didactic purposes, and were likely to be misleading. For example, an article published in the late 1940's stated that in two different regions of the USSR reconciliation occurred in 54 per cent and 56 per cent, respectively, of the divorce cases heard in the lower courts. Hazard, p. 270. One can guess that these statistics were published primarily to give lower court judges some idea of a reasonable norm and that "reconciliation" is to be interpreted mainly as a euphemism for the court's refusal to grant a divorce to the petitioner(s). Such an interpretation is supported by the additional information on the subject coming to light since the death of Stalin. See below, Chap. 9, under "A Major Social Problem."

64. The decree is translated in full in Schlesinger, pp. 269–279.

65. An example of how Stalin determined policy in an area closely related to family policy is the account of his decision to adopt a tolerant position toward religion. A speaker at the Tenth Congress of the Komsomol (1936) reported that Stalin had rejected a proposal to combat religion "decisively, mercilessly," and had said instead that it was necessary to "explain patiently" the harm of religious prejudices. Fisher, p. 353.

66. An exhaustive analysis would probably include still other considerations. One other is Robert E. MacMaster's provocative thesis about a practical, pragmatic strain in Russian culture, a kind of anti-analytical prejudice which might well have contributed to the downgrading of many aspects of classical marxism.

67. Hazard, pp. 252–253; Luke, p. 95.

68. *Semia i shkola,* No. 8, August 1951, p. 1; Svetlov, "Socialist Society," p. 333. See also, Hazard, who states that the new family policy was motivated largely by concern for the development of the children (p. 272).

69. "Iz otzyvov chitatelei *Pravdy,*" p. 274.

70. Volfson, "Socialism and the Family," p. 315.

71. For example, it is likely that a major aim of the 1944 divorce legislation was to help forestall divorce and other matrimonial problems of members of the Soviet armed forces arising during a time of war.

72. Mehnert, p. 21.

73. Solts, as quoted in Trotsky, *The Revolution Betrayed,* p. 151.

74. Chapman, pp. 145–148.

75. Svetlov, "Socialist Society," p. 334. For a recent implicit reference to the tradition of separation of public and private life, see Khrushchev's secret speech of 1956, in which he refers to a document purporting to be a

letter from Krupskaia to Lenin protesting Stalin's "crude interference in her private life." Inkeles and Geiger, p. 265.

76. Iaroslavski, *Voprosy zhizni i borby,* p. v.

77. Volfson, "Socialism and the Family," p. 311. See the exactly equivalent phrasing in Svetlov, "Socialist Society," p. 351.

78. Krupskaia, "Krepkaia sovetskaia semia," p. 146.

79. See, for example, Stepanian, or Svetlov, *Brak i semia,* pp. 3–13.

80. A similar development is observed by Fisher in his account of the changing content of the role of the Komsomol. Fisher, p. 210.

81. Volfson, "Socialism and the Family," p. 296; *Pravda,* April 4, 1936, as quoted in Trotsky, *The Revolution Betrayed,* p. 155; Svetlov, "Socialist Society," p. 330; Svetlov, *Brak i semia,* p. 107.

82. Svetlov, "Socialist Society," p. 323.

83. Svetlov, *Brak i semia,* p. 108. Unfortunately, this author fails to cite appropriate references for these assertions, which weakens them fatally.

84. *Ibid.,* p. 5.

85. See typical formulations *ibid.,* p. 151, and in Dodon, pp. 4–5.

86. Kharchev, *Marksizm-Leninizm,* p. 32.

87. Rabinovich, p. 268; Field, "The Re-legalization of Abortion," p. 15.

88. Field, "The Re-legalization of Abortion," p. 16.

89. *Ibid.,* p. 14; Mace, p. 239.

90. Gibian.

91. Vaksberg, p. 31.

92. See Chap. 9.

93. Vaksberg, p. 31.

94. Juviler, "Marriage and Divorce," p. 117.

95. Marshak; Dolinina.

96. Belyayev; Kaverin.

97. Vaksberg, p. 31.

98. "Birth of a New Law"; Decree of Presidium. The decree is translated in *CDSP* 17. 51:29.

99. By 1961 the obligatory publication in the newspapers of the intention to divorce was finding no defenders, at least not in the periodical press. For a wry account, see Veselovsky and Shabrov, who asked of M. A. Kapylovskaya, a deputy chief of the Russian Republic Ministry of Justice the purpose of this requirement. " 'I can't say,' she answered. 'I have often wondered about it myself. I think this must be changed.' "

100. See the reference on p. 312 of Kharchev, *Brak i semia,* to the sources of " 'the hunt' for materially well-off grooms and brides."

101. Kharchev, *Brak i semia,* pp. 63, 206, 215.

102. Kiselev, pp. 2–3.

103. Kharchev, "O roli semi," p. 63.

104. Kotovshchikova, "Neobychnye deti."

105. See the books by Abramzon et al., Bikzhanova, Kushner, and Terenteva and Shlygina.

106. Kharchev, *Marksizm-Leninizm,* pp. 14, 36.

107. Kharchev, *Marksizm-Leninizm,* p. 21; "The Nature of the Soviet Family," p. 5; *Marksizm-Leninizm,* p. 37.

108. Kharchev, *Marksizm-Leninizm,* p. 37.

109. Kharchev, *Brak i semia,* passim.

110. Strumilin, "Family and Community," p. 208. Quoted by permission of International Arts and Sciences Press.

111. N. Solovev, *Semia v sovetskom obshchestve* (Moscow, 1962), p. 120, as quoted in Bronfenbrenner, p. 21.

112. Triska, pp. 95–96.

113. Kotovshchikova, "O nikh dumaiut mnogie," p. 2.

114. Kharchev, "O roli semi," p. 63.

115. Triska, p. 93.

116. See the discussion of readers' reactions to Strumilin in Kolbanovsky. In Kharchev, *Brak i semia,* p. 262, the rearing of children is described as "the most important function of the family in the realm of spiritual life."

117. Juviler, "The Soviet Family."

118. Kharchev, *Marksizm-Leninizm,* p. 36.

119. Triska, p. 113.

120. Kharchev, *Brak i semia,* p. 314.

121. Strumilin, "Family and Community," p. 206.

122. Kharchev, *Brak i semia,* p. 307.

Five: What the Revolution Brought to the Family

1. David J. Dallin, *The Changing World of Soviet Russia* (New York, 1956), pp. 30–31.

2. Kushner, *Selo Viriatino,* pp. 207, 210.

3. Berman, "Soviet Law Reform," p. 1193; Chkhikvadze; Romashkin.

4. Fischer, pp. 49–50.

5. Gsovski, "Separation of Church from State," in Inkeles and Geiger, p. 419.

6. Curtiss, pp. 422, 426; Timasheff, "The Inner Life," pp. 427, 436.

7. Geiger, "Deprivation and Solidarity."

8. Eloquent claims of the advantages of Soviet communism compete with each other for space in the Soviet media of mass communication. An excellent recent source is the Program approved at the Twenty-second Congress of the party in 1961. See Triska.

9. Bischoff, pp. 306–307. According to Bischoff this outlook is a result of the extent to which party ideology is approved and the people admire the achievements of the regime; the great importance among the people of aspiration for social mobility; and the ideology itself, which presents a developmental theory prophesizing the attainment of communism, this in turn being the final goal of human development and bringing the redemption of all humanity. Bischoff believes that although this outlook is strongest

in the upper classes, it affects roughly two-thirds of the Soviet population in some way.

10. Triska, p. 90.

11. Timasheff, *Religion in Soviet Russia,* p. 65.

12. Curtiss, p. 424; Rossi, especially Appendix A, pp. 1–82.

13. Rossi, Appendix A, p. 70; Geiger, "The Urban Slavic Family," p. 235.

14. *Pravda,* August 4, 1954, in Timasheff, "Anti-religious Campaign," p. 342.

15. Newman, p. 146.

16. Kushner, pp. 40, 70, 232–233. The participants in the conference described in Trotsky, *Voprosy byta,* came to a similar conclusion. See chap. v, "The Family and Ceremony," and the appendix to the Russian edition.

17. Told to me by several respondents during interviews in Germany, 1950–1951.

18. Fisher, p. 190.

19. Bischoff, p. 97.

20. Grushin and Chikin, p. 55. The twenty-eight-year-old student and former construction worker continued: "Here is when our doubts took root and they, it is known, gnaw at the spirit . . . Later the rights of our fathers were restored, but there was no way to restore our fathers themselves . . . We cannot find consolation so easily." Ellipsis marks are in original source.

21. Kushner, *Selo Viriatino,* p. 223.

22. One can imagine the grim pleasure with which the feminists in the party read one of the conclusions of E. O. Kabo's 1928 study: "Even with the most superficial observation one cannot but notice how slowly, but truly, day after day the strength, health, and joy of life of even young women are undermined. While a worker, after his 8-hour work in the factory, devoted his free time to public activity, self-education or simply rest, *forever expanding his mental horizons,* the working wife, during her long workday ceaselessly struggles to economize and to improve and better organize the life of her family" (pp. 221–222). Almost thirty years later the Viriatino study offered much the same explanation of why the cultural level of women in the village was not so high as that of men. Kushner, *Selo Viriatino,* p. 48.

Six: Hardship and Opportunity: The Family in the Class System

1. Chapman, pp. 145–148.

2. *Ibid.,* p. 169.

3. *Ibid.,* p. 170.

4. See *ibid.,* pp. 155–164, for more details and analysis.

5. For a detailed account of the class system as it appeared in the two decades preceding Stalin's death, see Inkeles, "Social Stratification." See also, Chapman, especially chap. x, "Real Wages, Living Standards and Welfare," pp. 165–188.

6. Volkov.

7. "Sovetskaia semia."

8. Paustovsky, p. 157.

9. Bischoff, p. 194.

10. Question 17 in Section V, "The Family," of the paper-and-pencil questionnaire, Harvard Project on the Soviet Social System.

11. Lorimer, pp. 145–150; Kantner, p. 24.

12. The ramifications of this fact extend in many directions. For instance, had the real wages of urban workers remained on a constant or rising level from 1928 to World War II, the cities would have been even more completely overwhelmed by the mass exodus from the countryside, and the attendant social problems even more greatly magnified. In other words, it proved impossible to industrialize at the expense of the peasantry without also decreasing the living standard of the urban workers.

13. Bischoff, p. 300.

14. Many of the ideas presented here were corroborated by or stem initially from Bischoff.

15. Recht, pp. 16–17 et passim.

16. Bischoff, p. 293.

Seven: The Size and Organization of the Family

1. This is not meant to deny that the *direction* of change is nearly universal. See, for example, Bikzhanova, who states that many of the same patterns and directions of change can be observed in Uzbek collective farm families as in Slavic families. "In contrast with pre-revolutionary times they constitute a uniform type of Soviet family" (p. 133). She also takes some pains to emphasize that the changes, for example, the massive process of dissolution of the extended family, are going on at the present time (p. 135).

2. "Statisticheskie materialy: sostav semei," p. 93; Vostrikova, p. 46; Kharchev, *Brak i semia*, pp. 215–218.

3. Dodge, pp. 6–7.

4. *Ibid.*, p. 19.

5. Shimkin, p. 89.

6. Kushner, *Selo Viriatino*, p. 215.

7. Geiger, "The Urban Slavic Family," p. 155.

8. Ts. S. U., *Zhenshchiny i deti*, pp. 108–109. Corresponding percentages for the United States are less than 10 per cent.

9. Inkeles and Bauer, p. 206.

10. Yanowitch, p. 27. In an additional 17 per cent only the mother is employed, but it is hard to assign meaning to such a figure without knowing the family composition.

11. Hindus, p. 279.

12. Kharchev, *Brak i semia*, p. 253; Strumilin and Peremyslov.

13. "Chelovek i kollektiv."

14. Ilyina and Syrtsov, p. 7.

15. Letter to *Pravda,* January 6, 1962, in Field, "Workers (and Mothers)," p. 91.

16. Strumilin and Peremyslov.

17. Issue of March 16, 1960, as quoted in Hindus, p. 282.

18. See, for example, the study reported by Petrosyan.

19. Kharchev, *Brak i semia,* p. 259.

20. Dodge, p. 91.

21. Inkeles and Bauer, pp. 104–105.

22. Dodge, pp. 20–21.

23. Velt, pp. 179, 182.

24. There were 350,000 in the United States. Kantner, p. 52.

25. Brackett, pp. 565–567.

26. Kantner, p. 53.

27. Ts. S. U., *Zhenshchiny i deti,* p. 89.

28. Bronfenbrenner, p. 17. See also Dodge, who stresses the tendency of younger parents to favor state rearing for their children (pp. 87, 89).

29. Hindus, p. 291.

30. Winter, p. 146.

31. Kantner, pp. 51–52.

32. According to one source, *coitus interruptus* was common in pre-Soviet Russia. Kantner, p. 52. A recently published article on "The Hygiene of Marriage" states that *coitus interruptus* is "very widespread." Bogorov, p. 182.

33. Mace, p. 240.

34. *Sovetskoe zdravookhranenie* (Soviet health protection), No. 3, 1963; David M. Heer, paper read in Bryn Mawr, Penn., April 1964.

35. Kharchev, *Brak i semia,* p. 204. Conceptions of what makes a majority overwhelming and of how significant something less than 20 per cent is depends on the viewpoint of the writer. Kharchev feels the figure is high enough to support his argument that Soviet premarital intercourse has increased. Although his evidence is not strong, the argument could be accepted on other grounds.

36. For example, see Kotovshchikova, "Esli roditeli zhivy." Lady engineer M and her young son were abandoned by her common-law husband and she was neglected by her relatives, who felt she had disgraced herself and them by giving birth to a child outside marriage.

37. Kushner, *Selo Viriatino,* p. 68.

38. See Luke, p. 79, for evidence in the form of literary personalities.

39. There were no class differences in the use of condoms, abortion, and sexual continence as means of birth control.

40. See Kushner, *Selo Viriatino,* pp. 9–10.

41. *Ibid.,* p. 83.

42. *Ibid.,* p. 208. See also Shimkin and Sanjuan.

43. Kushner, *Selo Viriatino,* pp. 208–210.

44. *Ibid.*, p. 208.

45. *Ibid.*, p. 81.

46. *Ibid.*, p. 212 et passim.

47. *Ibid.*, pp. 209–210.

48. *Ibid.*, p. 215.

49. Madison, p. 527.

50. Mosely, p. 72; Kharchev, *Brak i semia,* p. 253; "Voters Meet Candidates."

51. Juviler, "Communist Morality," p. 21.

52. The discussion and data are taken mainly from Sosnovy.

53. Dodge, p. 94. See also Kharchev, *Brak i semia,* pp. 257–259.

54. Eliseeva.

55. Nash, pp. 397–398. In that year, the normal work week was seven hours Monday through Friday and six hours on Saturday.

56. Dodge, p. 94. See also Yanowitch, pp. 26–28.

57. For this reason also there is some evidence that elite families are little interested in owning their own homes, an obligation that would take up what little free time they have with extra travel hours and chores.

58. Novak, p. 35.

59. Kharchev, *Brak i semia,* p. 294.

Eight: Elements and Types in Soviet Marriage

1. Kushner, *Selo Viriatino,* p. 84. This attitude is now generally considered quite anachronistic, although parental desires are still treated as worthy of consideration in the village.

2. "Girls rarely wait for boys to come out of the army, for they fear that 'he won't want me!' " Kushner, *Selo Viriatino,* p. 225.

3. Bischoff, p. 175.

4. Kluckhohn, p. 618.

5. Kharchev, *Brak i semia,* p. 179. "Equality of rights and respect," so prominent in the official ideal, accounted for only 13.2 per cent of the responses.

6. Korbe, p. 85. See also, Kushner, *Selo Viriatino,* pp. 211, 214.

7. Kharchev, *Brak i semia,* p. 224. The first type of marital relationship accounted for 36 per cent, and in the remaining 4 per cent of families the wife held more authority than the husband.

8. Kushner, *Selo Viriatino,* p. 36.

9. *Ibid.*, p. 79.

10. Bischoff makes a distinction between two main subtypes in the equal-rights pattern of distributing power. He calls them "partnership" and "hedonistic individualism." This case is an obvious example of the latter.

11. Vera Dunham has discerned such a theme in both Russian and Soviet literature. See her article in Black.

12. Erikson, pp. 323–328.

13. Polunin, p. 6.

14. Bischoff, p. 190.

15. See the 1961 Program of the Communist Party of the Soviet Union. Triska, p. 99.

Nine: Marital Discord and Divorce

1. Vladimirov.

2. Bischoff, p. 314. I have transliterated phonetically rather than literally. *Nichevo* serves several purposes in the Russian language, the best meaning here being "So what?"

3. Bischoff, p. 131.

4. For another example, see the case of I. D. Sakhno, who had so many wives and children that he could not remember their names without the aid of a notebook. Narinyani, "A Rake's Progress."

5. Bischoff, p. 167.

6. See Bischoff; Geiger, "The Urban Slavic Family"; Kushner, *Selo Viriatino.*

7. Kharchev, *Brak i semia,* p. 140.

8. Bischoff, p. 156.

9. Koltsov, p. 170.

10. Schwartz, p. 460.

11. For the details of divorce legislation and procedure, as well as an excellent firsthand description of specific cases during the summer of 1960, see Mace, pp. 203–226. See also, Juviler, "Marriage and Divorce," for a more recent picture. For an excellent Russian-language treatment, historical and analytical, see Rabinovich.

12. Kurylev, p. 38.

13. Lenin, *Sochineniia,* 2d ed., XIX, 232.

14. Mace, p. 212.

15. Koltsov, p. 165.

16. Kharchev, *Brak i semia,* pp. 168–170.

17. See the case described in Narinyani, "Because of a Statistic," in which the vice-chairman of the Azerbaidjan Republic Supreme Court is alleged to have "closed his eyes to life" in denying a proper divorce, saying, "Just follow the instructions laid down by the USSR Peoples' Commissariat of Justice. Reconcile the couple." and so forth.

18. Oridoroga, pp. 23, 22.

19. Juviler, "Marriage and Divorce," p. 110.

20. Pochivalov.

21. Kiselev, p. 11.

22. Kharchev, "O nekotorykh rezultatov," p. 57.

23. Korolev, p. 12.

24. Kiselev, p. 11.

25. *Ibid.,* pp. 11–12.

26. Kurylev, p. 21.
27. Dolinina.
28. Kurylev, p. 21.
29. Juviler, "Marriage and Divorce," p. 115.
30. The figures come from Kharchev, *Brak i semia,* p. 212.
31. Kiselev, p. 11.
32. Korolev, p. 12
33. In the second half of the 1950's courts started to circumvent the 1944 decree, which had revoked the right of an unmarried mother to file a paternity suit. They began to rule that if a child had at any time been dependent upon a respondent he was entitled to further support on the basis of a proviso originally written to cover persons who had taken someone else's children into their homes as dependents for permanent upbringing. See Mironkin; Juviler, "Marriage and Divorce."
34. Korolev, p. 12.
35. Kiselev, p. 11.
36. Marshak et al.
37. Kaverin, p. 14.
38. MacMillan, p. 5.
39. For details see *CDSP* 17.51:29 and 18.31:21.
40. Mironkin.

Ten: The Rearing of Children

1. Rostovshchikov.
2. Lukin.
3. "Heartless People."
4. Kotovshchikova, "Esli roditeli zhivy."
5. Fedorov.
6. Kotovshchikova, "Esli roditeli zhivy."
7. DeWitt, p. 99.
8. *Ibid.,* p. 100.
9. Bischoff, p. 204.
10. *Ibid.,* p. 200. See also, Kushner, *Selo Viriatino,* p. 92, for a description that, although describing the pre-Soviet pattern, seems applicable to this type of family today.
11. Rossi, p. 81, records that 48 per cent of the respondents under forty years of age from worker and peasant families were coded in the Harvard Project life history interviews as showing "little affect" from their school experiences. In the group under thirty, 29 per cent were coded as having school experiences that were "generally unpleasant." These figures are surprisingly high for a country in which science and education otherwise rank very high in the popular regard.
12. In Viriatino in pre-Soviet days, for example, parents had "no special

interest in study for the children." An informant reports: "The boys studied, but they weren't forced into it. 'If you want to, study; if not, don't!' " (Ku 92).

13. This precept is still central. A definite time for every activity, a definite place for everything in the home, and a strict daily regimen are habits stressed in Soviet pedagogical literature. See, for example, Levshin, pp. 20, 70, et passim.

14. From *Semia i Shkola*, Nos. 1–2 (1946), p. 13, as quoted in Kramer, p. 151.

15. There is little evidence as to when or how widely fines were imposed, or whence came the initiative for them. Examples are at hand of children who brought parents who had punished them into court, often with the help of Pioneer and Komsomol delegations, but this practice apparently declined by the mid-thirties. One Western writer asserted in 1945 that childbeating remained a criminal offense, but that "a certain amount of physical coercion may be admissible." Teitelbaum, pp. 66–67. A 1949 Soviet source indicated that corporal punishment was a criminal offense for Soviet teachers but not for parents, although it was strongly deplored in the latter case. *Semia i Shkola*, No. 4 (1949), p. 14, as cited in Kramer, p. 145.

16. Krupskaia, *O bytovykh voprosakh,* pp. 48–49.

17. Bischoff, p. 201.

18. See, for instance, the description by Shimkin and Sanjuan of traits shared by families in three different regions in the nineteenth century. Physical punishment is described as a "rare and unpopular action" (p. 331). One suspects that Soviet sources arguing the contrary (for example, V. A. Murin, *Byt i nravy derevenskoi molodezhi* [The daily life and customs of rural youth], Moscow, 1926, pp. 18, 20, as cited in Teitelbaum, p. 44) are based largely upon the inclination to denigrate the backward and reactionary past for politico-ideological reasons.

19. Kabo, pp. 18, 32, reports that as of 1923–1924 physical punishment was used more by mothers than by fathers in Moscow worker families.

20. Bischoff comments about his sample that among these families "the chief traditional pleasure of the husband — drunkenness — is completely absent" (p. 208).

21. *Time, Events, People.*

22. Belfrage, p. 65. This comment, and the admiration commonly elicited in Western visitors by the demeanor of Soviet children, should be qualified by its restriction to the relatively affluent part of the population living in large cities.

23. "Speech by Comrade I. A. Kairov," p. 23.

24. Simmons, *Russian Fiction,* p. 111.

25. "Everything for the children" is described by Kushner, p. 213, as the principle that describes "the essence of contemporary relationships between parents and children."

26. Akishin, p. 33.

27. Fisher, p. 196.

28. *Ibid.*, p. 262. See also, Rossi, p. 73; Kassof, p. 233 et passim.

29. Much of the material in this chapter is based upon Bischoff, pp. 198–216.

Eleven: Old Parents and New Children

1. This subject is discussed at length in Inkeles and Bauer.

2. Rossi, pp. 4–6, 25, 28, 29, 55–56, 115–116, 307.

3. *Ibid.*, p. 53 et passim.

4. Boris Sluzky, translated and quoted in Dunham, "Eros in Contemporary Russian Poetry," p. 346. Quoted by permission of The Society for the Study of Social Problems.

5. "Be Equal to the Great Tasks," p. 6.

6. Rossi, pp. 54–59.

7. Kharchev, *Brak i semia*, pp. 180–181, 232–233.

8. Bischoff, p. 293.

9. *Ibid.*, pp. 199–208.

10. Kharchev, *Brak i semia*, pp. 290–291.

11. From *Sovetskaia Kultura*, January 18, 1955, as quoted in Deaton, p. 40.

12. Grushin, p. 68.

13. Grushin and Chikin, passim, give complete details of the 1961 poll conducted by *Komsomolskaia Pravda's* Institute of Public Opinion and express the opinion that "it is hard to doubt that the spirit of realism has at this time suffused the atmosphere of its [Soviet youth's] entire life" (p. 86).

INDEX

Abandonment: of children, 73–74; of wife, 328

Abolition of the family, in Marxist theory, 25, 323, 324. *See also* Withering of the family

Abortion, 61, 73, 76, 81, 93, 96, 99, 100, 106, 167, 188, 193, 195, 197, 322; rate of, 195; as contraception, 195–196, 270

Abraham, 307

Access to education, 156

Achievement: and social mobility, 130, 169; in upper-status marriage, 252

Adaptation: as mechanism of social change in marxism, 39; of family, 131–138; to society, 146–148; in marriage, 248; in upper social level, 291; political, 314, 315; as key problem in Soviet family, 324, 326–327

Adaptive parents, 287, 300, 303, 310–311

Adoption, 72–73, 88, 97, 108, 122, 322; of children in children's homes, 268

Adultery, 105, 246, 247, 248–249, 252; in marxist theory, 15–23; as source of true love, 36; in law, 94; and conflict over power, 249–250, 252; as cause of divorce, 252, 257

Advantaged social position, 154–158

Affiliation, need for, 223

Age: at marriage, 197; relative age of spouses, 225–226

Age and sex differences, role of in marxist theory, 27–29

Aid: for large families, 96, 103; to unmarried mothers, 260

Alcohol, 105

Alien elements, 121, 137, 138–139, 144

Alienated family, 144

Alimony, 51, 56, 60, 93, 96

American divorce rate, compared with Soviet, 258

American family, compared with Soviet, 112, 213–214, 235, 324

American Negro male, compared with nichevo man, 241

American women in labor force, compared with USSR, 177

Amoralism, sexual, 64

Analytical categories in marxist theory, 24–25

Analytical principles, clash of in marxist theory, 17–20

Anomie: and marital patterns, 238; created by family law, 262

Anti-semitism, 132, 158

Anti-Soviet attitudes, and loss of fatherly influence, 314

Appearance of wife, 224

Arrest, 121–126, 141; political, 126; and hardship, 139–140

Art, depiction of family in, 107

Asceticism, 88, 95, 147; sexual, 61–62, 64–65

Aspirations: and father role, 281; and childrearing, 282–283; and status of father, 312–314

Assimilation of politically alien, 120, 138–143

Atheism, *see* Religion

Attitudes: of women, 59–60; slow to change, 79–80; political, 101; religious, 122, 132–135; and social mobility, 130; differences within family, 137; of the alienated, 144–145

Attitudes toward: communal institutions, 58; sex equality in marriage, 58–59; work, 60; love, 67–68; sexual freedom, 71; contraception, 74–75; marxist theory of the family, 88; family law, 99; freedom, 99; prohibtion, 100; family policy, 99–101; private life, 102; divorce law, 110, 261; collectivization, 123–124; revolution and regime, 123, 125, 127–131, 132, 137; education, 156; social mobility, 164, 168; property, 167–168; women's work, 179–181; work, 182, 185–186, 243; marriage, 247; marriage policy, 254

Authority: of parents, 53–55, 91, 289–299; of Makarenko, 89–90; in the family, 220, 221; of working-class husband, 227–228; and individual capacity, 239

Avoidance, as response to conflict, 296

Baby-sitting, 222

Backward wife, 148

Baptism, 134, 135

Bargaining, as mechanism of social change in marxism, 39

RUSSIAN RESEARCH CENTER STUDIES

* Out of print.
† Publications of the Harvard Project on the Soviet Social System.
‡ Published jointly with the Center for International Affairs, Harvard University.